A NEW LOOK AT AMERICAN SOCIETY

EDITED BY
ROBERT HARTMANN MCNAMARA

PEARSON
Custom Publishing

Cover photograph courtesy of Stockbyte/Getty Images, Inc.

Printed in the United States of America

10 9 8 7 6 5 4 3 2

ISBN 0-536-15293-4

2005540090

EC/WH

Please visit our web site at *www.pearsoncustom.com*

PEARSON CUSTOM PUBLISHING
75 Arlington Street, Suite 300, Boston, MA 02116
A Pearson Education Company

Acknowledgements

This project originally began as a new edition to my social problems reader entitled *Understanding Contemporary Social Problems*. However, due to a number of unexpected changes, it evolved into a more robust and comprehensive anthology for an introduction to sociology course. This evolution was not without its problems and issues, however. As a result, I owe several people my thanks for their help, particularly in the latter stages of the project when the deadline for submitting the finished manuscript loomed. Most notably are two graduate assistants, Ashley James and Kristy Champagne. Both were exceptionally helpful in tracking down obscure facts as well as solving several logistical problems as I struggled to finish the manuscript. Gloria Maguire, our department's administrative assistant, was also invaluable as this manuscript went into its latter stages of development. As she does with everyone in this department, and most of our majors on campus, Gloria's calming influence made the frustrations of finishing a book project a relatively painless process. I would also like to thank all the contributors to this manuscript for their thoughtful and timely ideas. Class discussions will be greatly enhanced by their words and comments. Finally, I'd like to thank my wife for her support in this endeavor. Few people realize how taxing a book project is on a scholar and his or her family. This is true even of edited collections. Carey's support, encouragement, and patience with me was of great comfort during those stressful times and her gifts to me allow students to benefit from what is written in these pages.

To: Shelby, who taught me more about human behavior than anyone I have ever known.

A New Look At American Society

Edited by:
Robert Hartmann McNamara

INTRODUCTION
A first Look at the Sociological Study of Society and Social Interaction

If one were to look at the various introductory textbooks in sociology, most of them would include a definition of the discipline that says something like the following: *Sociology is generally defined as the scientific study of society, including the relationships between people and patterns of social life.* However, this brief definition says little about the subject matter of sociology and nothing about how sociologists approach their work.

The basic insight of sociology is that human behavior is largely shaped by the groups to which people belong and by the social interaction that takes place within those groups. While many scoff at the topic matter of sociology, it is import to understand that much of our daily lives and what we do in them is affected in a variety of ways by sociological investigation. Moreover our understanding of other societies is based largely on what is discovered by sociologists.

Another important issue in understanding the discipline of sociology is that the knowledge we derive from sociological inquiry is both subjective and objective. This implies that what people understand in the world around them goes beyond simply the objective recording of events. What a person sees or understands is colored by the social, political, and economic position they hold in society. These factors are of critical importance if we are to understand anything about society, the people in it, and the interaction that goes on between and among members of different groups.

THE SOCIOLOGIST

In writing *Invitation to Sociology*, Peter Berger (1963) states:

One conception of a sociologist is this. The sociologist is a person intensively, endlessly, shamelessly interested in the doings of man. His natural habitat or environment is all the human gathering places of the world and while he/she may be interested in other things, his/her consuming interest remains the world of people, their history, their passions, their organization. And since he is interested in Man, he will naturally be interested in the events that engage men's beliefs, their moments of tragedy and grandeur and ecstasy. But he will also be fascinated by the everyday, the mundane aspects of man as well. He may be shocked and repulsed in pursuit of his answers to questions about man, but he will continue his pursuit. Another way of saying this is to say that the sociologist, is similar to the man who must listen to gossip despite himself, who is tempted to look through keyholes, to open closed cabinets. In other words, what interests us is the curiosity that grips any sociologist in front of a closed door behind which there are human voices (p.18).

Because of what sociologists study and the techniques they employ, some people think sociology is little more than a common sense approach to society. At times, people read sociological accounts and become puzzled because they have heard the findings somewhere before or believe that they sufficiently understand the issues surrounding a problem That is, until they are suddenly brought up against an insight that radically questions everything they had previously assumed about this familiar issue or event. It is at this point that one begins to sense the purpose of sociology.

THE SOCIOLOGICAL PERSPECTIVE

Everyone understands something about life in society. Much of what we know is based on personal experience and on observation of the events that crowd into our lives. Personal experience can be a valuable teacher that enables people to understand the society in which they live and how they function in it. But personal experience does have its shortcomings.

First, it does not provide individuals with any understanding of social worlds other than their own, even within their own culture. Most people, for example, have no first hand experience with the world of heroin addicts. Second, using personal experience to understand society may lead to the acceptance of errors. For instance, many of America's "homeless" are considered by many to be lazy, shiftless drunks. However, while it may be true that some members of the homeless population are unmotivated and lazy, a major portion of the homeless have been driven to the streets by unemployment, lack of affordable housing, or domestic abuse. Additionally, many homeless people are children while others are mentally ill, who have nowhere else to live. Thus, it is easy to see how such "common knowledge" can be flawed.

In sum, personal experience usually provides firsthand knowledge of only a limited segment of a society, often leaving many unanswered questions and troublesome errors. But once we learn something in society, whatever its source, it is often very difficult for us to break loose from that understanding. We all have what Leon Festinger (1954) called a fundamental "need to know" or to understand the physical and social world around us. In an attempt to derive these answers, we tend to take cues from people and things and when enough cues emerge, we tend to categorize the person. If a person looks, acts, or dresses unconventionally, then people often make sweeping generalizations about who they are and what they believe.

This simplistic understanding of the world around us (and the people in it) leads to what phenomenologists call *typifications*. We put people and things into categories so that we are able to understand where they fit into our world and, conversely, we understand our place in it as well. This categorizing is what Fritz Heider (1958) referred to as a *naive psychology*. We all create "theories" to explain people's motives, attitudes, and behaviors. Most of us do this, and for the most part it is harmless. But is it? Some experts argue that it reflects a myopic view of the world, in that everyone and everything must fit someplace into some category.

Other experts argue that the reasons for categorizing people lies in part in people's perception. They tend to take their social world for granted, accepting their society and customs as unquestioningly as they do the physical world around them. Thus, while people want to understand their world, they do not want to understand too much of it. As such, people fall victim to their own attitudes and perceptions (which are often based on personal experiences or the experiences of people they know).

Since people see the world narrowly, this results in a narrowing of their own personal worlds. This is why many people have very firm but erroneous beliefs about "how things ought to be." They have not taken that next step in understanding, and for the most part, they do not want to. An added problem is that these typifications or simplistic understandings or categorizations can change over time, meaning that what constitutes a certain phenomenona in one instance may change dramatically at a later point in time. This is part of the idea that society and the world around us is socially constructed. It does not exist in a natural state for us to exist within, but there is a social construction to reality and to society (See for instance, Berger and Luckman 1968).

The way sociologists avoid this problem is by using the sociological perspective. C. Wright Mills, discusses what is called *the sociological imagination*. He reminds us that the value of sociology is not found by focusing on the personal troubles of individuals, but rather on the broader social context in which those individual issues emerge. He says, "our sociological imagination which helps us develop our perspective allows us a vivid awareness of the relationship between the individual and the wider society." The sociological perspective, then, allows us to expand our vision and objectively look at the society (of which we are a part) and see it as though looking at it for the first time. Another way of saying this is that the sociological perspective is a unique way of looking at the world: a lens of sorts which offers us a snapshot of the world that few others have a chance to see. Thus, the sociological perspective:

1. Removes us from familiar experiences
2. Forces us to examine critically and objectively
3. There is a conscious effort to question the obvious (Vander Zanden, 1993).

Using the sociological perspective is one reason why sociologists have continued to discover new and interesting things about social life that we thought we already understood. What you know or think you know has probably been discovered by a sociologist at one point in time. Thus, the first mission of sociology is that much of what may initially appear to be one way may not be that way at all in practice. Sociology offers a unique way of looking at the world and posing crucial questions. Sociology and the sociological perspective encourage us to look beyond individual cases and immediate events and to seek to understand them in the broader context of the society in which they occur. A specific crime, family breakup, or unemployment problem, is placed in the context of larger social events.

SOCIAL PROBLEMS vs. SOCIOLOGICAL ONES

So what exactly is a social problem? What is a sociological problem? There are a host of things in society that are problematic, but not all of them social problems. While there are some issues that practically everyone today agrees are social problems, such as crime or racial discrimination, on other issues, however, there is more disagreement.

The basic difference between a sociological problem and a social one is that a sociological problem attempts to document and understand a social phenomenon as accurately as possible. There is less of an emphasis on explaining the political reasons why a phenomenon exists as much as there is a focus on empirically explaining its presence and purpose in society. A social problem can best be understood in terms of "claimsmaking." That is, instead of trying to examine the phenonmenon and offer the most accurate explanation for it, social problems focus on how a phenomenon becomes the topic of discussion. This means that the process of constructing social problems is entirely political: who is making the claim? How is the claim being perceived by the public? Why is the claim being made in the first place? Are the solutions offered by the claims makers being received?

Recognize that whether it is a social problem or a sociological one, we are not interested in individual cases. When parents discover that their daughter has a serious drug problem, theirs is what C. Wright Mills called a "personal trouble" because the values and goals of only that family are threatened. In short, the trouble is seen as being primarily that family's difficulty. While it may be traumatic for that particular family to deal with the daughter's drug problem, this is not the focus of sociological investigation, although it might be for psychology or social work. Rather, the main focus for sociology are larger, more broad based issues, what Mills referred to as "public issues."

Public issues have an impact on large numbers of people, and are matters of public debate and collective solutions, rather than individual or familial ones. So when we examine statistics that indicate our society loses millions of dollars each year because of accidents, suicide, and worker absenteeism because of drug abuse, we are dealing with a public issue because the values of the group are threatened. Of course, public issues may translate into personal troubles in the lives of some people, but every personal trouble is not a public issue. The significance of this distinction reminds us that problems need to be viewed in the broad context of their impact on society.

So what is a social problem? According to Malcom Spector and John Kitsuse (1987) in their classic text on the subject, a social problem has the following elements:

1) **An influential group defines a social condition as threatening to its values:** An influential group is one that can have a significant impact on public debate and social policy. Personal troubles do not become public issues then unless an influential group defines them that way. The mere existence of a social condition does not make it problematic no matter how harmful it may be. Smoking tobacco has been a contributing factor in lung cancer for as long as people have used it, but it was not defined as a social problem until people became aware of the link between smoking and cancer and an influential group decided to label it a problem.

2) **When the condition affects a large number of people**: Conditions do not typically become social problems unless they affect a large number of people. When they affect relatively few people, they are private issues and there is little public debate over them or search for collective solutions. The more people they affect, the more likely they are to be publicly debated and defined as a problem that society should address.

3) **When the condition can be remedied by collective action.**
Finally, a social condition may satisfy the previous criteria but not be regarded as a social problem because the condition does not have social causes and cannot be remedied by collective human action. Earthquakes, tornadoes, and other natural disasters, are harmful to the society, but they would not be considered social problems because they are not produced by social conditions

and cannot be prevented by changes in social policy. Another thing we must bear in mind is that as objective conditions and subjective concerns change, social problems do as well. In other words, social problems are dynamic. In fact a social problem for some may be a solution for others.

This brief introduction helps us to understand the basic dimensions of the sociological enterprise as well as identifying a number of terms that will be used throughout this text. The articles in this reader are written by many of this country's leading experts and draw from some of the most up to date research available. Hopefully, they will illuminate the complexity of these problems as well as the difficulty in uncovering solutions to them.

REFERENCES

Berger, P. 1963. *Invitation to Sociology*. New York: Doubleday.

_____ and Luckmann, T. 1968. *The Social Construction of Reality*. New York: Anchor.

Festinger, L. 1954. "A Theory of Social Comparison," *Human Relations* 7:117-140.

Heider, F. 1958. *The Psychology of Human Relations*. New York: John Wiley and Sons.

Vander Zanden, J.W. 1993. *Sociology: The Core*. 3rd Edition. New York: McGraw-Hill.

An Exploration in Visual Ethnography

Stephen J. Sifaneck
Department of Sociology
City University of New York

Robert Hartmann McNamara
Department of Political Science and Criminal Justice
The Citadel

Ethnographic research is a type of research that seeks to produce a description of the way of life, or culture, of a society and to identify the behaviors, beliefs, understandings, attitudes, and values found in that social world. The central focus of the ethnographer is not the "things in themselves," if indeed there are such things, but things as they are grasped and shaped through the meaning-conferring responses of members. In his influential chapter beginning *The Interpretation of Cultures*, Clifford Geertz argues that ethnography should provide a "thick description" of cultural and social activities. Thick descriptions present in close detail the context and meaning of events and scenes that are relevant to those involved in them. They contrast sharply with most standard social science procedures, in which observers typically try to either ignore or to reduce the contextual meanings in the interests of standardization.

Some field research methods employ fixed, predetermined categories for coding behavior. For instance, in a number of studies of police decision making, Albert Reiss and others went into the field with code sheets to record all the interactions between police officers and civilians. Such code sheets are essentially predetermined questions about any incident (see Reiss 1971). While this is an important type of field research, the purpose of ethnographic description is not to determine the correlations and statistical significance of predetermined variables, but to understand the local meanings and contexts of human behavior.

Field notes are considered a central component to ethnographic research, but they also pose a problem. In their worst form, they are an attempt to vacuum up everything possible, often by interrupting observation to do so. In one field methods book, for instance, it is suggested that the ratio of recording time to observation time is six to one (Emerson 1993). Thus, while the researcher scribbles furiously, other important events are taking place, which are often overlooked. However, since the researcher does not usually know what is significant, especially early in the project, he or she often does not know what to record.

One strategy to compensate for this problem is to focus on only a few topics. At any given time during the early stages of fieldwork, there will be a couple of topics of interest, and the observations, conversations, and interviews should focus on them. Of course no one would advise ignoring everything that is unrelated to the topics of interest. However, the focus should be on the specific topics under consideration. Field notes, then, often consist of ideas and areas to purse that were generated either from observations or interviews. Some researchers add a personal diary that is separate from their working field notes. A diary focuses more on the reactions of the ethnographer to the field setting and the informants, the general sense of how the research is going, feelings of involvement, and so on.

Another approach to the problems of collecting and recording data is to use visual techniques that

Another approach to the problems of collecting and recording data is to use visual techniques that allow for a more comprehensive view of the topic. One of these techniques is referred to as *visual ethnography.*

VISUAL ETHNOGRAPHY

The concept of visual ethnography is designed to offer an image that allows an appreciation of the sociological imagination in a slightly different way. One of the principal advantages to visual ethnography is that the researcher and his or her subjects can convey subtle cues about what it feels like to be in a particular relationship or situation. In this way, sociologists can then focus on the ways in which people sort themselves out in space and time, the importance of meaning, and an array of other aspects of social interaction. We find that various visual techniques enhance our ability to record observations, to describe the setting more completely, and offer a vehicle by which the members of a chosen population may convey, in their own words, facial expressions, and body language, as well as how they see the world and react to it. This gives visual ethnography a decided advantage over traditional ethnographic methods, which focus primarily on the researcher's memory to reconstruct the setting or the dialogue generated from informal conversations and interviews.

Of course, this does not mean that visual ethnography is an overall superior technique to classic ethnographic methods. Rather, the visual approach represents one more tool in the researcher's repitoire to assist in capturing the essence of a phenomenon or understanding the members of a population. In fact, we would argue that this approach should be used in conjunction with other techniques to ensure a more comprehensive "picture." The following project serves as an illustration of the potential impact of the visual ethnographic approach.

THE PROJECT

In the spring of 1989, an experiment was conducted to explore the potential of using a video camera to conduct ethnographic research in one of the most unique urban settings in the world: New York City's Times Square. On one hand, this project was a descriptive endeavor, a traditional attempt at investigating social behavior in a particular urban environment. At the same time, however, this project involved a self-contained experiment in the methodology of visual ethnography. The subject of this inquiry was a "sound installation," which had become an unique environmental part of the urban ecology of Times Square. Max Neuhaus's Sound Installation was located under a pedestrian esplanade in New York City's Times Square. The installation was mounted here by the artist in September 1977, and it emitted a distinct, continuous, resonant sound that was about six times as strong as usual sound levels in Times Square. Neuhaus, the artist (a graduate of the Manhattan School of Music), has become a well-known interpreter of contemporary musical pieces. Having worked at length with notable figures of the musical avant-garde, particularly Karlheinz Stockhausen, Neuhaus quit performing in 1968 to construct "sound environments" around the world. The Sound Installation in Times Square was the first in this series of works, entitled "Underground Music." It is Neuhaus's intent to render music as a consciously applied ingredient of urban environments in a form that is accessible to all.

The sound of the installation was emitted by an electronic loudspeaker system positioned under the sidewalk in a triangular ventilation chamber. The chamber was a part of the New York subway system, and the metal grid covering it looked like countless others throughout the city. However, the project was not without its share of problems. Funding became an initial concern. The New York State Council on the Arts vetoed funding for the project on the grounds that it was not a responsible way to spend the public's money. Funding for the installation was ultimately generated in part by grants, but Neuhaus provided most of the money himself.

Additionally, various agencies were unwilling to commit to the project. For instance, The Metropolitan Transit Authority feared that the traffic island would have to be rebuilt to support the crowds of people that would gather there. Moreover, Con Edison, the electricity company, would not help install lines to power the work. Unable to negotiate with the Transit Authority as an individual, Neuhaus set up a nonprofit foundation, Hybrid Energies for Acoustic Resources, or HEAR, to proceed with his plan. It took him nearly four years to convince the Transit Authority to permit him to place his work in their facility.

The other focus of this project was an experiment in methodology: to explore a range of approaches in employing a video camera in the study of social behavior. Three visual methods were juxtaposed in the video presentation. These methods encompass varied levels of proximity, interaction, and intervention. These terms represent prominent methodological issues in the field of visual ethnography. For instance, how does proximity: closeness or distance of the lens, affect the object of study? What are the consequences of interacting with the people we are observing? Is intervention in a social scene a means to get in touch with its reality or does it act as a barricade to objectivity?

OBSERVATION

In the first segment of the presentation, the camera was placed on a tripod and left to record, in real time, how people move over and around the sound installation. The camera was placed in three locations, two of them providing close-range and one a long-range view of the installation. This method of visual observation was inspired by William H. Whyte's *The Social Life of Small Urban Spaces* (1980), where he utilized a time-lapse movie-film to study behavior in urban corporate plazas. He used the camera as a tool to observe social behavior, from a distance, during different times of the day. We attempted to use the video camera in a similar manner.

Employing this method enabled us to observe a certain level of reality, allowing us to make some general conclusions about how the sound installation was received by the general public. This type of observation also provided a quantitative assessment of how many people walk over and around the sculpture, or even notice the sound produced by it. We discovered that approximately 200 pedestrians an hour traversed the installation during the daytime on a typical weekday. From approximately twenty hours of daylight observation, our most general observation was that most people walked over the sound sculpture without expressing any acknowledgement of its existence. About a third of the people observed avoided walking over the center and walked around the perimeter instead. On occasion, a few individuals were seen gazing downward in an apparent search to "see" where the sound was coming from.

Observation with this method suggests that the installation evokes hardly any response from the people who walk over it. People did not interact with, or even react to, the presence of the video camera. Its presence was almost nonexistent, indicative of how most New Yorkers have become very accustomed to the constant presence of cameras in public spaces. By all conventional standards, this is "objective" observation, as no interaction or intervention affects the reality being observed--but how much of this reality are we forsaking in the name of objectivity? This removed level of observation was valuable in some respects, but in order to glean a more comprehensive understanding of the people in this setting, interaction and intervention were needed.

INTERACTIVE INTERVIEWS

The second visual method involved interviewing pedestrians as they walked across the sculpture, which engaged the video camera in an interactive role. The general format of the interviews varied, but as a rule, they began with the question, "Do you hear something?" From here, the direction of the interviews ranged from opinions about art, music, and city life to thoughts on existential philosophy. This method of interviewing is similar to the one employed by the anthropologist John Rouche and the sociologist Edgar Morin in the film *Chronicle of a Summer*. Capturing the mood of the summer of 1960 in Paris, the film opens with Morin interviewing a young woman and directing her to conduct street interviews by asking people, "'Are you happy?" In both cases, a standard, open-ended question launched the interviews, resulting in an array of responses.

While the interview allowed a somewhat more penetrating understanding of "what's going on" than the non-interactive method, some traditional claims to objectivity had to be neglected as the interviewer inevitably directs the interview process to some degree, thus augmenting its subjectivity. The interactive method that we used during the project represented a fair compromise between these objective and investigative interests.

ETHNOMETHODOLOGICAL INTERVENTIONS

As the work of Harold Garfinkel has shown us, the continuous, undisturbed flow of reality has to be disrupted so that the common, day-to-day, unconscious assumptions that comprise it can surface and manifest themselves to both the people who create that reality and those who wish to observe it. However, there is a price to pay for the disruption.

The third visual method involved not only interaction, but the intervening construction of a social scene. A party was organized on top of the work during a Friday afternoon rush hour in order to attract people to the sound installation. Intervening in the daily flow of activity on Times Square and creating a structured situation allowed for a greater involvement of the respondents. This was further enhanced by actually placing one of the video cameras in their hands. Here it is not simply "our" subjective observation of the group, but the group's own subjective observation of itself. Thus, in the spirit of the classic "breaching" experiment, we intervened into the daily social reality of Times Square and the sound installation, stopped it, restructured it, and then made this "new" reality reflective of itself.

But what kind of a reality were we able to probe so deeply? Can we say that it is "real life" on the sound installation, or has it become our own projection of it? The intervening and interacting approach to our subject has certainly done away with a lot of the traditional objectivity inherent in the first method of observation. However, it has provided a penetrating subjective interpretation of our topic that would have been inaccessible with the other approaches.

DISCUSSION

This experiment was an attempt to come to terms, not only with methods and a subject of interest, but also with the role of visual ethnography in sociological research. Throughout the project, we filmed and photographed ourselves while in the field and asked others to film and photograph us. Moreover, when employing the third method, we even encouraged the participants to engage in this reflection. In the completed video presentation, our moments of failure, the refusal of participants, and the cultural, and, of course, language obstacles were included, alluding to the realities of ethnography. This project enabled researchers to enhance their self-awareness, which is indispensable to ethnography, as its crucial role lies in helping subjectivity to be included in the investigation as a more "determined variable."

CONCLUSION

This project, which involved a methodological and thematical investigation, is a systematic attempt to further evaluate the basic relationships of objectivity and subjectivity in visual ethnographic research. We have shown that a tradeoff is involved in each method. Non-interactive observation allows for considerable objectivity, but little understanding. Penetrating intrusion in a social scene provides in-depth understanding, but is detrimental to objectivity. Neither approach can, or should be avoided.

In fact, we contend that the juxtapositioning of these methods, or "pastiche-work," fosters a greater understanding and robust appreciation for the topic being studied. Each method provides a different angle, a different segment of objectivity and subjectivity, while at the same time revealing its limitations. The graphic nature of the project also allows the viewer to reinterpret the "text."

Finally, perhaps the most important conclusion is that ethnography is inherently subjective. It cannot be value-free or meet the canonized demands of empirical science; it should not want to. Instead of shamefully hiding, it should exploit its subjectivity--and visual ethnography allows for enhanced reflexivity made possible by the employment of still, movie, or video cameras.

REFERENCES:

Emerson, Ralph. 1993. *Contemporary Field Research*. Prospect Heights, IL: Waveland Press.
Geertz, Clifford. 1973. *Interpretations of Cultures*. New York: Oxford University Press.
Reiss, Albert J. Jr. 1971. *The Police and the Public*. New Haven, CT: Yale University Press.
Whyte, William H. 1980. *The Social Life of Small Urban Spaces*. Washington, D.C.: Conservation Foundation.

Trust in the Hustler's World

Robert Hartmann McNamara
Department of Political Science and Criminal Justice
The Citadel

Gaining entry into hard-to-reach populations presents a host of problems for researchers (Luckenbill 1985; Douglas 1972; Karp 1980; Hammersley and Atkinson 1983). Often, the researcher must rely on informants to provide key information about the population as well as providing introductions to its members. Early on in my research, shopkeepers pointed out areas where a good deal of hustling takes place, offered opinions on the nature of the problem, and, in a few cases, introduced me to hustlers. My contacts with other researchers in the area and street people whom I had come to know were also helpful.

Through these networks, I was able to interview thirty-five hustlers. Because large segments of the population pride themselves on anonymity, I cannot make a claim about the representativeness of these interviews. However, I feel confident that what "the boys" have told me about the trade, the culture of hustling, and their lives has been accurate and consistent. When possible, I have verified the information through personal observation or by asking my informants or other hustlers for verification. These methods are obviously not without limitations, but they did serve to support the information provided by the boys. Nevertheless, it should be stressed that I am focusing on a select segment of the hustling population in New York City. My insights, assessments, and conclusions can only be applied to the hustlers in Times Square.

One of the most consistent questions people ask about this project, be they scholars or laypersons, is how I made initial contact with the boys. My first encounter with a hustler occurred after I had been in the field for about a month. I spent January making some preliminary observations as well as building a network to gain entrance into the population. I talked with people involved in the sex trade and the Times Square scene and attempted to learn more about the outreach programs in the area.

By February I felt I knew enough about the trade to begin interviewing hustlers. I encountered Eddie on the upper concourse of the Port Authority Bus Terminal. He was dressed in tight jeans, sneakers, and a hooded sweat shirt and was standing next to one of the doorways near the departure gates, a common pickup spot. Twice I saw him greet older men with a short conversation that ended with him shaking his head no. The men would depart and Eddie would remain, seemingly waiting for someone. He would make eye contact with a few passersby and in some cases quietly call out to them as they walked by. While this may appear to the casual observer as innocuous behavior, it led me to believe that Eddie was a hustler. I decided to approach him and determine if my initial assessment was correct: it was.

This was my first interview and I recorded it in my field notes immediately after it occurred. The verbal sparring was typical of the other encounters I had with hustlers who were not introduced to me.

> <u>MC</u>: How's it goin'. I'm Bob.
> <u>E</u>: I'm Eddie. How ya doin'.

MC: Listen I'm wondering if you could help me out, I'm writing a book about hustlers in Times Square. I was wondering if you knew anybody who hustled and would be willing to talk to me about it.

E: You writin' a book about hustlers? Here? How much?

MC: How much what?

E: How much you payin'?

MC: You don't understand, that's why I need your help. I don't have much money, but I could buy you lunch and we could talk about your experiences here.

E: You wanna what? Buy me lunch? What the hell am I gonna do with that? I can't spend that! You know my time is money, I can't be wastin' it talkin' to you or eatin' lunch.

MC: But you have to eat, right?

E: I'm not hungry.

MC: Okay, then how about I just stand here and hang out with you and ask you some questions until a trick comes along and then you leave?

E: If you stand around here, no tricks will come cause they'll think I'm talkin' to you.

MC: All right, what if you introduced me to some of your friends who hustle who aren't working now. You tell them what I'm doing and that I can't pay cash and basically say I'm okay. Then when you do have time and you are hungry, we can talk some more. That way you don't have to worry about losing money now and you can help out one of your friends who is hungry and who isn't hustling today.

E: So what do I get out of it?

MC: What you get out of it is that you help out one of your friends, you help me, and then the next time I see you, you can help yourself. You aren't always hustling. You have to eat at some point, so let me buy you lunch and all we're going to do is talk. If I ask you something you don't want to answer, then don't. So we would be helping each other and your friends. And if you and I get along, maybe you can introduce me to more of your friends or maybe you and I can hang out sometime. But right now, it doesn't cost you anything and all I want to do is meet other hustlers who aren't working so I can talk to them. After you introduce me and tell them what's up, you're done.

E: And all you want to do is talk? Nothin' else? And you can't pay? Oh, lord, what do I look like, some sort of social worker?

MC: You look like a guy who's smart enough to see what this is about and you are also smart enough to see that this could work out for everybody. You help your friends out and yourself at the same time. So how about it?

E: Okay, but I want to talk to you first. If you writin' a book I want my name in it. But I'm only gonna give you ten minutes. If I like you, I'll help you, but if I don't, I ain't doin' shit. Come on, you can buy me a slice over at that pizza shop.

That interview with Eddie lasted forty-five minutes. From that point on, he introduced me to many of his friends. Once he started talking he never stopped, but getting him to talk to me initially was a crucial step.

Many of my colleagues(and even some of the boys)have expressed surprise at how quickly and thoroughly I was able to gain access to this population. There were three primary reasons for my success. One of the things that helped establish my position in the culture was my willingness to deal with the same adversities the boys faced. They told me I earned their respect because, despite the freezing cold of winter or the sweltering heat of summer, I "hung out" and suffered from the elements along with them.

Moreover, unlike others in their lives, I was interested in what they had to say, did not pass judgment on them or their opinions, and was straightforward from the time of my initial contact with them. This, according to the boys, earned their respect. Prince told me:

> You never dissed [disrespected] us. You always straight up and you listen. You okay man, for a white boy, you okay. Like I never get to tell nobody how I feel about shit, you understand? Things like life and shit. But you, I know you interested in me and what I gots to say, I like that. And most of these other guys like that too. That's why you was accepted so fast. Like I said, you okay as far as I'm concerned. How many people you know will come out here, ask us how we doin', buy us lunch, ask us if we okay and then give us your phone number and say call if we need anything? You ain't really no researcher as far as I'm concerned, you a friend of ours.

While this is indeed speculation on my part, and based largely on my own beliefs and assessment, I think my immersion into the environment was successful in part because I went to the hustlers in their setting instead of having them come to me in mine. I also felt I could not, in good faith, represent myself to be something I was not. The trust that I engendered was tenuous in some instances, but I believe it may have been based on my fulfillment of any promises I made. For example, if I talked to someone on the condition that I would buy him lunch in return or meet him on a certain day to help him with welfare benefits, I felt obliged to show up as promised or else I should not have agreed to help in the first place. I believe they knew this and, as time progressed, they began to trust me and tell me more about themselves. This research approach granted me entrance into a hidden population in Times Square that few researchers have explored in any detail.

I was also very concerned about confidentiality and protecting the hustlers' identities. I applied for, and received, a Certificate of Confidentiality from the United States Department of Health and Human Services. This provided legal protection for my sources. I made a point of explaining what this document was and how it maintained their anonymity. I also took the added precaution of asking them what they wanted to be called rather than simply using their street names. In some cases, they said it did not matter, but I wanted to be clear about what I was doing and why. These boys appeared indifferent and said their street names could be used. Nonetheless, as an added precaution, in the text I use fictitious names for these individuals.

I also told the boys that I would bring them some of my field notes to read if they were so inclined. Later, I explained, I would also bring the completed chapters along so that they could give me their comments and offer any suggestions or clarifications that they felt were needed. This went a long way toward enhancing my credibility and standing in the community. My offer to share the contents of my work was perceived as an honest attempt to understand their world and learn from them, not to simply extract the information and depart, never to be heard from again.

A second factor in my success with the boys involved my passing a series of tests. For instance, a hustler would share a piece of information with me, make me promise it was to be held in the strictest of confidence, and then wait to see if I mentioned it to anyone else. When I did not, he would tell others that I was trustworthy. Other tests determined if I would uphold my end of an arrangement. Early on, I had established an agreement with the boys that I could not give them cash but would be willing to buy them lunch, cigarettes, or other incidentals in exchange for their time and insight. This was done to offset the income they would forgo by talking to me.

As they came to know and trust me, this issue became moot, and the boys would freely seek me out to tell me the latest news of their lives or what had happened since our last meeting. Our interaction became less an exchange and more a social relationship. I still purchased incidentals or lunch for them, but I would usually bring the subject up by asking a boy if he had eaten that day.

To test my resolve as well as their ability to "work" me, some hustlers would occasionally ask for a dollar or two to buy groceries for their family. I would remind them of our understanding, and, in turn, they would try to play on my sympathies. One parrying tactic I used was to offer to buy groceries for them and to have them take me to meet their "incredibly beautiful but hungry baby."

The point in all the tests or attempted scams was to determine whether I would make exceptions to our agreement. If I wavered even once, a precedent would be set and a deluge of requests might follow. Moreover, my standing in the community would be damaged: I could be "played." Knowing this, I remained steadfast in my position. As it turns out, this was the correct response. Within a short time, perhaps three or four months into the project, the tests had all but stopped. Occasionally a hustler reintroduced one, but it was usually a playful attempt, performed more as a joke coupled with a reminder of how the hustlers had "tested" me in the past.

Perhaps most important, the project benefited greatly from the active interest of three individuals.

Since they played leadership roles within the culture, my association with them was critical. Their introductions to other hustlers not only paved the way for those particular interviews, the effect snowballed and additional introductions came at a relatively rapid pace. These three hustlers became my cultural guides, pointing out new developments, providing and verifying information about others in the trade, and making important contacts for me. Although I will describe them in greater detail in the next chapter, they merit a cursory introduction here. Flacco is thirty years old. He has been involved in the Times Square scene for nearly seventeen years and his time spent there accords him respect by the other hustlers. Many come to him for advice and counsel when they are in need. Apache, who is twenty-one, has only seven years of experience in the trade. However, he possesses intelligence and business acumen far beyond his years or his tenth grade education. Since he is wise to the various street scams and possesses excellent powers of reasoning, he, too, commands respect within the culture. Finally, Raul, at twenty-eight, is bigger, stronger, and more tempestuous than most hustlers and therefore serves in a protector role for many people. His status is derived from intimidation and fear. As he is fond of saying, he never met a fight he didn't like.

OBSERVATIONS

I have come to know many hustlers in the area and have had numerous conversations with them, often in pairs or groups. I spent a great deal of time simply hanging out and observing their behavior, rituals, and activities. These observations occurred in a variety of places including coffee shops, fastfood restaurants, street corners, bars, and parks. A favorite pastime for the boys is to play handball in the nearby parks. The games are competitive and I learned a great deal about the boys by simply observing the games and how the players interacted. Some of the most interesting observations involved the dynamics of the transaction between the boys and their clients. Many of these took place on 42nd Street and 8th Avenue, especially in front of the peep shows.

INTERVIEWS

In order to learn as much about the boys as possible and to best understand their environment, I used a life history approach. Life histories can offer insight into a subject, including the individual's life situation and the state of the world, as he or she understands it, either at some particular point in time or over a long period. The interviews were of two basic types. One was a conversational interview in which there was no agenda and the subject controlled the flow and topic of conversation. The other type, while related to the first in that it was still open-ended, involved a general set of topics in which I guided the interview. In each type of interview, as well as in the informal conversations, I tried to get a sense of the boy's personal background, life style, relationships with others, and perceptions of how hustling has changed in recent times, as well as measures he took to adapt to these changes.

While I tried to understand the boys and their world, I made no attempt to fit an explanatory structure into the culture. I had no stated hypotheses, no theories to test. Rather, armed only with my "sociological hunting license" and an inexhaustible curiosity, I ventured into the field to learn something about the 42nd Street scene and the people who make their living there.

PROBLEMS AND SOLUTIONS IN THE FIELD

Despite my acceptance into the culture, I encountered difficulty from some hustlers who did not believe what they had heard about me. In an effort to remedy this, I often carried economy-sized packs of chewing gum, which I offered to those I knew and those I had just met. It was a great icebreaker and allowed me to inform them that I was simply trying to write about their lives. As time went on, my acquaintance with other hustlers served as a legitimizing mechanism. That is, my credibility was enhanced by having already talked to people the skeptics knew.

An obvious potential problem in working with this population was my personal safety. While I was accepted by most hustlers, who evinced a sense of responsibility for my safety, I could not rely on them completely in the event of trouble. One precautionary strategy that I adopted was to call home on an hourly basis. I also sent letters to the Port Authority Police and the mayor's Office of Midtown Enforcement explaining who I was and that I was conducting social science research in the area. I also explained that as a security precaution I would be checking in periodically at home and that if anything went wrong, my wife would contact their office with my description and last known location.

Whenever I arrived in Times Square, I would check in and tell my wife where I was and where I would be going during the next hour. An hour or so later, I would call and tell her where I was going next. If I did not check in within a two hour period, she was to call the police. I gave myself a two hour cushion in the event I could not easily break away to call, such as during a very personal or emotional interview with one of the boys. This was not a strategy without limitations and there were a few instances where I came extremely close to violating the two hour limit. Fortunately, my wife understood the difficulties of field research and remained calm. Interestingly, my informants understood my purpose in checking in and even reminded me to "go check in" on a few occasions. They would then explain my brief absence to others who might not know why I left.

Another problem that I confronted was my role in the culture. In deviant populations, members must always keep a wary eye out for the police, particularly undercover officers. This is especially true in Times Square, where the Port Authority Police as well as the New York City Police Department have escalated their undercover "sting" operations. As a result, strangers are given a great deal of scrutiny.

One problem in researching this population is that there are very few roles that an adult male can play. Essentially, one is perceived as either a client, a police officer, a commuter or "suit," or in some cases, an older hustler. Since I purposely avoided dressing like a "fly Puerto Rican," [hip, in style] the latter possibility was quickly eliminated. The role of researcher was not at all defined.

Many of the boys stated that they initially thought I was a police officer. They sensed something about my presentation of self, or in their words, I "smelled like a cop." There may be some accuracy to this assessment since I had six years experience as a security officer as well as some law enforcement training. In many ways, I may have indeed "smelled" like a police officer. Others thought I was a client, especially when they saw me talking to many different hustlers.

I had a few encounters in which one hustler propositioned me in front of another, which set off a round of arguments and angry threats. This occurred for two primary reasons. One was the aforementioned sense of responsibility my informants felt for my safety, while the other reason has to do with the normative system that regulates the boys' behavior. In either case, my role was not at all clear. Eventually, the word spread that I was writing a book about hustlers in Times Square and my place in the neighborhood became understood and accepted.

This role was carefully constructed for the reasons I just outlined. I needed to maintain a sense of distinction and separation so that others who did not know me would be able to understand who I was without cause for concern. I wanted to be part of the culture, but at the same time I needed a certain objective distance in order for my presence to be understood as well as to prevent my "going native." This role separation is a concept that Hammersley and Atkinson (1983) and Agar (1980) have discussed at length.

How I dressed played a very important role, especially early in the course of the project. While some researchers might find themselves thinking about how to dress like the natives lest they be identified as outsiders, I had the somewhat difficult task of trying to dress differently. This was especially important since I did not want to be mistaken for an undercover police officer.

Had I tried to dress like a hustler, I would have certainly been identified as a police officer, and if I dressed as I normally did, I would also be identified as one. The boys felt that white men, especially white men in their early to late thirties, who wore untucked tennis shirts and various sports-related clothing such as National Football League (NFL) jackets or hats, had various bulges around the waistband, and spent a lot of time standing around watching people, were cops. This made it very difficult to gain entry into the population. Here again, my informants played a key role. After I got to know them, they legitimized my presence by introducing me to other hustlers. Consequently, early on in the project I spent almost all my time with either Raul, Apache, or Flacco.

Finally, my relationship with outside agencies played a role within the culture. At the beginning of the project, I contacted some of the various outreach programs such as Covenant House, Streetworks Project, the Door, and Project Return. Due to problems stemming from client confidentiality, they rejected my requests to interview workers or any of the youths. However, what I thought initially would be an obstacle turned into an advantage as I became known in the hustling population. A few boys asked me if I was or had been affiliated with such groups. When they found that I was not, my credibility actually increased. This was especially true after I told them that the organizations had refused to help me.

It seems there is a good deal of animosity between some of these programs and many hustlers. While a few individuals will take advantage of the resources the programs offer, most want little to do with them or their staff. The fact that the agencies would not help me served as a bond between us. This was especially true of Covenant House, an organization for which most of the boys have a particular distaste. This is due largely to its rigid behavior code for clients.

I did have a few opportunities to learn about the programs from the inside, however. Apache, who was ever the enterprising soul, would occasionally go to Streetworks Project for groceries, and he simply brought me along and told everyone he wanted me there. Since I was accompanied by someone who was using the services, I was allowed access.

These are a few of the more problematic issues that I faced in my attempt to become a part of this population. In the following pages, I would like to tell you the boys' story and describe how hustling has changed dramatically in recent times. Since the boys capture the essence of a hustler's life, wherever possible I let them speak for themselves and tell their story in their own words.

The
Social Organization of
Peep Shows

Robert Hartmann McNamara
Department of Political Science and Criminal Justice
The Citadel

In *The Presentation of Self in Everyday Life* (1959), Erving Goffman argued that in order to maintain a stable self-image, people perform for their social audiences. As a result of this interest in the performance of roles and expectations, Goffman focused on dramaturgy, or a view of social life as a series of dramatic performances similar to those performed on stage.

He contended that when individuals interact, they want to present a certain sense of self that will be accepted by others, a process he calls "impression management." Specifically, impression management is oriented to guarding against a series of unexpected actions, such as unintended gestures, faux pas, or inopportune intrusions.

Following this theatrical analogy, Goffman spoke of a "front stage." This is the controlled or polished presentation of self. It is here that the actor attempts to convey a positive self-image and to elicit a favorable response from the audience. Moreover, the preparations, rehearsals, and creative methods employed to produce the "finished product" are not revealed to the audience. This is the area to which Goffman referred as "back stage."

Perhaps the most important way in which actors maintain a positive self-image with their audience is by controlling the amount and nature of private information. In this way, the actor is in a better position to convey a favorable impression to the audience, a process he refers to as the "information game."

Goffman continued his analysis of the control and management of information and image in *Stigma: Notes on the Management of Spoiled Identity* (1963). While most people engage in some form of impression management in their encounters with others, the need for impression management is greater for those who have either been stigmatized or have engaged in behavior that has the potential for a negative label. Goffman makes a distinction between "discredited" and "discreditable" individuals. The former are those whose stigma is easily identified and difficult to change. In these cases, as with those who are badly scarred, physically challenged, or disfigured, individuals can employ few strategies to manage their social identities.

Of greater importance, for our purposes, are discreditable individuals, whose stigma is not clearly identified by others. As Goffman states:

The cooperation of a stigmatized person with normals in acting as if his known differentness were irrelevant and not attended to is one main possibility to the life of such a person. However, when his differentness is not immediately apparent, and is not known beforehand (or at least known by him to be known to the others), when in fact this is a discreditable, not a discredited, person, then. The issue is not that of managing tension generated during social contacts, but rather that of managing information about his failing (p 41-42).

Goffman discusses the concepts of "passing" or "covering" as some of the ways in which individuals attempt to conceal discrediting information about themselves. In general, passing is a process by which individuals try to prevent discrediting information from being applied to their social identities. Covering, on the other hand, involves various techniques to minimize the impact of a clearly defined stigma. In sum, passing involves attempts to traverse the social landscape while avoiding dangerous obstacles to one's identity and covering involves the process by which individuals experience the least amount of possible damage.

This framework provides an interesting explanation of how individuals who patronize peep shows in Times Square attempt to avoid revealing their personal identities to others. In these instances, they engage in a form of "hiding," in that their stigma, if discovered, would be based on being "seen" in an establishment that is considered seedy and disreputable. Moreover, given the various sex acts that take place in peep shows (especially in the homosexual sections), it is often assumed by many non-patrons that if a person is found there, he or she must also participate in these activities. Thus, the setting of the peep show provides an interesting opportunity to examine the various techniques that individuals use to play the "information game." This chapter, then, attempts to shed light on the characteristics of peep show patrons and their attempts to conceal their behavior, both inside and outside the establishments.

METHODS

For the purposes of this study, I define peep shows as those establishments that offer magazines, books, and pornographic movies and contain video booths in which patrons may view a segment of a pornographic movie for a short period of time. This definition distinguishes it from those establishments that offer live entertainment (sometimes referred to as "lap dancing"), where the performers come into physical contact with customers, or those that offer live entertainment viewed from a booth.

The data collected for this study were part of a larger ethnographic study of male prostitution in Times Square. Since virtually every hustler uses the peep shows in some form, a great deal of time was spent inside the homosexual sections of these shops. As a result, I was able to make observations of clients or "tricks," employees, and other individuals who frequented the shops. It took only a short time to realize that there was an organized set of rules that regulates behavior when one enters the shop. I also learned that while prostitution is a common element in the peep shows, it is but one of the many activities that take place there.

While the observations took place both inside and outside the shops, the majority of the interviews and informal conversations with hustlers, clients, and other patrons occurred outside, often as we walked along 8th Avenue or 42nd Street. One exception to this were the interviews with store employees, which took place inside the shops. Interestingly, as the interviews progressed, the employees began to make many references to my research project. The reason for this, I believe, had to do with the fact that these individuals were violating one of the norms of the peep show setting which prohibits almost every form of conversation inside the shop. These employees were essentially engaging in a form of impression management to repair the damage to *their* social identities.

TYPES OF PATRONS

My time observing the peep show scene, interviewing its participants, as well as the contacts I established, revealed a number of patterns in terms of the characteristics of individuals who patronize the peep show. While it is indeed difficult to paint the picture of the "typical" patron, a typology of patrons is revealed.

Cruisers

This type of patron consists primarily of older gay men who frequent or "cruise" through the homosexual sections of peep shows. These men are usually on public assistance, live nearby, and considered "regulars" by the employees. They are looking for friends or perhaps someone interested in a brief sexual encounter. At times they have "picked up" hustlers, but their primary goal is companionship. Since they spend so much time in the shops and have been cruising for so many years, they know this is a central locale for hustlers and other companions.

Suits

This group, made up of middle- to upper-class professionals complete with briefcases and three-piece suits, are the commuters, whose primary purpose in using the peep shows is either to browse through magazines or, more often, simply to watch the movies in the booth while killing time before their trip home. They rarely purchase anything and are perhaps the group most concerned about being identified inside the shop.

Movie Buffs

The majority of these individuals use the peep shows for the purpose of purchasing homosexual pornographic movies. They seem to refrain from examining the other literature, the various sexual accessories, or the video booths and confine themselves to the sections of the shop where the movies are displayed. Interestingly, these tend to be older men, although they differ from the cruisers in that they seem uninterested in arranging a sexual encounter while in the peep show.

They remain in the peep show for the least amount of time, on average approximately ten minutes, and often leave without purchasing anything, only to return shortly thereafter and complete the transaction. The reason for this remains undiscovered: perhaps, like the average shopper, they need time to contemplate their purchase.

Shoppers

These individuals seem to be interested in the pornographic magazines that are located in various places around the peep show, as well as the sexual accessories section of the store, which includes items such as chains, dog collars, and various types of bondage equipment, as well as inflatable devices. Thus, of all the patrons, these are really the most product-oriented consumer, and the peep show managers prefer them simply because they spend the largest amount of money each time they come into the store. However, the employees showed this group no special consideration: they were viewed with disdain equal to that for other patrons. The number of times they entered the peep shows was less than with the cruisers, but they spent considerably more money each time.

Adventurers

This group, although small in number and visiting infrequently, makes up an important part of the peep show scene. It is made up of tourists, young adults, couples, and others who seem to be more interested in using the peep shows to satisfy curiosity than anything else. This is especially true in the homosexual sections of the shops. It is common to see a young couple enter this section of the peep show, make a cursory tour of the area, examine some of literature and movies, scrutinize the people congregating in this area, roll their eyes at each other in amusement, and depart quickly. These individuals pose perhaps the greatest danger to those who regularly frequent the shops, since they are "outsiders" who could recognize them.

Moreover, there is a noticeable difference in the behavior of the other patrons when adventurers arrive. The level of tension and anxiety noticeably increases and fewer patrons remain in the general area. Of those who do remain, there is a tendency for them to drift toward the darkest section of the shop, near the video booths.

Tricks

These are individuals whose primary purpose in patronizing peep shows is to locate a hustler and carry out a sexual encounter with him. Of course, finding a hustler is only one way in which peep shows are involved in male prostitution. For example, some clients may have already met their hustlers of choice at another location and agreed to meet him in one of the booths (see McNamara 1994).

Hustlers

Finally, we have perhaps the most important group of individuals in the peep show scene. Given its central place in the sex trade, the peep shows have been, and continue to be, an important part of the hustler's life. They provide a source of income, an area from which to operate, and a meeting place at which to socialize with other hustlers. An added advantage is that many hustlers have participated in the filming of homosexual pornographic movies. In a scene that almost resembles a book signing, hustlers will hang out near the movie section of the shop and try to pick up clients by telling them of their role in the movie. Additionally, hustlers can be found at various points in the hallway, where the booths are located. This is reminiscent of a "prostitution stroll" in that anyone walking down this hallway will be propositioned in various ways.

Because of the stigma associated with the sex trade in Times Square, and particularly, the peep show scene, most of the individuals who frequent these shops attempt to hide and to conceal information about themselves. This occurs at two levels: outside and inside the peep show. Outside, the risk factor of being seen is high but the association with being a peep show patron has not yet been confirmed. Once the person is inside, however, the risk of being identified and stigmatized is greater; consequently even more hiding takes place. This is largely due to the fact that adventurers may show up at any time and non-patrons may see the individual inside the shop as they pass by. Moreover, the concern for anonymity is especially true of those individuals who are interested in completing a transaction with a hustler.

BEHAVIOR OUTSIDE THE PEEP SHOW

There are a number of ways in which individuals attempt to demonstrate their social distance from the scene. That is, an individual who wishes to enter the peep show must find some way to conceal this fact from others. It is as if the individual were saying to all who might see him, "I am not the type of person who frequents these shops."

For instance, many patrons, and especially the suits, will stand outside the peep show entrance and give the appearance of casually waiting for someone in a place that just "happens" to be in front of the shop. At other times they may linger, standing near the curb as if waiting for a cab or bus. In either case, the intention is to demonstrate a clear distance between the shop and the individual. The person will stand in these places until it seems that "the coast is clear" and then quickly enter the shop.

Another technique involves walking by the shop and stopping, appearing to be a curious observer. The customer first looks through the window of the shop and then enters. Here there is no sense of rushing since, after all, the individual is simply a curious passerby.

The strategies are more elaborate and more surreptitious for an individual who is seeking a sexual exchange with a hustler. Because there are several peep shows in a relatively small geographic area, hustlers will often gather on the sidewalk in front of these shops to socialize. Moreover, a group of hustlers congregating in this area also signals potential clients of their availability. To the casual observer, these hustlers simply appear to be a group of friends who have met on the sidewalk.

A client who is interested in soliciting a hustler and wishes to complete the transaction inside the peep show must be extremely careful about his behavior in this type of situation. There are multiple levels of discrediting information revealed in this scenario: the risk of exposure by being seen entering a peep show, which is exacerbated by being identified as having solicited a hustler, and the possibility of getting caught engaging in the subsequent sexual activity inside a video booth. In an effort to offset some of these risks, clients employ a few strategies to limit their exposure.

For instance, one technique involves walking by a group of hustlers that has gathered, tapping the particular hustler on the back or shoulder, and continuing on toward the entrance of the shop. The client casually glances back to signal that this was not an accidental "bump," and his move toward the entrance indicates to the hustler that the client wishes him to follow. At this point, the client can enter the shop and the hustler will follow him a few moments later. Thus, the two men are not seen entering the peep show together, and there is no overt solicitation by the client.

Another technique involves attracting a hustler's attention and then indicating an interest in his services. For example, a client may act like one of the many commuters walking along 8th Avenue or 42nd Street and casually ask the hustler if he knows the time. The client then walks toward the preferred peep show, and the hustler will follow shortly thereafter. To the uninitiated, this type of behavior is seen as a relatively common exchange between two individuals in a large urban setting, an apparently innocuous interaction that prevents others from learning important and discrediting information about the client.

BEHAVIOR INSIDE THE PEEP SHOW

Once inside the peep show, the attempts at hiding become more pronounced. This is especially true in the homosexual section of the shop. Being seen in this particular section of the peep show has multiple ramifications. The person will be discredited for being seen in a peep show, for being in the homosexual section (which often leads to the interpretation that the individual is gay, which is another stigma), and will be perceived as attempting to engage in a sexual encounter inside the booths. Thus, there are fewer places in the Times Square scene where individuals are more concerned about their anonymity. As such, the environment and the interaction that takes place in it have led to a number of additional techniques, as well as the development of a set of norms to facilitate hiding behavior.

For one thing, the physical setting assists in fostering anonymity. The entire area is dimly lit, and the hallways that contain the video booths are almost completely dark. This is done ostensibly to allow patrons to view the movies more clearly, but an unintended consequence is that it allows the sexual transactions, and the solicitations that occur beforehand, to take place unnoticed.

Additionally, very few stores offer credit card sales, this is primarily a cash business. In the few stores that do allow credit card sales, employees usually avoid putting any type of explanation for the sale on the credit card slip. Once the sale is completed, whether by cash or other means, the items are put into a white plastic bag. The plain brown paper bag has become associated with the purchase of pornographic materials (Karp 1973) and as such, many shops have taken to using the white bags.

On a more personal level, patrons attempt to conceal their physical characteristics to avoid detection. Individuals in these settings avoid flashy clothing, opting instead for clothing of nondescript color and styles. Additionally, almost all patrons wear various types of hats and/or sunglasses in an effort to avoid recognition.

In addition to the individual techniques employed to remain anonymous, the nature of social interaction in the peep show has led to the development of a normative system that promotes appropriate behavior by the participants. For instance, patrons are very concerned about their own sense of personal space and careful not to violate the space of others. In fact, there are instances in which exaggerated efforts are undertaken to avoid any type of contact with another person. For example, as people browse through the different aisles, overt touching is not allowed. While some may contend that similar behavior is found in most bookstores, here it is especially pronounced. Wary patrons, who seem careful to avoid eye contact, give each other wide berths as they pass each other.

Similarly, there is little or no talking in the store. This is true among the patrons as well as between employees and patrons. For instance, there are usually three employees who work in this section of the shop. One employee monitors the cash register, another maintains security, and one employee's purpose is to provide change for patrons who wish to view the movies. When a patron requires change, he or she simply approaches this employee and hands over a dollar bill. The employee, in turn, takes the bill, makes change, and moves on to the next customer. No words are exchanged in this transaction. This lack of dialogue also applies when purchases are made. When customers approach the checkout counter with items such as movies, magazines, or accessories, they simply place the item and their money on the counter and wait. Without a word of greeting or acknowledgment, the employee will pick up the item and the money, make change and hand both back to the customer. Interestingly, Karp (1973) found that customers will typically lay the money on the counter and then retreat somewhat from the area. It is almost as if they do not wish to be seen making a purchase and, on the odd chance that someone will recognize them inside the shop, they try not to appear as if they were actually buying anything.

For patrons who seek to use the video booths for a sexual encounter with a hustler, there are a few other hiding techniques. Since there is a security guard posted in and around the area to prevent sexual activities from taking place inside the booths, clients must employ some means by which they can signal a hustler of their interest. Perhaps the most common method is for a client to pass by a hustler while holding a quarter between the index and middle fingers. This is done casually so that the security officer will not observe this type of proposition. If the hustler recognizes the sign and accepts, he simply enters one of the booths and the client will follow a moment or two later.

At times it is the hustler who initiates contact with the client. The way this is done is to simply linger near the booths and casually pull at the belt or touch the fly. At other times a hustler and a client have prearranged the meeting. The client will have already given the hustler a few quarters, which gives him a legitimate reason to be there: to watch the movies. The hustler remains near the booths until the client appears, whereupon the hustler selects a booth and the client sneaks in after him. This is known in the trade as "going for the coins" (McNamara 1994). In either case, the goal is to engage in the sexual activity and then leave the area with as little attention as possible.

Despite the various strategies employed to conceal one's identity, there are inevitably instances when individuals are recognized inside the shops. This is especially true of hustlers, who make little or no attempt to disguise their appearance. In these cases, a standing rule for both parties is to avoid showing any signs of recognition until outside the store. For the patrons, this prevents the situation from degenerating into an unpleasant scene, and for hustlers, it safely avoids any potential conflict with other hustlers, clients, or other individuals.

CONCLUSION

The behavior and activities of patrons in the peep shows in Times Square falls squarely within the dramaturgical tradition set out by Goffman's analysis of the presentation of self. Goffman's metaphor of the "information game" is perhaps best described in those situations where, not only does an individual wish to conceal information to those in his immediate social situation, he wishes to avoid disclosure of his public identity as well. Moreover, the potential risks to one's identity in soliciting the services of a male prostitute are many, and the discovery by others of such an attempt can have a sweeping and devastating impact on an individual's self-image. Thus, the need to remain anonymous and avoid revealing any personal information is of paramount importance in these transactions.

REFERENCES

Goffman, E. 1959. *The Presentation of Self in Everyday Life*. New York: Doubleday.
_____. 1963. *Stigma: Notes on the Management of Spoiled Identity*. New York: Simon and Schuster.
Karp, D. A. 1973. "Hiding in Pornographic Bookstores: A Reconsideration of the Nature of Urban Anonymity" *Urban Anthropology* pp.427-   451.
McNamara, R. P. 1994. *The Times Square Hustler: Male Prostitution in New York City*. Westport, CT: Praeger.

Male Prostitution in Times Square

Robert Hartmann McNamara
Department of Political Science and Criminal Justice
The Citadel

Historically, male prostitution has taken many forms, including "escort boys," those who worked in brothels, and even "kept boys," who served more as a companion to a client than a prostitute (Coombs 1974; Drew and Drake 1969; Weisberg 1985). While research on the subject of male prostitutes is still relatively sparse, there have been a few attempts to examine this population. For instance, the now classic study by Reiss (1961) found that most of the boys view prostitution as a job or simply a means of making money. He also found that many boys limit the scope of their activities which allows them to retain a sense of identity and control over their lives.

Other studies have attempted to identify common characteristics and describe the various motivations for becoming involved in prostitution (Weisberg 1985; Butts 1947; Jersild 1956; Ross 1959; Luckenbill 1986a, 1986b, 1985; Lloyd 1983; Campagna and Poffenberger 1988; James 1982; MacNamara 1965; West 1991; Bracey 1989). Most of the recent research has focused on the risks of AIDS and on the runaway population (see Ross, 1988; Elifson, Boles, and Sweat 1993; Calhoun and Pickerill 1988; Morse et al. 1991; Pleak and Meyer-Bahlburg 1990; Borus-Rotheram and Koopman 1991).

Thus, while it appears there is a growing body of AIDS related literature on this population, little is known about hustling in Times Square and even less is known about the ways in which hustlers develop a sense of cohesion as they share similar experiences. Part of the explanation is found in the way in which prostitution is practiced. In Times Square, male prostitution is more of an entrepreneurial activity occurring in an organized market area than is generally the case elsewhere. It is referred to colloquially as "hustling," a term whose meanings can include the activities of confidence men, drug dealers, those who deal with stolen merchandise and, in general, individuals who engage in a variety of illegal activities. However, the label "hustler" is also applied to males who engage in various sexual activities with other males for money, illegal drugs, or some other form of payment.

Hustling is incorporated into the definition of prostitution since the person seeks out and attempts to entice as many clients as possible without the benefit of a broker, client list, or other type of intermediary.

THE MARKETPLACE

Times Square possesses certain characteristics and institutions that facilitate prostitution. For instance, the peep shows, porno shops, hotels, bars, and the Port Authority Bus Terminal not only offer a centralized locale for the sex market, they also provide places for hustlers and clients to meet and carry out their transactions. Additionally, the influx of people who use the terminal and peep shows produces a steady supply of patrons to the market.

Virtually all these organizations are profit making, and the economic benefits they derive from hustling foster their acceptance. This is especially true of the hotels and peep shows, which have strong economic links to the sex trade. Consequently, the nature of hustling is predicated on the existence of these types of organizations as well as the manner in which they allow this type of activity to occur.

Moreover, the Port Authority Bus Terminal provides the market with a diurnal quality. In many ways, hustling is dependent on the work schedule of commuters and its frequency coincides with rush hours: hustlers are very busy early in the morning, as people make their way to work, and in the early evening, as they return home. There are also a number of older men who reside in the Times Square area who are either retired or living on public assistance. They, too, regularly solicit hustlers and know that the terminal serves as a central meeting place.

Another feature of the hustling market involves the activity's occupational structure. Because the vast majority of hustlers have few, if any, other means of economic support, hustling in Times Square is viewed as an income-producing activity. For most, it is a full-time job. While some are receiving public assistance, which would normally reduce participation in the trade, these hustlers usually have wives and children to support. Thus, the need to earn a living from hustling remains important.

In this way, hustling can be seen as an occupation for almost all the participants. Another illustration of this occupational role is demonstrated by the fact that most of the hustlers do not reside in the market area. In fact, many live outside Manhattan and, like so many other workers, must commute to Times Square every day. Additionally, part of the market is organized for the hustlers themselves. For instance, there are certain bars or parks where hustlers meet to socialize only with friends and colleagues.

In sum, there is a local market in which hustling exists, and it has a certain organization. There is a sense of territoriality in that it is found in a relatively small geographic area; it is organized along ethnic lines to the extent that most hustlers are Hispanic while almost all clients are Caucasian; there is a social class dimension; it is an income-producing activity rather than a recreational one; most of the hustlers work in the area and live elsewhere; the market depends to some extent on repeat clients, who either travel through on their way to work or reside in the area; and there are institutions and organizations that either facilitate hustling or provide places where hustlers can gather on their own. This article, based on a two year ethnographic study of hustling in Times Square, and consisting of numerous interviews and conversations with hustlers and those involved in the life, describes the nature of this market and its participants, as well as some of the important events which have affected it.

In addition to the organizational qualities of hustling, perhaps the most important contribution of this study may be to offer a way of thinking about hustling in Times Square. I view the hustlers of Times Square as a community within a structured marketplace. Moreover, the community's existence is due in part to the organizational features of the hustling market. The hustling community is currently being affected by a number of changes taking place in Times Square. Urban redevelopment, the emergence of crack, and an increased impact of AIDS, among other factors, have affected virtually every aspect of hustling in Times Square and each member of the population.

But what is life as a male prostitute like? Since this is a street level activity, one might think that everyone is concerned only with their own sense of survival. Being on the street usually connotes a desperate situation: one in which altruism and abiding by the rules do not apply. However, among the hustlers in Times Square, something unusual occurs. There are norms that regulate the trade, the boys' behavior, as well as various types of social control–which are understood and practiced by everyone involved. Because this is a rather unusual phenomenon, allow me to describe what the life is like and then demonstrate how this high level of social organization results in a predictable type of interaction whereby everyone involved in the trade comes away from the interaction achieving their objectives.

Do The Hustle

A typical day for a hustler begins early, often as early as 7 a.m., and ends as late as two or three the next morning. The weekend schedule is different, beginning and ending later and sometimes involving overnight stays with clients. The excitement of the weekend contrasts with the idleness of the remaining days of the week.

The Port Authority Bus Terminal is a special place for many hustlers. Much of the hustling in Times Square occurs either in the Terminal or in the peep shows. Both offer anonymity for the client because of the great deal of human traffic through both places. The exodus of commuters from the City, for example, especially at rush hour, offers clients the opportunity to lose themselves in the throng of people making their way home and to carry out transactions with hustlers without attracting much attention.

One particular area in the Terminal is known among hustlers and clients as the "Meat Rack." This is an area near some of the departure gates where the majority of hustling takes place. When the two parties reach an agreement, they go to a variety of places: the peep shows, a local hotel, the client's apartment or car, or one of the restrooms inside the Terminal. However, the latter are now considered less of a sanctuary for hustlers as a result of an aggressive police presence, which includes undercover operations. These areas are now used sparingly or for limited activities such as what Lite describes:

> I don't do nothin' that I... I don't do nothin'....the farthest thing I did was to jerk another man off you know what I'm sayin'? But I never sucked a dick, never fucked another person. I tell them straight up you know, like they say 'yo you wanna come with me? You know I'll give you $70.' But then when we start walkin' I'll say stop and what you all about man? What you want me to do? I'll say 'listen, I don't get fucked and I don't fuck nobody.' The only thing I do is jerk off and I will let them watch. I'll strip for them too and let them look at my body.
>
> But no kissing, I don't kiss no men. Sometimes you can catch the tricks early in the morning too. Like I had this trick at 9 o'clock in the morning. You can catch them before they go to work or sometimes a trick will get them when they goin' into the bathroom. That's another kind of trick. You only get five dollars for the bathroom. You go to the bathroom and make like you peein' and somebody's watchin' the door. You get it hard and then you jerk off and then they get off but you don't do nothin' though. You don't want to come, you definitely don't want to come. Cause then you can't make no more money. If you gonna come, it's gotta be a real expensive trick or the last one you

gonna do that day, and even then you charge him extra for that.

As Lite mentioned, hustling activities are marked by their diversity. A group of hustlers explain further:

Smokealot: It depends on who the trick is and what they want you to do. Like some guys will just come up to you and say how much? Right then you know they be Five-0 [the police] because they got to get you to admit the price first. But some of the tricks will come up to you and ask you what your name is, what you like to do, if you wanna get high or somethin' like that. We work out an arrangement depending on what the trick wants. I only go with tricks I know so I ain't gonna get picked up [arrested]. But other guys will pick up anybody. And usually, depending on what they want, you can make anywhere from 30 to 40 dollars a trick. See it depends on a lotta factors like what they want, how long they wanna go. It's just like females youknowhatI'msayin? But like for an average, it's about 30 dollars. But you always gotta be clockin' [observing or watching him closely] the man to make sure he ain't Five-0.

Canno: Well a lot of it depends on how long it takes them to come. Also you gotta know what kind of things that get them off. So you gotta have the knack. Sometimes they get off by watching you come. I mean I have a trick that wants me to come in, take my clothes off and pose for him, flexin' and shit you know. Sometimes there are people that can't come, you gotta make 'em come, that's your job. Then there's overnights. I tell them straight up. Fifty dollars alone for me just to go to your house. Then there's another $50 to do anything, and another $50 to stay over. So it's like a hundred and fifty dollars. And like different guys work out different arrangements. Like this one john he'll take a twenty dollar bill and rip it in half. He'll give you half and take half. So if he feels he's satisfied, he'll give you the other half and you just tape it and spend it. But if he's not happy, we both lose.

Raul: A lotta the hustling that goes on here ain't all that bad. I mean you go with a guy, maybe he's a member of the nickel and dime club. Those are the guys who pay you five or ten dollars and they blow you or jerk you off. We call them the nickel and dime club cause they be a lot of lonely old gay guys who are on welfare that come here and pick up guys. It takes maybe ten minutes. Sometimes they get off just watchin' you take off your clothes. Or they suck on your knob for a little bit and then they go.

But there's a lotta crazy motherfuckers out there too though. Like guys who will pay you good money, but the shit they want you to do is crazy man. So it depends, okay I met this guy. Another guy introduced me to him. He says 'yo you into bondage?' Yeah I could get into it. He says 'come on then.' We got into this taxi, the guy was in the middle. He said 'go and buy a carton of cigarettes.' I said 'a carton of cigarettes? I only want a pack.' He says 'no not for you, I want you to burn me.' He paid me a hundred dollars an hour to burn him with a pack of cigarettes every hour. I burned him all over his chest, his back, his legs, everywhere. At first I felt like throwin' up. I felt like weird, that was the first time I did that, puttin' the cigarette on him. I burned almost the whole carton on him. He paid me five hundred dollars for that.

I seen this other guy he took me to his house. You know them things that you see on TV they torture people, they put they head in things. [like a pillory?] Yeah yeah a pillory yeah. And he had a big old paddle man, with spikes in it. You know what I'm talkin' about the kind you got in schools? And he wanted me to beat him with it on his butt. I kept beating him and beating him and I asked him is it enough and he says 'no no I'll tell you when to stop.' Some weird shit man.

It appears then that hustling can consist of simply voyeurism, posing nude, masturbating clients, or sadomachoism, in addition to oral and anal sex.

The frequency with which the boys hustle also varies considerably. Some hustle every day, turning as many tricks as possible, while others are satisfied with one or two per day. The deciding factor, obviously, is how much money the boy needs to make. Those with drug habits, especially those addicted to crack, need to hustle as much as possible. Family men need a steady income, but since their income is supplemented by public relief, they usually hustle less frequently than other hustlers.

Lite: I hustle at least once a day. The most people I picked up in a day? Seven. I usually pick up like three or four. And if I get like thirty dollars each time then I chill for the rest of the day. Maybe I don't come back here for two or three days.

Apache: I come down here a good four times a week and most of the time I'll pull in two tricks a day. I could pull more, but I'll just pull two tricks. The average hustler around here? He'll pull I guess five to seven tricks and make himself a good 3-400 dollars in like five hours.

Dead Head: Like I gotta go with as many guys as I can cause I ain't got no money and no place to stay. Some days I'll do good and get four or five, which is maybe like a hundred and fifty bucks. That's cool cause then I can eat and stuff and maybe go to a movie, buy some pot or whatever. But I gotta do more than most of these guys cause I'm broke. [what is your average number for a day?] The average? Well, I guess it's probably like two a day. Yeah... probably one or two a day. But some days, just like anybody, I get skunked and nobody comes around.

Obviously, the amount per trick varies according to what the client requires, but the amount can also be determined by the talents of individual hustlers. For instance, some hustlers, such as Apache, are better negotiators and often convince clients to pay more than the usual fee.

While the Terminal is popular, the other primary location for hustling are the peep shows. As was mentioned, in the basement of many of these shops there is a section which caters to the homosexual client. Virtually every shop has a sign prohibiting hustling, prostitution, drug dealing, and the entry of minors, but one can easily find young men of questionable age standing in the long hallways of the shop.

The typical transaction in a peep show involves the hustler entering the peep show first and meeting the client near the booths. The client has already given the boy a few quarters which gives him a legitimate reason for being there: to watch the movies. This is known as "going for the coins." Each party enters the booth separately whereby the "coins" or quarters, are then put in the video machine while the sexual act(s) takes place.

The managers and clerks of these shops are adamant about not allowing hustlers in their stores. Zenith, a clerk in one of the more popular peep shows, describes it in this way:

> These kids come in here lookin' to hustle and shit. They come in here and they get a boot out the other way. They ain't supposed to be here and they don't stay. They got to be 21 and then they can't hustle even if they are over 21. I ain't gonna deal with none of that shit as long as I'm the guy who makes those decisions and I do. [how long have you worked here?] Me? I been here goin' on twelve years now. Look there's a sign on the door that says we don't want no prostitutes, no drug dealers, no boosters, none of that shit. Keep it outside these walls. And to make sure none of them little assholes slide in here, I got a guy who stands in that hallway back there and throws people out if they stand there too long. We ain't got none of that in here. Maybe in the other places you do, but not here.

As we are talking, several boys who don't appear anywhere near twenty one walk in and around the store. Moreover, the boys tell me it is quite easy to operate in these shops: they simply bribe both the clerk and the security officer. As long as the hustler is discreet and does not cause trouble, the employees are willing to ignore the illicit activity. Raul tells me of his experiences with the peep shows:

> See a lotta these places will let you in the booths and shit and sometimes there'll be more than one in a booth and that's how it goes,

but they ain't supposed to let you in there with them. [do they have guards or someone standing there?] Most of the guys they got working there are on parole and this is their job. And if they catch you, like across the street and shit, they beat the shit outta you and take whatever money you got on you. But that don't keep 'em from takin' your money for workin' in there.

Thus, the peep shows have been, and continue to be, an integral part of a hustler's life. They offer a relatively safe working environment as well as a steady source of income. An added allure of the peep shows is that the shops also sell homosexual porno tapes. According to Apache, a number of boys have participated in the filming of these movies, and it is not uncommon to see posters of them on the walls of the shops advertising one of their movies. Apache and I discuss this venture:

MC: I hear a lot about the movies and stuff do you know anything about it? What's the deal?

Apache: Um, you talkin' about Richie. Richie, he's the one who makes movies, but he makes sex movies. Sex movies. He's all right, he's cool people.

MC: How does that work?

Apache: He'll come down here and if he sees somebody that he likes, somebody who looks good and stuff, he'll ask them if they want to make a few bucks. If they do, he'll tell them what to do and stuff like that. And he gets them... and the most he'll pay is like $200 the most. So that ain't so good and shit. A lotta these guys around here will bullshit and say they got like $2,000 or $20,000 to do a movie. That's bullshit. I know, I did it and I seen other guys who did it and all they get is like $200.

MC: And how long does it take to make one of these movies?

Apache: It could take like two hours, and then he turns around and sells them to the video stores. And he sells them for forty or fifty bucks. I made what two, three movies.

MC: That's a good $600....

Apache: No but I mean, for me, for me he pays more, cause I charge him extra for pictures and stuff.

MC: So he takes pictures too for layouts and stuff in addition to the movie?

Apache: Yeah yeah. But those kids around here they don't know nothin' about pictures and shit, so they'll just do the movie and take pictures and shit for two hundred dollars. In the mean time, when they take pictures and do the movie with me, they pay a good, three hundred, three fifty.

MC: So he's paying you for both...You don't get a percentage or anything like that right? You just get a flat fee and he makes whatever he can off it?

Apache: You get paid for the movie but that's about it.

MC: This may sound like a weird question but, with these movies is there any safe sex involved?

Apache: Yeah I just thought about safe sex. I mean, he makes sure that when he's filming the two guys whatever they gonna be doing, he makes sure the camera sees the two guys taking the condom and opening and putting it on, so they're real safe and all that.

MC: So they'll show that right in the movie?

Apache: But I mean, that part is not in the movies. He films it, so it's legal for him to film it. He films it, but that part won't come out in the movie. You go to a peep show, you go into a peep show, you put in a quarter, they ain't gonna show a guy puttin' on no condom.
MC: So they have to do that while they're filming and then they edit it out.

Apache: Yeah while they're filming but then they take it out. It's like you have to be legal about it you know.

MC: Why do a lot of guys do these movies?

Apache: Well most of them are gay, but a lotta guys want the money. I hear all the time about guys bitchin' about not gettin' a percentage and how Richie is making money off them. Listen, Richie is makin' money off them, but so are a lotta people. He's the one who has to pay for all this stuff, it's his money and there ain't nobody puttin' no gun to nobody's head to do it either. All these guys out here who bitch about it, you don't hear them complain about how the drugs they bought are stepped on and full of all kinds of shit right? You don't hear them motherfuckin' the dealer right? But they bitch on Richie. They bitch but most of them have still done it.

According to the boys, clients like to seek out and solicit the actors of these movies. Raul states,

> It's like they think they rubbin' elbows with a celebrity or somethin'. I mean, they see the movie and then find the hustler and try to act out their fantasies with them like they in the movie or somethin'. They get off on it.

I had a chance to talk to Richie on a few occasions. His description and assessment of his business tended to verify what Apache and Raul had to say about it.

> Richie: Most of the guys come in here thinkin' they're gonna be stars and make millions. It ain't like that. When they find out how much I pay, some of them want a percentage of the profits. I tell 'em, who do you think you are, Slyvester Stallone? This is what I pay and that's it - you want it fine, if not, I got plenty of guys willing to do it. Some of these guys amaze me.

The Norms of Hustling

From the various types of activities to the movie making ventures, a pattern to hustling exists to which all the participants respond. There are agreed upon locations, a familiar dialogue, and a roughly established pricing policy for the various activities. This pattern fosters stability in hustling. For the most part, very few problems occur between the hustler and the client or among the boys themselves. In the vast majority of cases, the activities are completed without incident.

These patterns of behavior can be seen as a normative system that regulates the boys' behavior. One extremely important norm is that once a hustler and a client begin a conversation, another hustler should never intervene. This serves as a territorial marker that is not to be encroached upon. Violation of this norm can lead to severe and violent retaliation.

> Flacco: You see that's one thing among hustlers. You don't go and ask nobody, even if you are asking the hustler for money, you don't do it in front of the trick. You don't do that. You don't do that. This one kid caught a serious beat down from me around the corner for that. I had this one trick he was gonna give me $75 just for hangin' out with him and man, he was about to step off and get into the van to go to New Jersey. This hustler walks up and asks the guy for fuckin' ten dollars man. In front of me! And I looked at him and said 'Yo you should

have never done that.' And the trick got all roust and this and that and he said to me 'Look I'm sorry I just don't like people asking me for money.' And he stomped away all pissed off. I turned around and said 'Listen, first of all, you need money you come and see me. But don't you EVER EVER get in front of one of my tricks.' And then I kicked the shit outta him so he would never forget that.

Another related norm involves time and etiquette. There are times when a hustler and a trick cannot complete a transaction either because of price, type of activity, or some other reason. When this occurs another hustler may offer his services to the man provided he waits until he is certain this initial conversation has ended. This is often referred to as being a "free agent." Playboy explains:

Yeah well it's like this. See if Flacco is talking to this guy but they can't work it out, the guy or Flacco starts to leave. As long as he is far enough away so that everybody knows he ain't goin' with him, then he's a free agent and can negotiate whatever deal he wants with anybody else. I can go up to him now and there's no problem 'cause Flacco ain't got no claim on him see? That's what we mean by free agent. But I gotta make sure the guy ain't comin' back to Flacco before I approach him else I'm gonna get my ass kicked. I do that by waitin' until he is far enough away and then maybe I ask Flacco what's up?

Parenthetically, no one can give an exact time or distance that a client must be from the hustler in order to qualify as a free agent. There seems to be an implicit understanding about how far is "enough." In all likelihood, the longer another hustler waits and the further the client is from the initial contact, the less likely the norm will be violated.

Another important norm has to do with preserving and enhancing one's reputation within the community. While one's street reputation is always important in these circles (e.g. being able to handle one's self, showing courage, bravery, etc.), one's hustling reputation is quite important since it has far reaching implications. A cardinal rule among the boys is to never allow a client to publicly humiliate or insult him in front of his peers. This leads others to believe that the particular hustler is weak (which can lead to a loss of status and a violent retaliation by the group), and it serves as a reminder to other hustlers that they too can be treated that way. Additionally, an incident such as this sends a message to the clients that public humiliation of the boys is acceptable behavior. Thus, if a hustler does not respond to a challenge to his reputation, it has serious ramifications for him, his social standing, and it threatens the very structure and social order of the community.

Canno: See around here your reputation isn't everything, it's the only thing. If I let some fuckin' trick come in here and take advantage of me in front of everybody, then I'm lettin' myself down and I'm lettin' everybody else down too. They be thinkin' I'm nothin' but a punk and now I got to deal with them tryin' to get over on me. And every trick that sees this happen starts thinkin' 'hey why don't I do that too. He got away with it so why can't I?' So everybody has got to get involved now if I don't deal with it first. But it's better just to not let it ever come up in the first place.

Watchdog: I'm gonna tell you a little story. This is a story about a guy, I ain't gonna tell you his name. He likes to go out with guys and screw them and then gives them twenty dollars. So he walked up to me this morning, he never walked up to me before. He come up to me and asks me what I like to do. So I said 'Listen, first of all, you see me this morning, I cost a hundred dollars. Second of all this morning, I don't get screwed, I don't get screwed, I never got screwed by no asshole like you.' So he starts talkin' all this shit. So I tell him Listen... and before he even told me about the twenty dollars... so I told him 'if you think you gonna pay me twenty dollars for me to get screwed you must be outta your mind.'

So he gets all offended and starts talkin' shit to me about how he could do what he wants to me and all this shit. Then he called me a motherfucker. Well, that was it. He did this right in front of everybody thinking everybody gonna be laughin' and shit and on his side. Well it got real quiet all of the sudden up here. So I walk up to him and get right in his face and ask him real quiet what he said. He looks around and now everybody be lookin' real pissed off at him and he got scared. He be like 'nothin' I didn't say nothin' I was just fuckin' around you know.' And I said 'Listen, don't be fuckin' around like that around here. So don't say shit like that unless you lookin' to back it up.' So now he's real nervous and he apologizes and walks real quick to the escalators. We ain't gonna see him for a while now. But he can't be doin' that shit especially right in front of everybody.

The relationships that exist among the boys also plays an important role in the hustling culture. Some, such as Apache, look upon the hustling community as one big family. He says,

It's really like a family here. Everybody knows everybody else, everybody is basically friends with everybody else and there's kind of a support group you know. But it's like any big family of boys: you gonna have arguments and fights and people gonna get pissed off at each other but basically we all know what we're about and if somebody needs something and we know them, we help them out. The New Jacks (new hustlers) are different cause we don't know what they about yet. But after you been here a while and you straight up, you added to the family.

Like brothers, hustlers usually pair off and hang out together, sharing drugs, money, or other incidentals. Moreover, a sense of loyalty and responsibility develops between each boy and his partner whereby each boy tries to protect the other. When one goes with a client to a hotel for example, his partner will usually wait for his companion either outside the room or at the entrance to the hotel.

In some cases however, a hustler's partner is not always available. In those instances where a hustler has been picked up by an unknown client, there is an understanding among the members of the community that the boy will not go with him alone. There is usually someone who is hanging out or has just returned from a sexual exchange who will accompany the hustler. What is significant about this norm is that it also includes those situations in which a hustler would sacrifice his own trick to protect his comrade. While I believe this norm emerged as a result of survival rather than altruism, it is an important element in the nature of the trade.

Admittedly, I had some initial difficulty understanding this rule. The streets are such a desperate place, and this particular type of street life seemed, at first glance, to be particularly problematic for the participants. However, one must recognize that many hustlers engage in the trade to supplement their income. As a result, a number of hustlers are not involved in the mad scramble to earn every single dollar they can. In fact, in some cases, their situation allows them to forego the economic advantages in the name of maintaining strong social ties.

Consider Eddie and Jose's relationship. Eddie always goes with Jose when he takes a client to a nearby hotel. He waits outside the main entrance to ensure that Jose comes out safely. Jose, in turn, does the same thing for Eddie.

> Jose: This thing? It's a job, a constant job. You eat off it, you get clothes off it, you get drugs off it, you meet a lotta people, but you gotta know what you doin' or else you gonna get hurt. Every day somethin' happens... Every day me, him, everybody runs into somebody. Either 'Yo you wanna get high, you wanna make a few dollars, you wanna go eat and make a few dollars, let's go.' It happens, it happens. I turned Eddie on to a steady of mine. And every time the steady sees him, he throws me some money, maybe five or ten dollars. We know which ones pay more than others. Like if a guy wants me and he looks at me, and he looks at him I know him, I tell him 'Yo that guy is $35 take him.' Or he'll tell me 'Yo what is that date like, no that nigger fucks you,' or I'll tell him 'No don't go with him he wants you to suck his dick.' So Boom I'll let him know.

> Eddie: You gotta be careful of tricks though. They be like 'No you didn't do the job right' so you gotta get really really uptight sometimes and perform in there, 'I'm gonna beat the shit outta you you're not leavin' this room.' I usually bring him with me. He gets picked up and I see him go into a hotel, I'll wait in front of the hotel. Like if you go to their apartment and they do somethin' there, some of these guys they gotta realize they gotta pay. Like this one Japanese guy I had the

other day. We were in the booth, you can go in the booths with these guys. Well this guy didn't think he had to pay cause we went in the booth together. I took this guy and lifted him up by his neck in the booth and took his money.

He didn't think he had to pay. So for not payin' me the twenty dollars you owe me, I'm takin' your wallet. That was a hundred and fifty dollars, his quarters, and a lottery ticket. He was cryin' over that. I took his phone card too and brought it to the Port and sold it for $35. And where was my boy? He was right outside the booth waitin' to see if I needed him. We got high that night. [high fives partner]

This issue of loyalty also emerges when conflict arises. For instance, when conflicts and fights occur, it is expected and even demanded that a hustler's friends, and, especially, his partner, come to his defense. The issue of who's right is irrelevant; the only concern is how many friends will be fighting along side of him when fists fly.

For instance, one day Angel began arguing with another male in front of the bus terminal. As is often the case, the situation escalated into a brawl in a matter of minutes. The other young man had three associates with him, whereas Angel had but one companion, Nelson. Given the high police presence in and around the area, the fight began and ended quickly. Yet Nelson failed to join in and support Angel. Raul and I were walking down 8th Avenue when we saw what was happening. Running to the scene, Raul became furious when he learned Nelson did not react:

Raul: That stupid son of a bitch! What is this bullshit about bein' on parole? That's fuckin' bullshit! If I see my boy is gettin' a beat down, and that's my real boy, you think I'm on parole I can't do nothin'? I'm gonna jump on the motherfucker even faster cause I know I'm a go back upstate. He's talkin' about bein' on parole. I be like 'Yo man what's up I thought you were one of my boys man?' That's when he be gettin' a serious ass beatin' I should kick his ass now in front of everybody just to teach him a motherfuckin' lesson. I'm gonna get you man! You and me man!

Thus, the relationships between hustlers have far reaching effects. Most maintain close ties with one other hustler while being a part of the larger collectivity. The trade norms include personal protection from tricks as well as other outside threats, and a standing rule involves sharing drugs or money. If a hustler has one or the other, he is expected to share with his friends and associates. This allows everyone to endure and pass the time. Additionally, as Eddie mentions, there is an unwritten "book" about clients. Hustlers will share information on clients in terms of what is expected in terms of payment or any particular preferences the trick may have.

Judging from what the hustlers, clients, and others associated with the trade say, as well as my own observations of events, it seems clear that the sense of cohesion among the hustlers is quite strong. There is a sense of community felt among this population and this degree of social organization allows the trade to operate with a type of rhythm and flow. As long as everyone understands and abides by the rules, there are few problems. There is even a mechanism in place to socialize new hustlers to the rules of the trade.

Finally, a clearly defined mechanism of informal social control also operates within the hustler community. The threat of punishment has been a clear deterrent to those who might consider deviating from the norm. In fact, one could even argue that the hustlers of Times Square are a good example of a consensus model of society: as a group and as individuals, the hustlers believe that following the norms of the trade are in everyone's best interest.

However, having said this, as was mentioned, a number of social, political, and economic changes have taken place in Times Square which have posed threats to this established system. The emergence of crack cocaine as well as the massive redevelopment efforts in the Times Square area have caused more than a few problems for the community, both in terms of opportunities to hustle as well as the nature of social interaction between the participants. What remains to be seen is if these changes will have a permanent deleterious effect on the population and the trade.

REFERENCES

Borus-Rotheram, Mary, and Cheryl Koopman.1991. "Sexual Risk Behaviors, AIDS Knowledge and Beliefs about AIDS among Runaways." *American Journal of Public Health* 81(2):206-208.

Bracey, Dorothy. 1989. *Baby Pros: Adolescent Prostitution.* New York: John Jay Press.

Butts, William Marlin. 1947. "Boy Prostitutesof the Metropolis." *Journal of Clinical Psychopathology* 8:673-681.

Calhoun, Thomas, and Brian Pickerill. 1988."Young Male Prostitutes: Their Knowledge of Selected Sexually Transmitted Diseases."*Psychology: A Journal of Human Behavior* 25(3/4):1-8.

Campagna, Daniel J., and Donald L. Poffenberger. 1988. *The Sexual Trafficking of Children.* South Hadley, Mass: Auburn House.

Coombs, Neil. 1974. "Male Prostitution: A Psychological View of Behavior." *American Journal of Orthopsychiatry* 44(5):782-789.

Drew, Dennis, and Jonathan Drake. 1969. *Boys for Sale.* New York: Brown Book Company.

Elifson, Kurt, Jacqueline Boles, and Michael Sweat. 1993. "Risk Factors Associated with HIV Infection Among Male Prostitutes." *American Journal of Public Health* 83:79-83.

James, Jennifer. 1982.*Entrance into Male Prostitution.* Washington D.C.: The National Institute of Mental Health.

Jersild, Jens. 1956. *Boy Prostitution.*Copenhagen, Denmark: C. E. Gad.

Lloyd, Robin. 1976. *For Money or Love.* New York: The Free Press.

Luckenbill, David. 1985. "Dynamics of the Deviant Sale." *Deviant Behavior* 5(1): 131-51.

Luckenbill, David. 1986a. "Deviant Career Mobility: The Case of Male Prostitution." *Social Problems* 33(4):283-96.

Luckenbill, David.1986b. "Entering Male Prostitution." *Urban Life*

14(2):131-53.

MacNamara, Donal E.J. 1965. "Male Prostitution in American
    Cities: A Socioeconomic or Pathological Phenomenon?"
    American Journal of Orthopsychiatry 35:204.

Morse, Edward, Patricia Simon, Howard Osofsky, Paul Balson, and
    Richard Gaumer.1991. "The Male Street Prostitute: A Vector
    for Transmission of HIV Infection into the Heterosexual World."
    Social Science and Medicine 32(5):535.

Pleak, Richard R., and Heino Meyer-Bahlburg. 1990. "Sexual
    Behavior and AIDS Knowledge of Young Male Prostitutes in
    Manhattan." *Journal of Sex Research* 27(4):557-587.

Reiss, Albert J., Jr. 1961. "The Social Integration of Queers and
    Peers." *Social Problems* 9(2):102-20.

Ross, Laurence H. 1959. "The Hustler in Chicago." *Journal of Student Research*
    1:13-19.

Ross, Michael. 1988. "Social and Behavioral Aspects of Male Homosexuals" *The Medical
    Clinics of North America* 70(3):537-47.

Weisberg, Kelly D. 1985. *Children of the Night*. Mass: Lexington Books.

West, Donald J. 1991. *Male Prostitution*. New York: Harrington Park Press.

The Socialization of the Police

Robert Hartmann McNamara
Department of Political Science and Criminal Justice
The Citadel

The concept of socialization has been subjected to extensive analysis with the definitions of the concept varying widely. Generally speaking, we can say the term socialization is used to describe the ways in which people learn to conform to their society's norms, values, and roles. Many sociologists contend that people develop their own unique personalities as a result of the learning they gain from parents, siblings, relatives, teachers, and all the other people who influence them throughout their lives (Elkin and Handel 1989). What is important about socialization then, is that people learn to behave according to the expectations of their culture and transmit that way of life from one generation to the next. In this way, the culture of a society is reproduced (see for instance Parsons and Bales 1955; Danziger 1971).

It is also important to note that socialization occurs throughout an individual's life as he or she learns the norms of new groups in new situations. Generally speaking, there are three categories of socialization: *primary*, which involves the ways in which the child becomes a part of society; *secondary*, where the influence of others outside the family become important, and *adult socialization*, when the person learns the expectations of adult roles and statuses in society. This latter socialization includes learning the standards set by one's occupation.

The Socialization Process in Occupations

Of the many roles that a person is called upon to perform, few surpass the importance of possessing the skills and attitudes necessary for one's occupation. This is especially true in modern society where occupation has a central place in the life of the vast majority of adults. In fact, occupation is challenged only by the family and the peer group as the major determinant of behavior and attitudes (Moore 1968). To the degree that adequate socialization occurs to permit one to adequately perform in an occupation, an individual's world view, attitudes towards others, and general well being are influenced.

Interestingly, occupational socialization has not elicited the kind of scholarly interest that one might expect. While there are many studies on this topic, academic interest in socialization traditionally focused on infancy and childhood. It has only been within the last thirty years or so that researchers have become keenly interested in occupational socialization, or what is sometimes referred to as the sociology of work (see Erikson 1995). And the topics seem to focus on the normative dimensions of occupations; that is, the rules relating to the proper conduct and attitudes of an individual in a particular job or career.

For instance, in a classic study of socialization into an occupation, Becker et. al (1961) examined the process by which medical students are socialized into their profession. At the University of Kansas Medical School, Becker found that lower-class medical students, by virtue of their undergraduate education and commitment to becoming successful physicians, had clearly assimilated middle-class norms and values. Becker also found that first year medical students had idealistic reasons for becoming a physician: helping people was more important than making money. In the beginning of their profession then, there was a strong sense of idealism and many students felt that medical school would give them the opportunity to develop the skills needed to further that goal.

However, the process of medical training caused the students to alter their views. Early on, they adapted to the expectations of medical school and developed a strong appreciation of clinical experience (working with patients rather than reading about disease and studying it in the laboratory). They also learned to view disease and death as medical problems rather than as emotional issues. Additionally, despite their idealism, students in medical school quickly learned that they could not learn everything they need to know to practice medicine, and soon directed their efforts toward finding the most economical way of learning. Generally, this meant guessing what their faculty wanted them to know so that the material could be studied for the examinations. Thus, during the course of their medical training, idealism was replaced with a concern for getting through the program. Becker observed that medical students may in fact become cynical while in school, but he pointed out that these attitudes were often situational. As graduation approached, idealism seemed to return once the students were no longer under the intense pressure to "perform." That is, the immediate problem of completing their studies had passed. The lesson then is that when isolated in an institutional setting, the students adjusted to immediate demands. Once "released" from that setting, their attitudes changed to again conform to their new surroundings.

The broader implications of Becker's work are that individuals will be socialized to meet the expectations that important institutions or organizations place on them. Their attitudes, values, and beliefs will then become centered around fulfilling those expectations. In the case of the physician, where there is a great deal of autonomy, the original ideological concerns reemerge at the end of their training, largely because they have the ability to determine what type of medicine they will practice and under what circumstances. In those professions where there is an intense training period, less autonomy, and greater internal control by the organization, the individual is greatly influenced by the members of that organization. In other words, where there is greater freedom to practice one's profession, there is less of an impact in terms of the socialization process. However, in those professions where the individual is constrained by organizational rules and regulations, the more influential other members are on the thoughts and actions of the individual. This is exacerbated in professions that actively promote a sense of comraderie and solidarity among its members.

Resocialization

Perhaps the most significant aspect of the socialization process is that members within an organization (or, more broadly, within a society) internalize a set of norms which dictate appropriate behavior. When this fails to occur, the organization is forced to employ corrective methods to ensure conformity. Examples include deviants or criminals. Other people are resocialized because of a decision to join a new group. A good example of this occurs when an individual selects a particular career, such as soldier or police officer. It is here that the work of Erving Goffman plays a significant part in our understanding. In his now classic *Asylums,* Goffman (1961) contends that the resocialization of individuals often occurs in *total institutions*. These are places where the individual's physical and social freedom are constrained and channeled in a certain direction. Goffman describes resocialization as a two step process. First, there is what he calls the *mortification of the self*, where the attitudes, world views, and behavior patterns of the individual are stripped away. Goffman states:

> The recruit comes into the establishment with a conception of himself made possible by certain stable social arrangements in his home world. Upon entrance, he is immediately stripped of the support provided by these arrangements. In the accurate language of some of our oldest total institutions, he begins a series of abasements, degradations, humiliations, and profanations of self. His self is systematically, if often unintentionally, mortified. He begins to radical shifts in his moral career, a career composed of the progressive changes that occur in the beliefs that he has concerning himself and significant others. The process by which a person's self is mortified are fairly standard in total institutions; analysis of these processes can help us to see the arrangements that ordinary establishments must guarantee if members are to preserve their civilian selves (p.14-20).

This paves the way for the second step in resocialization, where a new set of attitudes, values, and beliefs are provided:

> . .Once the inmate is stripped of his possessions, at least some replacements must be made by the establishment, but these take the form of standard issue, uniform in character and uniformly distributed. These substitute possessions are clearly marked as really belonging to the institution and in some cases are recalled at regular intervals to be, as it were, disinfected of identifications. . .While the process of mortification goes on, the inmate begins to receive formal and informal instruction in what will here be called the privilege system. In so far as the inmate's attachment to his civilian self has been shaken by the stripping process of the institution, it is largely the privilege system that provides a framework for personal reorganization (p.20-29).

For instance, in the case of the military, the new recruit or civilian is brought to a "boot" camp and stripped of any individual characteristics: clothes are taken away, haircuts are given, and rules on every aspect of life in the institution are explained. It is during this process that the sense of self gives way and the individual becomes a cog in a much larger machine. Only after this process is complete can the organization implement the second part of the resocialization process. Upon completion of boot camp, the recruit has a different sense of self, along with a new set of attitudes and behavior patterns.

A similar process occurs in law enforcement. After selection, the police academy (also considered to be a type of total institution), represents the first overt process of socialization. In addition to the skills and techniques needed to become an effective police officer, recruits are indoctrinated and exposed to the vernacular used by its members, the cultural norms dictating acceptable and unacceptable behavior, as well as the world view from the law enforcement perspective. In addition, these values, attitudes, and beliefs are reinforced informally as new officers interact with more experienced ones outside of the classroom. The "war stories" told by more seasoned officers reinforces the point made by the formal classroom lessons. Over time, recruits develop attitudes and behaviors which provide a consistent framework in which to understand the role of the police and the individual officer (see for instance Radelet 1986).

This process continues after the academy, when the officer is usually assigned some sort of field training. The time spent in this phase of training varies by department, but can be up to six months. The field training officer (FTO) is responsible for teaching the new officer how to apply lessons from the academy to the tasks on the street. There is also an evaluative component to the process in that the FTO is charting the progress (or lack thereof) of the recruit. The style of the FTO, as well as the way in which the FTO interacts with citizens, will tend to be reflected in the recruit's behavior. In this way, FTO training is a part of the socialization process even though it may not be a consciousn process (Radelet 1986).

After FTO training, the officer remains on probation for a period of time, usually one year. During this time, a supervisor evaluates the officer in terms of progress and overall performance in the job. As described by Becker et.al (1961) most recruits will admit that part of the learning process involves knowing the unique expectations their supervisor/teacher has for them. When this is learned, the officer will modify his or her behavior to conform with that of the supervisor (See also Radelet 1986). If, for instance, the officer learns that the sergeant places a great deal of emphasis on police-community relations, the officer will, in turn, have more community contacts. These learned behaviors are part of what Goffman (1961) refers to as *working* the system. More importantly, these behaviors are the essence of occupational socialization.

For the most part, this is a normal part of the learning process. In order to be an effective police officer, the rookie officer must first learn the tricks of the trade and the most knowledgeable officers should impart their wisdom on their less learned colleagues. However, there is also the potential for various forms of misconduct to be taught as well as the proper procedures and attitudes.

NATURE vs. NURTURE IN POLICING

In 1991, Los Angeles police officers shocked the American public with the beating of Rodney King. In 1996, a South Carolina state trooper assaulted a motorist while she attempted to exit her vehicle after a traffic stop. Also in 1996, Los Angeles area officers have again been accused of assaulting Hispanic motorists after a prolonged pursuit. Incidents like these raise many questions concerning the attitudes, values, and behavior of police officers around the country. Social scientists have offered differing and sometimes conflicting explanations for police use of authority and misconduct.

Some contend that police officers have very different personalities than people in other occupations. Others maintain that there is a cultural distinction that separates law enforcement from other occupations. Still others contend that officers have neither personality nor cultural differences from other occupations. In sum, what we know about the police culture and personality is dependent on how one views police behavior. While no single perspective provides a complete understanding of the varieties of police behavior, there is a long history of debate as to whether they have unique personalities or whether socialization and subcultures play a significant part in the behavior of police officers. What can be said with some confidence is that the roles and functions of the police set officers apart from other members of society (Radelet 1986).

The Socialization Argument

A number of researchers argue that personality is not fixed and rigid and is subject to change based on different personal experiences and socialization. This school of thought focuses on the role of the police in society and how professionalization, training, and socialization influence an individual's personality and behavior. Researchers operating from this paradigm study how the work environment, peers, and academy training shape and affect a police officer's personality and behavior. Many of these researchers, such as Adlam (1982), still focus attention on an individual's unique experiences and the development of individual personalities.

A somewhat different approach contends that socialization occurs, but it is more of a group experience than an individual one (Stoddard 1968; Van Maanen 1978). For example, Van Maanen (1978) disagrees with the idea that police officers have certain personality characteristics, such as authoritarianism. He argues instead for a perspective based on both group socialization and professionalism. The latter is the process by which norms and values are internalized as an individual begins his or her new occupation. In this way, just as attorneys and physicians learn the values endemic to their profession, so too do police officers.

This perspective assumes that police officers learn their "social" personality from training and through exposure to the demands of police work. It follows then that if police officers become cynical or rigid, it is not because of their existing personality or individual experience, but because of the demands of the job and the shared experiences of others. Some research supports this idea. For instance, Bennett (1984) found that while probationary officers' values are affected by the training process, little evidence was available that personalities were shaped by their peers in the department was available. Part of this explanation involves the legitimacy of newly hired officers, who do not become "real" police officers until they are accepted as a member in standing of the police subculture.

Other studies, such as Putti, Aryee and Kang (1988) find that there may be a temporal factor at work in the socialization of police officers. That is, socialization into the subculture of police may occur at different points in the officers' careers. There is little evidence concerning the extent of how reference groups affect the personality of older officers, but it seems that in the beginning of his or her career, the officer's occupational values are shaped during the training and probationary process.

Still another model is offered by Kappeler et al. (1993) who contend that there is an acculturation process whereby the beliefs and values of police work are transmitted from one generation of officers to the next. In effect, the group socializes the individual officer into ways of acceptable and unacceptable behavior. This perspective draws heavily from an anthropological point of view and introduces the concept of the police subculture more concretely.

The Authoritarian Personality

Many researchers adopting this perspective feel that personality is fixed and does not really change by choice of occupation or experience. In other words, each person has a fixed personality that does not vary during the course of his or her life (Adlam 1982). This does not imply that personality is inviolate or does not have some degree of malleability, but generally speaking, it stays the same. As it applies to the police, most of the research in this area focuses on the personality characteristics of people who choose to become police officers. This perspective assumes that people with certain types of personalities enter law enforcement as an occupation and behave in certain ways.

One of the most influential experts in this area is Milton Rokeach. In comparing the values of police officers in Michigan with those of a national sample of private citizens, Rokeach found that police officers seemed more oriented toward self control and obedience than the average citizen and officers were more interested in personal goals, such as "an exciting life." Officers were also less interested in larger social goals, such as "a world at peace." Rokeach also found evidence that the experiences as police officers did not significantly influence their personalities. He concludes that most officers probably have a unique value orientation and personality when they embark upon their careers in policing.

In a similar study, Teevan and Dolnick (1973) compared values of officers in the Cook County, Illinois Sheriff Department with those Rokeach encountered in Lansing, Michigan. The findings suggest that the values of police officers in a large urban department are also far removed from those of the general public. Some of the reasons, according to Teevan and Dolnick, are that officers are isolated within society, they are required to enforce unpopular laws, and there is a sense of self-imposed segregation as officers think of themselves as a last bastion of middle class morality.

In describing the authoritarian personality, Adorno (1950) characterizes it in part by aggressive, cynical, and rigid behavior. People with these characteristics are said to have a myopic view of the world and that issues, people, and behavior are seen as clearly defined: good or bad, right or wrong, friends or enemies. They also tend to be very conservative in their political orientation (see also Niederhoffer 1976, Bayley and Mendelsohn 1969). Levy (1967) proposes that certain personality traits established early in life were clues to whether a person would be more likely to find policing attractive as a profession. She states:

> We find that the appointees most likely to remain in law enforcement are probably those who are more unresponsive to the environmental stresses introduced when thy become officer of the law than are their fellow-appointees. These stresses include becoming a member of a "minority" (occupationally speaking) group, need to adhere to semi-military regimen, community expectation of incongruous roles and the assumption of a position of authority complete with the trappings of uniform, badge, holster, and gun, and all these imply. The officers who remain in law enforcement may well be the sons of fathers who imposed a rigid code of behavior to which their children learned to adhere, and who do not feel a strong need to defy or rebel against authority (p.275).

On the other hand, some researchers have pointed to a few positive aspects of this type of personality in police officers. For instance, Carpenter and Raza (1987) have found that police applicants as a group are less depressed and more assertive in making and maintaining social contacts. Additionally they find that police officers are a more homogeneous group, which may be based on their similar interests in becoming police officers as well as sharing similar personality traits and world views.

Ultimately, many develop an occupational or *working personality*, characterized by authoritarianism, suspicion, and cynicism (Rubenstein 1973; Van Maanen 1978; Alpert and Dunham 1992; Neiderhoffer 1963). Skolnick (1994) provides perhaps the best description of the police personality:

> The policeman's role contains two principal variables, danger and authority, which should be interpreted in the light of a "constant" pressure to appear efficient. The element of danger seems to make the policeman especially attentive to signs indicating a potential for violence and lawbreaking. As a result, the policeman is generally a "suspicious" person. Furthermore, the character of the policeman's work makes him less desirable as a friend, since norms of friendship implicate others in his work. Accordingly, the element of danger isolates the policeman socially from that segment of the citizenry which he regards as symbolically dangerous and also from the conventional citizenry with whom he identifies (p.43).

An integral part of the police personality is cynicism: the notion that all people are motivated by evil and selfishness. Police cynicism develops among many officers through the nature of police work. Most police officers feel they are set apart from the rest of society because they have the power to regulate the lives of others. Moreover, by constantly dealing with crime and the more unsavory aspects of social life, their faith in humanity seems to diminish.

Probably the most well-known study of police personality was conducted by Arthur Neiderhoffer (1969). In *Behind the Shield*, Neiderhoffer builds off the work of William Westley (1970) that most officers develop into cynics as a function of their daily routines. Westley had maintained that being constantly faced with keeping people in line and believing that most people intend to break the law or cause harm to the officer led officers to mistrust the people they are charged to protect. Neiderhoffer tested Westley's assumption by distributing a survey measuring attitudes and values to 220 New York City police officers. Among his most important findings were that police cynicism did increase with length of service; that patrol officers with college educations became quite cynical if they were denied promotion; and that military-like academy training caused recruits to become cynical about themselves, the department, and the community. As an illustration, Niederhoffer found that nearly 80% of first day recruits believed the department was an "efficient, smoothly operating organization." Two months later, less than a third professed that belief. Similarly, half of the recruits believed that a supervisor was "very interested in the welfare of his subordinates," while two months later, those stil believing so dropped to 13%. Niederhoffer states:

> Cynicism is an ideological plank deeply entrenched in the ethos of the police world, and it serves equally well for attack or defense. For many reasons police are particularly vulnerable to cynicism. When they succumb, they lose faith in people, society, and eventually in themselves. In their Hobbesian view, the world becomes a jungle in which crime, corruption, and brutality are normal features of the terrain (p.9)

In sum, the police personality emerges as a result of the very nature of police work and of the socialization process in which most police officers experience. To deal with the social isolation that is derived from their use of authority, some of it self-imposed, officers use other members of the profession to cope with social rejection. As a result, many, perhaps most, police officers become part of a closely knit subculture that is protective and supportive of its members, while sharing similar attitudes, values, and understandings, and views of the world.

The Subculture of Policing

Occupational socialization creates occupational subcultures (Radelet and Carter 1994). The idea of the police being a subculture is not new and has been well documented (see for instance Westley 1970; Rokeach 1971; Kirkham 1976; Bittner 1970). For our purposes, subculture may be defined as the meanings, values, and behavior patterns unique to a particular group in a given society. Entry into this subculture begins with a process of socialization whereby recruits learn the values and behavior patterns characteristic of experienced officers.

The development and maintenance of negative attitudes and values by police officers has many implications. Regoli and Poole (1979) found evidence that an officer's feelings of cynicism intensifies the need to maintain respect and increase the desire to exert authority over others. This can easily lead to the increased fear and mistrust of the police by the general public. This, in turn, can create feelings of hostility and resentment on the part of the officer, creating what is sometimes known as *police paranoia* (Regoli and Poole 1979:43). Regoli and Poole also found that these negative attitudes result in conservative attitudes and a resistance to change among the officers.

As was mentioned, the creation of the police subculture also stems from this unique police personality. However, despite the evidence, many researchers disagree with the notion of a police subculture. Balch (1972) in his study of the police personality states:

> It looks like policemen may be rather ordinary people, not greatly unlike other middle Americans. We cannot be sure there is such a thing as a police personality, however we loosely define it (p.117).

Similarly, Tifft (1974) argues that while the attitudes of officers may be influenced by their work environment, the idea that officers maintain uniform personality traits developed through socialization or innate drives is fallacious. Thus, he argues that the activities and responsibilities most officers engage in have a role to play in how they see the world, but in many ways this is symptomatic of many other occupations. He states:

> Task related values, attitudes and behavior are occupationally derived or created out of specialized roles rather than being primarily due to the selection factors of background or personality (p. 268).

Thus, the debate over whether or not officers possess a distinct working personality, as well as whether or not the subculture of policing is pervasive, continues and no attempt will be made to resolve it here, especially in light of the recent community-oriented movement. What is important to remember is that the nature of police work remains complex and the issues surrounding law enforcement have not been completely understood. To that end, the purpose of this volume is to shed light on a number of issues of importance to the study of policing.

REFERENCES:

Adlam, K.R. 1982. "The Police Personality: Psychological Consequences of Becoming a Police Officer." Journal of Police Science and Administration 10(3):347-348.

Alpert, G. and R. Dunham. *Policing Urban America.* 2nd ed. Prospect Heights, IL: Waveland Press.

Balch, Robert. 1972. "The Police Personality: Fact or Fiction?" *Journal of Criminal Law, Criminology and Police Science* 63:117.

Bayley, D.H. and H. Mendelsohn. 1969. *Minorities and the Police: Confrontation in America.* New York: The Free Press.

Becker, H.; B. Greer; E. Hughes; and A. Strauss. 1961. *Boys in White: Student Culture in medical School.* Chicago: University of Chicago Press.

Bennett, R.R. 1984. "Becoming Blue: A Longitudinal Study of Police Recruit Occupational Socialization" *Journal of Police Science and Administration* 12(1):47-57.

Bittner, E. 1970. *The Functions of Police in Modern Society.* Chevy Chase, MD: National Clearinghouse for Mental Health.

Carpenter, B. N. and S. M. Raza. 1987. "Personality Characteristics of Police Applicants: Comparisons Across Sbugroups and with Other Populations." *Journal of Police Science and Administration,* 15(1):10-17.

Danziger, K. 1971. *Socialization.* Harmondsworth, England: Penguin.

Elkin, F. and G. Handel. 1989. *The Child and Society: The Process of Socialization.* 5th ed. New York: Random House.

Erikson, K. and Vallas, P. (eds.) 1995. *The Nature of Work: Sociological Perspectives.* Washington, D.C.: American Sociological Association.

Goffman, E. 1961. *Asylums.* New York: Anchor.

Kappler, V.E., M. Blumberg and G.W. Potter. 1993. T*he Mythology of Crime and Criminal Justice.* Prospect Heights, IL: Waveland Press.

Kirkham, G. 1976. *Signal Zero.* New York: Ballentine.

Levy, R. 1967. "Predicting Police Failures." *Journal of Criminal Law, Criminology and Police Science* 58(2):275.

Moore, W. 1969. "Occupational Socialization" in Goslin, D. (ed.) *Handbook of Socialization Theory and Research*, pp.861-884. New York: Rand McNally.

Neiderhoffer, A. 1967. *Behind the Shield: The Police in Urban Society.* Garden City, NY: Doubleday.

Parsons, T. and R.F. Bales. 1955. *Family, Socialization, and Interaction Process.* New York:

The Free Press.

Putti, J., S. Aryee and T.S. Kang 1988. "Personal Values of Recruits and Officers in a Law Enforcement Agency: An Exploratory Study." *Journal of Police Science and Administration* 16(4):245-249.

Radelet, L. 1986. *The Police and the Community*. 4th ed. New York: Macmillan.

Regoil, Robert and Eric Poole. 1979. "Measurement of Police Cynicism: A Facto Scaling Approach" *Journal of Criminal Justice* 7:37-52.

Rokeach, Milton, Martin Miller and Hohn Snyder. 1971. "The Value Gap Between Police and Policed" *Journal of Social Issues* 27:155-171.

Rubenstein, J. 1973. *City Police*. New York: Farrar, Strauss, and Giroux.

Skolnick, J. 1966. *Justice Without Trial: Law Enforcement in a Democratic Society*. New York: John Wiley and Sons.

Stoddard, E.R. 1968. "The Informal Code of Police Deviancy: A Group Approach to Blue-Collar Crime." *Journal of Criminal Law, Criminology, and Police Science*, 59(2):201-203.

Teevan, J., and B. Dolnick. 1973. "The Values of the Police: A Reconsideration and Interpretation." *Journal of Police Science and Administration*, 1:366-369.

Tifft, Larry. 1974. "The Cop Personality Reconsidered" Journal of Police Science sand Administration 2:268.

Westley, William. 1970. Violence and the Police: A Sociological Study of Law, Custom, and Morality. Cambridge, MA: MIT Press.

Van Maanen, J. 1978. "On Becoming a Policeman." in P. Manning and J. Van Maanen (eds.) *Policing: A View from the Street*. Santa Monica, CA: Goodyear.

Learned Helplessness and Homeless Women in Transitional Housing

Robert Hartmann McNamara
Department of Political Science and Criminal Justice
The Citadel

Carrie Flagler
Department of Sociology
Furman University

The faces of the homeless are changing: they are more feminine and younger than ever before. While the homeless population has been predominantly male for many years, the group that is presently growing the fastest are women and children (Bassuk et al., 1986; Brown and Ziefert, 1990; Salomon, Bassuk and Brooks, 1996; Weinreb, Goldberg and Perloff, 1998; Bassuk, 1995; U.S. Conference of Mayors 1998; Hertzberg, 1992; Mills and Ota, 1989; U.S. Department of Housing and Urban Development, 1994). In fact, homeless families with children constitute approximately 40% of people who become homeless (Shinn and Weitzmann, 1996). According to the U.S. Conference of Mayors Report (2003), on average single men comprise 44% of the homeless population, families with children 36%, single women 13% and unaccompanied minors 7%. The increase in the number of homeless families is underscored by the fact that they are almost always headed by women as single parents. In fact, in 1999, the Urban Institute estimated that 84% of these families are headed by single women.

Like their male counterparts, the number of homeless women in the United States is difficult to determine. For instance, an early estimate by Burt and Cohen (1989) reported between 500,000 and 600,000 homeless people nationally on a given day in 1987. Of this figure, they suggest that twenty-three percent, or 115,000 to 138,000, were families with children present, However, as McChesney (1995) argued, this number was probably underestimated due to methodological problems.

More recently, the Urban Institute estimates that between 2.3 and 3.5 million people, or approximately one percent of the population in this country, will have an episode of homelessness in 1999. They estimate that, as it was in 1987, about 700,000 people will be homeless on any given night[1]. There is also some variation due to factors such as when the study occurred as well as the affiliation of those conducting the study. Despite methodological problems however, the research has consistently shown that the number of homeless families have been increasing (see for instance U.S. Conference of Mayors, 1999; Bassuk 1993; Hausman and Hammen, 1993; Johnson, 1989; Johnson and Krueger, 1989; Crystal, 1984 and DiBlasio and Belcher, 1992).

Along with the increases in the size of the population comes a greater demand for services. The U.S. Conference of Mayors (2003) found that the average demand for emergency shelter increased by 15%, the highest one-year increase in a decade. Additionally, 76% of the cities in the study, the largest percentage since 1994, reported that demand for services had increased. Over the past 16 years, the average unmet demand for shelter was 20%. In 2000, the average demand for emergency shelter that went unmet was 23%.

---

[1] For instance, there is a tendency for service providers to inflate the size of the population while governmental agencies typically assess the population as smaller than may be the case.

Finally, the length of each episode of homelessness is increasing. According to the Mayor's study, on average, people remain homeless for about five months. However, of the twenty-five cities who participated in the study, 50% of them reported that the length of time people are homeless had increased in the last year. Unfortunately, while the numbers continue to rise, our knowledge of this population has remained rather limited—it is only recently that attention focused on women.

CHARACTERISTICS OF HOMELESS WOMEN

While there is obviously no single type of homeless person; the homeless come from all walks of life, recently, there has been a significant amount of research on homelessness among women. The average homeless mother is in her late twenties, unmarried, and has less than a high school education (Da Costa Nunez, 1995). Minorities are over represented in metropolitan areas (Bassuk, Rubin, and Lauriat, 1986) and most families are welfare recipients (U.S. Census Bureau, 1999).

Having divided the women into three groups: non-mothers, mothers without children present, and mothers with children present, Smith and North (1994) found that non-mothers were usually white, few were on welfare or married, were rarely substance abusers, and had minimal contact with family members. Mothers who did not have their children with them were likely to be white and often had problems with substance abuse and psychological functioning (the likely reason the children were not in the homes). Mothers who had older children who were not with them were the most likely to have been married, but least likely to receive welfare. Mothers who had their children with them as a family were the most vulnerable—they had difficulty providing for their children and finding jobs.

The race of homeless families tends to vary from study to study. Though it depends on geographic region of the country, African American families appear to be over represented among the homeless. Some studies show that nonwhite homeless men and women are younger and less likely to have been married than whites (Cummins et al., 1998; North and Smith, 1994). Nonwhite women were also more likely to be mothers. White women had been homeless for longer periods of time, but nonwhites depended more on welfare (North and Smith, 1994).

McChesney (1995) found that homeless mothers were an average of twenty-eight years old, while Hagen and Ivanoff (1988) discovered that the median age of homeless women was 26, with 37% under the age of twenty-one. Burt and Cohen (1989) found men to be the oldest group and women with children to be the youngest (McChesney 1995; Stanford Studies, 1991; Burt and Cohen, 1989). The majority of women are also single (Banyard, 1995).

Sixteen years ago, Burt and Cohen (1989) found that single women had the highest degree of education among the homeless. However, Smith and North (1994) discovered that single women without children were the least educated. In many recent studies, the majority of the women had not completed high school (Da Costa Nunez, 1995). In Hagen and Ivanoff's (1988) study, fifty percent had not finished high school, and eighteen percent had only some college experience. Obviously, the level of education, which is linked to employment opportunities, has slipped significantly since the mid 1980s.

As a consequence of poor nutrition, inadequate hygiene, exposure to violence, disease, and stress, homeless people suffer from ill health at a much higher rate than people living in stable housing. Many studies demonstrate that one-third to one-half of homeless adults have some form of physical illness (Bassuk and Rosenberg, 1988; Burt 1989; Gelberg and Linn, 1989), at least half of homeless children have a physical illness (Wood et. al 1990), and they are twice as likely as children living in stable housing to have such illnesses. Most important, mortality rates are three to four times higher among the homeless compared to the rest of the population (Morbidity and Mortality Weekly Report, 1991 and 1992, Hanzlick and Parrish, 1993; Hibbs et. al 1994).

The findings of studies on drug and alcohol abuse among homeless women were quite varied. Some studies found that as little as 8-9% of this population suffer from substance abuse (Bassuk, Rubin, and Lauriat, 1986; Bassuk and Rosenberg, 1988), while others report rates as high as 50% (Fischer, Breakey, and Nestadt, 1992). Compared to homeless men, homeless women typically abuse medication and drugs more often while men have higher rates of chronic alcohol problems (Roth, Toomey, and First, 1987).

The research on the topic of physical abuse tends to indicate that many homeless women are victims of this act at some point in their lives. Brown and Bassuk (1997) found that 67% of homeless women reported severe physical violence by a childhood caretaker, 43% reported childhood sexual molestation, and 63% reported severe violence by a male partner. In comparative studies of childhood victimization among homeless mothers, Bassuk and Rosenberg (1988) found that homeless mothers reported abuse eight times more often than housed mothers (see also Browne, 1993; Redmond and Brackmann, 1990). Many studies also disclose more abuse in adulthood among homeless mothers than among housed mothers (McMurray-Avila, Gelber and Breakey 1998; Bassuk and Rosenberg, 1988; Wood et al., 1990; Shinn, Nickman, and Weitzman, 1991; Knickman and Weitzman, 1989).

The length of joblessness varies among the homeless. The number of women with children who have not held a job for years is only slightly greater than the number of single men. In a study by DiBlasio and Belcher (1995), 35% of the sample were employed full-time or part-time. Of this thirty-five percent, most were men. One of the factors that plays a critical role in understanding employment patterns among homeless women, in addition to child care responsibilities, is the mother's health. This trend is underscored by Wolfe and Hill (1993), who argued that poor family health or health problems of the mother is one of the most important factors in understanding poverty among poor women.

Homeless women with children, compared to women without children, or compared to men, stay homeless the shortest amount of time (DiBlasio and Belcher, 1995; Butler, 1993; Stanford Studies, 1991; U.S. Conference of Mayors, 2001; National Survey of Homeless Assistance Providers and Clients, 2001). Men are homeless for the longest periods in comparison to women in all categories (Burt and Cohen, 1989). According to the Stanford studies (1991), the average length of homelessness was one year for singles and only one month for families.

For nearly a third of the homeless population, their current episode has lasted three months or less, but another third has been homeless for more than two years. Families were more than twice as likely as single persons to have been homeless for three months or less, while single persons were almost three times as likely as families to be homeless for more than two years (National Survey of Homeless Assistance Providers and Clients, 1996). According to the U.S. Conference of Mayors' (2003) people remained homeless an average of five months. Other research on the length of homelessness indicated a 40% of homeless people had been homeless less than six months and that 70% of homeless people had been homeless less than two years.

A common misconception is that homeless women and families move frequently. To be fair, this is a misunderstanding of homelessness in general. The image of the hobo of an earlier generation riding the trains from city to city is a pervasive one in our society (see for instance Harper, in Kornblum and Smith 1996), but this is simply not the reality for the vast majority of homeless people, especially women.

Bassuk and Rosenberg (1988) found that among the 82 families in their sample, the average number of moves in the last five years was 6.6, but 3.6 times within the last year. Where do the homeless go? Do they go to shelters that are close to their former residences? Hagen (1987) found that 75% of the women lived in their immediate area when they sought public assistance. The women interviewed by Roth, Toomey, and First (1987) were primarily born in the counties they were presently located or had lived there for at least one year. Similar findings were true for Bassuk, Rubin, and Lauriat (1986), who stated that the emergency shelter was usually located in the same vicinity where the mother had grown up. As with most of the homeless population, homeless families tend to seek assistance in areas close to home.

In summary, as a general rule, the characteristics of homeless families differ markedly from the rest of the homeless population. Compared to homeless single men and single women, homeless mothers are less frequently substance abusers, have fewer psychiatric disabilities, spend less time in prison, are homeless less frequently, and for shorter periods of time. Homeless mothers also seem to have better health and nutrition and more income due to welfare payments, food stamps, and Medicaid.

METHODS

This project consisted of classic ethnographic techniques of direct observation and semi-structured interviews of clients in a transitional housing program, also known as the *Helping Hands* program in South Carolina. We interviewed 20 women in this program from a list of clients provided by case managers. The total number of clients in the program when we began the study was 42.

In order to learn as much as possible and to best understand their lives, we used a life history approach. Life histories can offer insight into a subject, including the individual's life situation and state of the world as he or she understands it—either at some particular point in time or over a long period. The interviews were of two basic types. One was a conversational interview in which there was no agenda and the subject controlled the flow and topic of conversation. The other type, while related to the first in that it was still open ended, involved a general set of topics in which the researcher(s) guided the conversation. We tried to get a sense of the women's personal background, life style, relationships with family, friends, and others, and perceptions of how homelessness has changed in recent times as well as measures they took to adapt to those changes (Hammersly and Atkinson 1984).

While we tried to understand the women and their worlds, we made no attempt initially to fit an explanatory structure into the population. We had no stated hypotheses, no theories to test. Rather, armed with only our sociological licenses, we ventured into this population to learn something about homelessness among women and how they navigate their physical and social landscapes.

While the agency attempts to help single men and even married couples, we focused our attention on single women and those with children. Our group included women with children living with them, those without custody of their children, and single women. The interviews, which took place primarily in the clients' apartments, lasted an average of 90 minutes, with some as long as two and a half hours. Generally, we found that while clients were willing to provide us with information, perhaps due to the pain of reliving the events of their lives or the negative memories they generated, their interest in talking about their lives declined after about an hour and a half. The interviews were taped, transcribed and then erased. Assurances were given that their names would be disguised to protect their identities.

We attempted to interview clients at different stages of the transitional process. Given that the program lasts approximately two years, we felt it was important to derive a better understanding of how the process evolves for all clients. To accomplish this, we interviewed several at the intake stage of the program, some in the middle stages, and those that were nearing the completion of the process. Additionally, since we were interested in the long-term impact of the transitional housing program, we wanted to learn more about those that had already become self-sufficient.

Because some clients kept in touch with case managers on an informal basis after leaving the program, we asked the agency to provide us with a list of their names and addresses. While there is an element of self-selection that occurs, meaning that we do not have information about clients who were asked to leave the program or had left and did not maintain contact with the agency, this list provided us with an opportunity to learn something about what happens after clients leave the program.

LEARNED HELPLESSNESS AND HOMELESS WOMEN

One of the main findings of this study was that most of the women in the transitional housing program either did not complete it or, if they graduated, returned a short time later. They also expressed significant levels of fear and apprehension as they approached the completion date. Many clients would even violate the rules of the program so that they would be terminated, knowing they could reapply a few months later for admittance and begin the program again. What is significant about this trend is that many of the women seemed to possess the skills and determination to become self-sufficient. This was particularly evident in the middle stages of the program, where clients would complain about the restrictions placed on them by the agency. Many even lamented about simply being left alone to "get on with their lives." Many of these same women, however, when the time approached for them to do just that, suffered anxiety attacks, resorted to alcohol or drugs, or would find a way to get fired from their jobs so that they were again dependent on the agency for help.

Related to this is the almost overwhelming sense of loneliness and social isolation many of the women in this study experience. Granted, for some, this is self-imposed—they have so many issues and problems that they do not form social networks either from other clients or caseworkers. However, more women spoke of feeling overwhelmed by their situations, even as their circumstances improved and they tried to make friends. There was a sense of fear that many women felt as they approached the end of their time in the program, while others who had just entered the program said that they could not relax despite having a place to live and care for their children. Others felt that in addition to these fears, many felt as though they shut down at times, emotionally and physically. Still other women in the program became apathetic and simply stopped making the effort to improve their situations and engaged in behaviors that were obviously counterproductive.

Another interesting trend was the inconsistency between the women we talked to and their perceptions of other clients in the program. There was also an inconsistency in explaining how the individual client became homeless versus how most women become a part of the population. This is not as uncommon as one might first expect. In their study of welfare recipients, Davis and Hagen (1996) found that women tended to view themselves as atypical cases. While recipients are likely to condemn others for abusing the system, respondents saw their own acts as creative maneuvering within the existing system to make extra money.

In explaining the poverty and homelessness of others in the Helping Hands program, the women we interviewed were much more likely to attribute the cause of others' experiences to laziness, unwillingness to sacrifice, and lacking the work ethic to make something of themselves. When asked about their own reasons for homelessness, however, most of the women externalized the factors leading up to becoming homeless, contending that they were victims of forces beyond their control. Many offered comments such as, 'I was abused by my husband', 'There are no jobs for me', 'I had to drop out of school because I was pregnant and never had the chance to go back', 'I was given heroin at an early age and became addicted.'

One way to understand how these types of distinctions can be made by some women in the program is by using attribution theory (Jones and Nisbett, 1972). This theory holds that people tend to believe that another person's behavior is based largely on their individual traits and less on structural influences. At the same time, attribution theory suggests that we tend to understand our *own* behavior largely in terms of structural factors and less on individual ones.

While it is fair to say that there may be cultural factors preventing most of these women from achieving any meaningful level of independence, many of these behaviors are in response to structural barriers. In fact, one of the first studies of this population in the upstate area tried to answer the question of whether or not structural factors play a significant role in the lack of success of transitional housing (T/H) programs or whether cultural issues prevented many clients from achieving long-term self-sufficiency (see McNamara 1998). What we found in the present study is that there are a host of factors, both cultural and structural, that are interrelated and affect the outcome of clients' efforts.

Thus, while attribution theory offers an interesting glimpse into the inconsistency of homeless women's perceptions, we feel there is a more compelling and comprehensive explanation of homelessness, particularly for women—learned helplessness. At the outset, we encounter a significant barrier to accepting this theory: its name. The reason for this is that the name may suggest that homeless women have learned to be helpless, and, as a result, are incapable of living independently. This is an understandable but erroneous interpretation of learned helplessness theory[2]. It seems fairly evident that many of the women in this study, and in other T/H programs and shelters, are far from helpless in that sense of the term—that they have

---

[2] This is sometimes also referred to as "learned optimism" (Seligman 1993).

survived this long, particularly those with children, suggests otherwise.

We use learned helplessness theory to explain how and why some women remain unable to achieve self-sufficiency.[3] The women's situations, with a history of repeated failures in life, coupled with a stormy history of abusive, and even violent, relationships and interaction with others, has taught many of these women a kind of pessimistic way of coping with problems that results in a host of counterproductive behaviors and/or a sense of defeatism that prevents them from taking steps that are actually in their best interest.

We should point out that this framework is not based on a culture of poverty argument, rather it is a derivative of social learning theory: because of their experiences with abusive relationships, with living in shelters, a failure to adequately provide for their children or themselves, and the problems of finding a job that pays a livable wage, some women have become desensitized to constructive, productive behaviors and fail to realize their current responses actually perpetuate their current situation. This eventually becomes a self-fulfilling prophecy since those behaviors only reinforce the idea that they will never succeed. It is not a value system, as suggested by the culture of poverty assertion (Lewis 1969; Banfield 1970), rather it is a coping mechanism; one that many people, from all social classes, use in a variety of circumstances.

It is important to note that the theory is not designed to explain all behaviors of all homeless women. Rather, learned helplessness theory offers us important insight into a segment of the population that require alternative strategies in an effort to help them reach self-sufficiency.

Prior to a more concrete discussion of how this theory helps us to understand homelessness among the women we studied, we should explain the logic and empirical support for this theory.

LEARNED HELPLESSNESS THEORY

This theory has been misunderstood and often misapplied in explaining a variety of problems and situations.[4] It has also been severely criticized by psychologists, claiming that it too

---

[3] This interpretation of the theory is the one its founders have asserted to be the most accurate way of understanding the theory and its predictive value on human behavior. The name evokes so many negative connotations that many psychologists and sociologists reject the theory out of hand. To remedy this tendency, we propose a renaming of the theory to learned hopelessness.

[4] The theory of learned helplessness was actually an accident. 1964, Martin Seligman was a graduate student studying the relationship between fear and learning. Originally the experimenters thought there was something wrong with the dogs they were using in the project. During the early stages of the study, the dogs had been exposed to two kinds of stimulation: high pitched tones and brief shocks. The tones and shocks had been given to the dogs in pairs: first a tone and then a shock. The shock was a type of minor jolt and was designed to get the dogs to associate the neutral tone and the shock—to pair them so that later when they heard the tone, they would react as if it were a shock—with fear. After this was accomplished, the dogs were taken to a large box with two compartments, separated by a low wall. The experimenters wanted to see if the dogs would react to the tones in the same way they had learned to react to shock, by jumping over the wall to get away from it. If so, this would have shown that emotional learning could transfer across different situations; this is sometimes referred to as a *transfer experiment* (Seligman, 1992:19). However, in order for the experiment to work, the dogs had to learn to jump over the wall to escape the shock. This accomplished, they could then be tested to see if the tones alone would cause the same reaction. Since the wall was low and dogs usually learn this type of reaction rather easily, it should not have taken long to teach the dogs

easily alleviates people's responsibility for their actions. However, Seligman (1992) and other helplessness theorists argue that the best uses of learned helplessness theory are found among marginalized racial groups. Other empirical studies explore issues such as depression, overcrowding, and poor academic achievement. While the theory has not been directly tested on homelessness, the inference is easily seen and the theory provides a valuable framework for understanding homelessness, particularly among women.

There are three elements to the original version of learned helplessness theory. First, learned helplessness is present when a group or person (or animal) displays what is termed *inappropriate passivity*. This means that, although it is possible to effectively cope with a situation, the person fails to think or act in a way that allows them to overcome it. Second, learned helplessness follows in the wake of uncontrollable events. In other words, the individual could not have prevented or avoided the situation in the first place. Third, while exposed to this uncontrollable situation, the person begins to think, feel, and perceive things about this situation and then extrapolates these feelings and emotions to new situations that have not yet occurred. However, where and why these feelings, emotions, and perceptions occur is not known (Peterson, Maier, and Seligman, 1993).

The dramatic results of Seligman's studies led to a firestorm of controversy, particularly by behaviorist psychologists.[5] The obvious implications of learned helplessness theory led researchers to attempt to explain human behavior, particularly depression. The logic was that depressed people became that way because they learned that whatever they did was futile. During the course of their lives, depressed people also apparently learned that they had no control over them.

In a revision of the theory, drawn heavily from critics who took issue with the idea that individuals learned to be helpless but did not act that way, along with questions of exceptional cases (people who did not get depressed even after many bad life events), led Seligman to conclude that a depressed person thought about the bad event in more pessimistic ways than a non-depressed person. He called this thinking their *explanatory style of learning*. Pessimistic styles of learning result in very intimate, permanent and negative ways to explain events happening in one's life.

People who tend to explain bad things through internal, universal, and permanent causes are more likely to develop a pessimistic explanatory style of learning. Consequently, the most pessimistic explanatory style is correlated with the highest levels and incidences of depression (Seligman 1992). In sum, the basis of the learned helplessness theory, as it relates to depression,

---

to perform this way. However, the dogs did not try to escape the shocks at all. Rather they simply laid down, whimpered, and made no attempt to get away from the shocks. Seligman believed the explanation for the dogs' behavior was that they had been taught to be helpless. During the early stages of the experiment the dogs felt the shocks go on and off regardless of whether they barked, jumped, or did nothing at all. The dogs, then, concluded or "learned" that nothing they did mattered.

[5] Behaviorists insist that all of a person's behavior was determined only by his or her history of rewards and punishments. Actions that had been rewarded were likely to be repeated and those that had been punished were likely to be suppressed (Seligman, 1992; Peterson, Maier, and Seligman, 1993). Behaviorists argue that the human being is entirely shaped by his external environment, by rewards and punishments, rather than by his internal thoughts.

argues that people who have pessimistic styles of explaining events and who experience such events are likely to learn to be helpless and are much more likely to become depressed than people who have an optimistic explanatory style and suffer bad events.

The significance of this theory is that exposure to adversity and failure happens to everyone. When this occurs, people become momentarily helpless. Whether a person suffering from such an event bounces back quickly or stays mired in a depressive state is based on their explanatory style. The key to this process is hope or hopelessness (Seligman 1992). We believe that this is a key variable missing in the equation in the efforts to help homeless women reach their goals of self-sufficiency.

Evidence of Learned Helplessness

There has been a great deal of research on learned helplessness theory. Much of it relates indirectly to homelessness. Topics include depression (see Sweeney, Anderson and Bailey 1996; Riskind, Castellon, and Beck 1989; Firth and Brewin 1982; Brewin 1985; Zullow 1984), school failure (see Weiner, 1975; Dweck 1975; Butkowsky and Willows 1980; Metalsky et al. 1982), unemployment (see Baum, Fleming and Reddy 1986), and overcrowding (see Baum, et al. 1978; Baum and Gatchel 1981; and Baum and Valins 1977). Clearly all of these problems and others are experienced by homeless women. As was mentioned, Seligman and Maier (1992) have contended that either through methodological problems with the studies, a poor conceptual understanding of the theory itself, or simply applying the theory to inappropriate topics, many researchers have misused learned helplessness theory. Seligman (1992) asserts that the theory is best suited for understanding four main areas: depression, academic achievement, unemployment, and population overcrowding.

With regard to the research on depression, there are three consistent trends. First, symptoms of depression are a close match to the symptoms of learned helplessness. Second, depressed people make internal, stable and global explanations of bad events and then to make external, unstable, and specific explanations of good events. Finally, explanatory style is a risk factor for later depression: the more pessimistic the style, the more likely a subsequent episode of depression (Peterson, Maier, and Seligman 1993:223).

Second, one of the best known applications of the learned helplessness theory is in understanding school achievement. School represents a situation in which there are right and wrong answers and in which one's efforts really matter. Additionally, helplessness research began with the attributional determinants of performance (see Weiner 1979). Dweck (1975) was the first to apply helplessness ideas to academic achievement. In her studies, she defined helpless children as those who attribute failure to their lack of ability. When working on problems, they employed ineffective strategies, reported negative feelings, expected to do poorly, and spent a lot of time thinking about irrelevant matters. When these children encountered failure, they fell apart emotionally and academically, with prior success in school little consolation to them or having little effect. Butkowsky and Willows (1980) focused on poor readers in school. They found that fifth grade boys with reading problems expected little future success at reading skills, explained their failures with internal and stable causes, and failed to persist at reading

Third, several theorists have suggested that learned helplessness can be induced when one loses a job. The sense of demoralization that takes place upon finding oneself in a situation like this actually may make it more difficult for the unemployed person to find a new job. The research suggests that as the length of someone's involuntary unemployment increased, the person's ability to solve problems was increasingly disrupted by the uncontrollability of the event. With increasing unemployment, subjects in this experiment also tended to think less of their ability to meet the demand of difficult tasks (see also Feather 1982; Feather and Barber 1983 and Feather and Davenport 1981).

The fourth area of research on learned helplessness theory focuses on overcrowding. While the adverse effects of overcrowding have been well documented, and while the physical strain of living in crowded conditions plays a role in people's reactions to them, their perceptions of control also play a role (Peterson, Maier, and Seligman, 1993). Studies have shown that reactions to overcrowding are excellent examples of learned helplessness (Kuykendall and Keatin, 1984).

Whether it be depression, unemployment, poor academic achievement or overcrowding, the connections of learned helplessness to these topics is easily seen and documentable since many homeless women often experience overcrowding conditions, such as living in shelters or with relatives who have little or no space for them and their children. They also struggle with unemployment issues, poor academic achievement (their own as well as with their children), and suffer from episodes of depression because of the situation in which they find themselves. While it is true that no research exists clearly linking homelessness and learned helplessness, inferences are easily made that there is a connection between this coping strategy and the situation of many clients in T/H programs.

ASSESSMENT OF LEARNED HELPLESSNESS AND HOMELESSNESS

In some ways, it is relatively easy to be critical of learned helplessness theory. A main reason for this, particularly among sociologists, is that, at first glance, this theory appears to give credence to the poverty-as-pathology argument or its cousin, the culture of poverty. [6] Moreover, it

---

[6] In reality there are several sociological frameworks that explain poverty. Perhaps the best way to understand their differences is to use a continuum, with personal inferiority on one end of the spectrum and structuralism on the other. The personal inferiority perspective essentially states there are biological reasons to explain poverty. Poor people are in their current circumstances because they lack the talent to be successful. Thus, the more deficiencies a person has, the more likely they are to be (or become) poor. A variation on this theme suggests that since we are ultimately responsible for our actions, including our economic position, the reason some people are impoverished is because of poor decision making and/or a lack of an effective work ethic. At the other end of the continuum is structuralism, which contends that much of the inequality found in our society is embedded in the structure of society, such as the labor market and social policies. In other words, social structuralism argues that poverty and homelessness are a result of economic or social imbalances that exist within our society that inhibit opportunities for some segments of our population to succeed.

There are actually several structuralist explanations of poverty. One argues that poverty is an inherent feature of capitalism (Marx and Engels 1968). Social institutions exist to serve the interests of the wealthy in society and this means fewer opportunities for members of other social classes. As Marx's work clearly shows, there is a level of exploitation by the wealthy of the working class, both in terms of their wages as well as the amount of productivity that can be squeezed out of them. A second structuralist explanation of poverty points to the changes in

may be that many sociologists are reluctant to give credibility to the culture of poverty argument, or even a hint of it, largely because they may believe it ignores the structural factors that lead to poverty and homelessness. On one hand, it is clear, as the evidence shows, that structural factors are critical to understanding poverty and homelessness. However, an argument that attributes the problem only to these types of conditions limit the discussion to the possible solutions that can be developed to minimize or alleviate the factors that create and perpetuate poverty and homelessness. In other words, unless global changes in the economy, labor market, education, transportation, child care, and health insurance are forthcoming, little can be done to address poverty and homelessness. Given that such sweeping changes are unlikely, the futility of the situation stalls the discussion, leaving most social scientists lamenting the conditions and revisiting the issues only to come to the same conclusions.

Similarly, arguments in favor of a cultural explanation for poverty and homelessness, which use empowerment as the primary solution to the problem, are also limited in their ability to understand and address the problem. This argument suggests that because of some lack of motivation, work ethic, or value system that promotes present orientation, people remain poor. Thus, when programs are developed to empower the poor and fail to achieve the intended goal, the causes for this are attributed to the personal inferiority of the individuals involved. However, what this argument fails to address are the structural obstacles many recipients face. We discovered that even those who are highly motivated, and for whom some opportunities for success are present, numerous barriers for which motivation, perseverance, and determination cannot overcome. Clearly poverty, and its more severe cousin, homelessness, are influenced by structural factors and some people are able to navigate their way out of those circumstances and lead reasonably productive lives. Many, however, do not. So the question is not whether structuralism or the culture of poverty is the best tool to explain poverty: it is very evident that

---

the economy and job market. This view is expressed most often by William Julius Wilson and the *spatial mismatch hypothesis*. This concept suggests that there has been a significant amount of growth in the lowest paying sectors of the job market. As jobs have moved away from inner city areas, where most of the poor live, and relocated to suburban industrial parks or even to other countries (also known as deindustrialization), the number of jobs has dwindled. More importantly, the least skilled workers have the most difficulty obtaining alternative jobs (Wilson, 1987).

A third structural approach contends that welfare policies contribute to poverty by trapping people into poverty and homelessness instead of helping them to escape. This is a frequent claim made by Charles Murray (1988), who argues that people are inherently lazy and will not be motivated to work if they know the government will take care of them. Critics like Murray argue that the only way to reinstill a work ethic in people is to eliminate welfare programs all together. In between the two extreme positions of personal inferiority and structuralism is the culture of poverty explanation, which contends that the influences of the social structure result in attitudes, values, and beliefs that shape behavior. This behavior is not actually in the best interests of the person performing it, but these attitudes are very pervasive and are shared with many others within their communities. The culture of poverty explanation suggests that a set of values and expectations and world views have been created in response to the structural obstacles that many poor people have faced. Poor people are said to have a sense of present orientation, meaning they live for the moment. Proponents of the culture of poverty argument also contend that poor people have a sense of helplessness and resignation towards work (Burton, 1992).

There is also a sense that these traits are passed down from one generation to the next and this explains why poverty is intergenerational: it is part of the socialization of poor children much in the same way all children are taught about life and their place in it by parents and relatives. Further, present orientation, a central feature of the culture of poverty argument, puts it at odds with the notion of deferred gratification, sense of work ethic, and the belief in control over one's destiny found in middle class culture.

both play a role. The focus should be on the extent one or the other influences people's behavior. For some, it will be structural factors, for others, their coping mechanisms will not allow them to always act in what is actually in their best interests.

It is in this light that learned helplessness theory offers a way of understanding the psycho-social coping mechanisms that homeless women use that prevents them from achieving self-sufficiency. It is not simply the result of structural factors, but also a history of other forms of adversity that create an outlook on future circumstances.[7]

It is also curious that we continue to hold poor and homeless people to standards to which we do not hold ourselves. The fact of the matter is that few people respond well to adversity at all times. What happens after the event(s) and why remain less understood, but the reality is that there are portions of middle class and affluent society, as well as the poor and homeless, that do not respond well to different forms of adversity. Some adapt and move forward to overcome these obstacles, while others remain mired in poor decisions, emotional paralysis, and counterproductive behavior for years.

To underscore this point, Schulman's (2004) work shows that disorders such as anxiety, agoraphobia, and depression are a function of an interplay of factors, and that people have different abilities and adaptive responses to certain situations and they are intertwined with the way they have been socialized as well as what types of environmental or life stress they are currently experiencing.

In a similar way, it is indeed an intriguing commentary on our value system when we suggest that when bad things happen to poor people and they do not respond well, we feel entitled to offer condescending suggestions such as the existence of a culture of poverty, or that the homeless (and welfare recipients) abuse the services provided to them.

REFERENCES:

Abramson, L. Y., Seligman, M.E. and Teasdale, J. D. 1978. "Learned Helplessness in Humans: Critique and Reformulation." *Journal of Abnormal Psychology* 87:49-74.
Anderson, E. 1991. *Streetwise*. Chicago: University of Chicago Press.
Banfield, L. 1970. *The Unheavenly City Revisted*. Chicago: University of Chicago Press.
Baum, A., Fleming, R., and Reddy, D. M. 1986. "Unemployment Stress: Loss of Control, Reactance, and Learned Helplessness." *Social Science and Medicine* 38:471-481.
_____, Aiello, J. R. and Calesnick, L. E. 1978. "Crowding and Personal Control: Social Density and the Development of Learned Helplessness." *Journal of Personality and Social Psychology* 36:1000-1010.
_____ and Gatchel, R. J. 1981. "Cognitive Determinants of Reaction to Uncontrollable Events: Development of Reactance and Learned Helplessness." *Journal of Personality and Social Psychology* 40:1078-1089.

---

[7] The logic behind learned helplessness is not completely foreign. Historically, we have seen people in oppressive societies that learn to quit trying to be free and accept the exploitation forced upon them.

_____ and Valins, S. 1977. *Architecture and Social Behavior: Psychological Studies of Social Density.* Hillsdale, NJ; Erlbaum.

Bowman, P. J. 1984. "A Discouragement-centered Approach to Studying Unemployment Among Black Youth: Hopelessness, Attributions, and Psychological Distress." *International Journal of Mental Health* 13:68-91.

Bassuk, E. L. 1986. "Homeless Families: Single Mothers and Their Children in Boston Shelters. In E. Bassuk (Ed.), *The Mental Health Needs of Homeless Persons: New Directions For Mental Health Services* (pp.45-53). San Francisco: Jossey-Bass.

_____. 1993. "Social and Economic hardships of Homeless and Other Poor Women." *American Journal of Orthopsychiatry,* 63(3): 340-8.

_____. 1998. "Lives in jeopardy: women and homelessness" in Willie C, Rieker, P. Kramer, B., and Brown, B. (eds.) *Mental Health, Racism and Sexism.* Pittsburgh: University of Pittsburgh Press.

_____ and L. Rosenberg. 1988. "Psychosocial characteristics of homeless and children with homes." *Pediatrics* 85(3): 257-261.

_____., Rubin, L. and Lauriat, A. 1986. "Characteristics of Sheltered Homeless Families." *American Journal of Public Health,* 76(9): 1097-1101.

_____. and Rubin, L. 1987. "Homeless children: A neglected population." *American Journal of Orthopsychiatry,* 57: 279-86.

Brewin, C. R. 1985. "Depression and Causal Attributions: What is Their Relation?" *Psychology Bulletin* 98:297-309.

Browne, A. 1993. "Family Violence and Homelessness: The Relevance of Trauma Histories in the Lives of Homeless Women." *American Journal of Orthopsychiatry,* 63(3): 370-84.

_____. and S. Bassuk 1997. "Intimate violence in the lives of homeless and poor housed women: prevalence and patterns in an ethnically divers sample." *American Journal of Orthopsychiatry* 67(2): 261-278.

Browne, K.S. and Ziefert, M. 1990. "A Feminist Approach to Working with Homeless Women." *Affilia,* 5: 6-20.

Burt, M. R. and Cohen, B. 1989. *America's Homeless: Numbers, Characteristics, and Programs that Serve Them.* Urban Institute Report 89-3. Washington, D.C.: Urban Institute Press.

_____.1989. "Differences among Homeless Single Women, Women with Children, and Single Men." *Social Problems,* 36(5): 308-24.

Burton, C. 1992. *The Poverty Debate.* Westport, CT: Praeger.

Butler, S. S. 1993. "Listening to Middle-Aged Homeless Women Talk About Their Lives." *Affilia,* 8(4): 388-409.

Butkowsky, I. S. and Willows, D. M. 1980. "Cognitive-motivational Characteristics of Children Varying in Reading Ability: Evidence for Learned Helplessness in Readers." *Journal of Educational Psychology* 72:408-422.

Crystal, S. 1984. "Homeless Men and Homeless Women: The Gender Gap." *The Urban & Social Change Review,* 17: 2-6.

Cummins, L. K., First, R. and Toomey, B. 1998. "Comparisons of Rural and Urban Homeless Women." *Affilia Journal of Women and Social Work,* 13(4): 435-54.

Da Costa Nunez. 1995. "Family Values Among Homeless Families." *Public Welfare,*

53(4): 24-33.

Davis, L. and J. Hagen. 1996. "Stereotypes and Stigma: What's Changed for Welfare Mothers?" *Affilia*. 11:319-337.

DiBlasio, F. A. and Belcher, J. 1995. "Gender Differences Among Homeless Persons: Special Services for Women." *American Journal of Orthopsychiatry*, 65(1):131-8.

Dweck, C. S. 1975. "The Role of Expectations and Attributions in the Alleviation of Learned Helplessness." *Journal of Personality and Social Psychology* 31:674-685.

Feather, N. T. 1982. "Unemployment and its Psychological Correlates: A Study of Depressive Symptoms, Protestant Ethic Values, Attributional Style, and Apathy." *Australian Journal of Psychology* 34:309-323.

_____ and Barber, J. G. 1983. "Depressive Reactions and Unemployment." *Journal of Abnormal Psychology* 92: 185-195.

_____ and Davenport, P. R. 1981. "Unemployment and Depressive Affect: A Motivational and Attributional Analysis." *Journal of Personality and Social Psychology* 41:422-461.

Fernando, S. 1984. "Racism as a Cause of Depression." *International Journal of Social Psychiatry* 30:41-49.

Firth, J. and Brewin, C. R. 1982. "Attributions and Recovery from Depression: A Preliminary Study Using Cross-lagged Correlation Analysis." *British Journal of Clinical Psychology* 96:229-236.

Fischer, P. J., Breakey, W.R., and Nestadt, G. November 1992. "Victimization in Two Samples of Homeless Women." Paper prepared for the American Health Association, Washington, D.C.

Forward, J. R. and Williams, J. R. 1970. "Internal-external Control and Black Militancy." *Journal of Social Issues* 26:75-92.

Hagen, J. L. 1987. "Gender and Homelessness." *Social Work*, 32: 312-6.

_____. 1990. "Designing Services for Homeless Women." *Journal of Health And Social Policy*, 11(3): 1-16.

_____. and Ivanoff, A. 1988. "Homeless Women: A High-Risk Population." *Affilia*, (3)1: 19-33.

Hammersley, P. and D. Atkinson. 1984. *Principles of Ethnography*. London: Tavistock.

Harper, D. 1996. "Relations on the Road," in Smith, C. D. and Kornblum, W. (eds.) *In the Field: Readings on the Field Research Experience*, pp. 59-72. Westport, CT: Praeger.

Hausman, B. and Hammen, C. 1993. "Parenting in Homeless Families: The Double Crisis." *American Journal of Orthopsychiatry*, 63(3): 358-69.

Hertzberg, E.L. 1992. "The Homeless in the United States: Conditions, Typology, and Interventions." *International Social Work*, 35: 149-61.

Hilfiker D. 1984. *Not All of Us Are Saints*: A Doctor's Journey with the Poor. New York: Ballantine Books.

Johnson, A. K. 1989. "Female-Headed Homeless Families: A Comparative Profile." *Affilia*, 4(4): 23-39.

Johnson, A. K. and Krueger, L.W. 1989. "Toward a Better Understanding of

Homeless Women." *Social Work,* 34: 537-40.

Jones, E. and R. Nisbett. 1972. "the Actor and the Observer: Divergent Perceptions of the Causes of Behavior." In E. Jones, D. Kanoused, H. Kelly, S. Valins, and B. Weiner (eds.) *Attribution: Perceiving the Causes of Behavior.* New York: General Learning Press.

Knickman, J.R. and Weitzman, B.C. 1989. *A Study of Homeless Families in New York City: Risk Assessment Models and Strategies for Prevention* (Final report: Volume 1). New York: Human Resources Administration, Health Research Program, New York University.

Kozol, J. 1989. *Rachel and Her Children.* New York: Crown.

Kuykendall, D. and Keating, J. P. 1984. "Crowding and Reactions to Uncontrollable Events." *Population and Environment: Behavioral and Social Issues* 7:246-259.

Lewis, O. 1969. *Five Families: Mexican Case Studies in the Culture of Poverty.* New York: HarperCollins.

Metalasky, G. I.; Abramson, L. Y.; Seligman, M. E.; Semmel, A.; Peterson, C. 1982. "Attributional Styles and Life Events in the Classroom: Vulnerability and Invulnerability to Depressive Mood Reactions." *Journal of Personality and Social Psychology* 43:612-617.

McChesney, K. Y. "A review of the Empirical Literature on Contemporary Urban Homeless Families." *Social Service Review,* 69 (1995): 429-60.

McNamara, R. P. 1998. *Culture Versus Structure: Factors that Influence the Efficacy of Programs for the Homeless.* Greenville, SC: Sunbelt Human Advances Resources Incorporated.

Mills, C. and Ota, H. 1989. "Homeless Women with Minor Children in the Detroit Metropolitan Area." *Social Work,* 34: 485-9.

Murray, C. 1988. *Losing Ground.* Cambridge, MA: Harvard University Press.

North, C. S. and Smith, E. 1994. "Comparison of White and Nonwhite Homeless Men and Women." *Social Work,* 39(6): 639-48.

Peterson, C; Maier, S.F. Seligman, E.P. 1993. *Learned Helplessness: A theory for the Age of Personal Control.* New York: Oxford University Press.

Powell, L. 1990. "Factors Associated with the Under representation of African Americans in Mathematics and Science." *Journal of Negro Education* 59:292-298.

Roth, D., Toomey, B. and First, R. 1987. "Homeless Women: Characteristics and Needs." *Affilia,* 3: 6-19.

Salomon, A., Bassuk, S. and Brooks, M. 1996. "Patterns of Welfare use Among Poor and Homeless Women." *American Journal of Orthopsychiatry,* 66(4): 510-26.

Seligman, M.E. 1992. *Learned Optimism.* New York: Knopf.

_____. 1975. *Helplessness: On Depression, Development, and Death.* San Francisco: Freeman.

Shinn, M.; Knickman, J.R.; and Weitzman, B.C. 1991. "Social Relationships and Vulnerability to Becoming Homeless Among Poor Families." *American Psychologist,* 46: 1180-7.

Smith, E. M. and North, C. 1994. "Not All Homeless Women Are Alike: Effects of Motherhood and the Presence of Children." *Community Mental Health Journal,* 30(6): 601-11.

Smith, R. and Seligman, M. E. 1978. "Black and Lower Class Children are More Susceptible to Helplessness Induced Cognitive Deficits Following Unsolvable Problems. Unpublished Manuscript, University of Pennsylvania.

Spencer, M. B., Kim, S., and Marshall, S. 1987. "Double Stratification and Psychological Risk: Adaptational Processes and School Achievement of Black Children." *Journal of Negro Education* 56:77-87.

The Stanford Studies of Homeless Families, Children, and Youth. November 18, 1991. Stanford University.

Sue, S. 1977. "Psychological Theory and Implications for Asian Americans." *Personnel and Guidance Journal* 55:381-389.

Riskind, J. H., Castellon, C., and Beck, A.T. 1989. "Spontaneous Causal Explanations in Unipolar Depression and General Anxiety: Content Analysis of Dysfunctional-thought Diaries." *Cognitive Therapy and Research* 13:97-108.

Sweeney, P. D., Anderson, K. and Bailey, S. 1986. "Attributional Style in Depression: A Meta-analytic Review." *Journal of Personality and Social Psychology* 50:974-991.

U.S. Conference of Mayors. 2003. Sodexho: Hunger and Homelessness Survey: *A Status Report on Hunger and Homelessness in America's Cities.* Washington, D.C.: U.S. Government Printing Office.

U.S. Conference of Mayors. 2000. *A Status Report on Hunger and Homelessness in America's Cities.* Washington, D.C.: U.S. Government Printing Office.

_____. 1998. *A Status Report on Hunger and Homelessness in America's Cities.* Washington, D.C.: U.S. Government Printing Office.

U.S. Department of Housing and Urban Development. 2001. Homelessness: Programs and The People They Serve—Highlights Report. Washington, D.C., Office of Policy Development and Research.

U.S. Department of Housing and Urban Development. 1989. "A report to the Secretary on the Homeless and Emergency Shelters." Washington, D.C., Office of Policy Development and Research.

U.S. Department of Urban Housing and Development. 1994. "Priority: Home! The Federal Plan to Break the Cycle of Homelessness." Washington, DC: Author.

Weiner, B. 1979. "A Theory of Motivation for Some Classroom Experiences." *Journal of Education Psychology* 71:3-25.

Weinreb, L. and Buckner, J. 1993. "Homeless Families: Program Responses and Public Policies." *American Journal of Orthopsychiatry*, 63(3): 400-9.

_____, R. Goldberg, and J. Perloff. 1998. "The health characteristics and service use patterns of sheltered homeless and low income housed mothers." *Journal of General and Internal Medicine* 13(1): 389-397.

Weisz, J. R. 1981. "Learned Helplessness in Black and White Children Identified by Their Schools as Retarded and Non-retarded: Performance Deterioration in Response to Failure." *Developmental Psychology* 17:499-508.

Wilson, W.J. 1987. *The Truly Disadvantaged.* Chicago: University of Chicago Press.

Wolf, B. and S. Hill. 1995. "The Effect of Health on the Work Effort of Single Mothers." *Journal of Human Resources* 30(1): 42-62.

Wood, D.; Valdez, R.B.; Hayashi, T.; and Shen, A. 1990. "Homeless and Housed

Families in Los Angeles: A Study Comparing Demographic, Economic, and   Family
Function Characteristics." *American Journal of Public Health,* 80: 1049-52.
Zullow, H. M. 1984. "The Interaction of Rumination and Explanatory Style in Depression."
    Master's Thesis, University of Pennsylvania.

The War On Crime As A Social Problem

John Fuller
Department of Sociology, Criminal Justice, and Anthropology
State University of West Georgia

Crime is clearly a social problem. It represents a type of unfortunate behavior that seriously damages not only individual victims, but also the entire fabric of a healthy society. The level of crime in this country is high compared to other societies and has led the public to demand that politicians enact policies to do something, anything, to address this social problem.

Sometimes the cure is worse than the disease. To be sure, crime is a significant social problem in the United States, but the thesis of this essay is that the way we are addressing crime, by waging a war on it, is not only doomed to failure but also destroys the cherished rights of our citizens (Alexander 1996). The unanticipated consequences of the war on crime, particularly the war on drugs, has eroded the trust people have in the government, increased crime and the level of violence, and has made human life expendable because of the sensational nature of criminal penalties. These are serious charges to level at contemporary criminal justice policy, and to accept them causes one to envision alternative responses to the problems of crime and violence in society. The purpose of this essay is to do no less than propose the war on crime be ended and replaced by a peacemaking perspective that values the rights of victims, offenders, and society (Bartollas and Braswell 1993).

This essay is divided into three sections. The first section briefly discusses why war is an inappropriate metaphor to apply to social problems. The second section deals more extensively with the tactics of the war on crime and details how destructive to the social fabric of society this misguided policy has become. Finally, the third section proposes an emerging peacemaking perspective and suggests it will not only be more effective in addressing the problems of crime, but it will also allow a more comprehensive examination of social problems and provide a framework for a theoretically integrated and functionally-connected strategy to ameliorate their seriousness.

Of Metaphors and Wars

Metaphors are linguistic devices. They link two separate concepts and suggest a relationship whereby one takes on the characteristics and behavior of the other. They are also seductive devices because they suggest a simple way to comprehend or understand complex ideas by comparing them to more readily accessible concepts. The war on crime perspective is just such a seductive metaphor. By suggesting that the social problem of crime can be envisioned as an external enemy, we can employ the paramilitary methods and tactics of war to achieve the goal of victory. By couching the language of crime control in terms of a war, we obscure the true nature of criminal activity and give rise to all kinds of inappropriate and socially-destructive tactics to engage the problem (Czajoski 1990).

The most fundamental distinction between war and crime in the location of the problem. In a war, even a civil war, there is an identifiable enemy, an outside aggressor who can be subdued, defeated, or killed. Crime, on the other hand, presents no readily identifiable target for social policy. Criminals are drawn from within society and cannot be targeted for action until after they have committed the unlawful behavior. Unlike a wartime enemy, who conveniently wears a uniform and occupies a territory, the criminal is part and parcel of society. In a sense, we are all potential criminals and the tactics of war are unsuitable in a free and democratic society. To use the war on crime perspective is to essentially impose a police state, and this is something that most Americans are unwilling to consider.

The war metaphor is misleading in a fundamental way. While it is a concept that politicians can use to sound tough on crime, they do not literally mean that we should use the same tactics to address crime that we use to wage war against an external enemy. In a war we have to make significant sacrifices. During World War II, there was a massive mobilization of manpower into the armed forces and a change in the labor force, where significant numbers of women left the home and went to work in vital industries. This shift in the structure of the labor market was short-lived, however. When the men came back from overseas, they replaced the women in the labor force. The impact of the war on the way America worked was temporary. The sacrifices we were all willing to make were bearable and desirable because they did not entail a permanent change in society. They were necessary because of the external threat posed by the Axis powers.

When posed with the metaphor of a war on crime, the politicians are not talking about temporary sacrifices but about dismantling the protection of the Constitution that have been developed for over 200 years (Sutton 1991). There is no external enemy to conquer, as drug use is a social problem from within our society. Sure, we may hassle some Colombian drug lord or complain to Mexican politicians about drugs crossing our borders, but the demand for drugs in American society will be met by different entities even if we are successful in dealing with these two countries. The nature of the drug trade mutates as our policies change. At one time we believed the heroin distribution channel through France was the problem, but when it was successfully addressed, the heroin found other means to get to this country. Them problem is not in *Them*, but in *us*. This is the underlying reason why the war metaphor is so misleading and ultimately destructive. To wage a war on crime, especially on drugs, is to ask Americans to make permanent sacrifices in their protection from government. These sacrifices are not something the politicians emphasize when they espouse their campaign rhetoric (Gardiner and McKinney 1991).

Strategies, Tactics, and Sacrifices in the War on Crime

The war on crime has many fronts. While we may think the criminal justice system is where the war is being waged, the truth is that many of the institutions of our society have been enlisted to fight this war (Gottfredson and Hirshchi 1989). Schools, the family, health services, and other institutions have been drafted into this war, and the relationship with students, clients, and loved ones has been basically altered. This is done a great peril to the fabric of society. In the name of waging war, we have destroyed many of the delicate social bounds that hold us together in meaningful communities. By employing the simplistic war metaphor we have transformed the relationship between the individual and the government in ways that are producing unanticipated and unattractive consequences. Let's look are some of the methods and tactics employed by the war on crime and discuss their ramifications. This list is primarily taken from the book *Power, Ideology, and the War on Drugs: Nothing Succeeds Like Failure*, by Christina Jacqueline Johns (1992), and is presented here to highlight just how intrusive this policy has become and to demonstrate how the war on crime has, itself, become a social problem of far-reaching dimensions.

1. <u>The right to privacy and searches.</u> Americans treasure their rights of privacy and the proscription in the Constitution against unreasonable searches. In fighting the war on crime, the government has requested that restrictions on searches be eased so that they can find illegal drugs and weapons. This presents a conflict in values as most people would agree that lawbreakers should be caught, but at the same time, do not want be subjected to unnecessary and intrusive searches themselves. Some of the search tactics that citizens complain about include aerial surveillance where law enforcement agencies over fly private property looking for illegal drugs. Without probable cause, that is, without a good reason to suspect that someone is growing illegal drugs, it seems like a fishing expedition to fly over everyone's property in search drug activities. Another type of unfair search tactic is the targeting of individuals in airports because they fit a drug courier profile. These profiles are perceived to be racially and ethnically based and to select subjects for search based on stereotypes rather than on behavior. Law enforcement officers have gone through peoples' trash in an effort to find incriminating information and have used a variety of hidden electronic devices to listen to and record conversations. While these kind of information gathering activities have always been a part of law enforcement, the war on drugs has expanded their use into the lives of many citizens who do not consider themselves criminals and who resent this type of surveillance.

2. <u>The right of financial privacy.</u> The drug trade involves large sums of money. In an effort to prosecute drug traffickers the records of banks are routinely examined for evidence of money laundering. While most people might agree that the government should be allowed to freeze the accounts of criminals, they are also wary of the government secretly snooping into their private financial matters.

3. <u>Illegally-gathered evidence: The exclusionary rule.</u> One of the most vexing problems of law enforcement is when they find evidence of criminal activity and have the case thrown out of court because the evidence was not obtained legally. The Anti-Drug Abuse Bill of 1988 allows illegally gathered evidence to be used if, in the opinion of the court, it was gathered in good faith. To take a hypothetical example, let's say law enforcement officers entered a burning building with the goal of making sure there were no potential victims and in the search found illegal drugs. Normally, these drugs would not be admissible as evidence because the officer did not have a search warrant or probable cause to believe there were drugs in the building. But because he went into the building in good faith to rescue people, the drugs found can be used as evidence under the new law. The issue becomes one of deciding what is good faith and how it might be abused by law enforcement officers.

4.   <u>Drug testing.</u> One of the ways the war on crime is being fought in not only the criminal justice system, but also in other institutions is through drug testing. In an effort to make for a safer society, the intrusive practice of drug testing is utilized in a vast number of contexts, some of which have little prospect for achieving the goal of less crime and some of which are blatant violations of citizens' rights, common decency, and fairness. Take for instance the driving laws in Georgia, where the presence of marijuana in the blood or urine is sufficient evidence to convict a driver of driving under the influence. Because marijuana can be detected in the body weeks after it was smoked, it is possible that someone could be convicted long after the marijuana had any type of debilitating effect on the brain or body that could contribute to an accident. By testing for marijuana in the body of an accident victim, it is not possible to determine if any marijuana found actually was responsible for a miscalculation. The law does not promote traffic safety but merely regulates lifestyle. For DUI drivers who use alcohol, the blood alcohol level measured by a breathalyzer or blood test can give a reasonable indication of how much the driver was impaired by drinking. This is not the case with marijuana. Only the presence of marijuana can be detected, not the effect. We should not be fooled into thinking that drug testing can make the roads safer.

    Drug testing is used by the private sector also. Many employers test their workers to ensure a drug-free workplace. On one level this seems perfectly reasonable. Certainly none of us would want to fly on an airplane where the pilot was not in complete control of his/her faculties and we would not want our children on a school bus where the driver was under the influence of drugs. Unfortunately, drug testing cannot ensure that we are safe. Again, the question of impairment is not really measured. Additionally, there are many occupations that are subjected to drug testing where safety is not an issue. Employers are merely testing for lifestyle and imposing their own moral code on the employees. This is a controversial matter. If someone is doing a good job should they be fired because they use illegal drugs away from the workplace? Does the employer have the right to invade the privacy of the worker when there is no evidence that the worker is in any way affected by the drug use?

    There is one other use of drug testing that is of concern to many people. That is the home drug-testing kits that are being marketed to parents. One wonders about the family dynamics when parents randomly test their children for drug use. If the parents were truly involved with their children it would seem as if they would know from the child's behavior if there was cause for concern. By relying on drug testing, parents are attempting to get technology to do what they have been neglecting, that is, being intimately involved in the lives of their children. What is the effect of parents testing their children for drugs on the development of trust and responsibility? If these attributes are not taught early they may never be developed or refined in the youth. Drug testing is not a panacea for the problems of crime. In addition to being ineffective and intrusive, there are unanticipated consequences that make it a policy that should be considered only under very restricted and special circumstances, such as when the public safety in question.

<u>Due process and rights of defendants</u>. There is a widespread perception in the country that criminal suspects are protected by laws that allow them to escape justice by slipping through loopholes. People believe that guilty persons are routinely being set free because the hands of police and prosecutors are tied by the principle of due process. There are two types of law that govern the criminal justice system. Substantive laws proscribe acts such as murder and theft. Procedural law specifies how criminal justice practitioners may go about implementing the substantive law. Procedural law protects all of us from the arbitrary and capricious actions of the government (Sutton 1991). Many of the principles of the Constitution are embedded in our procedural law, such as the right to a jury of our peers and the right to confront hostile witnesses. The interpretation of the Constitution is an ongoing matter for the Supreme Court, and as the balance of liberal to conservative judges shift, we find that many of the principles of procedural law are being contested. Bills are routinely introduced in Congress that would diminish the right of criminal defendants and make it easier for the criminal justice system to convict. In addition to the exclusionary rule, the contested principles of due process include the number of appeals available to those under the sentence of death and the Miranda warnings, which advise suspects of their right to an attorney before they are questioned. There is tension in the criminal justice system as the rights of defendants and the rights of the victim and the public are being reconsidered in light of the war on crime (Levy 1996) Those who violate the law and do harm are hard to be sympathetic toward, but their rights against an overzealous criminal justice system protect all citizens and help ensure that innocent individuals are not railroaded through the system.

6.   <u>Public housing and public life</u>. The war on crime is not limited to the criminal justice system as witnessed by the laws concerning public housing. If drugs are sold in a public housing apartment, the occupants can be evicted. Even if the drugs are sold with out the knowledge of the parents, the entire family can be prohibited from living in public housing. This is a situation that has wide support given the conditions of crime and abuse in some public housing projects. The solution to economic crimes such as drug sales does not lie in punishing the whole family for the transgression of one of its members, however. By making public housing the instrument of law enforcement, the war on crime limits the role that other institutions can play in the prevention and treatment of social problems. If all our institutions do the bidding of the criminal justice system, then the supportive nature of these institutions is lost and the only approach to social problems is the punitive nature of the criminal justice system. That is not to say that other institutions do not play an important role in the development of social control. It is important, however, to recognize that there is a fundamental difference in not only the tactics, but in the missions of institutions. The separation of powers and purposes prevents the country from becoming a police state where we are under surveillance in all aspects of our lives.

7.   <u>Women, the unborn, and drugs</u>. In an effort to protect unborn babies from the addiction of their mothers to drugs and alcohol, there has been a great effort aimed at criminalizing the drug use of pregnant women. While using drugs when pregnant is clearly dangerous,

the best way to deal with this public health problem is not through the criminal justice system. There are really two issues here that speak to the problems associated with the war on crime. The first problem is of how to best help the mother to provide a healthy prenatal environment for the unborn baby. By holding the sword of the criminal justice system over her head, the war on crime pits the doctor and hospital against the mother. If she faces criminal charges for drug or alcohol use while pregnant, the woman will be less likely to seek prenatal care because her behavior could be discovered. The first time health professionals will become aware of the pregnancy is when there is a significant problem or when the baby is born. Much damage may already have been done by the time the woman's drug use and pregnancy are discovered. The alternative is to encourage women into prenatal programs and treat the drug use in a supportive way rather than in a punitive manner. Having a healthy baby can be a significant motivation for a women to address her addiction to drugs.

A second problem with the war on crime as it relates to pregnant women revolves around the issue of the "crack baby." There has been a massive campaign warning about the dangers of crack use on the unborn and the resulting behavioral difficulties these children face as they reach school age. Horror stories about the diminished brain capacity of crack babies are repeated to warn pregnant women about drug use. Laudable as these efforts may be it is now coming to light that the crack baby scare is exaggerated at best, and maybe even nonexistent (Welch 1996 426-27).

While no one is claiming crack is safe, no studies have scientifically established that there is such a thing as a crack baby. Women who took crack while pregnant also tended to drink alcohol. The indicators of fetal alcohol syndrome are the same indicators as those for what we call crack babies. The war on crime rhetoric has elevated crack use to crisis status when it may well be a legal drug, alcohol, that is responsible for this situation. Furthermore, there is some evidence that these babies are not doomed to a dismal life and that after two years they essentially catch up with their peers in terms of physical and intellectual development (Gavzer 1997).

8.   Expansion of the death penalty. The death penalty is used very sparingly in the United States. It is a rare occurrence that happens only after a long and protracted series of trials and appeals. Those who espouse the war on crime would like to change that. In addition to streamlining the process by limiting the number of appeals available to the defendant, those who advocate capital punishment would like to expand the range of crimes and circumstances for which the death penalty can be applied (Tobolowsky 1992). This is particularly true in the war on drugs where homicides revolving around drug sales would be held to a lesser criteria for application of the death penalty than are other murders. The thinking behind this policy is that it would deter individuals from engaging in the drug trade because if something went wrong and someone were killed, then death penalty could be more readily used. This reasoning naively assumes that people who make a great deal of money will be deterred from the drug trade by expansion of the death penalty. The unintended consequence of such a policy may well be to make drug trafficking more lucrative because of the increased risks, thereby drawing more people

into the drug trade rather than frightening them away. Additionally, drug traffickers who do kill may be more willing to use deadly force on undercover agents or innocent bystanders because of the increased risks if caught.

9. <u>Schools and the war on crime</u>. Like the family, schools have now been enlisted to fight the war on crime, and this can fundamentally alter the relationship between this institution and students. Of particular concern are the zero-tolerance policies adopted by some schools where minor and technical infractions of the rules can result in detention, suspension, or even dismissal. Discretion has been taken away from teachers and administrators by these zero-tolerance policies and the schools have been changed from institutions that exert informal social control to those that engage in a pervasive and formal type of social control. While school safety is certainly an important issue, the way students are stripped of their right and dignity has altered the affinity between the student and school. Schools routinely search students, their lockers, and their cars. Drug-sniffing dogs are used to detect deviant behavior even when there is no reason to suspect drugs. Small pocket knives or legally-prescribed drugs can be violations of rigid zero-tolerance policies and cause students to be disciplined. Student-athletes are tested for drug use and kicked off the team if they fail. Students can be denied financial aid if they have a history of drug use. While protecting children and youth from drugs and violence is a laudable goal, in many instances the schools have strayed too far from their primary mission of education and have become arms of the criminal justice system in the war against crime. Precisely those youth who need to stay in school the most are the ones being driven to the streets by the war on crime. As kids are kicked out of school for infractions of rules or alienated by an atmosphere of social control rather than learning, the schools forfeit their potential to make meaningful changes in the lives of students for the more limited goal of enforcing rigid rules and regulations aimed at uniformity and an atmosphere of discipline.

10. <u>Workplace surveillance</u>. In addition to drug testing many workers are finding their actions subject to greater and greater scrutiny at the workplace. Cameras are used to monitor not only job performance but also social interaction. Off the job behavior can also be used to discipline or fire employees. Drug use that does not effect job performance is not tolerated by many organizations. In short, the workplace is another institution that is assisting the criminal justice system in the war on crime.

This list of issues and concerns surrounding how the war on crime impacts the rights of citizens and the civility of everyday life is offered as a suggestion that fighting crime at all costs is too expensive. The costs in terms of the quality of life in a democratic society are being eroded by simplistic and political rhetoric aimed not at strengthening our institutions so they can do a better job in meeting the needs of people, but rather in enlisting them into fighting a war on crime which is destructive to the social fabric of the nation.

As mentioned previously, war is an inappropriate and misleading metaphor for the work of the criminal justice system. The consequences for employing such a destructive way of envisioning our crime problem is evidenced by this long and disturbing list of unintended consequences. It is required at this point to suggest an alternative way of addressing the very real problems of crime. It is not fair to criticize present policy if one has nothing to offer as a better way to solve the problem. What is offered here is not more of the same. What is advocated requires a fundamental change in thinking from the war on crime perspective. What is suggested is more in keeping with the values and principles of democratic institution, and hopefully, it will be more effective in dealing with crime and criminals than the status quo (Buckley 1996; Duke 1996).

A Plea For A Peacemaking Perspective

If the war on crime is failing, then what would be a sensible alternative? A peace perspective presents a framework for addressing criminal justice issues that not only holds more promise for dealing with those who have already broken the law, but also for the development of meaningful communities where citizens and government work together to meet the needs of everyone. A full explication of the peace perspective is beyond the scope of this chapter but can be found in *Criminal Justice : A Peacemaking Perspective* (Fuller 1998).

Where the war on crime perspective is based on deterrence and punishment, the peacemaking perspective is based on prevention and rehabilitation. Where the war on crime perspective finds the cause for crime in the motivation and personality of the individual offender, the peacemaking perspective looks at the culture and institutions of society to ask why certain environments so consistently produce high crime rates. Where the war on crime perspective is willing to sacrifice freedoms for the elusive goals of a drug-free and crime-free community, the peacemaking perspective realizes that a certain amount of deviant behavior is normal in society and that the ultimate answer to crime lies not in the criminal justice system but in other of society's institutions.

The peacemaking perspective is not new. The underlying fundamentals have been practiced not only in the criminal justice system but in many cultures for thousands of years. The peacemaking perspective requires us to step back from the ethnocentric way we view our country and to use our sociological imaginations (Mills 1959) to look historically and cross-culturally to see alternatives methods of dealing with crime. Pepinsky and Quinney (1991) locate the basis for the peacemaking perspective in three types of intellectual traditions. The religious and humanist traditions emphasize love, compassion, and forgiveness (Parrinder 1971). In order to reintegrate offenders into society we have to, at some point, stop punishing them and help them find meaningful relationships and fulfilling work. These traditions draw on the world's great religions for guidance on how to inspire and serve people so they become connected to the dominant culture. The feminist traditions look at how our society has developed patriarchal and sexist norms that limit the potential for women and men to develop their true human potentials.

Focusing on equal rights, equal opportunities, and cooperation, the feminist tradition requires that we rethink traditional sex-role behavior and look at how the relationships between and among women and men contribute to our crime problem (McDermott 1994). The critical intellectual traditions look at other variables, particularly social class, and emphasize social justice, enlightenment, and emancipation (Reiman 1995). These traditions all contribute to the peacemaking perspective which can be applied to more than the problem of crime. From the intrapersonal to the interpersonal to the institutional and societal to the global and international level, the peacemaking perspective provides an integrated and consistent guide for human behavior. It requires not only that the criminal justice system be reformed but also that we reconsider everything from our parenting skills to global economic systems. Crime, according to the peacemaking perspective, is intertwined in the patterns and relationships of society and can only be effectively addressed by getting beyond blaming the individual offender and looking at the entire way societies operate. This is not to say that individual offenders are blameless, but it does suggest that crime is a product of the organizational and institutional arrangement of countries and that it requires a more comprehensive look than just viewing the social deficiencies of individual offenders.

One of the most important principles of the peacemaking perspective is that it requires the criminal justice system to model the behavior it expects of its citizens. It is not surprising then that the peacemaking perspective opposes capital punishment, the war on drugs, and excessive use of police force (Skolnick and Fyfe 1993). Those who adopt the peacemaking perspective would support gun control and advocate a shift in criminal justice resources from punishment to prevention and rehabilitation. Maintaining law and order are only part of what our society should be striving for. We should, according to the peacemaking perspective, ensure that our institutions of social control accomplish their mandates in a non-violent way that promotes social justice (National Criminal Justice Commission 1996).

The key to making society work is to make it fair. Everyone must feel that they have a stake in obeying the law and acting in a civil manner. The war on crime fails to provide the underlying theoretical justification for this and thus has become a serious social problem itself. It is sometimes hard to distinguish which is more destructive to society: crime, or the way we address it with a war mentality.

REFERENCES:

Alexander, B.K. (1990) "Alternatives to the War On Drugs." *The Journal of Drug Issues* 20(1):1-27.

Buckley, W.F. Jr. (1996) "The War on Drugs is Lost." *National Review* 48(2):36-38.

Czajkoski, E.H. (1990) "Drugs and the Warlike Administration of Justice." *The Journal of Drug Issues* 20(1):125-129.

Duke, S.B. (1996) "The War on Drugs is Lost." *National Review* 48(2):47-48.

Fuller, J.F. (1998) *Criminal Justice: A Peacemaking Perspective.* Boston: Allyn and Bacon.

Gardiner, G.S. and R.N. McKinney (1991) "The Great American War on Drugs: Another Failure of Tough-Guy Management." *The Journal of Drug Issues* 21(3):605-616.

Gavzer, B. (1997) "Can They Beat the Odds? *Parade Magazine* July 27 4-5.

Johns, C.J. (1992) *Power, Ideology, and the War on Drugs: Nothing Succeeds Like Failure.* New York: Praeger.

Levy, L.W. (1996) *A License to Steal: The Forfeiture of Property.* Chapel Hill, NC: University of North Carolina Press.

McDermott, M.J. (1994) "Criminology as Peacemaking: Feminist Ethics and the Victimization of Women." *Women and Crimnal Justice.* 5(2):21-44.

Mills, C.W. (1959) *The Sociological Imagination*. New York: Oxford University Press.

National Criminal Justice Commission. (1996) "Ten Recommendations to Shift the Fundamental Direction of U.S. Crime Policy." http://www.ncianet.org/ncia/FIND.HTML.

Parrinder, G. (1971) *World Religions: From Ancient History to the Present*. New York: Facts on File Publications.

Pepinsky, H.E. and R. Quinney (eds.) 1991. *Criminology as Peacemaking*. Bloomington, IN: Indiana University Press.

Reiman, J. (1995). *The Rich Get Richer and the Poor Get Prison: Ideology, class and Criminal Justice*. Boston:Allyn and Bacon.

Skolnick, J.H. and J.J. Fyfe (1993). *Above the Law: Police and the Excessive Use of Force*. New York: The Free Press.

Sutton, L. P. (1991) "Getting Around the Fourth Amendment" in C. B. Klockars and S.D. Mastrofski (eds.) *Thinking about Police: Contemporary Readings*. New York:McGraw-Hill, pp. 433-444.

Tobolosky, P. M. (1992). "Drugs and Death: Congress Authorizes the Death Penalty for Certain Drug-Related Murders." *Journal of Contemporary Law* 18(1): 47-73.

Welch, M. (1996). *Corrections: A Critical Approach*. New York: McGraw-Hill.

The Interplay of Drugs, Gangs, and Violence

Robert Hartmann McNamara
Department of Political Science and Criminal Justice
The Citadel

Urban gangs have become one of the most pervasive problems confronting our society. Across the nation, we have become a society almost preoccupied with gangs and, especially, their relationship to drugs and violence. While it is true that there has been an escalation of violence among gang members, and although involvement in drugs in some form has been a feature of gang life for many years, gangs are now being exclusively blamed for the drug problems of the last decade (U.S. Department of Justice 1989). Part of the reason for this is that gangs have continued to grow in number and diversity across the nation, affecting both large cities and smaller communities. Thus, the problem has gone beyond merely the "urban jungles" to small town America as well.

As with many social problems, we have increasingly turned to the use of the legal norms for solutions (McNamara 1995). In the absence of effective informal means of controlling behavior, we have become dependent on the use of formal social control: the criminal justice system (Spergel and Curry 1990). This approach is clearly displayed with our response to the prevalence of gangs. However, while a more punitive approach may help to ease our fears about gang violence and drug-related crime, we cannot rely exclusively on one social institution to perform the work of five.

The criminal justice system continues to struggle to meet its responsibilities in an increasingly industrialized society. As a result, the problems stemming from the existence of gangs in our communities will require that we not only improve our understanding of the problem, a goal researchers have been hard pressed to achieve, but to reinstitute the influence of informal social control at the community level. As many sociologists, such as Emile Durkheim (1893), Robert Park and Ernest Burgess (1925), and Talcott Parsons (1951) remind us, the only way to solve the social problems of a society is by enhancing the level of integration members feel for the collectivity. As the number of people who feel they have a responsibility to the other members of their community increases, individuals are more likely to put the group's needs ahead of their own.

If this occurs, solutions to the problems emerge and are more likely to be effective. This is clearly the case as it relates to gangs: the most effective solutions must come from within the community itself. These solutions can only come, however, after a clear understanding of the nature of the problem. The purpose of this chapter is to explore the relationship between gangs, drugs, and violence, and to attempt to show this interplay of factors is anything but clear. Our understanding of the gang problem is clouded not only by the variability of gang life, but by the extent and type of information communities receive about gangs as well.

THE MEDIA'S SOCIAL DISTORTION OF GANGS

Is there a link between gangs, drugs, and violence? Common sense tells us that the answer to this question should be obvious. However, our understanding of the nature of the problem, as well as its possible solutions, may be colored by a distortion of information on these subjects. While part of the problem involves a denial of a gang problem, a strategy many police departments employ (Huff 1988a, 1988b, 1989; Hagedorn 1988) there is also a good deal of distortion of information concerning gangs in the media.

Throughout various periods in American history, gangs have received quite a bit of attention from the media. As Jankowski (1991) tells us, this was especially true during the 1970s and 1980s when the public's exposure to gangs in the media was very high. Gang life was described in all forms of the mass media and the general public's primary source of information about gangs, like most things that occur in our society, came from the media (see for instance Conklin 1992; Livingston 1990). Moreover, whether it was movies, television, radio, newspapers, even documentaries, the image created about gangs was a consistent one: they are heavily involved in the drug trade and are exceptionally prone to violence.

There are two primary reasons for this characterization. First, there is a commonality of interests that are being served with exaggerated portrayals of gangs and gang life. The news media, in whatever form, is in the business to make a profit. As such, the more exciting or dramatic the story, the more likely it is that it will garner the general public's interest. This raises the issue of our society's paradoxical relationship with crime. We are terrified of being victimized by crime, but at the same time, we are fascinated, almost enamored, with stories relating to it. Given the propensity to associate gangs with violence and mayhem, whenever a story carries with it a great deal of interest, members of the media often relate that drama to gangs. In short, the media attempts to increase their profit margin by providing the public with "glitzy" stories that relate to crime and violence, and increasingly, the most common vehicle with which to carry that message is to attribute the events to gangs.

Gangs also benefit from such a situation. Street life carries with it a need to enhance one's reputation. In the absence of more traditional status-conferring mechanisms, for many gang members one's reputation as being tough, savvy, or being a "bad-ass" (Katz 1989; Miller 1958) becomes the marker by which individuals can move up the social hierarchy. As the media continues to portray gangs in this negative light, it actually serves to enhance members' standing within their own communities. As such, the greater the characterization as violent, the more it serves the interest of the gang.

The second problem is one of access. The media has a limited amount of time and space in which to "tell the tale" (Van Maneen 1988), and very often the information they receive is either limited or reinterpreted by the reporter to fit the framework of the story. Thus, in those cases where the details of a particular crime are unknown, it is not uncommon for reporters to recast this description and broadly categorize it as "gang-related" (Jankowski 1991; Conklin 1992; Spergel and Curry 1990). In addition to these problems, reporters often have difficulty gaining access to gangs, especially for those who wish to spend an extended amount of time with members (e.g. documentaries). The most common method by which reporters learn about gangs involves reading other media accounts and attempting to interview gang members. This presents a host of problems, only one of which is the veracity of responses. Parenthetically, this is a problem that also plagues social science researchers. However, the difference is that reporters usually interview gang members only once, while researchers often spend months, and sometimes years, learning about the lives of gang members.

Thus, it is fair to state, for a number of reasons, that the information we obtain from the media on gangs is distorted to the point that the public believes gangs are extremely violent, are involved in drug trafficking, are highly organized, and are a pervasive part of the social landscape. In other words, a number of myths have recently emerged concerning gangs. This distorted view of gangs influences not only our understanding of the problem, but also impacts on social policy.

Another distortion the media portrays about gangs relates to their ethnic and racial composition. Gangs are not exclusively a minority phenomenon. Although poor nonwhite communities have produced the largest number of gangs, lower-class white communities have had gangs in the past and continue to produce them. What can be more accurately said about gangs is that it is not necessarily race that explains gang life, but that members usually occupy a marginalized social status (Miller and Fuller 1995).

Thus, while there may be highly dramatic accounts, these portrayals of gangs do little more than perpetuate existing myths which contribute to the problem and solutions concerning gangs in this country. If anything, an historical examination of gangs will show that there does not appear to be any exclusive pattern in which to identify gangs or gang life.

HISTORICAL OVERVIEW OF GANGS

Concentrations of gang research have occurred at three fairly distinct times in this century. The earliest studies were part of the more general concern for the effects of social disorganization in rapidly growing urban areas by researchers at the University of Chicago (Thraser 1927; Shaw 1930; Shaw and McKay 1942). The most influential study of gangs in the early part of this century is Thrasher's *The Gang*, published in 1927. Thrasher was able to identify 1,313 different gangs in the city of Chicago and provided the foundation for generations of researchers who are concerned with the gang phenomena. Thrasher's study is the first truly sociological analysis which attempts to do more than simply describe the gang problem. He addresses some of the social-psychological issues which prompt individuals to join gangs, such as the quest for adventure.

Thrasher also looked at how the gang is organized, how leaders emerge, and how authorities attempt to deal with the gangs. Similarly, Shaw and McKay (1942) argue that central areas of social disorganization, often the homes of the poorest and most recent immigrants, had high rates of street crime and delinquency due to the breakdown of their capacity for social control. Social disorganization theorists argue that the reason for the concentration of deviance in certain areas of the city was due to the breakdown of social relationships to the point where coordination, teamwork, morale, and social control are impaired. Thus, for this first wave of studies, the explanation of gangs focused on the squalor of certain parts of the city.

The second wave of studies began in the mid-1950s and lasted for approximately ten years (Cohen 1955; Miller 1958; Yablonsky 1959; Cloward and Ohlin 1960; Short and Strodtbeck 1965). This group of studies focus on community subcultures. Albert Cohen (1955) argued that delinquent gangs are primarily a lower-class, male phenomenon. Lower-class boys have the same aspirations as middle-class ones; the problem is that their legitimate opportunities to succeed are often severely restricted. Cohen argues that lower-class boys create a subculture, or gang, in reaction to their environment. In contrast, Walter Miller (1958) holds that there is no need to create a delinquent subculture because lower-class culture itself embodies a set of "focal concerns" or characteristics (such as toughness, smartness, trouble, and excitement) which account for higher rates of delinquency and gang life. Thus, crime is explained as a natural reaction to living up to the expectations found in a distinct and lower-class culture.

Building off the work of Merton's anomie or strain theory, Richard Cloward and Lloyd Ohlin (1960) offer an explanation that contends not only are legitimate avenues for success blocked for some individuals, but illegitimate ones are as well. Their typology of subcultures: *criminal, conflict,* and *retreatist,* plays an important role in identifying the types of activities in which an individual may engage. Recent research on gangs (see for instance Huff 1989) also identifies three types-- *hedonistic,* drug-oriented gangs; *instrumental,* theft-oriented gangs; and *predatory,* particularly violent gangs--which correspond remarkably well to Cloward and Ohlin's typology. Both waves of studies, in one way or another, attribute the creation of gangs, and the problems associated with their existence, to elements in the social structure: either the social ecology of the city or the opportunities associated with being a member of a particular social class.

In many ways, the research on gangs from the 1980s to the present, the third wave, resembles the gang research of the 1920s. As in previous eras, there is a tendency to associate gangs and violence with urban poverty, and gang life becomes a source of social identity in the face of impoverished living conditions. What has occurred, however, is that the lack of opportunities and the living conditions for some groups have not improved or have become worse. As a result, in many cases, gang life appears to have taken on much more severe or dramatic consequences. Short (1990) for example, has argued that members are involved in gangs for longer periods of time, are beginning their stints with gangs at a younger age and extending into early adulthood, and that gangs have become increasingly entrenched in the economically depressed communities. Hagedorn and Macon (1988) have found similar patterns in Milwaukee, and Fagan (1990) recently argues that gang membership may now be motivated more by the pursuit of profit than by the cultural or territorial reasons members used in earlier decades to join gangs. Fagan also notes that members tend to be more violent than in previous decades. However, gangs still serve the traditional role as surrogate families and provide a sense of belonging in addition to offering a queer ladder of social mobility (Bell 1953) for some members.

In sum, the study of gangs in this country demonstrates a wide variety of reasons why members become involved in a gang, as well as the benefits of gang membership. If policymakers, community leaders, and police officials are to design and implement effective strategies to control gang activity, they must understand the diversity of gangs in terms of their characteristics as well as the numerous functions they serve for members. This recognition of diversity also helps to organize the links between gangs, drugs, and violence.

TYPES OF GANGS

As was mentioned, our understanding of gangs in the U.S. has been colored by sensational accounts of gang activities and of gang life. This image has led many people to believe that gang membership means that violence and involvement in the drug trade is automatic. Many people also think that gangs are highly organized, with a specific division of labor. This is not necessarily the case. Taylor (1990) attempts to categorize the wide range of gang characteristics and contends there are essentially three different categories in which to identify gangs: *corporate, territorial, and scavenger.* Corporate gangs focus their attention on making money. There is a clearly defined division of labor, and the criminal activities members engage in is committed almost exclusively for profit. Territorial gangs focus on possession of turf, and members are quick to use violence to secure or protect what belongs to the gang. While there is some level of organization in these gangs, in that there is a clearly defined leader and particular objectives and goals of the group, it is less refined than what appears in corporate gangs. Finally, scavenger gangs have very little organizational structure and the motives for becoming a member focus on a need to belong to a group. The crimes that members of this category perform are usually impulsive and often senseless. There are no objectives or goals for the organization and the members tend to be low achievers who are prone to violent and erratic behavior.

While it is impossible to describe every characteristic of every gang, and while the popular conception of gangs focuses on African Americans and Hispanics, the following descriptions were chosen for their distinctive features, which run counter to the "conventional" gang. A discussion of these gangs also serves to identify the difficulty of making general statements about the violent nature of gangs and their involvement in drug trafficking. Finally, these characteristics will be used in a later section to illustrate the relationship between gangs, drugs, and violence.

Chinese gangs

In perhaps one of the most thorough examinations of Chinese gangs, Chin (1990) describes the differences of these gangs from other types of ethnic gangs. While there is some research to contradict Chin's findings (such as Robinson and Joe 1980; Joe 1994; Takagi and Platt 1978) these differences are based largely on skewed samples, or the findings have not been supported by other research. Chin argues that Chinese gangs are closely associated with, and are controlled by, powerful community organizations. In other words, they are an integral part of community life. These gangs are also influenced, to a great extent, by Chinese secret societies and the norms and values of the Triad subculture.

Second, the primary activity of Chinese gangs is making money. Members invest a considerable amount of money in legitimate businesses and spend a lot of time negotiating business deals. Chinese gangs develop in communities in which adult criminals serve as role models and mentors for gang members. In this way, Chin argues that Chinese gangs resemble Cloward and Ohlin's (1960) *criminal gangs*.

In keeping with their entrepreneurial efforts, drug use among Chinese gang members is rare. Although involved in drug trafficking, they themselves are not drug users. If a member begins using drugs, he is expelled from the gang. Thus, unlike Black and Hispanic gangs, the establishment of Chinese gangs is not based on illicit drug use or fads. Instead they are intertwined with the economic and social structure of their communities. Additionally, Chinese gangs do not experience the deterioration and poverty that other types of gangs members experience. Rather, Chinese gangs grow and become economically prosperous by maintaining ties with the economic and political structure of their communities. In other words, there is a cultural component to the success of Chinese gangs: they have a certain legitimacy within the community based on the historical experience of the Triad societies (Chin 1990).

Vietnamese Gangs

While still part of an overall "Asian" category, Vietnamese youth gangs, especially in

Southern California, are quite different in their characteristics from Chinese gangs. This group of immigrants, having experienced the racism and discrimination both in the job market as well as in the classroom, have had a number of significant problems assimilating into mainstream American culture. Essentially, there are three themes that best characterize Vietnamese gangs: mistrust, hiding, and self-control.

A pervasive cultural theme of mistrust runs through Vietnamese communities, one that gang members exploit. Members of the community distrust American banks and, as a result, keep their valuables and money at home. Knowing this, robbery of these families is a primary activity for these gangs.

As Vigil and Yun (1990) state,

> virtually all forms of behavior are calculated for their benefit and potential utilization. Rarely do these youth gangs engage in the persistent fighting that characterized African-American and Chicano gangs. This is not to say that gang fights do not occur, for they do. But our informants indicate that physical conflicts are relatively infrequent and usually the last alternative utilized in resolving a dispute (which commonly centers on money) (p.158 in Huff).

Drug dealing in Vietnamese gangs is perceived as too risky and is to be avoided. This is relatively easy to do since robbery is so lucrative. Thus, very few, if any, Vietnamese gang members are involved in drug dealing. Drug use, however, is heavy. The drug of choice is cocaine, while heroin is avoided since it is perceived to make one unreliable and crazy.

Vietnamese continue their low-profile approach to social life by avoiding conspicuous gang symbols such as tattoos or hand signs. Those that are used as indicators of gang affiliation (such as tattoos) are designed so that they can be easily concealed. Moreover, in manners of dress, Vietnamese gangs tend to opt for clothing similar to other youth in Southern California. In this way, they are able to blend in to the social landscape and to more easily avoid the attention of the police. Finally, the structure of Vietnamese gangs tends to be unorganized and fluid. Membership changes constantly and the rituals and practices of traditional gangs is noticeably absent (Vigil and Yun 1990).

In sum, Vietnamese gangs are loosely defined in terms of an organizational structure, disdain drug trafficking, and essentially attempt to conceal their gang affiliation to others. Vietnamese gangs do not claim turf, do not adopt similar modes of dress, and in some cases, avoid the use of gang names and "signs" (Vigil and Yun 1990).

Crack Crews/Jamaican Posses

In contrast to traditional gangs, there is now some evidence that violent drug-selling organizations, also known as *crack crews* have grown without gang connections (Fagan 1993). Although technically not gangs, these groups use violence to enforce organizational discipline or to resolve disputes with business associates. In short, violence is identified as a means by which to conduct business (Black 1983; Feyerherm et al. 1993). The development of this group has been the void created by those individuals who avoid street-level dealing due to the violent unpredictable nature of the activity (Fagan and Chin 1990). As a result, what remains is a hardcore group who are willing to engage in violence.

Perhaps one of the youngest and most violent criminal organizations (U.S. General Accounting Office 1989), the Jamaican Posses have become an important variable in understanding the intersection between gangs, drugs, and violence. These gangs, originated in Jamaica, have emigrated to the U.S. and have members in virtually every major city. The posses are said to be heavily involved in cocaine and crack distribution, as well as a variety of other criminal activities, such as money laundering, kidnapping, auto theft, and fraud. According to the U.S. Department of Justice, it is estimated that the posses control approximately 30 to 40 percent of the U.S. crack trade as well as approximately 20 percent of the marijuana trade.

A study by The General Accounting Office reveals that the posses are highly organized and possess considerable management skills in their illegal operations. What is perhaps most disturbing about this group however, is their willingness and propensity for violence. The explanations for this vary, but two factors appear to be central in explaining their brutality, both of which are cultural in nature. The first is that the willingness to use violence is status enhancing: it is associated with both economic and social power. Second, there is a long tradition in the use of violence by this group and it is in part based on their belief that violence is an occupational necessity (Kenney and Finckenauer 1995).

Biker Gangs

Outlaw motorcycle gangs essentially began in the late 1940s, and it is estimated that there are somewhere between 800 and 900 motorcycle gangs in the U.S. (Kenney and Finckenauer 1995). While there is a good deal of variability in the characteristics of these groups, for the larger and more organized ones, drug trafficking is their principal source of income. As Kenney and Finckenauer (1995) state, some of these gangs have ties to, and are involved with, other organized crime groups.

The larger and more organized motorcycle gangs engage in a variety of money making activities: prostitution, motorcycle theft, illegal arms dealing, counterfeiting, loansharking, and gambling. However, the most lucrative enterprise for these gangs is the manufacture of methamphetamines, LSD, and PCP. Since they both manufacture and sell their products, most researchers conclude that there is a significant level of sophistication in their organizational structure (Kenney and Finckenauer 1995).

GANGS AND DRUGS
Drug Use

Most researchers agree that drug use, drug selling, and crime, especially by youth, are strongly related. However, it is difficult to automatically associate these activities with gangs since, as we have seen, gangs are quite diverse in their characteristics and behavior (Fagan 1989). While it is true that gang members are involved in drug use, dealing, and criminal activity (see for instance Hagedorn 1988; Klein and Maxson 1989; and Spergel 1989), and it is true that these types of activities are higher among gangs than other youths (Fagan 1989), gang membership does not necessarily lead to involvement in any of those activities.

In some gangs using drugs is an important means of gaining social status, whereas in others, drug use is forbidden, especially if the gang is involved in selling them. Examples include the aforementioned Chinese gangs, who have strict rules regarding drug use (Chin 1990). In other gangs Cooper (1987) has found that members are discouraged, but not prohibited, from using their product. In still other cases, gangs will forbid the use of the drug they sell, but tolerate the use of other drugs (Mieczkowski 1986). Finally, some gangs will use drugs but not deal in them at all. For example, Vietnamese gangs will use drugs, especially cocaine, but avoid dealing since it is considered too risky and will attract attention (Vigil and Yun 1990) .

Drug Selling

As the economic climate and opportunity structure has declined in many cities, the underground economy has begun to play an even more important part in lower-class communities. It would seem likely that youths in these neighborhoods would become involved in drug dealing (Skogan 1990). It would also seem likely that gangs, which, in many cases, have formed in response to these conditions, would organize themselves around money making opportunities. However, again, the research is mixed. In some cases, gangs have become highly organized around drug selling (Skolnick 1990; Taylor 1989; Padilla 1992). For example, Skolnick (1990) makes a distinction between instrumental, entrepreneurial and cultural gangs. This distinction is based upon the degree to which gang organization revolves around the drug business. Based on interviews with 100 young drug dealers and 100 law enforcement officers in California, Skolnick concludes that gangs, especially entrepreneurial gangs, dominate the drug trade in northern California. Other examples include the aforementioned biker gangs (Kenney and Finckenauer 1995), African American gangs such as the Bloods and Crips (Bing 1984), or Williams's (1992) research on crack dealing in New York City (see also Padilla 1992) fit into this category. However, other research suggests that while individual members may sell drugs, it is not necessarily a function of the collectivity. That is, while gang members may engage in drug dealing, it is essentially an individual activity, not in connection with the gang (Waldorf and Lauderback 1993; Quicker, Galeai and Batani-Klhalfani 1991; Decker and Van Winkle 1994; Hagedorn 1994; Fagan 1989). An examination of five recent studies show a wide range of reported rates of involvement in drug sales (see for instance Maxson 1995; Esbenson and Huizinga 1993; Pennell, Melton and Hinson 1994; Decker and Van Winkle 1994; Hagedorn 1994). Maxson (1995) for instance, found that gang members were arrested in only 27% of the 1,563 cocaine sales arrests in two Los Angeles suburbs (Pasadena and Pomona), between 1989 and 1991, and gang members involved in arrests for sales other than cocaine was less than 12% of the 471 cases involved identified gang members. She concludes that gang members' involvement in crack cocaine sales is not overwhelming, as some have thought, and the even lower rates of gang involvement in other drugs raises the question of the need for special concern on the part of law enforcement. Maxson also asserts that the findings from her study have been replicated in other cities with similar results.

In sum, whether it be drug use or drug selling, the research on the relationship between gangs and drugs has not been clearly defined or understood. There are a number of gangs that are involved in using and selling drugs, while others are involved in selling but prohibit use by its members. Other gangs are highly organized, almost corporate in their organizational characteristics, while others are fragmented with individual members involved in drug dealing, but acting independent of the gang.

And still other gangs (and members) may be heavily involved in using drugs but do not attempt to become involved in selling it.

Drugs and Violence

As Collins (1990) has pointed out, there are essentially three ways to describe the relationship between drugs and violence. First, the physical and psychological effects of drug use can result in violent responses. This is especially true with regard to crack cocaine, whereby the user often experiences a sense of paranoia that leads to violent outbursts against another (Goode 1989; Lee 1980). Another example is PCP, which is known to cause extremely violent behavior. This relationship has little support in the academic community, however. In self-report studies, Collins et al. (1989) found that drug users typically report their drug use has no relation to violence.

Second, the most common association involves users committing crimes in which to support their habits. This can lead to instances of violent crime, such as street robberies. The available research does support this explanation (see for instance, Johnson et al. 1985; Chaiken and Chaiken 1982, Inciardi 1981). The third, which is the type of violence most commonly associated with gangs, is a function of the illegal sale and distribution of drugs, also known as *systemic violence*. Examples include issues of territory relating to the gang's share of the illegal drug market or, more simply, a transaction between seller and buyer in which a dispute occurs (Skogan 1989; Little 1995). This is the type of gang violence on which the media focuses its attention, perhaps because it extends beyond the participants in the drug trade and invades a neighborhood's sense of community and poses a risk to innocent bystanders. However, systemic violence has a number of advantages for individual gang members in terms of protection, a way by which a gang can control competitors and expand markets (see for instance Moore 1990; Fagan 1993; Goldstein 1985).

GANGS AND VIOLENCE

Of all the topics associated with gangs, perhaps none is more important to the general public than violence. As was mentioned, gang-related violence, itself a pejorative term (Spergel and Curry 1990) evokes the greatest fear by the public. However, gang violence is probably the least understood. Similar to the study of its relationship to drugs (and gangs in general), we have not yet developed a clear understanding of the relationship of violence to gangs.

Perhaps the act that best symbolizes the growing problem of gang-related violence is the drive-by shooting. In fact, given their notoriety in the media, the drive-by shooting has become synonymous with gang violence. In his book, *Gangbangs and Drive-bys* William Sanders describes the essential features of drive-by shootings as well as offering a symbolic interactionist explanation for its development. He contends that drive-bys are basically retaliatory measures against the offending gang based on the nature of the interaction between the groups. Additionally, the value of participating in drive-bys is grounded in the need to maintain and enhance members' status. There is also an economic side to Sanders' explanation. He contends that as the involvement in the drug trade expanded for a number of gangs, turf wars escalated. While the battle for turf has always been a common feature of inter-gang behavior, drug markets have exacerbated the problem.

Explanations for Violence Among Gangs

In general, past research on the causes of gang violence tended to focus on two factors. One body of research argues that gangs become involved in violence as a result of gang leaders who are psychologically impaired, and as a result, their need for violence translates into group violence by virtue of their leadership position. Yablonsky's (1959) work is an example of this school of thought. Many observers who subscribe to this line of thinking attribute the problem to the pathology of drugs, especially those drugs which induce violent and psychotic behavior.

The second body of research most often cites status deprivation as the primary cause of violence by gang members (see for instance Horowitz 1983; Miller 1958; Cloward and Ohlin 1960; Strodtbeck and Short 1965). These studies conclude that most gang members feel they have been deprived by society, or their own community, of the status they are due and their use of violence is a means by which their standing is reintroduced. The logic behind the development of this school of thought is based on the idea that violence emerges from low-income communities where violence is seen as a natural byproduct of social life. Violence becomes the means by which physical and social goals are achieved. As Jankowski (1991) argues, "violence is the currency of life and becomes the currency of the economy of the gang" (p.139).

There is also a tendency to view gang-related violence as intertwined with the gang's effort to achieve its goals. While this may be true in some cases, such as the case where an organized gang involved in drug dealing seeks to punish a noncompliant customer, some evidence exists to support the idea that much of what we refer to as gang violence is committed by individuals who are members of gangs, but do not undertake this activity to further the gang's objectives (Kornhauser 1978; Jankowski 1991).

As in the case of examining the relationship between drugs and gangs, the best possible explanation of the relationship between gangs and violence is that it depends primarily on the organizational characteristics of the gang. Many studies of gangs have found that there were different types of gangs, with some organized to fight while others to make money, and that the level of violence associated with each gang was dependent on its type (see for instance Block and Block 1993; Fagan 1993; Jankowski 1991; Skolnick 1995).

For example, using a variety of data collection techniques, Block and Block (1993) collected information from police records of lethal and nonlethal street gang motivated crimes, examined temporal and spatial patterns of those crimes and described the criminal activities of Chicago's four largest street gangs over a three year period. In this study, Block and Block make a distinction between *instrumental* and *expressive* violence. They argue that the dynamics of violence is based on the degree and type of motivation of the offender. In an expressive violent confrontation, the primary goal is violence or injury and the other motives are secondary in nature. The primary purpose of an act of instrumental violence is not to hurt, injure, or kill, but to acquire money or property. According to the Blocks, gang-motivated violence often contains many expressive aspects, such as defense of one's street reputation, membership in a particular gang and defense of gang territory. However, other gangs primarily engage in instrumental violence (such as possession or sale of drugs).

One of the most important findings from this study was that gang involvement in violence and homicide is more often turf-related than drug-related. Only 8 of 288 gang-motivated homicides were related to drugs. Moreover, the types of crime clustered in specific neighborhoods. Gangs specializing in instrumental violence were strongest in disrupted and declining neighborhoods, while street gangs involved in expressive violence were strongest in relatively prosperous neighborhoods. The value of this study is to show that gang-motivated crime is not random. It occurs in specific neighborhoods and during particular time periods. Some gangs spend a great deal of their time expanding and defending their turf while others were actively involved in the drug trade. The authors point out that to understand (and solve) the violence associated with gangs, one must understand the problem in light of the chronic conditions that exist in those particular neighborhoods.

Another important variable in understanding the extent of violence in gangs is the direction of their organizational structure. Gangs with a vertical/hierarchical organizational structure are likely to indulge in more organizational than individual violence, but overall these gangs avoid using it. The reason for this is that these types of gangs tend to have a larger goal of making money, which typically overrides individualistic acts of violence (see for instance, Williams 1992; Padilla 1992; Chin 1990). These gangs are also able to exert greater control over their members. Examples would include the aforementioned Chinese gangs, who are likely to use violence, but only in carefully prescribed instances. They are also able to exert control over individual gang members, which reduces the probability of attracting the attention of law enforcement (Chin 1990). In contrast, those gangs that have a horizontal structure tend to have less control over their members. While some of these gangs may be organized into cliques, which can be very organized and able to control its members, overall the gang is a loose collection of factions with limited organizational coordination.

While the organizational characteristics helps to explain the incidence and prevalence of violence by gangs, with money-making opportunities acting as an intervening variable, there are some exceptions. For instance, the aforementioned Jamaican Posses are highly organized in their drug trafficking operations, however, there is also the cultural influence in their propensity for the use of violence that must be taken into account. While the evidence on this inverse effect is scant, it is something to consider when discussing the explanations of gang violence. Thus, while it seems that as the level of organization of a gang increases, they are less likely to engage in widespread violence, this conclusion should be used with caution.

This is not to suggest that some gang members shun violence: there is a host of evidence in which members have indicated they enjoyed the use of violence against others. Violence is a common theme and is frequently lethal in gang life. Conflicts can arise from intra-gang authority struggles, inter-gang quarrels over turf (sometimes related to drug markets), and perceived threats to a gang's reputation and honor. What is especially disturbing in this regard is the increased firepower of heavy automatic weapons, which makes outbursts of violence more deadly.

THE INTERPLAY BETWEEN GANGS, DRUGS, AND VIOLENCE

Past research on the relationship between gangs, narcotics trafficking, and violence is inconclusive (Clark 1991). On one hand, it appears that gang-related violence is increasing. For instance, in 1993, gang members were involved, either as suspects or victims in about one-third of all homicides in Los Angeles county (Maxson 1995). Moreover, between 1980 and 1989 the homicide rate in Los Angeles was more than double the rate for the state of California (Meehan 1995). A prevalent theme in this city during the late 1980s was that a substantial proportion of the increasing incidence of homicide was attributable to the increasing involvement of gang members in both drug dealing and drug use. The theory had broad appeal and was accepted in the media as well as in official reports (California Council on Criminal Justice 1989). Skolnick (1989), for instance, found that street drug dealing in California is dominated by African American gangs organized specifically for the purpose of distributing cocaine.

In contrast, Meehan and O'Carroll (1995) suggest that it is possible that the violence relating to neighborhood cohesion is of a different type than the violence that exists for the purpose of dealing drugs. Despite its popularity, however, there is little evidence to support the theory that gang involvement in the drug trade is responsible for a substantial proportion of homicide (Klein and Maxson 1989; Meehan and O'Carroll 1995).

Moreover, some scholars contend the connection between street gangs, drug sales and violence appeared to have been overstated by media reports, especially during the mid 1980s when gangs became involved in the crack cocaine trade (Maxson 1995). This perception of a close relationship between gangs, drug sales and homicides have been challenged by a number of recent studies (see for instance Block and Block 1993; Meehan and O'Carroll 1995; Maxson, Klein and Cunningham 1992; Maxson and Klein 1993). For instance, in an elaborate study which drew from several different databases, Meehan and O'Carroll (1995) tried to assess the relationship between gangs, drug sales, and violence. They argue that this increase in homicides is predicated upon an increase in gang involvement in the drug trade, of which there is evidence that this has not been the case (Klein, Maxson, and Cunningham 1989; Fagan 1989). Meehan and O'Carroll conclude that gang-motivated homicides were less likely than other homicides to involve narcotics, and narcotics-motivated homicides were less likely to involve a gang member. Finally, victims of gang-motivated homicides were no more likely to have a history of narcotics arrests than other victims. In sum, they conclude that gang conflicts that result in a homicide are often independent of either involvement in the drug trade or the use of drugs.

Despite the recent increases in the use of violence by gang members, especially if their organizational viability or their competitive edge in the market is challenged (Fagan and Chin 1990), gang life may not be as dangerous as it appears to be. In fact, many researchers have found that much of gang activity is fairly mundane (Spergel 1992; Huff 1989; Sullivan 1989). In Cleveland and Columbus, Ohio, Huff (1989) found that gang members spend most of their time acting like typical adolescents (e.g. disobeying parents, skipping school). Similarly, Sullivan's (1989) study of Brooklyn gangs reveals that gang members derive a sense of satisfaction by engaging in relatively minor acts that are perceived as taking advantage of a system that they feel is stacked against.

Consequently, despite the fact that there is a greater prevalence of individual gang violence, especially in those gangs that can be characterized as having a horizontal organization, we must also understand that much of what passes for "gang-related" violence is not gang-related at all. This does not suggest that gang violence is random, unrestrained, or even confined to certain groups. What it does suggest, however, is that the relationship between these phenomena are complex and have yet to be completely understood.

In summary, what most gang members find attractive about violence are the things it sometimes can secure for them. Violence is understood to be the vehicle by which objectives can be achieved when other alternatives are unavailable. Gang violence, like drug use, varies considerably, but one characteristic that helps to explain gang violence is the level of organization a particular gang possesses. This, in turn, is based on the money-making ventures in which the gang is involved. Those that are able to secure lucrative illegal ventures seem to be less likely to engage in violence. Thus, the type of gang that emerges or moves into a community depends, in large part, on the availability of legal and illegal opportunities within it. This is consistent with Merton's (1958) classic examination of anomie. Additionally, the availability of illegal opportunities is also an important factor. As Cloward and Ohlin (1960) pointed out several decades ago (and continues to be relevant today), in highly organized communities with many illegal opportunities, entrepreneurial gangs may arise (Taylor 1990). In contrast, in disorganized communities, where there are a lack of illegal opportunities, as well as the absence of criminal role models to regulate illegal behavior, "fighting" gangs may emerge, which include the aforementioned, highly competitive and violent drug-selling organizations. Finally, in those cases where gang members have failed to succeed in the legitimate market as well as the illegitimate one, what Cloward and Ohlin (1960) and more recently Fagan (1993), describe as *double failures,* retreatist gangs, which rarely engage in violence, may emerge. These gangs are perhaps the least harmful to a community since their activities pose little threat to the social order of a neighborhood.

COMMUNITY RESPONSES TO THE PROBLEM

The review of the literature on gangs essentially leads to two important conclusions: gang activities vary widely and are tied to the particular characteristics of the particular gang's community, and the sources of dangerous and illegal gang activities are found in the deteriorating economic conditions of our inner cities. With respect to the first point, it seems clear that the interdiction efforts that have traditionally been employed have only a limited effect on the problem. As such, communities must take a more active role in developing less coercive intervention techniques that will complement the more traditional law enforcement approaches. It is also important to distinguish between hard-core gang leaders who are involved in the most serious forms of criminal behavior and the peripheral members of the gang. One should be the focus of the criminal justice system, the other by community or diversion efforts.

As the research clearly indicates, the solutions to the problems associated with gangs are inextricably woven into the changes in the economic structure of American society. Deindustrialization, due largely to technological advances, competition in the global economy, and the relocation of industry, have led to the decline of numerous jobs for many unskilled or semi-skilled workers. This is especially true for teenagers in inner cities, whose unemployment rates are much higher than the national average. Thus, our early understanding of gangs as caused by social structural constraints continues to provide a compelling explanation. As Huff (1989) has argued:

> Youth gangs are symptomatic of many of the same social and economic problems as adult crime, mental illness, drug abuse, alcoholism, the surge in homelessness, and multi-generation "welfare families" living in hopelessness and despair. While we are justly concerned with replacement of our physical infrastructure (roads, bridges, sewers) our *human* infrastructure may be crumbling as well. Our social, educational, and economic infrastructures are not meeting

the needs of many children and adults. Increases in the numbers of women and children living in poverty (the "feminization" and "juvenilization" of poverty) are dramatic examples of this recent transformation. To compete with the seductive lure of drug profits and the grinding despair of poverty, we must reassess our priorities and reaffirm the importance of our neighborhoods by putting in place a number of programs that offer hope, education, job skills, and meaningful lives. It is worth the cost of rebuilding our human infrastructures since it is, after all, our children whose lives are being wasted and our cities in which the quality of life is being threatened (p.536).

Researchers have examined the effectiveness of intervention programs and three basic strategies seem to be the most common. The first intervention involves organizing neighborhoods in such a way that leads to the reduction in the number of gangs in a particularly community. The second targets the problems identified by Huff (1989, 1990). It involves creating jobs, training, and other opportunities to lure individuals away from gang life. The third strategy is the most commonly used in dealing with gangs. It is an interdiction approach with arrest and incarceration as its primary features. The fourth strategy involves an amalgamated approach by involving the cooperation of various agencies developing various community-based approaches to solving the gang problem in that particular community, as well as various media campaigns to target potential gang members (Spergel and Curry 1990; Spergel et al. 1994).

One of the most recent attempts to address the gang problem in this country is the Comprehensive Gang Initiative (CGI) by the U.S. Department of Justice. This manual is an attempt to recognize the variability in the study of gangs and to offer assistance to communities facing gang-related problems. The essence of this initiative is that the best approach to dealing with gang-related problems involve several agencies or groups handling a number of facets of local gang problems, which focus not only on suppression, perhaps the most common strategy, but intervention and prevention. Thus, while the traditional community response has been to address the gang problem by increasing the number of police officers and targeting members of the gang, the CGI recognizes that the variation in the characteristics and activities of gangs calls for a more customized approach, which use different strategies to target the different problems presented in those particular communities.

Thus, the Initiative encourages communities to focus on what can be described as *retail changes* instead of wholesale ones. In other words, when a community attempts to solve the "gang problem," there is a tendency to become overwhelmed with the large scale implications of the problem. Instead, building upon the work of Weick (1984), the CGI asserts that the focus of community programs targeting gangs should be on "small wins." This approach is designed to take large problems and break them into smaller ones. In this way, concrete and manageable steps can be taken to deal with the particular aspect of the problem, and if enough "small wins" occur, the more global issue is dealt with. As it relates to the gang problem, the small wins approach means that communities should reduce the problem of eliminating gangs into a series of specific problem statements and developing solutions for them. The success of each individual strategy will, in turn, increase the likelihood that the larger problem will be solved.

CONCLUSION

Despite their portrayal in the media, which seems to make the connections to drugs and violence clear and obvious, the study of gangs and gang life remains complex and difficult to understand. This is especially true if one attempts to identify the intersection between gangs, violence, and drugs. The literature suggests that the causal links between these three phenomenon have not been clearly established. There is a great deal of diversity in terms of the characteristics of gangs. Some are highly organized, with a clear division of labor, and whose sole motivation is to make money, while others are loosely organized and the establishment of the gang seems to be based on an inability to cope with the discrimination and racism they experience as new immigrants to the United States.

There is also a great deal of diversity in terms of the relationship between drugs and gangs. While many gang members use drugs, some do not. Some gangs deal in drugs, while others do not. While some gangs who deal in drugs prohibit members from using their product, other gangs only attempt to discourage members from it, or permit the use of other recreational drugs.

With regard to violence, it seems that there has been a recent increase among gang members, but again, the research does not identify any clear trends. While an important variable in explaining gang violence is the degree of organizational structure, with those highly organized gangs being less likely to use violence, there are some notable exceptions to this trend as well. Part of the violence can be explained as a function of gangs competing for drug markets. Here, gangs are fighting over turf and profit. However, this is only one of many circumstances that lead to gang violence. Violent behavior occurs among most gang members, but it occurs regardless of involvement in the drug trade. As was mentioned, some gangs are able to achieve the status in their communities by engaging in violence, largely because there are few other opportunities to obtain it. What does seem clear is that the changing economic climate in this country has led not only to the perpetuation of gangs, but their concentration in lower-class communities, where unemployment and poverty are widespread. The effects of deindustrialization appears to be a driving theme behind much of the crime, drug use and involvement in drug trafficking of many gangs. It can also explain the behavior of some of the *retreatist* gangs and the *fighting* gangs, whose adaptations are rather different from the gangs that seek to turn a profit. In each type of gangs, the legitimate opportunities for status-enhancing jobs has led many members to seek other outlets in which to achieve their goals: for some it is involvement in dealing drugs, in others it is to use them heavily, for still others, it is to violently lash out at society.

It seems obvious that a great deal more work needs to be done in an attempt not only to understand the nature of gang life, but to devise effective programs to solve the problem. Community leaders and law enforcement officials need to understand that the type of gangs, and the activities many members are likely to become involved in, are related to the structure of the community in which they live. In other words, the opportunity structure will determine, to some extent, the nature of the gang problem in that community. Since the problem begins in the neighborhoods in which gangs reside, so too, do the solutions. A clear understanding of the community is necessary before any other steps are taken. Additionally, the focus on small wins must become a driving theme behind any community's effort to deal with the problem.

REFERENCES:

Bell, D. 1953. "Crime as an American Way of Life" in Marvin E. Wolfgang, Leonard Savitz and Norman Johnston (eds.), *The Sociology of Crime and Delinquency*. New York: John Wiley and Sons, pp.213-225.

Bing, L. 1991. *Do or Die*. New York: Harper Perennial.

Black, D. 1983. "Crime as Social Control" American Sociological Review 48:34-45.

Block, C. R. and R. Block. 1993. "Street Gang Crime in Chicago" in *The Modern Gang Reader*, Malcolm Klein, Cheryl Maxson and Jody Miller (eds). Los Angeles, CA: Roxbury, pp.202-210.

California Council on Criminal Justice. 1989. *Task Force Report on Gangs and Drugs*. Sacramento, CA: Council on Criminal Justice.

Chaiken, J. and Chaiken, M. 1982. *Varieties of Criminal Behavior*. Santa Monica, CA: RAND.

Chin, K. 1990. "Chinese Gangs and Extortion" in *Gangs in America*. C. Ron Huff (ed.). Newbury Park, CA: Sage, pp.129-145.

Clark, C.S. 1991. "Youth Gangs" *Congressional Quarterly Research* 22:755-771.

Cloward, R. and L. Ohlin. 1960. *Delinquency and Opportunity*. Glencoe, IL: The Free Press.

Cohen, A. K. 1955. *Delinquent Boys: The Culture of the Gang*. New York: The Free Press.

Collins, J. 1990. "Summary Thoughts About Drugs and Violence" in *Drugs and Violence*. M. de la Rosa, E. Lambert and B. Groper (eds.). Rockville, MD: National Institute on Drug Abuse.

Conklin, J. 1992. *Criminology*. New York: Macmillan.

Cooper, B.M. 1987. "Motor City Breakdown" *Village Voice*, p.23-25.

Curry, D. and I. Spergel. 1988. "Gang Homicide, Delinquency and Community" *Criminology* 26:381-405.

Decker, S. and B. Van Winkle. 1994. *Slinging Dope: The Role of Gangs and Gang Members in Drug Sales*. St. Louis, MO: University of Missouri Press.

Durkheim, E. [1893] 1947. *The Division of Labor in Society*. New York: The Free Press.

Esbensen, F. and D. Huizinga. 1993. "Gangs, Drugs, and Delinquency in a Survey of Urban Youth" *Criminology* 31(4):565-587.

Fagan, J. 1993. "The Political Economy of Drug Dealing Among Urban Gangs" in *Drugs and Community*. R.C. Davis, A. Lurigio and D. Rosenbaum (eds.).

Fagan, J.and K. Chin. 1991. "Social Processes of Initiation into Crack Use and Dealing" *Journal of Drug Issues* 21:313-343.

_____. 1990. "Violence as Regulation and Social Control in the Distribution of Crack" in *Drugs and Violence*. M. de la Rosa, E. Lambert and B. Gropper (eds.) Rockville, MD: National Institute on Drug Abuse.

Fagan, J. 1990. "Social Processes of Delinquency and Drug Use Among Urban Gangs" in *Gangs in America*. C. Ron Huff (ed.). Newbury Park, CA: Sage, pp.129-145.

_____. 1989. "The Social Organization of Drug Use and Drug Dealing Among Urban Gangs" *Criminology* 27:633-669.

Feyerherm, W.; Pope, C; and Lovell, R. 1993. *Gang Prevention Through Targeted Outreach*. Washington, D.C.: Office of Juvenile Justice and Delinquency Prevention.

Goldstein, P. J. 1985. "The Drugs/Violence Nexus: A Tripartite Conceptual Framework" *Journal of Drug Issues* 14:493-506.

Goode, E. 1989. *Drugs in American Society*. Third Edition. New York: McGraw-Hill.

Hagedorn, J. 1994. "Neighborhoods, Markets and Gang Drug Organization" *Journal of Research in Crime and Delinquency*.

_____. 1990. "Back in the Field Again: Gang Research in the Nineties" in *Gangs in America*. C. Ron Huff (ed.). Newbury Park, CA: Sage, pp.129-145.

_____. 1988. *People and Folks: Gangs Crime and the Underclass in a Rustbelt City*. Chicago, IL: Lakeview Press.

Huff, C. Ron. (ed.). 1990. *Gangs in America*. Newbury Park, CA: Sage.

_____.1990. "Denial, Overreaction and Misidentification: A Postscript on Public Policy" in *Gangs in America*. C. Ron Huff (ed.). Newbury Park, CA: Sage, pp.129-145.

_____. 1989. "Gangs, Organized Crime, and Drug-related Violence in Ohio" In Governor's Office of Criminal Justice Services, *Understanding the Enemy: An Informational Overviw of Substance Abuse in Ohio*. Columbus, OH: Governor's Office of Criminal Justice Services.

_____. 1988a. "Youth Gangs and Public Policy in Ohio: Findings and Recommendations." Paper Presented at the Ohio Conference on Youth Gangs and the Urban Underclass, Ohio State University, Columbus.

_____. 1988b. "Youth Gangs and Police Organizations: Rethinking Structure and Functions" Paper Presented at the Annual Meeting of the Academy of Criminal Justice Sciences, San Francisco, CA.

Horowitz, R. 1983. *Honor and the American Dream: Culture and Idtneity in a Chicano Community*. New Brunswick, NJ: Rutgers University Press.

Inciardi, J. (ed.) 1981. *The Drugs-Crime Connection*. Newbury Park, CA: Sage.

Jankowski, M. 1991. *Islands in the Street: Gangs and American Urban Society*. Berkeley, CA: University of California Press.

Joe, D. and N. Robinson. 1980. "Chinatown's Immigrant Gangs" *Criminology* 18:337-345.

Joe, K. 1994. "Myths and Realities of Asian Gangs on the West Coast" *Humanity and Society* 18(2):3-18.. 1994.

Johnson, B.D.; Goldstein, P.J; Preble, E; Schmeidler, J; Lipton, D.; Spunt, B.; and Miller, T. 1985. *Taking Care of Business: The Economics of Crime by Heroin Abusers*. Lexington, MA: Lexington Books.

Katz, J. 1989. *Seductions of Crime*. New York: Basic Books.

Kenney, D.K. and J.O. Finckenauer. 1995. *Organized Crime in America*. Belmont, CA: Wadsworth.

Klein, M.; C. Maxson; and L. Cunningham. 1991. "Crack, Street Gangs and Violence" *Criminology* 29:623-650.

Kornhauser, R. 1978. *Social Sources of Delinquency: An Appraisal of Analytic Models*

Chicago, IL: University of Chicago Press.

Lee, D. 1981. *The Cocaine Handbook: An Essential Reference.* San Rafael, CA: What If? Publishing.

Little, C. 1995. *Deviance and Control: Theory, Research and Social Policy.* Istaca, IL F.E. Peacock Publishers.

Livingston, J. 1992. *Crime and Criminology.* Englewood Cliffs, NJ: Prentice-Hall, pp. 30-35.

Maxson, C. 1995. "Research in Brief: Street Gangs and Drug Sales in Two Suburban Cities" in *The Modern Gang Reader,* Malcolm Klein, Cheryl Maxson and Jody Miller (eds.). Los Angeles, CA: Roxbury, pp.228-235

_____ and M. Klein. 1990. "Street Gang Violence: Twice as Great or Half as Great" in *Gangs in America.* C. Ron Huff (ed.). Newbury Park, CA: Sage, pp.71-102.

_____. 1989. "Street Gang Violence" in *Violent Crime, Violent Criminals.* Weiner, N.A., and Wolfgang, M.E. (eds.). Newbury Park, CA: Sage, pp.198-234.

_____. 1986. *Street Gangs Selling Cocaine "Rock": The Confluence of Two Social Problems.* Los Angeles, CA: Social Science Research Institute, University of Southern California.

_____. 1985. "Differences Between Gang and Nongang Homicides" *Criminology* 23: 209-222.

Maxson, C., M. Klein, and L. Cunningham 1991. "Crack, Street Gangs, and Violence" *Criminology* 29:623-650.

Mieczkowski, T. 1986. "Geeking Up and Throwing Down: Heroin Street Life in Detroit" *Criminology* 24:645-666.

McNamara, R. 1995. "The Emphasis of the Legal Norm in Solving Social Problems" *Free Inquiry in Creative Sociology* (under consideration).

Meehan, P. J. and O'Carroll, P. W. 1992. "Gangs, Drugs, and Homicide in Los Angeles" *American Journal of Diseases of Childrren* 146:683-87.

Merton, R. K. 1968. "Social Structure and Anomie" in *Social Theory and Social Structure.* New York: The Free Press.

Miller, R. G. and Fuller, J. R. 1995. "Historical and Sociological Aspects of Gangs" in *The Urban Landscape: Selected Readings.* Kristy Maher McNamara and Robert McNamara (eds.) New York: University Press of America, pp.227-246.

Miller, W. 1990. "Why the United States Has Failed to Solve Its Youth Gang Problem" in *Gangs in America.* C. Ron Huff (ed.). Newbury Park, CA: Sage, pp. 263-287.

_____. 1958. "Lower Class Culture as a Generating Milieu of Gang Delinquency" *Journal of Social Issues* 14:5-19.

Moore, J. W. 1990. *Gangs, Drugs, and Violence.* Rockville, MD: National Institute on Drug Abuse.

Office of Juvenile Justice and Delinquency Prevention. 1989. Community-wide Responses Crucial for Dealing with Youth Gangs.Washington, D.C.: United States Department of Justice.

Padilla, F. 1992. *The Gang as an American Enterprise.* New Brunswick, NJ: Rutgers University Press.

Park, R. E. and E. W. Burgess. 1925. *The City.* Chicago, IL: University of Chicago Press.

Parsons, T. 1951. *The Social System.* New York: The Free Press.

Pennell, S., Evans, E. Melton, R. and Hinson, S. 1994. *Down for the Set: Defining and Describing Gangs in San Diego*. Report to the Administration of Children, Youth and Families. San Diego, CA: San Diego Association of Governments.

Quicker, J.C., Galeai, Y.N. and Batani-Khalfani, A. 1991. *Bootstrap or Noose: Drugs in South Central Los Angeles*. New York: Social Science Research Council.

Sanders, W. 1994. *Gangbangs, and Drive-bys: Grounded Culture and Juvenile Gang Violence*. New York: Aldine de Gruyter.

Shaw, C. R. 1930. *The Jack-Roller: A Delinquent Boy's Own Story*. Chicago, IL: University of Chicago Press.

_____. and H. D. McKay. 1942. *Juvenile Delinquecy and Urban Areas*. Chicago, IL: University of Chicago Press.

Short, J. F. Jr. 1990a. "Cities, Gangs, and Delinquency" *Sociological Forum* 5:657-668.

_____. 1990b. "New Wine in Old Bottles? Change and Continuity in American Gangs" in *Gangs in America*. C. Ron Huff (ed.). Newbury Park, CA: Sage, pp. 223-239.

_____ and Strodtbeck, F. 1965. *Group Processes and Gang Delinquency*. Chicago, IL: University of Chicago Press.

Skogan, W.G. 1990. *Disorder and Decline: Crime and the Spiral of Decay in American Neighborhoods*. New York: The Free Press.

_____. 1989. "Social change and the Future of Violent Crime" in *Violence in America* Vol. 1. T.R. Gurr (ed.). Newbury Park, CA: Sage.

Skolnick, J. H. 1995. "Gangs and Crime Old as Time: But Drugs Change Gang Culture" in *The Modern Gang Reader*, Malcolm Klein, Cheryl Maxson and Jody Miller (eds.). Los Angeles, CA: Roxbury, pp. 222-227.

_____ . 1992. "Gangs in the Post-Industrial Ghetto." *Amercian Prospect* 8:109-120.

_____, Correl, T., Navarro, E., Rabb, R. 1989. "The Social Structure of Street Drug Dealing" in *BCS Forum: The Social Structure of Street Drug Dealing*. Los Angeles, CA: University of Southern California.

Spergel, I. A.; R. Chance; K. Ehrensaft; T. Regulus; C. Kane; R. Laseter; A. Alexander; S. Oh. 1994. *Gang Suppression and Intervention: Community Models*. Washington, D.C. Office of Juvenile Justice and Delinquency Prevention.

Spergel, I. A. 1992. "Youth Gangs: An Essay Review:" *Social Service Review* 66: 121-140.

_____ and D. G. Curry. 1990. "Strategies and Perceived Agency Effectiveness in Dealing with the Youth Gang Problem" in *Gangs in America*. C. Ron Huff (ed.). Newbury Park, CA: Sage, pp. 288-309.

Spergel, I. "Youth Gangs: Continuity and Change" in Crime and Justice *An Annual Review of Research*, Vol. 12 N. Morris and M. Tonry (eds.). Chicago, IL: University of Chicago Press.

Sullivan, M. 1989. *Getting Paid: Youth Crime and Work in the Inner City*. Ithaca, NY: Cornell University Press.

Takagi, P. and T. Platt. 1978. "Behind the Gilded Ghetto" *Crime and Social Justice* 9(2):2-25.

Taylor, C. S. 1990. "Gang Imperialism" in *Gangs in America*. C. Ron Huff (ed.). Newbury Park, CA: Sage, pp.103-115.

_____. 1989. *Dangerous Society*. East Lansing, MI:Michigan State University Press.

Thraser, F. M. 1927. *The Gang: A Study of 1,313 Gangs in Chicago.* Chicago, IL: University of Chicago Press.

United States General Accounting Office 1989. *Nontraditional Organized Crime: Law Enforcment Officials' Perspectives on Five Criminal Groups.* Washington, D.C: U.S. Government Printing Office.

Van Maanen, J. 1988. *Tales of the Field: on Writing Ethnography.* Chicago, IL: University of Chicago Press.

Vigil, J. D. "Cholos and Gangs: Culture Change and Street Youth in Los Angeles" in *Gangs in America.* C. Ron Huff (ed.). Newbury Park, CA: Sage, pp.106-128.

_____ and Steve Chong Yun "Vietnamese Youth Gangs in Southern California" in *Gangs in America.* C. Ron Huff (ed.). Newbury Park, CA: Sage, pp.146-162.

Waldorf D. and D. Lauderback. 1993. *Gang Drug Sales in San Francisco: Organized or Freelance?* Alameda, CA: Institute for Scientific Analysis.

Weick, K. 1984.

Williams, T. 1989. *The Cocaine Kids.* Boston, MA: Addison-Westley.

Yablonsky, L. 1959. "The Gang as a Near Group" *Social Problems* 7:108-117.

Battered Women's Experiences
With Leaving Violent Relationships

Denise Donnelly
Department of Sociology
Georgia State University

"My early home life wasn't so good--my dad was an alcoholic, and he'd always get drunk and yell at my mom and me. I don't think he ever hit my mom, but he'd break things and stomp around and yell. My mom, she was scared of him, and tried to stay out of his way. When I was 16, I got this job working at McDonald's so I wouldn't have to be home much and because I needed the money. That's where I met Bart. He was older, around 20, and he'd come in all the time on his breaks [from working construction]. We got to talking, and he asked me out. He was really the only boyfriend I had, and we got married right after I finished high school. Our little girl Jessie was born a year later, and Johnny ... 14 months after that. Jessie's almost two now, and Johnny is 9 months old. Bart really didn't get violent until after we were married, but he was jealous of me from the first...even when we were dating. You know, always thought I was looking at other guys, trying to attract them....wanted to know where I'd been, and always calling me. If he couldn't find me, he'd get mad, and accuse me of seeing someone else. I just thought it was cute, and that he did it because he loved me. I'd never had someone love me like that--he was my first real boyfriend and all. The first time he hit me was the day I found out I was pregnant with Jessie. I forgot to take my birth control pills, and when I came home from the doctor and told him I was expecting, he was furious. He called me retarded and said that any stupid idiot could remember to take a pill every day. He didn't want the baby, and I started crying because I wanted to be a mother, I wanted to have his child. My crying made him mad. The madder he got, the more I cried. Finally, he said, 'Why don't you shut the hell up?' and he slapped me across the face. I fell into a end table and cut my back, and he left. When he came back three days later, he smelled like...ummm...that he'd been with another woman. But, he apologized, and I thought he meant it. He went right out and bought a bunch of baby stuff, like a crib and furniture, to show me how sorry he was. For a while, things were really good between us, but then he started pushing and slapping me maybe once or twice a month....just about whenever we'd fight, he'd shake me, or slap me, or pull my hair. When he'd get mad, he'd always bring up how he didn't want kids and how I was a cow who kept making babies. He'd tell me how stupid I was, and how no man would ever want me. About three months ago, he decided that he didn't want to be married anymore, and that he wanted to see other people. He said he felt trapped, and that he was too young (He's 24) to be saddled down with a wife and kids. I mean two kids later, and he doesn't want to be married? What am I supposed to do? He started seeing this other woman, and he moved in with her for a while. When he came home

to get his stuff, I begged him to stay. So he stayed the night, and things went really well....he said he missed me, and we made love and all. I thought we'd be okay, but then he didn't come home from work the next Friday night. I had my friend Sheila take me to where this girl he's seeing lives. I went in to talk to him, and he got really, really mad because he hadn't told her he was married. He pulled me by my hair all the way to the car and drove back to our apartment. He was driving really fast, and I was scared we'd have a wreck. He kicked me in the butt all the way from the car to the apartment, and was screaming about how I'd embarrassed him, and he was tired of me and these babies and he never wanted them in the first place. When we got in the apartment, he...hit me several times, knocked me on the floor and kicked me in the ribs. It hurt so bad I couldn't get up, so I lay there for a long time. It got real quiet, and I thought he'd left. I finally was able to crawl to the bathroom, and I was washing my face. Well, he'd been in bedroom upstairs, and when he heard the water running, he came back downstairs, and when he saw me, he ran down the hall and tackled me like a football player or something. I hit my head on the top of the vanity (it was marble) really hard and blacked out for a second. My friend came in with the kids a little later and found me, and took me to the emergency room. I had a concussion, and a couple of cracked ribs. One of my teeth was chipped, and both my eyes were black. I had to have over 30 stitches where my head split open.... I spent the night in the hospital, and then they brought me and the kids here to the battered women's shelter. All I want....all I've ever wanted...is to be Bart's wife and to be the mother of his children. I'm a religious person--I truly believe that marriage is forever, and I want to make this work. I mean, I don't understand, he never wanted me to even look at another man, and now he's gone and found another woman. It just doesn't make sense....you know? I don't know what I'm going to do now.... I know he's wrong to hit me, but I really wish we could make it work."

> --Jenny, aged 20, mother
> of two, married three years,
> clerical worker.

Women's Experiences with Violence

Stories such as this one are repeated every day in every city around the country. Even though public awareness and disapproval of woman battering have grown tremendously, researchers estimate that one in ten American women are beaten by their husbands and partners each year (Straus and Gelles, 1986). The American Medical Association predicts that as many as one quarter of women will be physically abused by a partner during their lifetimes (Flitcraft, 1992). For many women, violence is not a one time occurrence; it is a fact of everyday life, occurring with frightening regularity (Langan and Innes, 1986). Woman battering is a social problem of truly enormous magnitude.

Not all battered women are as young as Jenny, and not all are working class. In fact, while woman battering is more common among the young and those at the lower end of the socioeconomic scale, it occurs across all age, race, and income groups (Straus, Gelles, and Steinmetz, 1980). Contrary to popular beliefs, alcohol or drugs are not always factors in woman battering (Kaufman-Kantor and Straus, 1990). Nor are heterosexual women the only victims of battering--lesbian women, gay men, and even straight men--can also be the targets of intimate violence (Renzetti, 1992; Donnelly and Kenyon, 1996). Because heterosexual women make up make up the overwhelming majority of battered women, however, this chapter focuses on their experiences.

Often, when stories such as Jenny's appear in the news, people ask "Why did she stay with someone who beat her?" They assume that since the woman is an adult, she can leave any time she wants. In many ways, this view blames the victim, and doesn't take into account the numerous complicated reasons that prevent women from leaving men who beat them. Rather than focusing on why the man felt that he had the right to hit his wife or partner, on how he continued to get away with battering (many times over months or years), or on whether she tried to get and received help, we focus instead on why she stayed.

In my research, I examined women's experiences with intimate violence, their decisions to leave (even temporarily) abusive relationships, and their help seeking behaviors. My aim in doing so was not to blame battered women for their problems, nor was it to relieve the batterer of responsibility. Rather, the research focused on giving women a chance to tell their own stories, in their own words, in an attempt to better understand the barriers and decisions that women face when they leave their abusers.

The stories told in this chapter come from in-depth interviews conducted with battered women in one rural Southeastern county. I began this research after three years of volunteer work (as hotline counselor and shelter worker) which brought me into contact with a variety of battered women and children in a number of situations. In all, I talked with 32 women over a six-month period. Each gave permission for her interview to be used in research publications. While names were changed and minor details altered slightly or omitted to insure safety and preserve privacy, the stories presented here are as the women actually told them.

Twelve women were residing in a battered women's shelter at the time of the interview, and 20 were living alone or with their children, friends, or family members. Most of the non-sheltered women were approached as they waited for their requests for temporary protective orders to be heard by the judge, or while waiting for other social services. I asked the women a series of questions about their lives, previous experiences with violence, decisions to leave, and their help seeking behaviors. If they agreed, the interview was tape recorded and transcribed later. If not, I took detailed notes, and reconstructed the interview immediately upon returning to my office.

The women who participated in this study were for the most part white, reflecting the racial/ethnic distribution of the county where the interviews were conducted. Of the 32 women I talked with, only three were women of color (one African American, one Latina, and one Pacific Islander). Most were young, and all but one had children (though three were not living with their children at the time of the interview). Only four women were over 35, and none were over 45. Most came from the working or lower middle-class, and most had been homemakers or were working at low-paying jobs when the violence took place. All the women in my sample were living apart from their partners at the time of the interview.

The types of violence perpetrated on the women in my study ran the gamut from fairly minor physical violence such as pushing or hair pulling, to moderate violence such as slapping, hitting and kicking, to severe violence such as being threatened with a weapon, hit with a fist, pushed out of a moving vehicle, pushed down stairs, or dropped from a window. Thirteen percent had experienced only minor violence, 68% at least moderate violence, and 19% severe violence. Every woman that I interviewed had been emotionally abused in some way (such as name calling, ridicule, or humiliation in front of others), and sexual abuse (ranging from unwanted sex to bondage, torture, and rape) occurred in all but two cases. Economic abuse (such as destroying property or withholding money) was reported by 81% of the women.

Sarah, who was living with Bennie when he became abusive, is an example of a woman who experienced fairly mild violence, yet decided to seek help because of past experience. I met her while she was waiting for her court case to be called.

> *"Bennie wasn't that violent before [the incident that lead to his arrest], but he's always threatening me and calling me names. Sometimes he'd shake me or say he was gonna hit me, but he never did. He's not working right now, and we completely ran out of money a couple weeks ago. He wanted me to borrow money from my mom, but I was too embarrassed. We started fighting, and I told him that if he wasn't too lazy to hold a job, we might have some money. So, he got really mad, and turned over the [dining room] table and then he started punching his fist through the wall. I got scared and asked him to stop because we'll lose our deposit [on the trailer], and he came and stood over me and grabbed my shoulders and started shaking me. Then, he lifted me up and shoved me back in the chair really hard. He went in the kitchen and got a beer, and walked out. I put the baby in the stroller and walked to my moms. I went down and took out a temporary protective order the next day. I was married to an abuser before, and I don't intend to take this from Bennie."*
>
> --Sarah, age 27, stay-at-home
> mother of a 6 mos. old daughter.

Stories like Sarah's are fairly rare, since most women don't leave the first time physical abuse occurs, and if they do, they tend to return to their abusers (Gondolf, 1988). Sarah, because of past experience, recognized the potential for violence to escalate, and left before the situation worsened. Sarah's two older children (from her first marriage) were living with her mother because their father (Sarah's ex-husband) had abused them, and child protective services had removed them from the home. Since Sarah was working towards being reunited with her children, she was especially motivated to leave Bennie at the first sign of violence. When I talked with her six months after the original interview, she was working at a fast food restaurant (having been promoted to assistant manager), and living with her mother and three children.

Other women, like Melanie in the case presented below, experience violence over a longer period of time. Typically, the violence escalates until it becomes so bad that they leave, the abuser is arrested, or all too frequently, the woman is murdered (Browne, 1987). Often, women only leave their batterers (as Jenny did) when they are seriously injured, they believe they will be killed, or when a child is hurt (Snyder and Fruchtman, 1981). In Melanie's case, the abuse had gone on over a long period of time, and continued to worsen as time passed. She left her situation only after her husband was violent towards her son. An articulate and obviously middle-class woman in her early thirties, Melanie commented:

"I am in my second marriage. The first one was abusive too. I have a 11 year old son from my first marriage and a 4 year old daughter from my second. My second husband, Tony, was so nice when we were dating. So gentle, and so different from my first husband. But then it started. A couple of months after we were married he started grabbing me. When he'd get mad, he'd grab me and hold me and make me listen to him. I was a little scared, but figured that he wasn't really hitting me, so I never thought about leaving. But it didn't stop, and it got worse. By the time our daughter was born, he was slapping me and shoving me. And he started kicking me on my legs, or he'd grab my arm and not let go, and I'd have fingerprints. Or, he'd hold me down and pin my arms down and slap me. He'd always apologize after it was over, but things kept getting worse. The last time, before I left him, I don't even remember what we were arguing about. He got me on the couch, and he laid down on top of me so I couldn't get up and he yelled right in my face. Then he straddled my waist with his legs and started slapping me in the face. The children saw, and they were begging him to stop. He picked my son up and tossed him across the room. The baby was crying so hard she was losing her breath, and my son was so startled and stunned (he wasn't hurt) that he just sat there. I knew then that I had to leave, so I waited until Tony left for work the next day, and I took the car and came to the shelter."

--Melanie, aged 33, twice
married mother of two, working
as a dental hygienist.

The abuse that Melanie experienced was fairly typical of the experiences of women in the sample, but 1 in 5 (19%) had experienced even more severe attacks. Sandra's story is an example of a woman who was almost killed because of her partner's violence. Sandra is a 22-year-old woman who was living with her boyfriend at the time of the violent incident which led to his arrest. After she was released from the hospital, she came to the shelter. Her story illustrates the impact of a life-time of abuse:

"As far back as I can remember, men have been violent with me. First my daddy, then my step-father, even my boyfriends. My step-father raped me when I was 11 or 12, and I started using drugs to deal with that. Two years ago, I was back at the []

hospital to get dried out, and I met Mike. He was working maintenance at the hospital, and we used to talk when I'd go out for a smoke. When I got out of the hospital, I moved in with him. He wasn't violent at first, but he destroyed some of my clothes because they were too sexy, and some of my country music tapes because he thought they were trashy sounding. Then I started using drugs again, and he hated that, and that's when he started hitting me. Said I was a whore, and an addict, and worthless bag of bones. I got pregnant, and quit using, and he stopped [hitting] for a while. But after our daughter was born, he got bad again. He wouldn't let me work, and had the phone taken out so I couldn't use it. He wouldn't let me see my friends. I wasn't supposed to leave the apartment--he even went grocery shopping with me. The day I had to go to the hospital [because of injuries from abuse], he came home from work, and accused me of taking some of his pain pills [for a back injury]. He said he was missing a bunch of pills, and accused me of taking them. He beat me up really bad, and would dunk me in the bathtub [filled with cold water] to wake me up when I passed out. He did this several times, and finally he calmed down and apologized. He told me that he was sorry for hurting me, but that it was my fault. Then he wanted to have sex to make up and all. I couldn't, just couldn't, because I hurt all over. So, he got mad again, and said that I must be sleeping with someone else. When I told him I was hurt too bad, he got even madder and held me out the window of our apartment by one arm, and dropped me in the bushes under our window. We live on the second story, so I was all scratched up and bleeding, and I crawled under the shrubs to rest. He came down after a while, and said he'd take me to the hospital. After we were in the car, he got mad again, and said that I was a no good whore, taking his pills and sleeping around. I wouldn't answer him or look at him, so he slowed down and opened the car door while we were going down the highway and pushed me out. I rolled into a ditch, and the people behind us stopped and carried me to the hospital. The police arrested Mike the next day. He's still in jail right now.

--Sandra, age 22, never
married, recovering addict,
mother of one, unemployed.

Sandra's story was one of the most heartbreaking I heard. She also told of Mike destroying her property (once, when he thought she was dressing too provocatively, he threw all her clothes in the bathtub and dumped an entire bottle of bleach on them). Sexual abuse and torture were also common. He often forced Sandra to have sex with his friends while he videotaped, she told of waking at night with his hand over her mouth as he forcibly anally raped her. Sandra was afraid to leave because Mike had threatened to kill her and their daughter if she tried. Given his past behavior, she had every reason to believe that he would.

Common Themes in the Stories of Abused Women

While I was soon to learn that there is no such thing as a "typical" case of intimate assault, the stories presented here share common elements and help to illustrate what family violence researchers know about abusive relationships. For example, many victims of violence have histories of growing up in violent households and of experiencing violent relationships as adults (Doumas, Margolin, and John, 1994). All four of the women discussed above had experienced violence in past relationships. Sarah and Melanie had been in battering relationships previous to their current relationships, and Jenny and Sandra had grown up in violent households. In fact, of the 32 women I interviewed, only 2 (6%) said that their current relationship was the first in which any sort of violence had taken place. Family violence researchers speculate that growing up in a violent household may lead one to see violence as a normal and expected part of adulthood (Doumas et al., 1994; Hotaling and Sugarman, 1986), and women who have experienced intimate violence as adults may become desensitized to warning signs in future relationships (Holiman and Schilit, 1991).

Another common theme that ran through the interviews was that violence started early in the relationship. For many women, like
Sandra, violence occurs almost from the time they meet their future partners (Roscoe and Benaske, 1985). For others, like Sarah, Jenny, and Melanie, violence begins in the first year of marriage or cohabitation. In fact, all the women I talked with noted that violence did not suddenly start after five, ten or fifteen years--it was there from almost the beginning.

For most of the women in my sample, violence escalated over time. What started out as psychological abuse, or very mild physical violence, later became severe abuse that caused (or had the potential to cause) permanent physical or mental impairment. For Jenny, Bart's violent behavior started out as jealousy and control, but escalated into physical abuse early in the relationship. Likewise, Sandra's abuse began with her property being destroyed, then almost immediately progressed to physical violence, and from there to sexual abuse and torture. Melanie's abuser began with grabbing (which she didn't define as "real" violence), and subtly moved on to more severe forms of violence, such as pinching and slapping. In every case, physical abuse was accompanied by at least one other type of abuse. Psychological abuse was most common, with batterers literally wearing down their victims through intimidation, control, and humiliation.

Though researchers have found no causal relationships between drug and alcohol use and violence, these substances are often used (by both the batterer and the victim) in violent relationships. While substance use doesn't cause violence, it may be used by the abuser as an excuse to batter (Collins and Schlenger, 1988) or to relieve the guilt of battering (Kaufman-Kantor and Straus, 1990). Victims often use alcohol or drugs as a way of mitigating the physical and emotional pain of abuse (Hotaling and Sugarman, 1990). In my sample, alcohol or drugs were present in over half the battering incidents described.

Another element associated with battering is stress. Finn (1985) found that financial problems, unemployment, alcoholism, unplanned pregnancies, and other family problems were more common in families where abuse was taking place. My sample was no exception. In Jenny's case, as with many battered women (Helton, 1987), an unplanned pregnancy preceded physical violence. For Sarah, financial problems and unemployment seemed to contribute, while in Sandra's situation it was drug abuse. Although stress may have contributed to the violence, we should not forget that the male partner in each of these situations made a conscious decision to use violence, as opposed to another way of dealing with stress. In fact, one woman that I talked with noted that her husband explained hitting her as "his way of calming down." It is also possible that stress is used as an excuse for battering, as a way of relieving the batterer of responsibility for his actions after a violent incident has taken place.

As all the stories presented above illustrate, battering is about power and control (Paymar, 1993). Husbands and boyfriends believe that they have the right to control every aspect of the woman's life. They disregard boundaries, and fail to respect their partner's body, her possessions, or her mental well-being. Jealousy is common among batterers, and because of this, they may try to isolate their partners from friends, co-workers, and families, or they may try to keep tabs on her every movement, as Sandra's story illustrates.

A final commonality in the stories that I heard was that after the battering, the abuser was sorry for what he'd done, and often very apologetic. Lenore Walker (1979) noted that violence may occur in cycles consisting of a buildup phase (where tension mounts), a blowup phase (where battering occurs), and a makeup phase (where the batterer is apologetic and romantic after the battering event). According to the women I interviewed, batterers often used charm and manipulation to get them to stay. In Jenny's case (at least initially), it was new furniture for the baby. Sarah's partner continued to call and beg her to come back for several months after she left, and Melanie's husband always apologized and seemed truly sorry for what he'd done. Sandra's boyfriend also apologized for hurting her, but then would hurt her again, often almost as soon as he'd apologized. Each of these men was using kindness and apologies as ways to manipulate the women in their lives into continuing the relationship. And sadly, when they agreed, they were likely to be battered again.

Reasons for Staying in a Battering Relationship

For most battered women, the decision to end an abusive relationship is difficult. Women stay with their abusers for a variety of very complicated reasons. Many stay because of a lack of money. Women with fewer financial resources and limited educations are more likely to stay and more likely to return after leaving, because they can't afford to live as single parents (Johnson, 1992; Strube, 1988). Even women with relatively high family incomes may hesitate to leave, because they know that their standards of living will drop substantially. Women who have never worked, have small children, or low levels of education, often find the costs of housing, food, transportation, and childcare simply beyond their reach. Melanie, for example, was able to leave her batterer only because she moved in with her mother, who provided housing, transportation, and childcare.

Some women stay in abusive relationships because of the psychological consequences of prolonged battering and emotional abuse. These injuries may hinder their ability to be employed productively, to make daily decisions regarding their own or their children's well-being or safety, and to sustain family and social relationships (de las Fuentes and Wright, 1991). For some women, such as Sandra, the abuse is so severe that it results in Battered Woman Syndrome, (Walker, 1989) which is recognized as a sub-category of Post-Traumatic Stress Disorder (PTSD). Women with Battered Woman Syndrome frequently experience recurring nightmares, diminished responsiveness, loss of interest in activities, detachment from others, disturbed sleep, memory loss, difficulty concentrating, and avoidance of activities.

Because of past experience, victims of domestic violence may feel that they can do nothing to change their situations, and may simply give up trying. They may have tried to leave, without success, or their batterer may have convinced them (through psychological manipulation) that they would be unable to survive if they left (Johnson, 1992). For some, like Jenny in the opening story, the predictability of staying in an abusive situation is more comfortable than the unpredictability of leaving.

Other women stay because they love their batterer, or feel that they have invested too much in the relationship to end it (Strube, 1988). They may feel responsible for their partner, and guilty over leaving because they believe that the partner cannot make it without them (Ferraro, 1979).

Still others hesitate to leave because they are embarrassed for others to find out about the battering, or because they believe that marriage is a lifetime commitment (Vaughn, 1987). They may be pressured by friends, family and clergy into trying to preserve the relationship. Some stay because they believe it is better for the children to be with their father (even one who is violent) than to be raised by a single parent. Others simply believe the batterer when he says that he will stop the abuse, and stay with him in hopes that the physical violence will end (Aquirre, 1985).

Jenny, whose story was presented at the beginning of the chapter, loved her husband, and didn't want to leave him. Even when he began seeing other women and asked for a divorce, she hoped to make it work. As a deeply religious woman, she believed in "the sanctity of marriage," and truly felt that her commitment was "till death do us part." Ending the marriage was simply not an option for her.

Another reason that women stay with their batterers is fear. Abusive men often threaten to harm the woman, her children, or family members or pets if she attempts to leave. Research shows that these fears are not ungrounded. Battered women are most at risk for serious harm or death from their abusers when they make life changes, threaten to leave, or actually leave (Snyder and Fruchtman, 1981).

Finally, many women stay because they have nowhere to go. Most people assume that everyone is aware of hotlines and shelters for battered women, and that we have sufficient resources to assist women and children in need. As the findings discussed later in this chapter show, however, battered women are often unaware of available services, and even if they are familiar with agencies that can assist them, they may not be able to get the help they need.

The Decision to Leave

When asked why they decided to leave, the women in my sample gave a variety of answers. The most common reason for leaving was concern for their children. Like Melanie in the case presented above, Wanda left her husband when she felt her his behavior was beginning to endanger her children. Jeff, aged 9, is her son by a previous marriage. Hannah, aged 2, is her daughter by her current husband.

> *"I left because of my kids--I didn't want them in danger. My son, especially. His step-father was spanking him way too hard--beating him really, and expecting too much of him. And Jeff was becoming just like his step-father. He was getting aggressive, he'd lost compassion, and he behaved to his sister like his step-father behaved to him. He started trying to control Hannah...stuff like where to sit and what she was doing. If she wouldn't cooperate, he'd slam doors or blow up and yell. He even backhanded her across the face once, and she's just a little kid. He'd get this 'I hate you' look in his eyes. He used to be such a sweet kid. Now, I dunno....I hope it's not too late. I left his father on account of violence, and then married*

another violent man. I feel like this is my fault."

Wanda aged 28, mother of two, retail sales clerk, married for the second time.

Wanda was seeing first hand the effects of raising her children in a violent household. While concern for her own safety wasn't enough to motivate her to leave, her hopes for a better life for her children were. Like many battered women, she blames herself (rather than her violent husband) for the damage her children have suffered.

Connie was also concerned about her children, but left her husband because of a different type of danger. She suspected him of sexually abusing their 6-year-old daughter,

> *"Butch was abusive throughout our marriage, but I never really thought of leaving him until he started in with Christy. He'd hit the boys, but he always treated her like she was a doll...very special....daddy's little girl. Over the last few months, he got to where he wanted to spend a lot of time with her alone. I didn't really think much about it, until she started complaining that her 'pee-pee' hurt. When I asked her what made it hurt, she said that daddy hurt it when he rubbed her down there. I started asking her questions, and I think he's been fondling her. It just made me sick.... physically sick....and I knew I had to leave him. I mean, hitting me is one thing, but to do sexual things to his own daughter? That's disgusting."*

> --Connie, aged 31, mother
> of two teenaged boys and a
> 6 year old girl, married to
> Butch for 14 years.

Like Wanda, Connie never contemplating ending the relationships until it began to explicitly endanger her youngest child. Only when she suspected Butch of abusing their daughter did she decide to end the relationship and report him to Child Protective Services. Six months later, he was still denying these charges, and had sued for joint custody.

Another common reason for deciding to leave an abusive relationship was serious injury or hospitalization, as was the case with Jenny and Sandra, whose stories were presented earlier. Several of the women in my sample mentioned leaving because they feared that next time, their husbands or partners might kill them. Barbara was one of these women. She left her husband after he held a gun to her head.

> *"What finally made me leave was when he took a gun and*
> *threatened to shoot me. He'd hurt me bad before, and threatened to kill me, but I*
> *never believed him till then. I'd threatened to leave, and he'd promised me that he'd*
> *stop drinking. He came in drunk, and I got mad because it was the same old story,*
> *and I'd believed it. I told him that I was leaving. That made him angry, and he*
> *shoved me into the kitchen sink. The door was open and I fell under it. He kicked me*
> *a few times and went out to his truck. I looked out the window, and saw him getting*
> *his gun. I picked up the phone to dial 911, and when he walked in and caught me, he*

pulled the phone out of the wall. I started out the back door, and he yelled that he'd shoot me if I didn't stop. So, I did, and he held the gun to my head for [what seemed like] hours, and said that if he couldn't have me, nobody else would either...he wasn't having his kids raised by another man [Charles wrongly suspected Barbara of having an affair with a neighbor who had intervened in an earlier violent incident]. All this time, he was crying and ranting, but not hitting me. But he wouldn't let me go. I finally told him to just go ahead and do it. After a minute he let me go and went in the bedroom, and passed out. You know, I think if he hadn't been so drunk, he'd of done it. I found the truck keys, picked the kids up from school, and went to a gas station and called the police. Then I called the hotline and came to the shelter. I'm leaving to go back to Colorado, where my parents live, next week. I'm afraid he'll kill me if I stay."

> --Barbara, aged 33, mother
> of 2 girls. Married to
> Charles for 10 years.

Women sometimes used the arrest of their husband or partner as a window of safety in which to leave. Lisa's husband of 5 years had battered her since before they married. Each time she'd make plans to leave, he'd take the children and go to his brother's house in another state, wouldn't let her take the children, or would threaten to come back and hurt Lisa and her two toddlers.

"Greg had been hitting me for years, and at times it would get so bad that I'd threaten to leave. Whenever I'd do that, he'd take the kids and go to his brother's house in [another state] and tell me to go ahead and leave. I'd worry about the kids--let me tell you, he is not a responsible father--and I'd call and apologize and beg him to bring them back. Or, anytime I'd try to go somewhere, he'd keep one of the kids at home and not let me take both with me, like he knew I was about to leave. For the last year, I don't think I ever even left the house with both kids. He'd either come with us, or he'd keep one of them at home. I was finally able to leave because one of our neighbors happened to drive up while Greg was beating me, and called 911 on his car phone. When the police got there, Greg had our daughter in his arms, and was telling our little girl, "Mommy is being bad, she's making me hit her, she wants to take you away from me, and I won't let her." They took one look at me, and arrested him. Since I was afraid he'd get out on bond, they brought the kids and I right to the shelter. We're leaving day after tomorrow to move to another state. I'd probably still be there if that neighbor hadn't driven up when he did."

> --Lisa, aged 26, stay-at-home
> mother of two children under
> age 4.

Sadly, it is the woman and her children who often have to leave their homes and rearrange their lives in order to escape battering. Even when the court awards the family home and financial support to the battered woman, many times she is afraid to stay, since the batter can find her so easily. Although protective orders offer some protection (the batterer can be arrested for coming near his victim), many batterers simply disregard the order. After all, these are men who violate the law when they batterer their wives. Why should a piece of paper suddenly turn them into law abiding citizens?

One of the women that I interviewed briefly while waiting for a hearing on her husband's violation of a protective order told me that even though she was awarded the house and furniture, her ex-husband kept a garage door opener, and would routinely let himself in. He damaged furniture and electronic equipment (he once poured crazy glue into her VCR), smoked and left his cigarette butts in evidence, masturbated on her pillow, and even fixed himself meals and left dirty dishes in the sink. Although he never came into the house while she was there, she felt violated and lived in fear of what he might do. Even though her finances were stretched to the limit, she didn't feel safe until she bought a new garage door opener and had an alarm system installed.

Asking for Help

Even when women made the decision to end an abusive relationship, they often ran into difficulties when they tried to leave. Some were too ashamed to ask for help, but most eventually did. Many sought informal assistance from friends, neighbors, and relatives, while others sought help through more formal channels such as the clergy, hotlines and shelters, the legal system, and social services.

Brenda was a stay-at-home mom who left with only the clothes on her back. Friends let her live in their basement until she found a job and apartment. Angela found the courage to leave her abusive husband when her friend Nancy (also a battered women) decided to leave her husband. They came to the shelter together, and later shared a rented apartment with their children. Several other women that I interviewed told similar stories of support from friends.

Some women, like Monica, sought and received help from their families. I met Monica and her mother, Mrs. Johnson, outside the courtroom while they waited for her TPO hearing. They were obviously very close, with Mrs. Johnson talking Monica through her fears of seeing Danny (her husband) at the hearing. Monica acknowledged how fortunate she was,

"I don't know what I'd have done, if it hadn't been for my mom and sisters. When they saw how bad the abuse was getting, they kept telling me that I needed to leave. The last time he beat me, my brother-in-law invited Danny hunting for the weekend, and my sisters and mother came over with a U-Haul and helped me move out. My mom put a deposit down on an apartment, and we took all my furniture and moved it in. When Danny got back, we were gone."

--Monica, aged 28, mother
of two school aged
children.

Other women got no support from families and friends. Often, family and friends had tried in the beginning, but became less supportive as time went on. Many of the women in my sample told of how their husbands or partners had antagonized friends and family with their behavior, cutting the women off from valuable social supports. Often, batterers would deliberately isolate their victims to keep friends and family from seeing signs of abuse and to keep their victims from leaving.

Some of the women I talked with left abusive situations in spite of their families. Sasha, aged 20, was in her third battering relationship. Her parents were divorced, and she described both her mother and father as alcoholics. After sending her money to leave the first battering relationship, they refused to assist her any further. She came to the shelter pregnant and penniless, and later returned to her abuser. Jenny, whose story appeared at the beginning of this chapter, was estranged from her parents, and had not seem them in several years. Asking them for help was not a viable option. Angela was told by her mother, "You made your bed, now lie in it."

Some families and friends even encouraged battered women to stay with their husbands and partners, and to work on the relationship. In several cases, the batterer put on such a good "front" that the woman was accused of making up stories. As Carol, a middle class mother of two shared with me,

> *"No one believed that Mark was beating me. He never hit me where it showed, and he was always so charming and caring around my family. He turned into a different person when we were alone. He'd hit me on my head or punch me in the stomach, since no one would see what he had done. I knew about the women's shelter and all, but didn't want to ask for help. I mean, our families are well known and respected in this community. Mark is a teacher. It would be too embarrassing."*
> --Carol, age 36, real estate
> agent and mother of two
> school aged children.

Carol finally got help when her family physician confronted her about her injuries during a routine visit. Only when she had "evidence" to back her statements did her family believe her. I talked with her briefly by phone after her case came before the judge. While the court believed her and gave her possession of the family home and children, some relatives still accused her of trying to "ruin a good man's name."

Although most women sought help from friends and family members first, it was often not until professionals were involved that they were able to leave battering relationships. In many instances, battered women sought help from the clergy before turning to other professionals. Eight of the women in my sample called their pastors first before deciding to leave abusive relationships. Although other researchers (Alsdurf, 1985; Bowker and Mauer, 1986) found that the clergy tend to encourage the woman to stay with a batterer, to do her "duty," or to honor her marriage vows and "submit" to her husband, I found quite the opposite. In only two cases did the clergy recommend that the woman stay and try to work things out. One of these was quite disturbing, however, since the pastor put a battered woman in serious danger. After coming to the shelter, Doris's pastor (who was a close friend of her husband) tried several times to get in touch with her, calling friends and family, and even leaving messages with the shelter office. When she eventually returned his call, he asked her to come to his office to "talk about all this." When Doris arrived at the church, she noticed that her husband's truck was parked in the lot, and drove by without stopping. Apparently, the pastor had planned to use the session to try and get the couple to reconcile.

In all other cases where women contacted their pastors, they were advised to call the domestic violence hotline or shelter, or were given material on battered women's programs. Two of the women noted that their churches had given them assistance with finances, transportation, or housing. One pastor even helped a battered woman find a job that enabled her not to return to her abuser. Keep in mind, however, that the women in my study were all living apart from their batterers when I interviewed them. It is possible that those women whose clergy advised them to stay, did in fact stay, and were not included in my sample.

The police also received high marks from the women I talked with. For many, the police were the first persons outside the to intervene in their violent relationships. Often, the women or their children called 911, and in several cases, a neighbor or family member had called police. For the most part, the police acted appropriately, arresting the batterer, advising the woman of her rights, and arranging to transport her to a safe place, hospital, or shelter, if needed.

It seems that when problems did occur, it was after the initial incident. Eight of the twenty-four women who had contacted the police had problems with paperwork. Police reports were sometimes not filled out correctly, not noted as domestic violence cases, or had portions missing, resulting in problems when hearings were held.

In four cases, the woman was taken to the hospital because of her injuries. Each noted that the hospital assisted her in locating a safe place when she was released. Two women came directly to the battered women's shelter, one went to a shelter in another county, and another was released to her mother.

The women I talked with were also pleased with the hotline and shelter. Twenty had contacted the hotline, and twelve had actually used the shelter. Many were not aware of the services offered to battered women until told of them by their clergy, the police, or the hospital. Hotline callers felt that they were given good information, and that counselors were both supportive and knowledgeable. Shelter residents were pleasantly surprised with the shelter (which is a 4 bedroom, 2 bath house), noting that they expected, "a gym filled with rows and rows of bed and lockers." Most said that their shelters stays had given them a safe environment in which to "get their heads together and make plans."

The safety net for battered women broke down, however, when the legal system and social services stepped in. Women often felt the courts were unresponsive, asking them to share blame, or putting them or their children in danger. One woman noted that,

> "I'd just gotten out of the hospital, and went to my TPO hearing. This guy [her husband] had beaten me within an inch of my life. The judge decided to order visitation for my husband, and wanted me to meet him at Burger King every other weekend to drop the children off. I mean, this man almost killed me, and now I'm supposed to entrust my children to him and have to see him every two weeks? It seems like I'm the one being punished here."

> --Robin, aged 26, mother of
> two toddlers.

Other women felt that going to court was a frightening experience, since in the state where this research took place, the batterer was told of the TPO hearing date, and had the right to present his side of the story in court. Often, batterers threatened women while waiting cases to be heard, tried to intimidate them with stares or gestures, or tried to convince them to return. I observed one ex-partner smile at his victim in the hallway before court, and slowly run his finger around his neck in a throat slitting gesture. Another brought a dozen red roses to court in an attempt to reconcile with his wife.

The greatest amount of dissatisfaction was with social services and follow up care. Since the shelter had room for only 4 families, stays were limited to 30 days, and decisions and arrangements had to be made very quickly. Other than a support group, the shelter offered no follow up or after-care (because of a lack of funding). Social services (such as welfare, food stamps, housing, and job services) were not located in central locations, nor were they convenient to the shelter. Women often had to go to as many as five different offices in order to arrange for services. Often, they lacked the transportation, funds, or childcare to do this. Bureaucratic regulations were difficult to understand, and the paperwork they needed to qualify for assistance was many times left behind when fled the abusive relationship.

Sadly, it was at this point that many of the women in my sample returned to their batterers. Feeling overwhelmed and lacking necessary supports, it was sometimes easier to return to the batterer than to continue to seek assistance, and to locate housing, jobs, and childcare. I was able to keep in touch with only 10 of the women in my sample after the interview. Of those, seven had returned to their batterers within six months of the interview. This is consistent with Gondolf's (1988) findings that women return to their batterers an average of 6 times before they leave for good.

Conclusion

As the stories presented here illustrate, battered women face a daunting array of barriers in leaving their abusers. Several social actions are needed to combat this problem. First, even though the public is becoming better informed regarding domestic violence, additional education is necessary in to continue to raise awareness of the problem, help people to understand the dynamics of woman battering, and to make sure that all women are aware of the services available in their communities. Second, improved follow up services for battered women are of vital importance in helping them to stay free of their batterers. With cuts to social service budgets following recent welfare reforms, services for battered women are likely to become even harder to obtain. Our society must work together to insure that no woman becomes trapped with an abuser simply because she lacks the funds to leave. Finally, after almost thirty years of attention to this problem, it is time that we begin to shift the focus of our efforts from treating victims of battering to preventing violence from occurring in the first place.

REFERENCES:

Aquirre, B. (1985). Why do they return? Abused wives in shelters. Social Work, 30:350-354.

Alsdurf, J. (1985). Wife abuse and the church: The response of pastors. Response, 8(1):9-11.

Bowker, L., and Mauer, L. (1986). The effectiveness of counseling services utilized by battered women. Women and Therapy,5:65-82.

Browne, A. (1987). When Battered Women Kill. New York: Free Press.

Collins, J. and Schlenger, W. (1988). Acute and chronic effects of alcohol use on violence. Journal of Studies on Alcohol, 49: 516-521.

de las Fuentes, C. and Wright, D. (1991). Surviving Rape: A Structured Group Manual. Austin, TX: Counseling and Mental Health Center, University of Texas at Austin.

Donnelly, D. and Kenyon, S. (1996). "Honey, we don't do men: Gender stereotypes and the provision of services to sexually assaulted males. Journal of Interpersonal Violence, 11(3): 441-448.

Doumas, D., Margolin, G., and John, R. (1994). The intergenerational transmission of violence across three generations. Journal of Family Violence, 9:157-175.

Ferraro, K. (1979). Hard love: Letting go of an abusive husband. Frontiers, 4:16-18.

Finn, J. (1985). The stresses and coping behavior of battered women. Social Casework, (June):341-349.

Flitcraft, A. (1992). Diagnostic and Treatment Guidelines on Domestic Violence. American Medical Association, Chicago, IL.

Gondolf, E. (1988). The effect of batterer counseling on shelter outcomes. Journal of Interpersonal Violence,3:275-289.

Helton, A. (1987). Battered and pregnant: A prevalence study. American Journal of Public Health, 77:1337-1339.

Holiman, M. and Schilit, R. (1991). Aftercare for battered women: How to encourage the maintenance of change. Psychotherapy, 28: 345-353.

Hotaling, G. and Sugarman, D. (1986). An analysis of risk markers in husband to wife violence: The current state of knowledge. Violence and Victims, 1: 101-124.

Hotaling, G. and Sugarman, D. (1990). A risk marker analysis of assaulted wives. Journal of Family Violence, 5:1-13.

Johnson, I. (1992). Economic, situational, and psychological correlates of the decision-making process of battered women: Decisions to return home after shelter termination. Families in Society, 73:168-76.

Kaufman-Kantor, G. and Straus, M. (1990). The "drunken bum" theory of wife beating. In M. Straus and R. Gelles (Eds.), Physical Violence in American Families (pp. 203-224). New Brunswick, NJ: Transaction.

Langan, P. and Innes, C. (1986). Preventing Domestic Violence Against Women (Bureau of Justice Statistics special report). Washington, DC: U.S. Dept. of Justice (NCJ No. 102037).

Paymar, M. (1993). Violent No More: Helping Men End Domestic Abuse. Alameda, CA: Hunter House.

Renzetti, C. (1992). Violent Betrayal: Partner Abuse in Lesbian Relationships. Newbury Park, CA: Sage.

Roscoe, B. and Benaske, N. (1985). Courtship violence experiences by abused wives: Similarities in pattern of abuse. Family Relations, 34, 419-24.

Snyder, D. and Fruchtman, L. (1981). Differential patterns of wife abuse: A data-based typology. Journal of Consulting and Clinical Psychology, 49:878-885.

Strube, M. (1988). The decision to leave an abusive relationship: Empirical evidence and theoretical issues. Psychological Bulletin, 104:236-250.

Straus, M. and Gelles, R. (1986). Societal change and change in family violence from 1975 to 1985 as revealed by two national surveys. Journal of Marriage and the Family, 48:465-79.

Straus, M., Gelles, R., and Steinmetz, S. (1980). Behind Closed Doors: Violence in the American Family. Garden City: Doubleday.

Vaughn, D. (1987). The long goodbye. Psychology Today, (July): 37-38, 42.

Walker, L. (1979) The Battered Woman. New York: Harper and Row.

Walker, L. (1989). Terrifying Love: Why Battered Women Kill and How Society Responds. New York: Harper and Row.

The Current State of Welfare Reform

Robert Hartmann McNamara Department of Political Science and Criminal Justice, The Citadel

Carrie Flagler
Department of Sociology
Furman University

The Personal Responsibility and Work Opportunity Reconciliation Act of 1996 was signed into law by President Clinton on August 22, 1996. As Clinton signed the bill, he commented, "[t]his is not the end of welfare reform, this is the beginning...Today, we are not ending welfare as we know it. But I hope this day will be remembered not for what it ended, but for what it began—a new day that offers hope, honors responsibility, rewards work, and changes the terms of the debate..." (State Guidance for the Temporary Assistance for Needy Families Program, 1996). With these words, President Clinton let the world know this new system would be one that honored hard work and would compel participants to become more involved in bettering their own lives.

If one were to read the news or listen to broadcasters over the last seven years, one might think that the U.S. is making great progress to end poverty. The media is replete with stories that welfare is a resounding success. This is especially true in the late 1990s when the economic boom created millions of new jobs. However, some experts and social advocates question if this is really true. Have the lives of the poor really improved? Has mandating personal responsibility really resulted in the achievement of the American dream for many people? This is especially true given our cultural belief in the idea that hard work results in rewards. Where exactly are we in our understanding of welfare reform and its effects? What are the measures used to define success? It seems clear that the public and many politicians believe welfare reform is working, but by what standard?

The "success" of welfare reform was readily evident in 2002, when President George W. Bush challenged states to increase the standards used for welfare recipients. Among his proposed changes were to increase the number of hours a welfare recipient must work each week (NPR, 2002). Additionally, because of the evidence supporting the benefit of children raised in intact two parent families, and based on the idea that single mothers represent a substantial portion of welfare recipients, President Bush also proposed ways to improve the marriageability of welfare mothers. Bush contends that there is a great deal of social science research that suggests children tend to be better off, financially and emotionally when their parents are married to each other. This is also controversial, as Ooms (2004) describes. Finally, President Bush continues to promote the idea that private organizations, such as churches, should provide the lion share of the assistance to the poor. Many of these ideas are ambitious and raise questions about the viability of welfare reform.

When welfare reform legislation was passed, many service providers and researchers worried that the lifetime eligibility stipulation of welfare reform, which would have been reached for many recipients in 2002-2003, coupled with the structural problems in the labor market, might increase the size of the homeless population if changes were not forthcoming (National Coalition for the Homeless, 2002). However, in 2004, there remains considerable debate about whether or not the gloomy forecasts were realized. For some, such as Christopher Jencks (2004), things really are not that bad for former welfare recipients (see also Robert Rector's *Broadening the Reform* 2000, the Heritage Foundation). There are others who see welfare itself as the problem, but tolerate welfare reform due to its ringing success in supporting the idea that the poor would not be in their current situation were it not for welfare policies that have spanned generations (see Banfield 1970; Murray 1984).

Others, however, disagree and argue that the lives of the poor are not very different from pre-welfare reform days since the structural problems facing America's poor have gotten worse, not better, by a stumbling economy and an administration that focuses only on narrowly defined measures of success (Hilfiker 2004; O'Gorman 2002; Tanner 2001; *BusinessWeek* 2000). There are also issues of the cyclical nature of welfare, where many recipients who leave welfare commonly are forced to return (Anderson, Halter, and Gryzlak 2004). There are also many experts who focus on institutional issues, such as the amount of money provided to states, the lack of adequate oversight of state spending on welfare programs, and the prioritization states are giving to welfare issues (Friedman 2002).

While there is a tendency for many opposed to welfare reform to attribute these problems to Republicans and President Bush, some experts and scholars, such as Hilfiker (2004), argue that the problems of welfare reform are not uniquely attributable to conservatives (see also Jencks 2004). Rather, it is the result of how most Americans view the poor over the last few decades. In 2000, George W. Bush campaigned as a "compassionate conservative," expressing concern for the poor. Since coming into office, he has continued to be a strong voice in favor of helping the less fortunate. However, Hilfiker (2004) argues that many of the Bush administration policies, particularly tax policies, which have led to unprecedented budget deficits, as well as the ripple effect it has had on state budgets, will have serious implications for the poor and disenfranchised.

Before discussing these issues, however, it is necessary to provide an overview of the welfare reform legislation, including the highly controversial faith-based initiative.

THE ESSENTIALS OF WELFARE REFORM

More commonly known as the 1996 Welfare Reform Act, the Personal Responsibility and Work Opportunity Reconciliation Act (PRWORA) established the Temporary Assistance for Needy Families Program (TANF) and replaced the sixty-one year old system of public assistance. Under the previous system, according to *Washington Post* writer, Dan Froomkin (1998), "[t]he federal government provided fairly uniform benefits to the nation's poor...without regard to the details of their personal circumstances, and with no time limit" (p. 1).

The TANF program consists of block grants, where each state (which must commit state funds to their welfare systems to be eligible for TANF funding) determines how to run its own welfare system in a manner that will meet its specific needs. The TANF program focuses on creating "a working poor" rather than "a welfare poor." Work, marriage, and independence, are the central themes of this program, and temporary assistance is offered while recipients look for a position in the labor force. The Administration for Children and Families (2000) declares that individual states must use TANF funding "to provide assistance to needy families so that children can be cared for in their own homes; to reduce dependency by promoting job preparation, work and marriage; to prevent out-of-wedlock pregnancies; and to encourage the formation and maintenance of two-parent families" (p. 1).

While each state determines eligibility limits, amounts paid for assistance, and establishes programs to distribute the services provided, federal guidelines must also be followed. According to Palen (2001), "[f]ederal guidelines generally limit cash benefits to two years at a time and a total of five years in a lifetime for adults and a work requirement of 30 hours per week. Additionally, at least 50% of all single parents have to work by at least 2002" (p. 53).

State work requirements, as described by the Administration for Children and Families (2000), must be imposed and "recipients will be required to participate in unsubsidized or subsidized employment, on-the-job training, work experience, community service, and 12 months of vocational training" (p. 3). With the help of federal funding and incentives, such as bonus rewards for states that move welfare recipients into the workforce, "each state [is to] be held accountable for moving families from welfare to self-sufficiency through work" (Summary: Final Rule, p. 3).

After two years of receiving assistance, recipients are required to participate in work or a work-related activity. The act set state-based work participation requirements at 30% in 1997, 40% in 2000 and 50% in 2002 (Holcomb and Thompson 2000 in Lee and Curran 2003). As Congress wrestled with the reauthorization of the PRWORA legislation in 2002, the Bush administration proposed raising the work participation rate to 70% by 2007. However, PRWORA allows states to exempt up to 20% of their caseloads from the time limits and grants states considerable flexibility in their implementation of work requirements. States can design their own welfare to work programs, decide who will be exempt from work requirements, and determine who will be exempt from time limits all together. They can also transfer block grant monies and maintenance of funds to pay for additional services to recipients, including mental health services (Derr, Douglas and Pavetti 2001; Lee and Curran 2003). Additionally, legal immigrants are not eligible under welfare reform laws.

The original amount of funding allocated for TANF was $16.5 billion. Since 1996, that figure has remained the same, which means it has suffered a real value decline of more than 11% due to inflation. To add to the problem, states have had to make up the difference in the lack of federal funding increases from their own budgets. However, over the next four years state spending is expected to cut TANF funding from $19.3 billion in 2003 to $16.9 billion as they struggle to recover from the last few years of budget crises.

Another dramatic change in the current reform legislation relates to education and work requirements for welfare recipients. Recently, the U.S. House of Representatives approved sweeping changes to federal welfare policy that some argue will make it tougher for recipients to obtain an education. In passing H.R. 4, the House endorsed a series of changes including a 40 hour work week for welfare recipients. The jump from 30 to 40 hours per week would allow 16 hours for job preparation (Bernstein and Starr 2003). In response to the increases in work requirements, as well as targeting the provision that prohibits legal immigrants from receiving TANF funds (see Kandula,

Grogan, and Lauderdale 2004), Senators Clinton and Kennedy signed a letter calling for restoration of welfare for legal immigrants, who were cut off in 1996, and boosting child-care funds by $11 billion over five years. However, there is no effort being made by Congress or the Bush administration to include legal immigrants or to increase the federal funding beyond its current $16.5 billion budget.

In addition to imposing new work requirements, H.R. 4 also limits time in educational programs to no more than four months over a two year period. Current law allows 12 months in education over five years. Tommy Thompson, former U.S. Health and Human Services Secretary has said, "Welfare reform is working in America because we're helping people go to work and build better lives for themselves and their families" (Black Issues in Higher Education 2003).

Another important dimension of the original and more recent versions of welfare reform relate to a concern about "family breakdown." Ooms (2002) contends that although it was not really noticed at the time, three of the four purposes of the welfare legislation refer directly or indirectly to marriage and family formation. The Bush administration plans to make marriage an even more central feature of welfare reform in the coming years. In his reauthorization proposal, Bush included $300 million for demonstration grants to focus on promoting healthy marriages and reducing out-of-wedlock births. This, in the view of the administration, is the principal cause of welfare dependency and a host of other social problems. It is not surprising that many states have followed the lead of the federal government on this issue.

As Ooms (2002) describes, Oklahoma, Arizona, Florida, Louisiana, Michigan and Utah have all embarked upon a marriage initiative for welfare recipients. Unlike other states in the past, where such initiatives were designed to minimize the high divorce rates and the effect an absent father has on children, these initiatives are designed to provide incentives to welfare mothers to marry. The justification for this change in policy is based on ample social science research that shows children living in two parent families fare better than those in single parent families. How one goes about creating a stable environment for children is the central question and primary source of the debate. We will have more to say on this in our evaluation section of welfare reform. However, all of these initiatives: increasing the work requirement, reducing the amount of time for job preparation and education, marriage incentives, and the forthcoming discussion on faith-based helping, are all part of the reauthorization package that remains, as of this writing, stalled in Congress. However, given the popularity of welfare reform by most Americans, as well as its support by Congress and by the President, there is every reason to believe that these new dimensions to welfare reform will become a reality in the near future.

Faith-Based Organizations and Welfare Reform

Charitable Choice was a provision of the 1996 welfare reform legislation and it gave the faith-based community service providers an equal opportunity at federal money for secular community services. It is important to note from the outset that Charitable Choice and Bush's Faith-Based Initiatives do not create more funds; they merely allow more people access to preexisting ones. Charitable Choice also changes the regulations on how states can spend federal grants, allowing the creation of partnerships between faith-based programs and the states (Spain, 2001). The Act also exempts religious organization from the Civil Rights Act because it defends their rights "to hire and fire employees using religious criteria" (Svanoe, 2001). On the other hand, federal money cannot be used for direct religious purposes of proselytizing, and they may not refuse services to people based on religious criteria. This helps to ensure government accountability (Svanoe, 2001). Prior to Charitable Choice, social service programs were required to be secular in nature. Now, they may "keep their religious symbols, [and] use their religious language" (Glennon, 2000). Consequently, Charitable Choice protects the religious liberty of the beneficiary, forbids discrimination against the recipient, and mandates that a secular alternative be available for those who do not feel comfortable receiving assistance from a religious provider.

On January 29, 2001, during his second week in office, President George W. Bush proposed a new government plan entitled "Rallying the Armies of Compassion," which created a new strategy for fighting poverty. The new strategy became known as the *Faith-Based and Community Initiatives*. The Faith-Based and Community Initiatives center around three lines of action: identification and elimination of federal barriers to faith-based and community serving, increasing private giving to non-profit, faith-based and community groups, and expanding the involvement of faith-based and community groups.

The creation of the White House Office of Faith-Based and Community Initiatives (OFBCI) was the first step towards elimination of the "bureaucratic red tape" (Edwards, 2001:24). According to President Bush, the office was formed "to help promote public/private partnerships that enable diverse sacred places and grassroots secular programs to achieve civic purposes" (Bush, 2001:8). However, aside from these goals, it also performs many other tasks. It ensures that Faith-Based Organizations (FBO) are receiving an equal opportunity to compete for federal funds; it works at improving and expanding Charitable Choice; it coordinates programs to increase public support; and acts as the liaison between organizations and the President. It also provides guidance to state and local officials during implementation and works to develop "new programs that exemplify the President's agenda" (Bush, 2001:15).

The second step toward the elimination of federal barriers is the creation of state-level offices, which enforce the implementation of the agenda, thus transferring a large amount of responsibility from the federal to the state level. The third and final step in eliminating federal barriers was the expansion of Charitable Choice (Bush, 2001:9).

President Bush also wants to expand the trend of giving to local charities. Presently, there are many factors that result in some people choosing not to donate to charity. President Bush intends to eliminate many of these obstacles through tax deductions and other initiatives. Specifically, there are six planned changes.

The first is to grant charitable deductions for those who do not itemize and thus currently cannot claim this benefit. Hence, anyone would get deductions for donating to charity. In November 2001, Bush is quoted to believe that it would be "a wise use of the tax code to encourage giving to programs that are positively affecting people's lives" ("President Urges Support..." 2001). The government estimates that by allowing charitable deductions "billions of dollars in new donations" will be produced (Bush, 2001:10).

The second change would be to limit the liability of corporations who donate. By eliminating the obstacles that are preventing the corporations from donating, Bush hopes to encourage more organizations to contribute to their communities. Third, Bush wants to change the law, which presently will not allow elderly (people over the age of 59) to withdraw money from Individual Retirement Accounts (IRA) for charitable purposes without being taxed. Fourth, the government will encourage people to become more involved in their community in the fight against poverty by giving more to the anti-poverty cause. For example, credits will be given against certain taxes if the person contributes to charities that address poverty. Fifth, President Bush plans to increase the allowance of corporations to deduct donations to 15% of the company's taxable income (Bush, 2001). Prior to this change, the allowance was at 10% of the company's taxable income (Bush, 2001). This slight change could generate billions of dollars in donations.

The final change is the creation of a Compassion Capital Fund. The fund will match private giving with federal dollars. The Compassion Capital Fund has two goals: to increase monetary assistance, which will help the programs grow in capacity and competence, and to "provide start up capital to enable smaller groups to expand their programs" (Bush, 2001:11). In essence, with every increase in private giving, an increase in government funding will follow.

HAS WELFARE REFORM REALLY WORKED?

Success of welfare reform is predicated in large part on how "success" is defined. On one hand, many politicians and policy makers argue that the goal of welfare reform was to get people off welfare. This was based on the belief in a "culture of poverty" to explain poverty. This perception suggests that poor people are pathologically lazy or feel entitled to assistance from the government despite the fact that they are perfectly capable of working and being self-sufficient. Additionally, poor choices, such as drug abuse, teenage pregnancy, and dropping out of school, are individual choices that should not become the responsibility of the government to solve. This, coupled with the lingering image of President Regan's "welfare queens" is the catalyst behind welfare reform. Thus, success of welfare reform is operationalized to be a reduction in the number of people on welfare.

By this standard, welfare reform has been a ringing success. The Third Annual Report to Congress (2000) found that there has not only been a reduction in the number of welfare recipients, but the percentage of recipients that are employed "reached an all-time high in fiscal year 1999 at 33% compared to...11% in 1996" (p. 1). The report also suggests that the average monthly earnings of employed welfare recipients have increased from $466 in 1996 to $589 in 1999.

As was mentioned, the Welfare Reform Act has also been successful in reducing the number of welfare recipients. According to one estimate, "[c]urrent numbers on welfare are at the lowest rates in over a quarter of a century" (Palen, 2001:53-54). Across the country the number of people on welfare rolls is decreasing, and "[a]s of 1999, welfare recipients were down 46% (14.1 million to 7.6 million) compared to six years earlier" (Palen, 2001:54). By 2003, the number of people removed from welfare rolls is approximately 6.6 million.

Table 4-1
Declines in Welfare Caseloads

Fiscal Years	Estimated U.S. Populations (000's)	AFDC/TANF Recipients	Percent of U.S. Population
1994	259,935	14,225,651	5.5%
1995	262,392	13,660,192	5.2%
1996	264,827	12,644,915	4.8%
1997	267,346	10,823,002	4.0%
1998	269,845	8,778,815	3.3%
1999	272,286	7,187,753	2.6%
December 1999	274,076	6,274,555	2.3%

From the Introductory and Executive Summary section of the "Third Annual Report to Congress," 2000, p. 3.

The issue of single mothers has long been a problem related to welfare, but between 1995 and 2000, Ryan Streeter of the Hudson Institute (2001) found that "the number of children living with single mothers dropped 8%...[and] [t]he percentage of children living with married parents held constant at 70%, halting a previous downward trend in the number of married-with-children households" (p. 1). Streeter (2001) believes welfare reform has been successful because it "took away the advantages of being unemployed and unmarried--two conditions required by the old welfare system for public assistance," (p. 1).

These changes not only positively affect welfare adults, but they also offer children in welfare homes more hope for growing up in a financially and emotionally stable environment with the support of a family. "Numerous studies have confirmed that children from two-parent households fare much better economically and socially than children from single parent homes. To the extent that welfare reform has encouraged more two-parent households, it is a victory for children" (Streeter 2001, p. 2).

Jencks (2004) argues that many experts initially thought that welfare reform would result in disaster for many families. However, his main argument is that welfare reform has not been as detrimental to poor families. Jencks begins his assertion that the 1996 legislation sent a powerful statement: America was no longer committed to supporting women who wanted to be full-time mothers. Single mothers judged capable of working can get short-term assistance, but they will not get any long-term help unless they have a job and they cannot expect the government to find them one. Jencks cites three primary reasons for the success of welfare reform.

One reason Jencks thinks welfare reform has worked is largely due to the Earned Income Tax Credit (EITC). In 1993, President Clinton expanded the EITC and in 2003, EITC distributes more money to working parents than AFDC ever gave to mothers who stayed home. For a minimum wage worker with two children, the EITC means a 40% increase in annual earnings. Second, the improved income of working mothers has been aggressive child support enforcement. Additionally, extending Medicaid coverage to some of the working poor also reduced some mothers' out of pocket medical expenses.

Third, TANF funding did not reduce as welfare caseloads decreased and this allowed states to supplement child care costs, which made it more likely that a poor mother could survive on low paying wages. Jencks describes the new system as a "wage subsidy state" in which assistance is tied to employment.

In addressing the mothers who left welfare but did not find regular work, Jencks argues that they are still doing better than most of the welfare reform critics expected. He contends it is difficult to find evidence that their situation has gotten worse.

Another proponent of the success of welfare reform is Robert Rector of the Heritage Foundation, who asserts that reduction in poverty was never a statutory goal of welfare reform. Rather, the primary goal was to reduce the number of people dependent on government support in lieu of employment. Some people thought, from the emphasis on self-sufficiency through employment, that jobs were the paths out of poverty. Additionally, according to Rector, many people think that poverty reduction should be the benchmark for assessing the reform's success.

In a survey by the Packard Foundation, 74% of respondents said that decreasing the number of families in poverty should be very important in judging welfare reform. However, there is little agreement on the existence, causes, and meaning of poverty. Rector believes that the extent of poverty is essentially determined by the way in which the government calculates the data, which artificially inflates the incidence of poverty. In his view, poverty is a result of poor choices. He states, "The culture of the underclass is marked by a cluster of behavioral pathologies, eroded work ethic, collapse of marriage, indifference to education, drug and alcohol abuse and pervasive crime."

Thus, despite the public's perception that welfare reform should have the ultimate objective of alleviating or reducing poverty, Rector and many others believe that this is an unrealistic goal. This is particularly true if there exists a belief that poverty is a result of poor choices and individual pathologies, one of which is an abuse of the very system that tried to help them to become productive members of society. The better marker, they believe, should be a reduction in the number of people on welfare and forcing people to take responsibility for their own actions.

However, studies cited in Rector's report indicate that over one-third of welfare fraud under the old system was illegal employment, which casts some doubt on the pathological laziness-causes-poverty argument. The general pattern in the pre-welfare reform era was that most recipients would receive welfare for a time, leave and then return, largely because they were unable to find steady employment. Thus, about as many people exited welfare rolls as those who came on each year (O'Gorman 2004).

According to Wade Horn, Assistant Secretary of Health and Human Services, the right question to ask of welfare reform is whether children are better off than before. Rector argues in his report entitled *Broadening the Reform* that "The decline in welfare dependence has been greatest among the most disadvantaged and least employable single mothers—the group with the greatest tendency toward long-term dependence." He sees in this a confirmation that welfare reform affected the entire welfare caseload, not merely the most employable mothers. Another way of saying this is that Rector believes if the children of the most disadvantaged are better off, then certainly the children of the less disadvantaged are faring much better as well.

THE OTHER SIDE OF THE "SUCCESS" OF WELFARE REFORM
Does Leaving Welfare Result in Self-Sufficiency?

There is little question that welfare caseloads have declined dramatically since 1996. It is also fairly clear that, as Bernstein and Starr (2002) contend, lawmakers are focused on making the reform policies even more restrictive. Stricter work rules could force already financially strapped states to set up costly public-job programs to get enough recipients off the rolls. At the same time, Bernstein and Starr (2002) argue that Bush administration officials have been reassuring governors that there are plenty of loopholes they can use to avoid workfare programs. The result could be tougher standards, but only in states willing to bear the cost of enforcing them. Michigan Governor John Engler, a Republican, says that "Many in Congress, on both sides, are playing 'who can be more pro-work than the other guy'" (Bernstein and Starr 2002). Such an approach has dramatically altered the nature of welfare in this country.

Early studies found that about 50-70% of TANF leavers were employed immediately after leaving welfare (Acs and Loprest 2001; Tweedie, Reichert, and O'Connor 2004 in Anderson, Halter and Gryzlak 2004). However, these studies also showed that average earnings were usually below the poverty level. Further, job instability was common because those who leave welfare are employed in temporary or low skilled jobs (Anderson, Halter, Julnes and Schuldt 2004 in Anderson, Halter and Gryzlak 2004). Studies also showed that public support like the Earned Income Tax Credit, transitional Medicaid and child care were underused (Anderson Halter, and Schuldt 2001).

As Anderson, Halter, and Gryzlak (2004) assert, there is little information available concerning the principal reasons that those who leave TANF often return. However, pre-TANF studies found that welfare returns resulted largely from structural employment problems (Harris 1996; Pavetti 1993 in that article). Edin and Lein (1997) reported that those who left welfare often concluded they were worse off after leaving because of work disincentives and tenuous employment. Anderson, Halter and Gryzlak (2004) also contend that because TANF placed little emphasis on job development, the structural problems identified by others may continue to undercut successful welfare exits. What we do know is that most who leave TANF return, largely due to low wages and unstable jobs.

"[T]he long-term success of welfare reform depends largely on whether the economy can create enough jobs to employ those with limited skills" (Palen, 201:54). In 1996, when Clinton passed the reform bill, the economy was booming, and this initially helped decrease the number of people on welfare, primarily because it was easier for individuals to find work.

The Council of Economic Advisors finds that "more than 40% of the decline in the number of welfare recipients is due to growth of the economy, while more than 30% is due to changes in state welfare laws. The rest are due to other factors, such as more aggressive collection of child support" (p. 54). The strong economy was responsible for a majority of welfare decline, but the recession that began in March 2001 is slowing the economy and it is estimated that we can expect an increase in the number of people needing assistance (Achievements of the Welfare Reform Law of 1996, 2002).

Second, most experts agree that welfare reform has so far focused on the easiest, most employable cases. With a five year time limit, one that has seen the first wave of recipients permanently removed from caseloads, welfare reform may finally begin to affect the hard core cases. Studies show that those who are still on the rolls have less education, fewer basic skills and less previous work experience (Tanner 2001). Thus, an increasing proportion of remaining welfare recipients are people who have been on assistance for more than five years. This is the group most conservatives target as the core problem relating to welfare. It is this segment of the population that President Reagan referred to as "welfare queens" or those that Charles Murray and others describe as an entrenched segregated underclass of people (see Tanner 2001). It remains to be seen if the reform legislation will have the same impact on this group now that the easiest cases have been removed.

A third issue concerning the problems of welfare reform also relates to the changing economy: income. Many experts contend that the poor are unable to gain access to jobs that pay wages sufficient to achieve self-sufficiency. An article from *the Atlanta Journal and Constitution* in August 2001 stated that, "at today's minimum wage of $5.15 an hour, working 40 hours a week, a worker can only earn $10,712 a year. (The poverty rate for a family of four is $17,999; $13,290 for a family of three)" ("Poverty, Income and Wealth, 2001, p. 3). Even if a person is able to secure a minimum wage job, often he or she is unable to support their family with the income derived from it. Under these circumstances, many people turn to welfare for assistance. Unfortunately, the amount of assistance offered and available is declining.

"Between 1993 and 2000, earnings increased dramatically while income from welfare fell. The figures show that welfare income, primarily from cash and food stamps, has declined by about $2,500 per family" (Achievements of the Welfare Reform Law of 1996, 2002, p. 3). While the amount of money offered is decreasing, programs such as Earned Income Tax Credit, which will be discussed later, are attempting to offset this decline in money offered to families receiving welfare.

Critics of welfare reform argue that finding a job does not automatically lead to self-sufficiency. While it is clear that the poverty rate of single mothers has declined since the early 1990s, those in the bottom fifth of the income scales, which include most of the welfare-eligible population, earned an average of only $7,900 in 2000, according to the Office of Management and Budget. While that is a 24% increase since 1993 after inflation, it is still more than 40% below the poverty line. Moreover, in 2003, just 25% remain consistently employed for two years, versus 57% of all women, according to the Economic Policy Institute. In some states, up to 40% of welfare leavers say they are worse off than when they were on welfare.

It is not simply that there are only low paying jobs in the marketplace; simply finding a job can be a challenge. As Butterbaugh (2004) shows, the unemployment rate for low income single mothers has risen faster than for the general population, averaging 12.3% compared to 4-6% for the nation overall. The key labor market sectors for single mothers: retail trade and services, have seen even greater losses. Vacancies in retail trade fell by over 20% in 2003 and currently for every job opening in the retail sector, there are 3.2 people (all workers not just single mothers) to fill it. The main thrust of this argument, then, is that the employment market is over-saturated and unable to absorb more workers, no matter how many hours Congress legislates that TANF recipients work.

Some argue that workfare is the answer. However, workfare only works when there are sufficient numbers of jobs available. Otherwise, those jobs are taken by welfare recipients, leaving the near poor without adequate job opportunities (Wilson 1998). Second, workfare is not likely to result in a permanent job for welfare recipients. Studies show that workfare recipients often do not find private-sector jobs. New York officials recently testified before Congress that only 10% of workfare participants in that state found jobs lasting more than 90 days (Bernstein and Starr 2002).

On a more cynical note, O'Gorman (2002) argues, perhaps the plan all along has been to create a pool of low-wage workers. She says, "how else can we call the reform a success when 60% of employed leavers are living at or below the poverty level—the majority in jobs that do not carry health insurance? In 1999, 59% of single mothers in families with incomes below 200% of the poverty level, were working. And studies that track leavers over longer periods show no significant earnings growth after leaving welfare. In 1999, amid a booming economy, the poorest 700,000 single mothers living only with their children had lower earned income than similar women in 1985, even though their earnings increased.

In other words, the lowest-income single mothers had become poorer. More recently, President Bush was moving to allow states to place welfare recipients in jobs that pay less than minimum wage as a form of supervised work experience. Replacing the term *employment* with *supervised work experience* removes the recipient from any minimum wage requirement and labor protections. (O'Gorman 2002). It also alleviates the states from the responsibility of creating workfare employment for welfare recipients.

State Spending on Assistance

Another criticism of welfare reform focuses on how states are spending TANF funds. As Friedman (2002) describes, there are essentially two issues related to welfare reform. First, given how many families have left the welfare rolls, states have spent less money on basic assistance to poor families than they have received in block grant funds. What has happened to those funds? Second, in recent times, particularly due to economic fluctuations, caseloads have increased. Given that the block grant amounts have not risen since the initial passage of reform legislation, how have states allotted for the additional costs?

In an attempt to address the first question, a U.S. General Accounting Office (GAO) issued a report in 2001 that examined how some states were allocating their funding as well as how much money was set aside for emergencies. Nine of the ten states in the GAO study were using TANF money to pay for state programs formerly financed with state funds, and then using the state funds for other purposes. Texas, for example, used at least $320 million in TANF money to replace state spending, most notably for child protective services and foster care. Critics of this practice, while acknowledging the importance of such programs, argue that the state should commit its own resources for those types of programs, not federal funds designated for welfare. While Texas officials contend that they are spending more money on welfare-related issues, critics point out that the state general revenue was about the same and in some cases, spending per client went down dramatically. At the same time, there have been allegations made that state funds, offset by TANF money, helped to pay for $2.3 billion in tax cuts to homeowners and businesses over a five year period.

Critics also argue that left over funds, about half of the total given to states in 2000, is often already committed to other projects (see Friedman 2002). According to the Center for Law and Social Policy, nearly 63% of the leftover funds were already obligated but not yet spent, and even the unobligated category, meaning those funds that were free to be spent by states, included funds already slated for future use. Additionally, the Center found that 11 states had no uncommitted funds at all. The upshot of this is that there is no "rainy day fund" for many states in the event welfare caseloads increase. Rather, most states have taken the federal funding and used it to offset their state costs, whether for other social services programs or for tax refunds.

Obviously, for those states that actually have unspent money available, economic downturns will result in most of the funding being used quickly. For other states that have committed that money for other projects, the problem becomes more acute. In Texas, for example, it ended its fiscal year 2000 with 25% of its funds unspent. However, it was unable to replace its state funds with federal funding since it spent more than it received. Wisconsin witnessed a 25% increase in caseloads in the last year, which leaves them with a projected $107 million deficit. To make up the differences, states are going to have to find additional sources, probably from state budgets, to make up the differences. Unlike the federal government, most state constitutions do not allow for deficit spending. The result will be a reduction in services for recipients or attempts to locate additional funding. The likely scenario, say many advocates for the poor, will be that many poor families will not get the assistance they need.

Marriage Incentives

As was mentioned, there is an overwhelming amount of social science research that children from two-parent families fare better than those from single parent families. For instance, children living with single mothers are five times as likely to be poor as those in two-parent families. Growing up in a single parent family also roughly doubles the risk that a child will drop out of school, have difficulty finding a job, or become a teen parent. About half of these effects appear to be attributable to the lack of income available to single parents, but the other half remains more difficult to explain. It is not simply the presence of two adults in the home that helps children.

As evidence of this trend, critics point out that children living with cohabiting partners and in stepfamilies generally do less well than those living with both married biological parents (Ooms 2002). Married adults are more productive on the job, earn more, save more, have better health and live longer (Haney and March 2003; Ooms 2002). However, it is not simply the case that single mothers find themselves poor because they are unmarried; they find themselves unmarried because they are poor. Successful marriages are more difficult when husbands and wives are poorly educated, lack access to well paying jobs, and cannot afford decent child care. Thus, economic hardships and other problems associated with poverty (e.g. education, occupational prestige) have significant influences on couples' relationships (see Haney and March 2003; Ooms 2002).

Still, many states and policymakers believe it is better to be married than unmarried when it comes to welfare. For instance, in West Virginia, married families receive an extra $100 per month in welfare benefits as a "marriage incentive." The Heritage Foundation has proposed the idea to give $4,000 to welfare recipients who marry before they have a child and stay married for two years. Many critics point out that marriage by itself is too simplistic a solution to the complex problems of the poor. Marrying a low-income, unmarried mother to her child's father will not magically raise the family out of poverty when the parents often have no skills, no jobs, and substandard housing, and may be struggling with substance abuse, domestic violence or other emotional problems. Additionally, the decline in marriage is worldwide, a result of a number of social and economic forces that result in different forms of families. The incentives also suggest that we know how to help people create better relationships. Most Americans have problems, as evidenced by the extraordinarily high divorce rate in this country. It also sends a mixed message to children about the value marriage holds in our culture. What example do we set for children about why people should marry when they see people doing it for financial reasons, with the state providing the subsidies? Will they interpret marriage to be a financial solution to a problem, as the government seems to be suggesting? Critics also wonder what will this do to future generations of adults and their ideas about morality, love, family, and marriage as an institution of those concepts.

Faith-Based Helping

Finally, there remains the issue of whether or not faith-based organizations should be eligible for federal funds. This plan, like many dimensions of the overall package, has caused great controversy; both the religious organizations and the secular groups are concerned about its effects. The four main fears center on constitutional issues, resources, accountability, and the unintended consequences of the plan. The constitutional issue focuses on religious freedom. This proposal could put government officials in the awkward position of having to determine which program to fund; hence, which religion to support. Theoretically, it is based on merit—the programs that work will get funded. However, if the government funds only those "programs that work," it will become logical for the agencies to accept into the program only those with a higher likelihood of success, so that their program's statistics reflect a program that 'works' (Buckstead, 2001). By creaming the clientele, agencies will be guaranteeing their 'success'. Unfortunately, those that need help the most might become the ones least likely to receive it because no one will want to invest in them.

Many people also fear that the government will be put in the position to choose which organizations are legitimate religious organizations (Darden, 2001) and which "faiths are out of bounds" (As cited in "Will the Office..." 2001:17). Another constitutional issue is that the beneficiaries' religious liberty will be jeopardized. The White House recognizes that it will be difficult to keep "volunteers, who would not be paid with federal money," from preaching or attempting to convert the participants in the programs, but they do not attempt to challenge it (Becker, 2001:2).

Another potential problem relates to the funds themselves. While there will be more people eligible to receive federal funding there will not be an expansion of "The amount of funding available for the provision of human services" (Buckstead, 2001:3).

In other words, the pie is not getting bigger, but more people are getting pieces, which means each agency will get "a smaller piece of the federal pie" ("Faith-Based Questions" 2001:13). This increased competition for the already inadequate funds could potentially, according to critics, "become an instrument of division and separation" (Glennon, 2000:839). Related to this is that needy individuals may be forced to attend a religious organization. As Elena Matsui and Joseph Chuman (2001) remind us in their critique of Charitable Choice, "no person should ever be placed in the demeaning position of having to compromise his or her religious conscience in the face of neediness and dependence on others"(p.33).

In the original proposal, there was a mandate that every religious organization must have a secular alternative; however, the Community Solutions Act, which the House voted on and approved by a vote of 233 to 198 ("Faith-Based Initiative..." 2001) in 2001 did not have this mandate (Homeless Conference 2001). If there was one, which required a secular equivalent for every religious organization, people fear that government will be purposefully funding a duplication of services, causing the existing funding to be further divided (Buckstead, 2001). On the other hand, some believe that instead of division, this proposal could lead to collaboration between religious organizations.

The accountability issue deals with the Faith Based Organizations (FBOs) not having to adhere to the same standards as secular organizations. For example, the FBOs "are exempt from the non-discrimination provisions of the Civil Rights Act" because they are allowed to discriminate on the basis of religion in their hiring practices, so they may hire people only within their own religion (Buckstead, 2001:4). Many churches fear that this freedom in hiring will be challenged if they accept federal funds ("Bush's Faith-Based Office" 2001). Employees of secular organizations also fear the accountability issue. They worry that if they lose their jobs in secular organizations and are forced to seek employment with a religious organization, they might not be hired for religious reasons, even if they have the necessary skills needed for the position (Glennon, 2000).

Finally, the unintended consequences of concern are not of "religion intruding on government, [but] government intruding on religion" ("Bush rallies support..." 2001:2). Many churches fear that they will lose autonomy by making themselves dependent on tax money (Buckstead, 2001:4). Related to this is the fear that the over-dependence on government money will cause the organizations to begin secularizing in order to remain in compliance to receive funding. Although the organizations are not required to take government funding, they may do so because they need the money to remain viable. Therefore, the pressure to take the money might create unintentional secularization.

Another concern is that religious organizations are no more trustworthy than the secular ones when it comes to managing funding (Homeless Conference 2001). Therefore, Wilson (2001), among others, fear that the funds will not be used appropriately. Although many poor people see religion as a support mechanism, it does not necessarily make the religious organizations more apt to deal with poverty and its associated problems. The President believes "that religious programs can transform the lives of drug addicts, criminals, welfare recipients and troubled teenagers and that it can do so for less money than government programs" (Goodstein, 2001:A12). However, according to Professor Byron R. Johnson, a Social Science Professor for the Center for Research on Religion and Urban Civil Society at the University of Pennsylvania, there is little reliable evidence on the effectiveness of religious programs, and even less empirical evidence showing that religious programs produce the best results (Goodstein, 2001).

CONCLUSION

In the end, the issues are not simply that there are fewer people on welfare, clearly there are. Questions about how one defines success is also important--such semantics detract from the real issues. On balance we think that leaving welfare does not necessarily mean becoming independent. Few who leave welfare for work are earning enough through wages alone to be better of in work than on welfare. As a result, around two-thirds of former recipients remain dependent on the government to meet their health care, child care, food, housing, and transportation needs. There should be no disagreement on these issues. Almost everyone agrees that moving people from welfare to work signifies progress of some kind, but an honest assessment would assert that this group has attained or perhaps can attain self-sufficiency. The real measure of success is how to turn dependence into self-reliance (Tanner 2001).

Is this possible or even realistic? Somehow we feel as though we are willing to help as long as someone is trying to make their lives better. However, where we fail is in our perceptions and definitions of what constitutes "trying." To most people, working is better than not working. However, there are conditions in which this is simply not the case. Until we address those issues, as well as addressing the problems of operationalizing "capable of working" and being realistic on what can be expected of those who can find a job, we will remain mired in the 'poverty is caused by individual pathology' discussion since we created workhouses in Boston generations ago.

Clearly, there will be some segments of the poor population who will not be able to meet a middle class definition of independence, for a variety of reasons. What is also clear is that they will require assistance from the government in some form, for some period of time. What we also may have to face is that for some clients, states may have to make long-term commitments to helping, something we are reluctant to do. If we are not willing to commit to helping poor families in the form of welfare, then we must also recognize that this problem will resurface in other areas.

For instance, in attempting to address the question "Are children better off because of welfare reform?" there are not fewer children who are poor, only fewer who are receiving assistance. As was articulated by others, there is no essential connection between a family leaving TANF and a family leaving poverty. But to more directly answer the question, it is simply not clear at this point how TANF has affected children. Of the studies of pre-TANF programs in states, two findings are of particular interest.

First, TANF's positive effects depend on improved income, not just increased employment. Without increased income, academic achievement and behavior of young and adolescent children were negatively affected. TANF programs that led to increased earnings but not increased incomes (because benefit losses offset earnings gains) show no clear positive effect on children (Anderson, Halter, and Gryzak 2004).

Second, studies showed a negative impact on TANF-type policies on rates of child maltreatment, particularly neglect. Between 1995 and 1999, the estimated number of children in foster care grew from 483,000 to 568,000 and increase of 85,000. As more single mothers went to work, there was an increase in child neglect, a pattern concentrated among the most disadvantaged, those with the fewest resources to overcome the combined effect of low wage work and welfare loss (O'Gorman 2002).

Studies also show a trend indicating that TANF grant reductions increased entries into the child welfare system. Trends also showed an increased delay in family reunification—employed mothers who experienced TANF grant reductions were reunified with their children nine times more slowly than other mothers. In short, the loss of benefits combined with low-wage employment appears to increase neglect (O'Gorman 2002).

Thus, it appears that homelessness is closely related to poverty and any changes implemented to help the poor, especially women and children, will have an impact on the homeless population and their service providers. While some states, such as Wisconsin, have made significant strides to greatly limit the problems of dependency among welfare recipients, a changing economy threatens the success stories seen thus far. More importantly, the problems relating to poverty and homelessness are found in the structural elements of the labor force. As long as the jobs available to poor mothers remain in the lowest paying sectors of the market, so low in fact, that a family cannot adequately survive, other measures will be necessary to fill the gap.

What must also be remembered is that these additional measures will only serve as temporary stopgap mechanisms and will accomplish little in the way of resolving one of the most chronic problems of our time. Programs such as Bush's faith-based initiative, while creative and potentially plausible, will not achieve the level of success promoted since these organizations are ill-equipped to deal with the chronicity of poverty. Furthermore, they ignore the infrastructure to make the necessary structural changes which could result in self- sufficiency for most poor women. Most important, the failures of welfare reform to reduce or minimize poverty will inevitably lead to the increase in other social problems. As was noted by O'Gorman (2002), while the number of welfare caseloads has been reduced, we have seen an increase in child welfare cases. While not a direct correlation, there is ample evidence to suggest that as one problem appears to be "solved" the nature of the problem is so complex that it merely transforms itself in some other way. Similarly, as we witness more poor families being reduced from welfare rolls, we will likely see an increase in the use of emergency shelters, soup kitchens, and other forms of assistance (Hilfiker 2004).

In many ways, the study of homeless women is also the study of poor women. The problems many welfare recipients experience are identical to those found among the homeless. In fact, homelessness and poverty for women are two sides of the same coin. In the next chapter, we explore the idea of transitional housing for homeless women as well as describe the setting in which the present study occurred.

REFERENCES:

Acs, G. and Loprest, P. 2001. *Initial Synthesis Report of the Findings from ASPE's "Leavers" Grants.* Washington, D.C.: U.S. Department of Health and Human Services.

Anderson, S., Halter, A. P., and Gryzlak, B. 2004. "Difficulties After Leaving TANF: Inner City Women Talk About Reasons for Returning to Welfare." *Social Work,* 49(2):185-195.

_____, A. P., Julnes, G., and Schuldt, R. 2000.. "Job Stability and Wage Progression Patterns Among Early TANF Leavers." *Journal of Sociology and Social Welfare,* 27(4):39-58.

Banfield, E. 1970. *The Unheavenly City: Revisited.* Chicago: University of Chicago Press.

Becker, E. 2001. "Bush's Plan to Aid Religious Groups Is Faulted." *New York Times* http://www.nytimes.com/2001/04/27/politics/27FAIT.html?searchpv=site08.

Bernstein, J. and Greenberg, M. 2001. "Reforming Welfare Reform." *American Prospect* 12 no1: 10-16.

Bernstein, A. and Starr, A. 2002. "Welfare Reform: Round 2: Keeping Poor Moms Working Won't be Cheap." *Business Week,* June 24, p.60.

Blau, P. 1992. *The Visible Poor.* New York: Oxford University Press.

Buckstead, J. 2001. "Letter to Community Action Executive Directors." http://www.nacaa.org/FBOletter.doc.

Bush, G. W. 2001. "Rallying the Armies of Compassion." United States Government Printing Office.

"Bush's Faith-Based Office. (George W. Bush establishes Office for Faith-based and Community Initiatives." *Christian Century* 118 (5): 9.

"Bush Rallies Support for 'Faith-Based' Services package." *CNN* Online. Internet Explorer.May52001.Available: http://www.conn.com/2001/ALLPOLITICS/stories/01/30/bush.faith/index.html.

Butterbaugh, L. 2004. "More Pain Less Gain: Reauthorizing Welfare." *Off Our Backs,* 34(1-2):17-20.

"Charitable Choice." *Christian Century*118 (5): 67.

Collins, S. Goldberg, G. 1999. "South Carolina's Welfare Reform: More Rough than Right." *Social Policy,* Spring. http://vweb.hwwilsonweb.com.

Darden, C. 2001. "ACLU Worried about Bush's Faith-Based Initiative." *CNN* Online.Available: http://www.cnn.com/2001/ALLPOLITICS/stories/01/30/aclu.faith/index.html.

Edelhoch, M. 1999. "South Carolina's Welfare Reform" *Social Policy,* Spring. http://vweb.hwwilsonweb.com/cgi-bin/webclient

Edin, K. and Lein, L. 1997. *Making Ends Meet: How Mothers Survive Welfare and Low-Wage Work.* New York: Russell Sage Foundation.

Edwards, C. 2001 "The Truth about Charitable Choice." *Insight on the News 17 (12): 22.*

"Exposing the Poverty Line." *Poverty, Income and Wealth, August 9, 2001.* http://www.epn.org/ideacentral/welfare.

"Faith-Based Experiment. (United States Office of Faith-Based and Community Initiatives)." *The Christian Century 118 (5): 5*

"Faith-based Initiative: Current Status. Part 1: House passes Faith-based Initiatives Act." *US Government Information/ Resources* Online. Internet explorer. July 19, 2001. Available: http://usgovinfo.about.com/library/weekly/aa053001a.htm.

"Faith-based Questions. (Newly established Office of Faith-Based and Community Initiatives)." *The Christian Century* 118 (7): 10.

Friedman, T. J. 2002. "How States Are Spending Their Welfare Money—Or Not." *Dollars and Sense,* March, pp.46-48.

Froomkin, D. 1998. "Welfare's Changing Face. *Washington Post*, July 23rd.
http://www.washingtonpost.com/wp-srv/politics/welfare.

Garfinkel, I. and McLanahan, S. S. 1986. *Single Mothers and their Children: A
New American Dilemma* Washington DC: The Urban Institute Press.

Glennon, F. 2000. "Blessed be the Ties that Bind? The Challenge of Charitable
Choice to Moral Obligation." *Journal of Church and State* 42 (4): 825.

Goodstein, L. 2001. "Church-Based Projects Lack Data on Results." *New York Times*
National Report: A12.

Green, J. 2000. "Tough Sanctions, Tough Luck." *American Prospect,* July 3rd.
http://www.vweb.hwwilsonweb.com

Haney, L., March, M. 2003. "Married Fathers and Caring Daddies: Welfare Reform and
the Discursive Politics of Paternity." *Social Problems*, 50(4):461-482.

Harris, K. M. 1996. "Life After Welfare: Women, Work, and Repeat Dependency."
American Sociological Review, 61:407-426.

Hilfiker, D. 2004. "On Poverty: Despite Massive Wealth, The United States is
Abandoning its Poor Citizens." *The Other Side*, 40(2):11-19.

Holcomb, P., and Thompson, T. 2000. *State Welfare-to-Work Policies for People with
Disabilities: Implementation Challenges and Considerations*. Washington, D.C.:
United States Department of Health and Human Services.

Homeless Conference in Greenville, SC. 28 September 2001.

House of Representatives. 2001 (House) "Congressional Record" From the
Congressional Record Online via GPO. Access [wais.access.gpo.gov] Page:
H4222-H4281 July 19.

Jencks, C. 2004. "Liberal Lessons from Welfare Reform" *The American Prospect*
13(13):A9-13.

Kandula, N. R., Grogan, C. M., and Lauderdale, D. S. 2004. "The Unintended Impact of
Welfare Reform on the Medicaid Enrollment of Eligible Immigrants." *Health
Services Research*, 39(5):1509-1527.

Koralek, R. and Pindus, N. 2001. *South Carolina Family Independence Program Process
Evaluation Report of Overall Findings, Context and Methods*. Washington, D.C.:
The Urban Institute.

Lee, R. and Curran, L. 2003. "Servicing the 'Hard-to-Serve:" The Use of Clinical
Knowledge in Welfare Reform." *Journal of Sociology and Social Welfare*,
30(13):59-80.

Lenkowsky,L. 2001. *Ending Welfare as We Knew It*. Washington, D.C.:Hudson
Institute. www.hudson.org/wpc/LESLENK.
_____.2001. "Funding the Faithful: Why Bush is Right." *Commentary*.
http://vweb.hwwilsonweb.com

Levesque, R. 2001. "Mis-Diagnosing Poor People." *Policy Evaluation* 7 no 2: 15-
21.

Lindsey, E. W. 1998. "Service Providers' Perception of Factors that Help or Hinder
Homeless Families." *Families in Society: The Journal of Contemporary Human
Services* 78 (2): 160-173.

Massing, M. 2000. "Ending Poverty as We Know it: a Report from Washington
State." *American Prospect* 11 no15: 30-38.

Matsui, E. and Chuman, J. 2001. "The Case against Charitable Choice." *The*

Humanist 61 (1): 31.

Miller, M. 1995. "The War on Poverty: A PBS Special." *Social Policy* 25:53-61.
 Poverty: 2000 Highlights United States Census Bureau. Available:
 http://www.census.gov/hhes/poverty/poverty00/pov00hi.html.

Murray, C. 1984. *Losing Ground*. Cambridge, MA: Harvard University Press.

Nather, D. 2001. "Diminished Faith-Based Initiative Heads Towards House."
 Congressional Quarterly 59:1687-1689.

O'Gorman, A. 2002. "Playing by the Rules and Still Losing Ground." *America*
 187(3):12.

Ooms, T. 2002. "Marriage Plus: Most People Agree That It's Healthy For Kids to Grow
 Up in a Two-Parent Family." *The American Prospect*, 13(7): 24-30.

Palen, J. J. 2001. *Social Problems for the Twenty-First Century*. New York: McGraw-
 Hill.

Pavetti, L. A. 1993. *The Dynamics of Welfare and Work: Exploring the Process by Which
 Women Work Their Way Off Welfare*. Unpublished doctoral dissertation, Harvard
 University, Cambridge, MA.

Piven, F. F. 1999. "What's Really Happening in South Carolina?" *Social Policy*, Spring.
 "Revised Welfare Rules Would Hinder Educational Pursuit" *Black Issues in
 Higher Education* 20(3):7.

"President Urges Support for America's Charities: Remarks by the President." *White
 House*. Available: http://www.whitehouse.gov/news/releases/2001/11/20011120-
 5.html

Rector, R. 2000. *Broadening the Reform*. Washington, D.C.: The Heritage Foundation.

Renwick, T. J. 1998. *Poverty and Single Parent Families: A Study of Minimal
 Household Budgets* New York: Garland Publishing, Inc.

Rossi, P. 1989. *Without Shelter: homelessness in the 1980's* New York: Priority Press
 Publications.

Schwartz, J. 2001. "What the Poor Need Most." *The American Enterprise* 12 (no2):
 52-53.

Shank, H. and Reed, W. 1995. "A Challenge to Suburban Evangelical Churches:
 Theological Perspectives on Poverty in America." *Journal of Interdisciplinary
 Studies* 7 (no1-2): 119-134.

Sherman, A. 1999. "Children's Poverty in America." *Forum for Applied Research
 and Public Policy* 14 no. 4: 68-73.

Sherman, A. L. 2000. "The Lessons of W-2." *The Public Interest*.

Skocpol, T. 1995. *Social Policy in the United States: Future Possibilities in
 Historical Perspective* Princeton: Princeton University Press.

Spain, D. 2001. "Redemptive Places, Charitable Choice, and Welfare Reform."
 Journal of American Planning 67 (3): 249-269.

State of South Carolina, 1998. *Legislative Audit Council Report Summary on Impact of
 the South Carolina Family Independence Act: 1996-1998*.
 http://www.lpitr.state.sc.us/reports/lafi98bf.htm

Streeter, R. 2001. *Happy Fifth Birthday, Welfare Reform*. Washington, D.C.:
 Hudson Institute.

Svanoe, T. 2001. "Charitable Choice Dance Begins: Controversy over Government
 Funding of Religious Charities." *Christianity Today* 45 (5): 28.

Tanner, M. 2001. "Welfare Reform: How Successful?" *World and I* 16(10):1-4.

Tweedie, J., Reichert, D., and O'Connor, M. 2000. "Tracking Recipients After They Leave Welfare." Washington, D.C.: National Conference of State Legislatures.

United States Department of Health and Human Services. 2002. "Final Rule: Summary." http://www.acf.dhhs.gov/programs/ofa/exsumcl.htm

_____. 2002. Introduction and Executive Summary. *Third Annual Report to Congress*. Washington, D.C.: U.S. Government Printing Office. http://acf.dhs.gov/programs/Opre/annual3execsum.htm

_____. 2001. "Temporary Assistance for Needy Families." *Administration for Children and Families*. Washington, D.C.: U.S. Government Printing Office.

_____. 1996. *State Guidance for the Temporary Assistance for Needy Families Program*. Washington, D.C.: U.S. Government Printing Office.

Wax, A. L. 2000. " Rethinking Welfare Rights: Reciprocity Norms, Reactive Attitudes, and the Political Economy of Welfare Reform." *Law and Contemporary Problems* 63 (no1-2): 257-297.

"Will the Office of Faith-Based Initiatives Fund All Religions?" *Fund Raising Management* 32 (2): 17.

Wilson, W. J. 1996. *When Work Disappears: The World of the New Urban Poor*. New York: Alfred A. Knopf.

"Working Toward Independence: Achievements of the Welfare Reform Law of 1996." 2002. *The White House*. http://www.whitehours.gov/news/releases/2002/02/print/welfare-book-02.html.

The History of Homeless Women

Robert Hartmann McNamara
Department of Political Science and Criminal Justice, The Citadel

Carrie Flagler
Department of Sociology, Furman University

Homelessness has existed in the United States since its formation. Hopper states, "[t]hroughout most of our history the homeless have been regarded at least with indifference and often with contempt, fear, and loathing" (Rossi 1989: 17). Both males and females have been victims of homelessness throughout history, but more information about males is available, as "[h]omeless women have been something of a sociological mystery" (Golden 1992 : 151). This lack of documentation pertaining to women results in missing information within this book and others regarding homelessness among women. These gaps are typically filled with general information about the concept of homelessness, the majority of which pertains specifically to males. It is uncertain exactly why homeless women have been largely ignored, but the reality is that they have been overlooked throughout most of history.

When they have been noted, homeless women throughout history have been frowned upon, despised, and labeled as witches, prostitutes, and the stereotype that survives today, the mentally ill bag lady (Glasser 1994; Ralston 1996).

COLONIAL AMERICA

Colonial America's homeless population consisted primarily of single men and women. Typically men served as artisans, mariners and laborers while women played the role of domestic servants in society (Wright 1989). Women's position in society was defined by their role as a mother and wife, and those who did not fulfill these roles were regarded with contempt and considered undeserving of help or relief. Poor women were often denied residency and economic relief because they did not conform to society's idea of the family ethic. Unmarried women had a difficult time proving to town officials that they were self-sufficient and moral--virtually any woman living on her own was immediately stereotyped as immoral, a probable prostitute, and a disease to society (Golden 1992). The relief systems in place during colonial times were composed of a combination of local and religious assistance, which provided enough support to prevent the deserving poor from resorting to begging (Hopper and Baumohl 1996).

The colonial relief systems for the poor were modeled after the British system of Elizabethan Poor Laws (Rossi 1989), but vagrancy and settlement laws within America were made even stricter (Golden 1992). In Colonial America, relief provided to the poor was tied to settlement rights. Settlement rights were granted to children born into previously settled families or to individuals or families that succeeded in petitioning the town to settle there. These rights were granted depending on the ability of a family or individual to be self-sufficient as well as the length of time a family had been residents of a town.[3] When town members with established settlement rights fell upon hard times, the town helped these individuals, but those denied settlement rights were ignored.

The classification of the homeless and poor as either "deserving" or "undeserving," distinguished between who was and was not eligible to receive relief. The undeserving poor typically consisted of paupers (the extremely poor surviving solely on charity), vagrants, and runaway slaves, while the deserving poor were respectable individuals falling on hard times with no family or social networks to turn to for support (Hopper and Baumohl 1996). The undeserving poor were denied outdoor relief (direct cash assistance) and were often sent to almshouses. Almshouses were established to protect and help those who were truly needy while simultaneously rehabilitating the undeserving poor. Residents of almshouses were expected to work so as to remain active parts of society and avoid the "disease" of idleness. However, the conditions that existed within the almshouses were less than ideal: overcrowded quarters, illness, and the presence of alcoholism and mental illness among many residents (Baum and Burnes 1993).

Various methods were established throughout colonial towns to control the size of relief rolls. In highly populated areas, individuals were employed to walk door-to-door questioning town members about strangers in an effort to have them removed. In the 18th century, towns sent the poor to workhouses and poor farms, which served the same purpose as almshouses. Residents of these institutions were expected to work for the relief and public aid they received. The poor were also sent to families in need of labor to work as indentured servants. The most common procedure for dealing with the poor was the process of "warning out." This was a sort of banishment that resulted in many individuals becoming wanderers or transients as they were continuously rejected from settling anywhere. In Massachusetts, the names and information of potential town members were presented to the colonial courts, and upon judicial review, a person could be commanded to leave a town (Wright 1989). Strict rules were in place distinguishing between those allowed to settle in an area. Individuals deemed unacceptable by societal standards, and those who would likely need assistance, composed the majority of the population warned out (Golden 1992). By not granting an individual settlement rights, he or she was placed in a geopolitical limbo, with no one responsible for his or her care. When warned out of a town, individuals were often physically removed from the city and taken to the jurisdiction boundary where they were left to fend for themselves. This method of dealing with the poor was later known in the 20th century as *Greyhound Relief*. While the minutes from many town meetings throughout the 17th century mention a concern about the growth of the homeless population and how such situations were dealt with, there was no mention of the problems and dangers for those who were warned out of town (Rossi 1989).

The practice of warning out unwanted or problem individuals created a large transient population of typically young, single individuals, many of whom were formerly indentured servants (Golden 1992). Wright (1989) believes as many women as men were warned out of colonial towns and Golden (1992) found that possibly half of the vagrant population of the 18th century was composed of women. Female vagrants were usually young unmarried mothers, divorced or abandoned wives, or older widows. This transient

---

[3] Usually one or more years of self-sufficiency was required to obtain residency rights.

poor was a group large enough to cause alarm and inspire legal measures in many towns of Colonial America.

NINETEENTH CENTURY

The 19th century experienced multiple economic downturns, each of which resulted in increased homelessness and overwhelming demands on public relief rolls. While this century was characterized by a lack of sympathy for the poor and the homeless, better records were kept, resulting in more knowledge of the 19th century poor than those of previous times (Rossi 1989, Rossi 1989a). During this era, poverty was connected with criminality, insanity, and other moral defects creating " the morphology of evil" (Golden 1992). There was little tolerance of the homeless and the police often blamed crimes on the homeless in order to solve them (Rossi 1989a). Poverty was seen as a moral condition that resulted from inferiority, weakness or laziness, and offering relief to the poor was thought to encourage idleness and only increase the problem of homelessness (Golden 1992).

While helping the poor was not encouraged, some institutions were available to provide relief. Charities were typically religiously-based and able to provide for only a small number of people. These institutions distinguished between the worthy and unworthy poor, helping only those thought to be acceptable, which usually included the sick, the elderly, and children. Unmarried mothers, abandoned wives, and widows in a nonreputable neighborhood were denied relief on the grounds that they did not uphold the woman's responsibility to the family ethic. Women were viewed as part of a cult of domesticity, and those who did not comply with the family ethic were deemed undeserving and immoral (Golden 1992). If the early part of the century saw large numbers of transient individuals who were ignored and offered little assistance, the late 19th century homeless were gathered together to live in skid row areas (Rossi 1989a). Skid row areas emerged in most major cities to house homeless and transient individuals searching for seasonal industrial work.

> The name derives from the street in Seattle that paralleled the log chute, or 'skid,' that the lumberjacks used to slide their cuttings down to the sawmill below on the waterfront of Puget Sound. In time the area around the 'skid' became characterized by its shanties, cheap rooming houses and saloons. Somehow, in the cant of homeless men, the 'road' became a 'row,' 'skid row' became a synonym for the bottom rung of the urban social ladder... (Miller 1991:46).

Skid rows typically formed on the outskirts of towns to hide the poor so their presence would not be obvious to the townspeople.

Municipal lodging houses emerged in the 19th century to supplement the almshouses and work farms in sheltering, punishing, and deterring the homeless (Baum and Burnes 1993). Municipal lodging houses required those who could work to do so, and created many strict rules to prevent laziness and ensure that only those willing to participate actively in society would receive help. "On the whole, supporters and administrators of the municipal lodging house saw it first as a weapon against unwanted tramps and the demoralized unemployed, and only second as a service to a legitimate sector of the laboring population" (Schneider 1989: 96).

Municipal lodging houses proved ineffective for a number of reasons. While these houses had strict rules, they varied from city to city, resulting in different expectations and varying methods of enforcing rules. Other options for housing were available in the commercial market, resulting in a decreased demand on municipal housing as individuals decided not to deal with the rules and regulations, and instead found cheap housing in other areas (Schneider 1989).

Society defined the transient population of the 19th century as *tramps, hobos* and *bums*. Transients wandered from town to town typically finding work with railroads or within the expanding commercial agriculture industry (Rossi 1989). Transients were not respected by or accepted within society, and were warned out of towns when work ran out. The terms *tramp, hobo* and *bum* are often used interchangeably in describing the transient population, but distinct characteristics exist between these three groups. The term *hobo* stems from the early nineteenth century itinerant workers who traveled to find labor as railroad builders, canal diggers, lumberjacks, and farm hands. The term hobo had a relatively positive connotation compared to bums and tramps. Hobos were seen as aggressive workingmen with meaning and purpose in their lives. They published literature, such as the pamphlet *Hobo News,* and books that described the excitement of the road (Golden 1992). *Bum* is a term used later in history as the population of hobos declined. In the early 20th century, as machines replaced manpower in the agricultural field, hobos were left without the seasonal work they depended on for survival. Thus the hobos of the early 1920's became bums. They were unable to find work and thus stopped searching, depending on handouts and begging for survival. The term *tramp* was first used during 1870's when many transient workers lost their jobs as a result of the Depression of 1873. Tramps were considered "lazy, dishonest, and menacing to ordered society" (Golden 1992: 135).

Tramps were more common than hobos or bums in the 19th century. While it was thought at the time that the majority of tramps were men, it appears that many women were among the population of tramps, the majority of which disguised themselves as men. These women often disguised themselves to avoid being singled out, harassed or discovered. Disguised female tramps were viewed with disdain because they were not only defined by their sexuality, but they were also shunned because they exhibited power and assertiveness by disguising themselves as opposed to playing the proper woman's role of passivity. In the New York winter of 1875-1876, approximately 4,310 tramps applied for public aid. Of these tramps, 6.3% were found to be women (Golden 1992).

The onset of the Civil War diminished the number of homeless individuals as many unemployed, poor, and homeless were employed into both the Confederate and Union armies. When the war ended, these individuals returned to their lives of poverty along with the addition of needy widows, orphans, freed slaves, and injured war veterans (Baum and Burnes 1993). Local charitable organizations and relief programs were overwhelmed, forcing the federal government to become involved in the care of the poor and the homeless for the first time. Following the Civil War, men returned to their previous roles and jobs, pushing women out of the marketplace. As the number of jobs available to females decreased, women were forced to find work in cities as secretaries, waitresses, and even prostitutes (Hopper and Baumohl 1996).

The 19th century presented many dangers to unsheltered homeless women ranging from abuse to rape and death. Women on the edge of poverty often resorted to scrounging for items in the trash and working as street finders or street sellers. Street sellers were typically elderly widows or women on the verge of destitution who failed at or were unable to work. These women stocked light and cheap items such as matches, pincushions, pins, and needles to sell on the street for a minimal profit that would only provide a cheap room and very little food. Street finders were considered the predecessors of today's homeless, who earn money collecting bottles and cans. The street finders of the 19th century made a living by collecting items such as bones, rags, cigar ends, and fresh dog excrement used to purify leather. Single women were also sometimes forced to send their children to the streets to beg for money and food (Golden 1992).

Women traveling alone on the roads faced many of the same concerns as homeless women in cities, such as food, money, and the dangers presented by men. Rape and abuse were common crimes committed against homeless women. Men often viewed homeless women as common property and had little respect for them. Some women voluntarily used their sexuality as a means to get what they needed from men, such as food or "hitching". On the other hand, many did not voluntarily give themselves up to men, but rather "accepted the fact that it was easier for a women to get along on the road if she was not too particular" (Golden 1992: 140).

Alcohol was a strong contributor to homelessness in the 1800's, as women either deserted or widowed often turned to alcohol for comfort and help in handling their situation. Homeless women had little hope for sustaining themselves, and any woman abandoned or widowed by her husband was doomed to eviction as a result of her inability to pay rent. During this time period, a homeless women on the streets could expect to be arrested for vagrancy. Once released from prison, she would return to the streets to again be arrested, and eventually sent to a poorhouse (if she were older) or to a poor farm (if she was young and able to work).

Prostitution became a more common practice during the 19th century, as more women were forced to provide for themselves and were unable to find adequate work. In 1858, Dr. William Sanger conducted a survey of 2,000 prostitutes in New York and found that over 25% of the women claimed they felt pressured into prostitution as a result of the destitution they were experiencing. He also found that the remainder had jobs but chose prostitution as a means to make more money. Many women turned to a life of prostitution to escape the poor treatment they received as domestic servants, the insufficient wages, and a lack of employment opportunities (Golden 1992).

TWENTIETH CENTURY
1900 to 1930

During the 1920's, the demand for labor decreased as a result of technological advancements. Unemployment was high and job opportunities were low, sending many people into a downward spiral ending in poverty (Rossi 1989a). Skid row communities continued to grow and develop, reaching their peak population during the first decades of the twentieth century. By the end of the century, skid row communities existed in all major cities. Nels Anderson, a transient worker turned sociologist wrote *The Hobo: Sociology of the Homeless Man* in 1923. Anderson argued that transients played a functional role in society by providing temporary labor where and when it was needed. He also argued that tramps and hobos were different from bums, who did not want to work and instead chose to beg or steal (Rossi 1989; Rossi 1989a).

The Great Depression and World War II

The Great Depression began with the collapse of the Stock Market in October 1929. The onset of the Depression greatly increased the homeless population and caused the number of individuals in skid rows to increase dramatically (Miller 1991). Few Americans were exempt from the suffering created by the Depression, as evidenced by the fact that unemployment drastically increased during the Depression, and by 1932, approximately 25% of the population was unemployed (Miller 1991).

Many of the recently dislocated built shantytowns in their communities so as to remain in the area while others turned to a life on the road. Many community residents were resentful of the homeless population's continuous demands for help. Feeling overtaxed financially and emotionally, many communities denied relief to transients on the grounds that they were unattached outsiders (Golden 1992). Homeless individuals continued to be classified as deserving or undeserving of aid, the latter of which consisted of "worthy" women, children, the elderly, or the blind. By 1934, twenty-eight different states provided relief to these three groups (Golden 1992).

During the Depression, the composition of the homeless population changed. Soon, the majority of the homeless were young, single men who moved from town to town looking for work. They often lived with their families prior to becoming homeless, but either chose to leave or were asked to leave so as not to further burden the family because they were unable to find work in the struggling economies of their hometowns (Rossi 1989).

Prior to the Depression, relief for the poor was provided by private charities, donations, and the local government. These funds allowed for outdoor relief and the operation of municipal lodging houses and poorhouses. With the onset of the Depression, however, it became apparent that local governments and charities could no longer support the poor, and the federal government became more involved in the problems of the nation's poverty and homelessness (Baum and Burnes 1993). The Federal Emergency Relief Act was passed in 1933, and it created the Federal Transients Bureau, which helped states fund shelters and meals for non-local transients (Snow and Anderson 1993). This first government involvement was a big step in addressing the nation's homeless and impoverished and "marked a change in how the nation viewed its social responsibility" (Miller 1991: 64).

While there was no exact count of the homeless conducted during this time period, evidence for the growth of the homeless segment of the population was seen in the records of relief agencies. For example, in 1933 the Federal Emergency Relief Administration housed 125,000 people in its transient camps (Rossi 1989; Wright 1989). A 1934 survey of social agencies estimated 200,000 homeless people during this time, while some estimates were as high as one and a half million during the worst years of the Depression. Glasser (1994) found estimates that 30,000 women took to the roads during the Depression to join the ranks of the transients. The March 1933 census, conducted in 765 U.S. cities, found 1.25 million people to be homeless, and women accounted for

150,000 of these individuals. Golden (1992) argues that the number of women are undercounted in this study because many women were not in the shelters where the counts took place. The majority were sent to furnished rooms or cheap hotels because most cities did not have shelters available for women. A better estimate is that 300,000 women were homeless at this time (Golden 1992).

Schubert (1934) studied the transient population in Buffalo, New York. He gathered data on 20,000 individuals applying for aid. Schubert found the transient population to be "predominantly young (median age was 30), unattached (89% single) white (82%) males (98%)" (Rossi 1989: 23). These transients had an education level slightly below average and had been out of work for approximately one and a half years. Transients were refused relief in towns and were often removed from a city or kept from entering it. Similar to Colonial America, homeless individuals were often physically removed from territories using the aforementioned Greyhound Relief. During the Depression, New York City spent more money on Greyhound Relief than was spent on direct benefits (Rossi 1989).

While Schubert found the vast majority of transients in Buffalo to be male in 1934, there were still a number of homeless and transient females during the Depression. As previously mentioned, the number of women in poverty was underestimated in part due to the fact that agencies sent women to cheap hotels since there were few women's shelters. Women were also undercounted because they avoided shelters since the majority of shelters adopted a policy of attempting to send any single woman back to her home or to any known relatives. The rationale for this was that shelter officials believed women belonged at home with their families. Moreover, African-American homeless women were not counted because agencies refused to acknowledge their need for help and simply turned them away.

Large municipal housing for homeless women was available only in large cities where the necessity of settlement rights to receive help complicated a woman's ability to receive relief. In New York, settlement rights of a woman were tied to her husband, and therefore she was considered settled only where he was. Even if a woman was abandoned by her husband or separated from him, unless they were legally divorced, she was considered settled wherever he was, whether she knew where he was or not. Without settlement rights, a woman was unable to receive public charity and the agency could only send her away or to her family (Golden 1992).

The most desperate homeless women of this time were the elderly. These women were worse off than the young and were even more invisible. Unlike the younger homeless women, who had a chance at becoming self-sufficient in time, the elderly needed permanent care. A 1933 study by social workers in Philadelphia found less than half of the elderly homeless women had relatives, the majority of which refused to help their kin. While Schubert found that the vast majority of transients in 1934 in Buffalo, New York were male, there were still many homeless and transient females during the Depression (Golden 1992).

Skid rows were unable to accommodate the large number of transients entering major cities, and thus emergency shelters were set up to house the transient population flooding into cities. Emergency relief shelters usually provided shelter only for a month, and many of the homeless and transients could not find a job, much less a means of housing themselves after only one month in a shelter. The Federal Emergency Relief

Administration created several transient camps during the Depression. These shelters were usually outside towns where the unsightly conditions would not bother citizens. This made it difficult for residents to access the few jobs that were available at the time. The camps were also often reserved for older men, usually over the age of 40, who were considered unemployable, further limiting the number of people able to receive help (Rossi 1989).

Once the United States became involved in the second World War in 1941, the Depression ended and the number of homeless and the unemployed dropped drastically as the American population enlisted in the army or found jobs in the booming industrial market created by the war. Skid row areas remained for the few transients left behind, but despite the continued presence of homeless individuals, many programs and shelters for the homeless were closed. The homeless that remained during and immediately after World War II, though few in number, were left to fend for themselves with little support or help offered to them (Rossi 1989).

1950's and 1960's

During the mid-twentieth century, while there were few homeless women, society explained the phenomenon as either those individuals who posed as female hobos and bums, women who did not want to deal with or could not maneuver the complexities of the welfare system, or women who were released from mental hospitals during the period of deinstitutionalization (Golden 1992). Despite the decrease in homelessness during the war, skid rows remained a common feature of the urban landscape, which affected the value of those areas. With the onset of urban renewal, cities were renovated and the unsightly low-income areas were replaced by modern offices, buildings and apartments (Rossi 1989).

However, as cities expanded, the unsightly skid row areas became neighbors to respectable businesses and buildings. Clearly, skid rows stood out as stark contrasts to urban progress, but it was unclear what to do with the residents once the skid rows were demolished. Between 1958 and 1964, the Housing and Home Finance Agency, which would later become the Department of Housing and Urban Development, provided grants to study these areas in the hopes of developing a solution. In 1960, Blumberg and his associates found that Philadelphia's skid rows consisted of 2,000 homeless individuals. Donald Bogue used 1950 Census data to estimate that 100,000 homeless people lived in skid rows in 41 large cities throughout the U.S. in 1950. Another study by Bogue, an actual count of Chicago's homeless skid row population, provided a more accurate count than his estimate in 41 cities. Bogue found 12,000 people living in skid rows in Chicago, most of which were men, and no more than three percent of this population were women (Rossi 1989). While homeless women were few in number during the 1950's, those present were characterized by their invisibility within society. These women did not want to draw attention to themselves and stayed away from heavily populated and visible areas (Golden 1992).

During the 1960's, the number of homeless women slowly began to increase, primarily as a result of increased divorce rates and the deinstiutionalization of mental hospitals. Divorce rates began to rise in the 1960's, continuing until the early 1980's, which created an increase in the number of homeless women. When a couple with children divorced, the female usually gained custody and responsibility for the children, creating a financially difficult situation for many women (Timmer & Eitzen 1994). Female headed households were at an increased risk of poverty compared to male headed houses (Ferman, Kornbluh & Haber 1968). In 1969, Jencks found that "91 percent of women with extremely low personal incomes were married," but the number dropped to 89% in 1979 and 82% in 1989 (Jencks 1995: 55). The increase in divorce rates during the 1960's not only led to more women becoming homeless and poor, but also to an increased number of children living in poverty. Jencks states that in 1969, only 16% of all working-age, unmarried women with extremely low incomes had children. By 1979, 23% of these women had dependent children, and in 1989, this increased to 31%. The decline in the standard of living for single mothers, beginning in the 1960's, led to increased numbers of females and children living in poverty (Jencks 1995).

The process of deinstitutionalization began in the late 1940's and early 1950's, and took place in five stages over a thirty year period, and is arguably, one of the main reasons the homeless population began to grow in the 1960's and boomed in the early 1980's. The first round of deinstitutionalization resulted from changes and advancements in the treatment of patients. The advent of new drugs, namely Thorazine, revolutionized the treatment and release of patients. Thorazine, a tranquilizing drug used to treat psychiatric disorders, allowed thousands of previously hospitalized patients the chance to participate as active members of the community. After the deveopment of this new drug, the number of patients in state hospitals dropped by 25%, although the fact that the effectiveness of hospitalization was beginning to be questioned may also account for part of the drop in numbers (Jencks 1995).

The process of deinstitutionalization stemmed from more than the advent of new drugs, however. The second round of deinstitutionalization occurred in 1965 when Congress established Medicaid for poor patients, but the costs of patients in state hospitals were not covered since they were already paid for by the individual states. While this decreased the number of patients in state hospitals, the number of patients in short-term psychiatric care at general hospitals increased since Medicaid covered these expenses (Jencks 1995).

The third round of deinstitutionalization began in 1972, when Congress passed a federally financed program known as Supplemental Security Income (SSI). Those eligible for SSI consisted of individuals who were unable to keep a job as a result of physical or mental disabilities. SSI provided its recipients with a monthly check, food stamps, and Medicaid. In 1992, the value of these benefits was $500 a month (Jencks 1995).

The fourth round of deinstitutionalization occurred in the 1970's as advocates of the deinstitutionalization movement turned to the courts to prevent physicians from committing patients to mental hospitals. Reformers attempted to convince the public of the inhumanity and cruelty of mental institutions. This movement was successful, and in the 1970's it was understood that mental illness alone was not a sufficient justification for institutionalization unless the individual posed a serious threat to themselves or others (Jencks 1995). Thus, the push for deinstitutionalization stemmed in part from a concern of the rights of patients who were confined and also from the idea that the medical conditions of some patients could be better served by local centers that would provide treatment while also allowing individuals to live a normal life. In New York, as well as other major U.S. cities, the money that was to finance these outpatient centers never surfaced, and those who were released from mental institutions were given few options and opportunities to receive the help they needed to assimilate into mainstream society (Golden 1992).

The fifth and final round of deinstitutionalization took place in the 1980's when state officials urged hospitals to cut their costs. In order to cut budgets, psychiatric wards across the country were closed and individuals committed at the time were released, directly resulting in an increased number of mentally ill people on the streets. More women than men were patients in mental hospitals at the time of deinstitutionalization, and this movement increased the number of homeless women on the streets during the late 20th century. These new homeless women were more visible than in the past, in part because there were more of them, but also because there were not enough shelters and agencies available to help these women and care for their specific problems. The increase in number and visibility of these homeless women resulted in the stereotype of homeless women as mentally ill bag ladies (Jencks 1995).

1970's

Homelessness increased throughout the 1970's due to a number of factors, including a world-wide recession, the continued deinstitutionalization of mental institutions, decreased marriage rates, and a lack of housing (Ralston 1996). Marriage rates declined between the 1970's and 1980's. The decline of marriage rates paralleled the decrease in men's wages, making it more difficult for a man to support a family. Marriage rates also declined due to an improved job market for women. As women were granted more job opportunities and advancements, they became more careful about the person they chose to marry. No longer did women need to marry for financial security, and many chose a career over marriage or delayed marriage in order to have a fulfilling career.

A change in sexual norms of society was also partially responsible for the decline in marriages during the 1970's. Prior to the 1970's, few communities approved of sexual relations outside of marriage, but as society became less conservative, sexual involvement outside of matrimonial vows was more accepted and common. This liberalization of society allowed men and women to satisfy their sexual desires without the bonds of marriage, thus decreasing the number who chose to marry. Marriage lost its appeal due to other changing social factors, such as the growing uncertainty over the proper division of labor among households. Women were more educated and many were not content with the traditional household roles women had played in the past, and refused to accept marriage under similar terms or expectations. The decline in marriage during the 1970's increased the number of homeless women and children among low-income, low-educated populations. Despite the empowerment of women, marriage still served as a source of financial support. While many poorly educated and unskilled women married less, they found their inability to provide for the family drove them into poverty and homelessness (Jencks 1995).

Cheap single room units, known as *SRO's*, (Single Room Occupancy units) provided affordable housing for the elderly living on pensions, welfare recipients, and individuals who had previously lived in skid rows that were destroyed. SRO's were often a last resort for individuals and families on the fringes of destitution and homelessness. Many of the women living in these units suffered from mental or physical disorders but refused treatment. A 1976 report by Bahr and Garrett revealed the dangers women faced in shelters or SRO's in New York City. The women were often victims of street crimes, such as muggings and robbery, and their pleas to the police for protection often went unnoticed. Public women's shelters were avoided due to their depressing and dismal nature, but SRO's were not necessarily a better option than shelters. The women living in SRO's were in poor financial positions and under extreme stress, which led to the higher than average rate of alcohol consumption among this population (Golden 1992).

In the 1970's, many SRO's were destroyed sending men, women, and families to the streets. In the 1970's, approximately half of the SRO population was destroyed, totaling a loss of approximately one million units (Wright 1989), and between 1973 and 1983, four and a half million low-income housing units were destroyed (Blau 1992). In New York City, between 1970 and 1982, approximately 87% of the city's SRO's were lost, and across the nation former residents of these low-income housing units were left without shelter. At the same time low-income units were being destroyed, rent prices prevented individuals from finding affordable housing, resulting in more individuals living on the streets (Golden 1992).

During the 1970's, the definition of homelessness to the average American became one involving a deprivations of basic shelter and the homeless were more visible (Rossi 1989). Prior to this decade, the homeless remained out of sight, concentrated in skid rows or areas outside of towns. The new visible homeless were seen sleeping and living in public areas, such as railroad depots, bus stations, doorways, cardboard boxes and abandoned automobiles (Rossi 1989). As vagrancy was decriminalized and the number of skid rows demolished increased, the number of visible homeless rose. Without vagrancy laws, the homeless could wander through the streets of downtown without being arrested or sent to jail, and much of this wandering population was composed of females previously released from mental hospitals. It was during this time that the label of shopping bag lady became popular in describing the increased visible female homeless population (Golden 1992).

The late 1970's and 1980's were characterized by changes in the homeless population that resulted in this group being defined as the "new homeless." The new homeless were much more visible to the public, they were not as likely as the previous homeless to be employed, more minorities became homeless, and there was an increased number of women composing the homeless population (Rossi 1989). There were two phases of growth among the homeless during this decade. In the early 1980's, the portion of the population that was economically vulnerable grew, yet the odds of members of this population becoming homeless remained the same as before. In the latter portion of the decade, there was less growth of the economically vulnerable population, but the odds of these people becoming homeless was far greater than earlier in the 1980's (Jencks 1995). The homeless of the 1980's differed from those of previous decades due to their increased visibility within society. The homeless were not concentrated in skid rows, they were not arrested if they wandered streets, and they increasingly began to frequent populated areas (Glasser 1994).

The increase in homelessness resulted from many factors that had been building during the previous years. The increase in homelessness parallels an increase in the poverty rate, contributing to the many individuals becoming poor and later homeless. Golden (1992) claims homelessness was not a personal failure as much as it was due to the failure of the housing market. During the early 1980's, available cheap housing declined as rents rose, incomes dropped, and many people lost their jobs. The number of evictions increased and many individuals and families on the border between self-sufficiency and poverty crossed the line into homelessness. Little help was available to the homeless as programs to help the poor were eliminated or cut, federal housing subsidies declined, and few low-income housing units were constructed. Many Americans of the 1980's were sobered as people once thought exempt from poverty faced homelessness and destitution. The decade was characterized by the fact that people "like us" became homeless.

The number of homeless women rose greatly during the 1980's, and women were considered the poorest of the poor (Ralston 1996). By the middle of the decade one in four homeless persons was a woman (Wright 1989). Domestic violence contributed to the increased homelessness among women, and a 1988 study in New York found that 35% of women in the shelter system had been battered prior to becoming homeless. Changes in the labor market and the decline of marriages also increased the number of homeless women (Jencks 1995). Women were most commonly employed in clerical positions, with a distinct wage gap existing between the salaries of men and women (Timmer & Eitzen 1994).

The number of homeless families rose during the 1980's because, according to Jencks (1995), there were more single mothers, welfare recipients' purchasing power eroded, and the increased use and abuse of crack cocaine on the streets. The number of homeless single mothers with children increased during the 1980's, as women and children made up one-third to two-fifths of the homeless population (Wright 1989). Homeless women were typically younger than in previous decades, under the age of 40 (Golden 1992), and those with children often avoided shelters for fear of having their children taken away (Timmer & Eitzen 1994).

Women on the streets dealt with many indignities and stereotypes. The stereotypical homeless woman was a young, black mother on welfare who continuously birthed illegitimate children solely to receive additional welfare benefits. Street life was harder for women than men, and women faced problems and indignities that the male homeless were able to avoid. Issues of privacy were a concern, as it was harder for a woman to use a public restroom than a man, and women were more concerned with other issues, such as showering. As the number of low-skilled jobs decreased during this time period, obtaining employment became harder for all people, especially homeless women, who were unable to find employment without proper hygiene and clean clothes. If a woman walking along a street looked homeless, she was ridiculed and harassed, while a businesswoman or shopper walking on the same street was left alone. Living on the streets presented many dangers for women, as men often felt that women who lived on the streets were common property. Rape among homeless women was not uncommon, and the instability of these women's lives prevented them from receiving proper medical care, counseling, or police action (Golden 1992).

The concept of transitional housing was first introduced during the 1980's when it was discovered that the same women and children were readmitted to shelters time and time again. Glasser (1994) points out the fact that there were theoretically enough housing units available for the urban population, but the housing was too expensive to accommodate those who truly needed it. As more low-income housing was demolished and replaced with offices, quality apartments, and shops, more women and children lost their homes. Transitional housing programs aimed to help women and kids who were living doubled up or in shelters as well as those women who had a high risk of becoming homeless. Transitional housing programs differ throughout the country. Some offer counseling and help in finding a place to live while others provide individual apartments for women and their children as well as counseling (Glasser 1994).

As homelessness became more visible, an increasing number of studies were conducted to discover more about this population. A 1987 study by Burt and Cohen (Glasser 1994) found approximately 194,000 homeless adults using shelters and soup kitchens in large cities. Seventy-three percent of the homeless population studied was composed of single men, nine percent of single women, and nine percent of single women with at least one child in their care. Burt and Cohen also found that single, homeless women were typically non-white and the most educated of the homeless population. In 1989, these two researchers found that single homeless women and mothers with kids had the poorest levels of self-reported health, and the highest levels of hospitalization for mental illness (Glasser 1994).

CONCLUSION

Our description of the history of homelessness and of homeless women in particular, ends in the 1980's for a number of reasons. First of all, this decade marks the last major change in the composition and characteristics of the homeless. Since the emergence of the "new" homeless population, few significant changes have taken place.

Like the homeless of the 1980's, the decade of the 1990's saw an increased number of visible homeless living in public places, such as city streets, bus terminals, train stations, etc. The homeless population is concentrated in cities and the poor are still vulnerable to unemployment (Timmer and Eitzen 1994). The number of women who were homeless increased as well as the number of women with children living in poverty or without shelter. Ralston (1996) reported that women and their children composed 40% of the homeless population. As in the 1980's, the homeless of the 1990's were faced with housing problems, a discriminating wage gap in favor of men, and lack of affordable services such as childcare, which, in turn, made employment more difficult than under normal conditions (Timmer and Eitzen 1994).

Another reason for ending the history of homeless women in the 1980's stems from the fact that many of the previous chapters focus specifically on the problems and aspects of homelessness among women in the 1990's, which is the time period that this transitional housing study took place. Therefore, statistics on the numbers of homeless women and reasons behind homelessness can be found in the initial chapters of this book.

It is undeniable that homeless women need assistance and support in order to overcome the factors that brought and keep them into poverty. The following chapter focuses on the welfare system as a means to help the poor. The chapter concentrates on faith-based initiatives, welfare reform, and how the system pertains specifically to and affects women. While welfare is considered helpful by some and flawed by others, it is currently one of our society's main forms of dealing with homelessness and poverty. The history, successes, failures and reforms of the welfare system must be thoroughly discussed in order to better understand homeless women.

REFERENCES:

Baum, A.S. and D.W. Burnes. 1993. *A Nation in Denial: The Truth About Homelessness.* San Francisco, CA: Westview Press.

Bell, C. S. 1970. *The Economics of the Ghetto.* New York, NY: Pegasus.

Birch, E. L.. (ed.). 1985. *The Unsheltered Woman: Women and Housing in the 80's.* New Brunswick, NJ: Rutgers.

Burt, M. R. and B. E. Cohen. 1989. *America's Homeless: Numbers, Characteristics, and Programs that Serve Them.* Washington, DC: Urban Institute Press.

Burton, E. 1992. *The Poverty Debate.* Westport, CT: Greenwood Press.

Blau, J. 1992. *The Visible Poor: Homelessness in the United States.* New York, NY: Oxford University Press.

Ferman, L. A., J. L. Kornbluh, and A. Haber. (eds.). 1968. *Poverty in America: A Book of Readings.* Ann Arbor, MI: The University of Michigan Press.

Glasser, I. 1994. *Homelessness in Global Perspective.* New York, NY: G.K. Hall & co.

Golden, S. 1992. *The Women Outside.* Berkley and Los Angeles, CA: California Press.

Harrington, M. 1984. *The New American Poverty.* New York, NY: Holt, Rinehart and Winston.

Hopper, K. and J. Baumohl. 1996. "Redefining in Cursed World: A Historical Interpretation of American Homelessness. In J. Baumohl (ed.) *Homelessness in America.* Phoenix, AZ: The Oryx Press.

Jencks, C. 1995. *The Homeless.* Cambridge, MA. Harvard University Press.

Miller, H. 1991. *On the Fringe: The Dispossessed in America.* Lexington, MA: Lexington Books.

Ralston, M. L. 1996. *Nobody Wants to Hear Our Truth: Homeless Women and and Theories of the Welfare State.* Westport, CT. Greenwood Press.

Rossi, P. H. 1989. *Down and Out in America: The Origins of Homelessness.* Chicago: University of Chicago Press.

_____. 1989a. *Without Shelter: Homelessness in the 1980's.* New York: Priority Press Publications.

Snow, D. A. and L. Anderson. 1993. *Down on Their Luck: A Study of Homeless Street People.* University of California Press.

Timmer, D. A., D. S. Eitzen and K. D. Talley. 1994. *Paths to Homelessness: Extreme Poverty and the Urban Housing Crisis.* Westview Press.

Wright, J. D. 1989. *Address Unknown: Homelessness in America.* Hawthorne, NY: Aldine de Gruyter.

Wright, T. 1997. *Out of Place: Homeless Mobilizations, Subcities, and Contested Landscapes.* Albany, NY: State University of New York Press

Ripping Off The Band-Aid: A Permanent Solution to End Homelessness Under the Bringing America Home Act

Amy Presley Hauser, J. D.

"…[E]nd the disgrace of the worst form of poverty in the richest nation in the world. It's time for Americans to take a stand to help our most vulnerable citizens. It's time to Bring America Home."[1] Homelessness is not a new phenomenon or problem in the United States or even across the world.[2] The new phenomenon is the growing number of people, including children, who it is affecting. A minimum of 3.5 million people will experience homelessness during a single year in this country.[3] Some of the characteristics of these individuals are as follows: 42% are employed, 39% are children, 55% are without public or private health insurance, and 38% of families that seek shelter are turned away because there is no room for them.[4] Veterans compose approximately 500,000 of those that will be homeless.[5] The cycle of homelessness has been described as "costly and inhumane."[6]

The public sentiment toward the homeless population is typically not favorable, though the public opinion of the homeless is often incorrect. Some even describe them as "worthless."[7] However, a person who is homeless deserves the same human and fundamental rights as every other person, because having a place to stay does not change these rights. The argument has been made that the indigent homeless population should be a protected class, though they have not received this label.[8] This argument is grounded in America's adoption of the Universal Declaration of Human Rights[9] that protects every member of society.[10] The effects of granting the homeless this much needed suspect classification would be more freedom and protection under the law, particularly in a court's review of laws affecting the homeless.[11]

Current problems for the country create even more troubles for its citizens in poverty.[12] The state of the economy, the high rate of unemployment, and the fact that there is less affordable housing than ever before further complicates the situation of the homeless.[13] Other causes of homelessness include substance abuse, inadequate services, mental illness, domestic violence, family crisis, and extreme poverty.[14]

The most modern effort to address homelessness has recently reached the eyes and ears of the 108th Congress, entitled *the Bringing America Home Act* (hereinafter the Act).[15] This legislation proposes to eliminate homelessness, by focusing primarily on housing, civil rights needs, health care, and economic issues. We believe this Act is an important step and an adequate presentation of solutions for this voiceless group of Americans who are in need. Though success of the Act is uncertain, homelessness can and should be reduced by following the measures presented in the Act.

The Legislative Endeavors

In 1987, the Stewart B. McKinney Homeless Assistance Act, Public Law 100-77, was the first legislation evaluating and addressing the needs of the homeless population in America and providing a general definition of a homeless individual.[16] This Act was developed as a response to the crisis caused by insufficient shelters for elderly persons, handicapped persons, families with children, Native Americans, and veterans.[17] The purpose of the Act included establishing an Interagency Council on the Homeless, coordinating better public programs and resources, and delivering funds to programs assisting the homeless.[18] As years have passed, more people have become homeless and need intervention of the government to provide for their needs.

In response to the need, seven simple words capture the purpose and goal of this new legislation: "To end homelessness in the United States."[19] Though likely met with some snickers and raised eyebrows, the legislation was presented to the U.S. House of Representatives on July 25, 2003.[20] For over a year, various academics, social service providers, Congressmen, and homeless advocates, worked to create H.R. 2897.[21] As Representative Julia Carson, who presented the legislation, stated: "America has been blessed with incredible wealth and resources. There are no excuses for permitting families to live in sub-standard housing, or to be homeless."[22]

Believing with Carson that homelessness can end,[23] twenty-seven initial cosponsors were on board when the legislation was proposed,[24] and this number has since increased to thirty-eight.[25] Resolutions have already been passed in some cities across the nation that support the proposal.[26] For example, the National Alliance to End Homelessness set its sights on a ten-year plan to accomplish this goal.[27] Other supportive organizations include the U.S. Conference of Mayors,[28] the Corporation for Supportive Housing,[29] and the National Housing Trust Fund Campaign.[30]

The goal of the Act is generally to bring resources together to assist the homeless in becoming self reliant.[31] Primarily, the Act will provide for housing, economic security, health care, civil rights, opportunities for job training, vouchers for childcare and public transportation, and emergency funds for families facing eviction.[32] As Congress recognized in the Stewart B. McKinney Act, "There is no single, simple solution to the problem of homelessness."[33] Though it is not simple, the advocates of the Bringing America Home Act believe there is a solution. The solutions suggested for each problem in the Act must be evaluated in comparison to the actual problems presented. The issues center around: inadequate housing, the criminalization of homelessness, and healthcare and economic security.

Inadequate Housing

The importance of housing is obvious.[34] The importance reveals a significant problem for those without it. As one commentator said, "In the absence of [a] decent place to call home, it is foolhardy to expect people to succeed as citizens. Yet in no jurisdiction in the country can a full-time minimum wage worker afford the fair market rent."[35] Individuals, families, veterans, and former inmates all are in need of low-income housing.[36] The right to housing has not been officially recognized, as reflected in decisions of the Supreme Court.[37] However, some countries throughout the world have taken the position that housing is a basic human right.[38]

Lack of affordable housing is widely known to be a main cause of homelessness in America.[39] The problem in Kentucky is likely representative of the problem nationwide. The cycle that is occurring looks like this: someone gets evicted or is suddenly without housing, then he or she goes to a shelter. From a shelter, a person would normally then go to Section 8 housing; however, due to the poor economy and other factors, persons in Section 8 housing are unable to leave, meaning the persons in the shelters have no place to go. This ultimately overcrowds the shelters so that they are at full capacity.[40] Thus, the problem is that there is simply not enough available affordable housing for the number of people who need it.[41] Donald Whitehead, Executive Director of the National Coalition for the Homeless, communicated this message by stating that the true problem was the need to "increas[e] the number of houses and apartments for low-income residents."[42]

Reflecting the urgent need for more housing, legislation has been proposed by the National Housing Trust Fund that would provide funds for building new housing, rehabilitating current private market affordable housing, and preserving existing federally assisted housing. This would apply to 1.5 million units of rental housing over a ten-year period.[43]

The Act has offered many solutions to the deficient number of affordable housing options. In support of the legislation, Sheila Crowley, President of the National Low Income Housing Coalition, commented that homelessness "will not end without a federal investment in affordable housing,"[44] and this appears to be the driving force in the Act. Title I of the Act boldly takes the stand that housing is a basic human right, as recognized by numerous groups, though presenting a new approach by the government.[45] Congress would declare that providing each American the right to life, liberty, and the pursuit of happiness requires a national goal to act according to such rights and "fulfill the basic human need of shelter by ending homelessness in the United States and to provide the security of a home to people in cases of sickness, inability to work, old age, unemployment, and in any other case in which one is deprived of the means of subsistence."[46] The Act also alters the definition of homeless to include more specific details, in effect, expanding the number of people included.[47]

Title II of the Act, which focuses on housing security, begins to address the housing issue and methods of meeting these needs. The National Affordable Housing Trust Fund will be established in the Treasury of the U. S. to assist in supplying and preserving affordable housing.[48] The point of this will be to achieve: 1) a halt in the growing gap in the ability to build affordable housing through using profits from federal housing programs to fund more housing activities; 2) building of rental housing in mixed-income settings where there are opportunities for economic growth; 3) promotion of homeownership for low-income families; and 4) production, rehabilitation, and preservation of a minimum of 1,500,000 units of affordable housing over the next ten years.[49] This is incorporation of the legislation by the National Housing Trust Fund.[50] Allocation of the funds from the Trust Fund will be a product of a formula based on need and several factors.[51]

Title III of the Act involves homeless intervention and prevention. One group covered under this title is families. Section 303(a) maintains that shelters cannot have policies denying family units admission. This section also ensures that residential facilities will act to make certain that a person being discharged will not be homeless. Section 304 provides emergency rent relief grants from HUD to nonprofit organizations that will distribute the funds when tenants face eviction. A nonprofit organization can pay to prevent eviction if seven requirements have been met.[52] The requirements include the fact that the tenant's nonpayment was due to circumstances out of his control, it is reasonably likely that the payments are only temporary, and the payments would be repaid by the tenant to the group that paid for him.[53] Section 304(g) and (h) provide details on the emergency rent relief fund to be established in the U.S. Treasury and the regular report that must be submitted to Congress regarding current rates of eviction and delinquent rent payment.[54]

Title IV of the Act calls for a consolidation of homeless assistance programs under the McKinney Act and for codification in federal law of the continuum of care planning process. This is said by experts to be an essential function at the local level for producing strategies to bring an end to homelessness.[55] Section 402 calls for Homeless Assistance Planning Boards, half of those involved being former or current homeless individuals, advocates for the homeless, those who assist the homeless, or superintendents of local educational agencies, that will plan and develop programs, policies, and practices to prevent and end homelessness.[56] Additional provisions addressing housing purport to do the following: increase authorization levels of HUD, United States Department of Agriculture, and Veterans' Administration Housing Program; authorize use of surplus federal property for permanent housing; provide a Mutual housing demonstration program for housing cooperatives; reauthorize HUD McKinney-Vento programs for five years; and require that federal funds used for demolition be applied to replace units so none are lost.[57]

Each solution presented by the Act appears to assist agencies in addressing the actual problems presented. However, there are some concerns about the proposed solutions. One of them is the ten-year projection placed on creating all of the affordable housing, which may not be realistic. Further, placement of the housing also must be addressed because it is important to build the units where economic growth is or will be occurring. It is difficult to ensure this while dealing with traditional problems of "not in my backyard."[58] Cost is another major issue because the Act simply creates a trust in the Treasury, but does not locate the source of funding. The requirements for the emergency rent relief present a problem because it seems unlikely, in the current situation, that most would be able to repay the rent paid on their behalf. Additionally, these provisions require major time, perhaps more than Congress is willing to give.

Criminalization of Homelessness

According to the National Coalition for Homeless, the civil rights of homeless people are being violated instead of protected.[59] The constitutional rights that are constantly at risk include the First Amendment, the Fourth Amendment, the Eighth Amendment, and the Fourteenth Amendment.[60] The violation of such rights is exemplified through the disproportionate number of hate crimes and violence against homeless persons,[61] lack of adequate legal representation in court,[62] selective enforcement of laws against homeless, creation of laws aimed at moving homeless persons out of specific areas,[63] and restricting access to public places.[64] The use of ordinances and laws to target everyday activities that a homeless person must carry out in public since he is without a private place to do so has been termed "criminalization of homelessness."[65] [66] [67]

Often, city ordinances or local laws call for this sort of action against homeless persons, but these kinds of laws are not new.[68] As one author recounts, "Throughout American history, such policies [toward the homeless] have been based on the assumption that the homeless are lazy and irresponsible—a deviant group, perhaps incorrigible, but in any case outside the boundaries of mainstream society."[69] Laws may exist in two forms: 1) "homeless" laws that explicitly target homeless persons and their activities, and 2) "status" laws that punish persons for their economic condition not for the way they act.[70] A recent study conducted by the National Coalition for the Homeless reveals numerous civil rights violations and implementation of laws targeting homeless people since January 2002.[71] The effects of these laws have been observed by Brian Davis, Executive Director of the Northeast Ohio Coalition for the Homeless,

Imagine the loneliness and feeling of helplessness, when every shelter is full and then the city's police force adds insult to injury by confiscating all your belongings or issues a ticket for sleeping in a park. It takes a special person to be able to cope with the daily struggle to survive while the city government throws added barriers into your path toward stability.[72]

In Cordova v. City of Reno,[73] a homeless alcoholic challenged the city ordinance which imposed criminal liability on anyone "engag[ing] upon a public street, highway, alley or premises to which the public has access or other public place within the city in conduct having a tendency to annoy, insult or disturb offensively any person passing or being therein."[74] The court found that the Reno ordinance was unconstitutional and noted selective enforcement is a risk against people "whose behavior is 'annoying' 'because their ideas, their lifestyle, or their physical appearance is resented by the majority of their fellow citizens.'"[75] However, the court would not grant Mr. Cordova an injunction on future enforcement of this ordinance.[76] In fact, many ordinances are never challenged so they are still enforced in violation of rights.[77]

Advocates for the homeless realize that criminalization is poor public policy[78] and counterproductive with regard to cost and the effect of having a criminal record in terms of creating barriers to finding employment and housing.[79] [80] Currently, homeless persons are shuffled between jails, emergency rooms, shelters and the streets.[81] Sometimes, there is no place to go: [82] the shelters are full, the low-income housing is unavailable, and the laws make it illegal to sleep or be in public places.

The Act presents some remedies for these problems. First, if a community is obtaining assistance for the homeless, that community must provide a guarantee through formal certification that it is not participating in criminalizing homelessness. This portion of the Act is under the selection criteria of HUD McKinney-Vento Act. If a city is receiving Community Development Block Grants and HOME Investment Partnership Program funds, that city is not permitted to pass laws that punish or have a disparate impact on homeless people for performing daily activities in public areas since no alternative public spaces are available to them.[83] Cities also receiving these same funds must not pass zoning ordinances that will in effect prevent placement of facilities serving the homeless. For civil rights concerns, the Act additionally provides a post office box for homeless or indefinite general delivery service.[84]

Though this type of accountability sounds good in theory, it is less likely to be effective on a practical level. One problem relates to monitoring to ensure that communities and cities are in compliance. Also, it must be considered whether this formal certification will achieve the desired result. For example, are there implications of breaking the commitment? Can the state claim ignorance when the police continue to enforce these laws anyway? The protections and safeguards to avoid the criminalization of homelessness is weakly stated in the Act. Perhaps the drafters were acting under the thought that if all the other provisions of the Act are carried out, then provisions against criminalizing homelessness would be unnecessary. If so, the problem must be addressed for the interim period until the execution of the Act and provision of housing.

Health Care and Economic Security

The healthcare and economic situation of homeless individuals are also central concerns of the Act. With healthcare, some of the problems that the homeless face include access and treatment. [85] For the homeless who are mentally ill, facilities for treatment are very limited and recovery is unlikely.[86] Homeless individuals are thus more likely to access costly healthcare services because homelessness is a cause and result of serious health care problems.[87]

[88] The Act proposes to expand Medicaid to all individuals with incomes below 200 percent of the federal poverty line.[89] Further, accelerated enrollment for homeless applicants will be required.[90] Mental health services and treatment also occupies a large portion of Title VI. The Act also stipulates that a facility receiving funds under a grant must give preference to homeless individuals seeking treatment at their facility.[91] In addition, Section 676 amends the Public Health Service Act, 42 U.S.C. 300ff-14, to provide priority status to homeless persons, including children, youth, and families, with HIV disease and to require Health and Human Services to address issues and policies addressing these individuals.[92] The Act also provides food stamps within seven days of application if any members in the household are homeless.[93]

Economic problems for the homeless include the inability to work or find work, low wages, and/or barriers to receipt of government assistance. Title VII of the Act speaks to economic security for homeless persons.[94] Based on numerous findings grounded in the typical inadequacy of incomes and other factors, Congress would recognize the right to a living income that is stated in this manner: "Every person who works 40 hours or more per week should receive a wage sufficient to provide for safe, decent, and affordable housing, which should be ensured through a living wage that is indexed to the local cost of housing."[95] If a person cannot work or cannot get work, he should receive public benefits at a level that provides a livable income.[96] Additionally, the Act will add to the Cranston-Gonzalez National Affordable Housing Act, a provision that provides training to homeless persons sufficient to helping them gain employment as skilled or semi-skilled residential construction workers.[97] Those qualified will be employed by a Homebuild program, which builds affordable housing for low-income people.[98] The Act also requires the Social Security Administration to be proactive in locating and making benefits available to homeless persons. [99] Other provisions include repealing the statute that permits homeless to receive SSI only six of every nine months they live in a public emergency shelter; giving presumptive eligibility to homeless for SSI; and increasing the authorization of the Homeless Veterans Reintegration Program.[100]

This utilization of the homeless to assist in building the housing units seems to be a primary strategy. However, the training is limited to this area and would be insufficient without further consideration. Also, the Social Security Administration may be unwilling to perform this kind of outreach that it is not required to do for others. The Act does not address the need to create wealth, educating the homeless on issues like managing money, or educational opportunities in general.

Can America Be Brought Home?

A review of this legislation reveals ambitious plans for providing adequate care for the homeless population. Overall, the Act presents solid ideas and appears to cover nearly every aspect of difficulty facing the homeless. Critics will say this is too lofty—the budget nor the administration can survive the scope of these plans. Funding is obviously the life of the Act so allocation of funds is crucial. A price tag has not been given to this legislation,[101] but it will obviously not be small. Currently, insufficient funds exist to satisfy the need and prospects for the future are not positive considering the tight budgets. In early September, the Senate VA-HUD appropriations committee passed a bill that severely undercut funding to HUD. The National Coalition for the Homeless sees three ways this action will only continue to assure the rise of homelessness, especially among families.[102] Further, HUD has not supported the National Housing Trust Fund nor acknowledged the need to build more housing that is affordable.[103] Funding is also being cut both at the federal and state levels. As an example, New York City cut its 2004 budget in areas of existing housing programs and is ending one-third of the city shelter cleaning and maintenance staffs.[104] It is also discouraging to notice that nationally the housing budget has been cut over seventy percent in the last twenty years.[105] Under the current administration, the needs of those in poverty have not been at the forefront of urgent action; instead, the reduced funding and services, tax cuts, and diminished supply of subsidized housing has likely set a tone for reaction to this major legislation.[106] [107] Though the states can still seek to attain the goals outlined in the Act, these efforts will not likely reach full potential without adequate funding. Some states will not even get its programs off the ground.

Does this legislation have a future? It has been suggested that survival is a long shot in the Republican-controlled Congress. This legislation also has lots of competition—national security[108] and other such measures are likely more pressing issues to legislators than the homeless population. Plus, the homeless are relying on the voices of their advocates because they, as a group, do not have political power. It is hard to determine which aspects can or will be eliminated, but it is almost certain that some provisions will not survive. To complicate the matter further, the problems are intertwined in many ways. For instance, residential stability is a large component of effective healthcare.[109] Congress will have to decide if it is worth the effort to only partially help the homeless without addressing many of the problems. The next piece of legislation that is likely to survive include the economic provisions, because this helps fulfill the self-sufficiency goal. The civil rights concerns will not likely receive much attention, and the healthcare issues will probably be diverted. The passage of the Act will not be accomplished swiftly but instead will require a great amount of continuing supervision. The country needs an abundant supply of resources and public support to accomplish each of these goals in order to Bring America Home. The attitude should be that we will do this not to get the homeless off the streets to help tourism and the aesthetic appeal of our cities, but because they deserve not to be homeless.

Conclusion

Does this Act give "hope" to the homeless?[110] The drafters certainly had high hopes. It seems clear that the Stewart B. McKinney Act has been inadequate and has not achieved the necessary goals. The temporary measures to address homelessness must also be terminated because they have not been successful.[111] This Act presents an opportunity for dramatic change. [112] Despite concerns that have been raised, the Bringing America Home Act is an admirable effort to make a difference for homeless people across America. Though it may have some provisions that cannot be accomplished, it is certainly an important beginning. The problems of the homeless are not someone else's problems. They belong to the entire country.[113] When reflecting on helping the homeless in his book, *The Homeless*, Christopher Jencks stated, "Because we can, we should."[114] This Act successfully presents the message that we can assist this group of people in need and we should. The time to do so is now.

---

[1] *Congresswoman Julia Carson Introduces Comprehensive Legislation to Address Homelessness in America*, July 25, 2003, *available at* http://www.juliacarson.house.gov/issues2.cfm?id=6554 (last visited Oct. 9, 2003). Statement made by Donald Whitehead, Executive Director of the National Coalition for the Homeless.

[2] For information on homelessness generally, *see* Martha Burt, et. al., HELPING AMERICA'S HOMELESS 1-22 (2001). An overview of homelessness is provided in Maria Foscarinis, *Downward Spiral: Homelessness and Its Criminalization*, 14 YALE L. & POL'Y REV. 1, 8-12 (1996). For information on the views of the homeless by countries around the world, *see generally* Valerie Polakow and Cindy Guillen, editors, INTERNATIONAL PERSPECTIVES ON HOMELESSNESS (2001).

[3] *America's Homelessness Crisis & the FY 2004 Budget Request*, National Coalition for the Homeless, *available at* http://www.nationalhomeless.org (last visited Oct. 3, 2003).

[4] *Id.* For a closer look at families and single individuals who are or will be homeless, *see A Plan, Not a Dream: How to End Homelessness in Ten Years*, A Snapshot of Homelessness, National Alliance to End Homelessness, *available at* http://www.endhomelessness.org/pub/tenyear/demograp.htm (last visited Oct. 10, 2003).

[5] *Congresswoman Julia Carson Introduces Comprehensive Legislation*, *supra* note 1.

[6] *The Bringing Home America Act*, 2003 Adopted Resolutions, 71st Annual Meeting, *available at* http://www.usmayors.org/uscm/resolutions/71st conference/cdh 14.asp (last visited Oct. 9, 2003).

[7] *Equality in the Courts?*, Civil Rights, Atlanta Task Force for the Homeless, *available at* http://homelesstaskforce.org/rights comments.php?id=P237 0 3 0 C (last visited Oct. 3, 2003).

[8] The National Coalition for the Homeless created a resolution to this effect that declares protection for homeless from laws against sleeping in public; acts interfering with the right to travel; denied access to housing due to bottom wages; practices that ignore their rights of ownership of their personal belongings; being targeted with hate crimes; and being treated as noncitizens. *NCH's Protected Class Resolution*, National Coalition for the Homeless, *available at* http://nch.ari.net/pcresolution.html (last visited Oct. 3, 2003).

[9] The Universal Declaration of Human Rights has been accepted by the United States and it defines food, housing, and living wage jobs as human rights. *See KWRU Stands Up for the Homeless*, Shelterforce Online, July/August 1999, *available at* http://www.nhi.org/online/issues/106/brown.html (last visited Oct. 3, 2003).

[10] *NCH's Protected Class Resolution*, *supra* note 8.

[11] The criteria for a suspect class are not precise, but Supreme Court decisions indicate that a group qualifies if they are "'saddled with such disabilities, or subjected to such a history of purposeful unequal treatment, or relegated to a position of political powerlessness as to command extraordinary protection from the majoritarian political process.'" Jennifer E. Watson, Note, *When No Place is Home: Why the Homeless Deserve Suspect Classification*, 88 IOWA L. REV. 501, 510 (2003) (quoting San Antonio Independent School District v. Rodriguez, 411 U.S. 1, 28 (1973)). *Id.* at 533. The review applied would be strict scrutiny which is the most demanding level of review. *Id.*

[12] *See Bill Introduced Today to End Homelessness in America*, National Coalition for the Homeless, July, 25, 2003, *available at* http://www.nationalhomeless.org/bah/intro.html (last visited Oct. 18, 2003).

[13] Kathryn Lewis, *Gimme Shelter*, TomPaine, Aug. 26, 2003, *available at* http://www.tompaine.com/feature2.cfm/ID/8722 (last visited Oct. 9, 2003).

[14] Foscarinis, *Downward Spiral, supra* note 2, at 8-12. For poverty statistics from 2001 and 2002, *see* U.S. Census Bureau, American Community Survey, *available at* http://www.census.gov/acs/www/. Some say being homeless is a choice. Foscarinis, *supra* note 2, at 11.

[15] Bringing America Home Act, H.R. 2897, 108th Congress (2003), *available at* http://thomas.loc.gov.

[16] Stewart B. McKinney Homeless Assistance Act, Pub. L. No. 100-77, 101 Stat 482 (1987). The definition of a homeless individual is
> (1) an individual who lacks a fixed, regular, and adequate nighttime residence; and (2) an individual who has primary nighttime residence that is- (A) a supervised publicly or privately operated shelter designed to provide temporary living accommodations (including welfare hotels, congregate shelters, and transitional housing for the mentally ill); (B) an institution that provides a temporary residence for individuals intended to be institutionalized; or (C) a public or private place not designed for, or ordinarily used as, a regular sleeping accommodation for human beings.

§ 103(a). This definition excludes prisoners. § 103 (c).

[17] *Id.* at § 102(a).

[18] *Id.* at § 102(b). Title IV attempted to address the housing issues of these groups. It provides a comprehensive homeless assistance plan. The areas of emergency shelter grants, supportive housing demonstration program, supplemental assistance for facilities assisting homeless, and other provisions regarding the use of funds are addressed.

[19] *Id.*

[20] *Congresswoman Julia Carson Introduces Comprehensive Legislation, supra* note 1.

[21] *Id.*

[22] *Id.* This statement was made by Julia Carson in discussing the legislation.

[23] *A Plan, Not a Dream: How to End Homelessness in Ten Years*, Executive Summary, National Alliance to End Homelessness, *available at* http://www.endhomelessness.org/pub/tenyear/executiv.htm (last visited Oct. 10, 2003). The National Alliance to End Homelessness has stood up to say that "ending homelessness is well within the nation's grasp." *Id.*

[24] The fellow sponsors were: Mr. Conyers, Mr. Kucinich, Ms. Lee, Mr. Gutierrez, Ms. Corrine Brown, Mr. Cummings, Ms. Jackson-Lee, Mr. Owens, Ms. Millender-McDonald, Mr. McGovern, Mr. Sanders, Mr. Wexler, Mr. Grijalva, Ms. Woolsey, Mr. Reyes, Ms. Schakowsky, Mr. Rangel, Ms. Majette, Ms. Slaughter, Mr. Thompson, Mr. Evans, Mr. Payne, Mr. McDermott, Mr. Capuano, Mr. Weiner, Mc. McCollum, and Mr. Emanuel. H.R. 2987, *supra* note 15, at Introduction.

[25] *Supporters of the Bringing America Home Act*, Bringing America Home Act, Oct. 27, 2003, *at* http://www.bringingamericahome.org/endorse.html (last visited Nov. 2, 2003).

[26] *Id.* Some of the cities that have acted include Providence, Rhode Island, and Lakewood, Ohio.

[27] *A Plan, Not a Dream: How to End Homelesness in Ten Years,* Executive Summary, *supra* note 23. This requires preventing homelessness rather than causing it. This involves four steps occurring at the same time: 1) plan for outcomes- gather better local data and focus on the outcome of ending homelessness, 2) close the front door- invest in prevention, 3) open the back door- have permanent supportive housing so people are not homeless for long, and 4) build the infrastructure- need permanent housing, adequate incomes, and necessary services.

[28] *The Bringing Home America Act,* 2003 Adopted Resolutions, *supra* note 6..

[29] *Corporation for Supportive Housing Lauds Introduction of Bringing America Home Act,* Aug. 18, 2003, *available at* http://www.bringingamericahome.org/csh.html (last visited Oct. 9, 2003).

[30] *Campaign applauds introduction of Bringing America Home Act,* Aug. 1, 2003, *available at* http://www.nhtf.org/pressroom/release.asp?rel=32&sty=plain (last visited Oct. 9, 2003).

[31] *Congresswoman Julia Carson Introduces Comprehensive Legislation, supra* note 1; H.R. 2897, *supra* note 15.

[32] *Congresswoman Julia Carson Introduces Comprehensive Legislation, supra* note 1.

[33] Stewart B. McKinney Homeless Assistance Act, *supra* note 16, at § 102(a)(4).

[34] For the history of housing problems and the effects of living without housing, *see generally* Christopher Jencks, THE HOMELESS (1994).

[35] Background, The National Housing Trust Fund Campaign, *available at* http://www.nhtf.org/background.asp?sty=plain (last visited Oct. 3, 2003).

[36] *Incarceration, Homelessness, and Health,* National Health Care for the Homeless Council-2003 Policy Statements, *available at* http://www.nhchc.org/Advocacy/PolicyPapers/2003/10IncarcerationHnHealth.pdf (last visited Nov. 2, 2003).

[37] *See* Lindsey v. Normet, 405 U.S. 56 (1972).

[38] *See* INTERNATIONAL PERSPECTIVES ON HOMELESSNESS, *supra* note 2.

[39] *Making the Connection?: Homelessness & Housing in the President's Budget Request,* National Coalition for the Homeless, *available at* http://www.nationalhomeless.org (last visited Oct. 8, 2003). To understand the combination of insufficient affordable housing and extreme poverty in causing homelessness, *see Affordable Housing: A Quiet Crisis for Families and Children,* Children's Defense, *available at* http://www.childrensdefense.org/pdf/houscrisis_OCT02.pdf (last visited Oct. 3, 2003).

[40] Telephone Interview with Bart Smith, Director of Programs, Wayside Christian Mission (September 28, 2003).

[41] For history of the problems, *see* Jencks, *supra* note 34, at 61-74, 81-102.

[42] A very recent decision by the Salvation Army in Louisville to begin charging homeless persons and families five dollars a night to stay in the shelter after a week was met with outrage by advocates. Donald Whitehead, executive director of the National Coalition for the Homeless, stated that he disagreed with the fee, noting that this was action not focused on the true problem. Chris Poynter, *Homeless Pay for Stay,* The Courier-Journal, Sept. 28, 2003, *available at* http://www.courierjournal.com/localnews/2003/09/28ky/wir-front-shelter0928-11458.html (last visited Oct. 2, 2003). Approximately 10,900 people used homeless shelters in Louisville last year. Louisville can house

about 1,000 people a night in its 25 shelters. The point was also made that the National Coalition for the Homeless and the national Salvation Army were unaware of any other shelter nationwide charging families. *Id.*

[43] *Campaign applauds introduction of Bringing America Home Act, supra* note 30; *The Campaign's Policy Proposal*, National Housing Trust Fund Campaign, *available at* http://www.nhtf.org/about/proposal.asp?sty=plain (last visited Oct. 9, 2003). The Trust Fund specifies the term of affordability, distribution, compatibility with other programs, and the source of capital. This proposal already has support form 205 cosponsors and 4,300 various organizations and local leaders. *Id.*

[44] *Campaign applauds introduction of Bringing America Home Act, supra* note 30.

[45] H.R. 2897, *supra* note 15, at § 101. These groups include some religious and faith organizations, states, cities, and counties, national and local organizations, and international organizations. *Id.*

[46] *Id.* at § 102(1)-(3).

[47] *Id.* at § 402(a). The definition is as follows:
(1) [ ] an individual who lacks a fixed, regular, and adequate nighttime residence; and (2) include (A) an individual who (i) is sharing the housing of other persons due to loss of hosing, economic hardship, or a similar reason; (ii) is living in a motel, hotel, trailer park, or camping ground due to the lack of alternative adequate accommodations; (iii) is living in an emergency or transitional shelter; (iv) is abandoned in a hospital; or (v) is awaiting foster care placement; (B) and individual who has a primary nighttime residence that is a public or private place not designed for or ordinarily used as a regular sleeping accommodation for human beings; (C) an individual who is living in a car, park, public space, abandoned building, substandard housing, bus or train station, or similar setting; and (D) migratory children (as such term is defined in section 1309 of the Elementary and Secondary education Act of 1965) who qualify as homeless for the purposes of this Act because the children are living in circumstances described in any of subparagraphs (A) through (C); and Such term includes individuals who have been released form prison on parole.
Id.

[48] *Id.* at § 221.

[49] *Id.*

[50] *See supra* text accompanying note 43.

[51] H.R. 2897, *supra* note 15, at § 221. These factors include the percentage of families in the jurisdiction of the eligible recipient that live in substandard housing and that pay more than fifty percent of annual income to housing expenses; the percentage of persons in that jurisdiction with an income at or below the poverty line; the cost of developing or rehabilitating housing in that area; percentage of the population that resides in counties with very low vacancy rates (if the eligible recipient is a State); the percentage of housing stock in the area that is very old; and any other factors deemed appropriate. *Id.*

[52] *Id.* at § 304(c)(1)-(7). The seven requirements are as follows: 1) the land lord has notified the tenant of his intent to evict due to failure to pay the rent; 2) the property involved is the tenant's principal residence; 3) the rent is not above the median rent for units that are similar in the area; 4) the tenant is not in control of the reasons that rent is not being paid; 5) only payment will prevent eviction; 6) it is reasonably likely that tenant will be able to pay full rent in the specified time; and 7) the tenant will likely repay what was paid for him. *Id.*

[53] *Id.* at § 304(c)(1)-(7).

[54] *Id.* at § 304(g)-(h).

[55] *Id.* at § 401.

[56] *Id.* at § 412.

[57] *Bringing America Home Act*, National Coalition for the Homeless, *available at* http://www.bringingamericahome.org (last visited Oct. 16, 2003).

[58] "Not in my backyard" is a common response and consideration in placement of federal, Section 8, housing. *See* Timothy L. Thompson, *Promoting Mobility and Equal Opportunity: Hollman v. Cisneros*, 5-SPG J. AFFORDABLE HOUSING & COMM. DEV. L. 237, 257 (1996).

[59] *People Need Their Civil Rights Protected*, National Coalition for the Homeless, *available at* http://www.nationalhomeless.org/facts/civilrights.html (last visited Oct. 1, 2003).

[60] *Combating the Criminalization of Homelessness: A Guide to Understand and Prevent Legislation that Criminalizes Life-Sustaining Activities*, National Law Center on Homelessness & Poverty, Oct. 2002, *available at* http://www.nlchp.org/FA_CivilRights/CR_crim_booklet.pdf (last visited Nov. 2, 2003).

[61] *See Civil Rights*, Greater Cincinnati Coalition for the Homeless, *available at* http://homeless.cincy.com/pages/content/civil rights.html (last visited Oct. 3, 2003). According to studies by the National Coalition for the Homeless, these hate crimes include beating, murdering, setting on fire, and urinating upon homeless people. Many of these crimes are not reported, but the National Coalition for the Homeless 2000 Hate Crimes Study showed 43 homeless deaths and 23 non-lethal acts of violence against the homeless in forty-two cities.

[62] *Equality in the Courts?*, *supra* note 7. In Georgia, it appears that homeless individuals have two choices when they go into a Georgia court: 1) plead guilty to any charges, or 2) wait for a hearing without adequate representation. "Homeless individuals no longer hope for justice in the courtroom; they can only hope for a speedy escape from the criminal justice system." *Id.*

[63] As Maria Foscarinis suggests, "'Punishing homeless Americans for living in public- when thousands literally have no other alternative- is inhumane, immoral, and unjust—and it just won't work. What will work is affordable housing, healthcare, and living-wage jobs." *Advocates Decry Increasing Civil Rights Violations Nationally*, Civil Rights, Atlanta Task Force for the Homeless, *available at* http://homelesstaskforce.org/rights comments.php?id=P248 0 3 0 C (last visited Oct. 3, 2003).

[64] *People Need Their Civil Rights Protected*, *supra* note 59.

[65] *Combating the Criminalization of Homelessness*, *supra* note 60. Generally, "criminalization" includes the "practices of local jurisdictions in legislating against basic life-sustaining activities such as sleeping, sitting, or storing personal belonging in places where people are forced to exist without shelter....include[s] the selective enforcement of other laws like loitering or public intoxication against people who appear to be experiencing homelessness." *Id.* According to another source, the definition of criminalization is stated in two parts: 1) it encompasses all legislation penalizing life-sustaining activities conducted by people who are without homes, 2) enforcing pre-exiting ordinances in a discriminatory manner. *See* Illegal to be Homeless: The Criminalization of Homelessness in the United States, 10, *available at* http://www.nationalhomeless.org/civilrights/crim2003/report.pdf (last visited Nov. 2, 2003).

[66] Maria Foscarinis, Kelly Cunningham-Bowers, & Kristen E. Brown, *Out of Sight—Out of Mind?: The Continuing Trend Towards the Criminalization of Homelessness*, 6 GEO. J. ON POVERTY L. & POL'Y 145, 152-56 (1999).

[67] Some ways homeless become victims include having all of his or her possessions thrown into a garbage truck while being arrested under a warrant for not paying citations he could not afford to pay or when police perform "sweeps" in an area. *Politics of Homelessness*, Coalition on homelessness, San Francisco Bay Guardian, November 7, 2001, *available at http://www.sfbg.com/News/36/06/06oped.html* (last visited Oct. 3, 2003). The Coalition on Homelessness in the area initiated legislation for a twenty-four hour notice requirement to let homeless people know before arbitrarily taking their property, but this effort was defeated, in part due to the Mayor's opposition to protecting rights of homeless people. *Id.* "Sweeps" are when the property of the homeless in a certain area or street is removed and destroyed. This often happens, non-coincidentally, only days before a certain political or other big event is happening in the city. Andrea Grant-Friedman, *"Out of Sight, Out of Mind?"* International Committee of the Fourth International, *available at* http://www.wsws.org/articles/1999/jan1999/home-j22.shtml (last visited Oct. 3, 2003).

[68] For a history of such ordinances and laws, *see* Jason Leckerman, Comment, *City of Brotherly Love?: Using the Fourteenth Amendment to Strike Down an Anti-Homeless Ordinance in Philadelphia*, 3 U. PA. J. CONST. L. 540, 546 (2001).

[69] Kenneth L. Kusmer, DOWN & OUT, ON THE ROAD: THE HOMELESS IN AMERICAN HISTORY at Preface (2002). *See id.* on how homeless have been an integral part of American civilization for over two centuries.

[70] Dave Oehl, *The American Criminalization of Poverty*, Peacework, *available at* http://www.afsc.org/pwork/0200/0208.htm (last visited Oct. 3, 2003).

[71] This practice continues to grow. For general analysis, *see* Foscarinis, *Downward Spiral, supra* note 2. *As homelessness increases, number of laws targeting homeless people rise*, National Coalition for the Homeless, *available at* http://www.nationalhomeless.org/civilrights/crim2003/index.html (last visited Oct. 1, 2003). For example, it was reported that Mayor Bloomberg of New York City conducted a joint conference with the police providing a list of "seven deadly sins" that the city should be tackling. One of the "sins" was homelessness. Melissa Williams, *Public sleeping, urination debated by City Council*, Citizen-Times, Oct. 15, 2002, *available at* http://cgi.citizen-times.com/cgi-bin/print/21852 (last visited Sept. 25, 2003). An Asheville ordinance provides another example. This ordinance would ban all panhandling downtown and prohibit public urination and sleeping on public property. *See* Leckerman, *supra* note 68.

[72] *As homelessness increases, number of laws targeting homeless people rise, supra* note 71.

[73] Cordova v. City of Reno, 920 F. Supp. 135 (D.Ct. Nev.1996).

[74] *Id.* at 137. *See* Reno Municipal Ordinance 8.22.040.

[75] Cordova, 920 F. Supp. at 139 (citing Coates v. City of Cincinnati, 402 U.S. 611, 616, 29 L. Ed. 2d 214, 91 S.Ct. 1686 (1971)).

[76] *Id.*

[77] Foscarinis, Cunningham-Bowers, & Brown, *supra* note 66, at 145. Ordinances resembling this one are often found by a court to be overly broad. *Id.*

[78] Such action is poor public policy for these reasons: the laws will not reduce the occurrence of these activities or keep homeless people out of public spaces when there is no alternative, it causes burdens on the criminal justice system that are unnecessary, and it does not provide long-term benefit to the homeless or solution to conflicts in public spaces. Kristen Brown, *Outlawing Homelessness*, Shelterforce Online, Issue #106, July/August 1999, available at http://www.nhi.org/online/issues/106/brown.html (last visited Oct. 3, 2003).

[79] The evidence overwhelmingly shows that continuous mistreatment and criminalization of the homeless is occurring across the nation. *See* Illegal to be Homeless, *supra* note 65, at 14. This report examined 147 communities in 42 states. *Id.* at 5. Advocates for the homeless have fought many of these discriminatory ordinances For examples of successfully challenged ordinances in different states, *see* Homeless Civil Rights Successes/Victories (1994 to Present), National Coalition for the Homeless, *available at* http://nch.ari.net/crsuccesses.html (last visited Oct. 3, 2003). Advocates realize that criminalization of homeless activities is not the answer if cities want to reduce or eliminate homelessness. *Combating the Criminalization of Homelessness, supra* note 60.

[80] *Civil Rights*, Greater Cincinnati Coalition for the Homeless, *supra* note 61.

[81] The better answer is addressing chronic homelessness through provision of permanent housing and appropriate. services. *New Report on Criminalization of Homelessness Highlights Need to Refocus efforts*, National Alliance to End Homelessness, *available at* http://www.endhomelessness.org (last visited Oct. 10, 2003). Cities have more productive options to pursue. Kristen Brown, *supra* note 87. Some options will likely be best if they include collaboration between two groups: 1) city officials, police departments, and business people, and 2) homeless people and advocates. For examples of what some cities are doing, *see Id. See also Out of Sight—Out of Mind?*, supra note 70, at 159. *See also* Illegal to be Homeless, *supra* note 68, at 21-23. As one advocate has noted, "Local policymakers must recognize the distinction between intolerance of homeless people and intolerance of the manifestations of the problem of homelessness." Kristen Brown, *supra* note 78.

[82] Without sufficient facilities, some homeless persons will be put in jail unnecessarily. *See As homelessness increases, number of laws targeting homeless people rise, supra* note 71.

[83] H.R. 2897, *supra* note 15, at § 310.

[84] *Id.* at § 306. To receive a post office box, the person must meet one of these: 1) be personally known by the postmaster or clerk; 2) be able to submit proper identification such as a driver's license; or 3) give a verifiable point of contact like a place of work, shelter, etc. If the person cannot meet any of these or would prefer not to do those, then he has the option to get indefinite general delivery service. *Id.*

[85] Illegal to be Homeless, *supra* note 65, at 12.

[86] *Id.*

[87] *A Plan, Not a Dream, supra* note 4.

[88] H.R. 2897, *supra* note 15, at § 601.

[89] *Id.* at § 602.

[90] *Id.* at § 602 (b)(3).

[91] *Id.* at § 626.

[92] *Id.* at § 676 (a)-(c). The Act goes a step farther to require creation of a plan by the Secretary of Health and Human Services regarding policies at all levels addressing homelessness and HIV prevention, treatment, and care; administrative and statutory access and care barriers for homeless persons with HIV; and recommendations for administrative and legislative actions improving the access and quality of care for necessary services for HIV homeless patients. *Id.* at § 681(a). This plan must be submitted to the Committee on Energy and Commerce of the House of Representatives and the Committee on Health, Education, Labor, and Pensions of the Senate within a year of enacting the Act.

[93] H.R. 2897, *supra* note 15, at § 703 (a)(3).

[94] *Id.* at Title VII.

[95] *Id.* at § 701(1).

[96] *Id.* at § 701(2).

[97] *Id.* at § 705. The Act provides qualifications for homeless individuals who can participate in this program and for how long.

[98] *Id.*

[99] *Id.* at "Outreach and Application Assistance to Homeless Applicants for Benefits and Beneficiaries under Title II and Title XVI."

[100] *Bringing America Home Act, supra* note 57.

[101] Greg Barrett, *Plan by Conyers aids working poor*, The Detroit News, Dec. 23, 2002, *available at* http://www.detnews.com/2002/politics/0212/23/a08-42756.htm (last visited Oct. 9, 2003).

[102] This Senate bill creates these three problems: 1) it underfunds the Section 8 program and requires the HUD McKinney-Vento Homeless Assistance goes toward a national mandate, disallowing communities from meeting their local needs; 2) cut funding for the Section 811 program which will hurt homeless with disabilities; and 3) has HUD develop requirements on implementing plans in communities yet cut important resources at the same time. *Senate Appropriators Deny Critical Resources to Families, Remove Local Flexibility in Meeting Homeless Needs*, National Coalition for the Homeless, Sept, 10, 2003, *available at* http://www.nationalhomeless.org/senhud03.html (last visited Oct. 3, 2003).

[103] Illegal to be Homeless, *supra* note 65, at 11.

[104] Kathryn Lewis, *supra* note 13.

[105] *Id.*

[106] Illegal to be Homeless, *supra* note 65, at 5.

[107] *Representatives Julia Carson and John Conyers join with National Coalition for the Homeless to Rally for the Bringing America Home Act*, Rep. Julia Carson Website, Oct. 8, 2003, *available at* http://www.juliacarson.house.gov/issues2.cfm?id=6982 (last visited Oct. 28, 2003). One such state effort is the Indianapolis Blueprint to end homelessness. *See Facts About Homelessness*, Coalition for Homelessness Intervention & Prevention, *available at* http://www.chipindy.org/factstats.html (last visited Oct. 28, 2003).

[108] Greg Barrett, *supra* note 101.

[109] *Homelessness and Health*, National Health Care for the Homeless Council- 2003 Policy Statements, *available at* http://www.nhchc.org/Advocacy/PolicyPapers/2003/01HealthcareHomelessness.pdf (last visited Nov. 2, 2003).

[110] Kathryn Lewis, *supra* note 13.

[111] *Id.*

[112] Attorneys need a more informed perspective of the nature of this problem and what their role can be. Wes Daniels, *"Derelicts," Recurring Misfortune, Economic Hard Times and Lifestyle Choices: Judicial Images of Homeless Litigants and Implications for Legal Advocates*, 45 BUFF. L. REV. 687 (1997). This includes aiming for legal relief, perhaps that produces social programs, that truly and significantly improves the situation of homeless individuals because it successfully addresses the actual problems of the homeless. Lawyers can also try one of these: argue in a way that acknowledges that the homeless exercise autonomy in a place with limited and insufficient options; join a push for changing present social conditions; or get involved in forming coalitions with community activists. *Id.* The necessity defense is another avenue that attorneys should be familiar with. For explanation and evaluation of the necessity defense, *see* Antonia K. Fasanelli, *In Re Eichorn: The Long Awaited Implementation of the Necessity Defense in a Case of the Criminalization of Homelessness*, 50 AM. U. L. REV. 323, 337-54 (2000).

[113] As Julia Carson expressed, "It is a national disgrace and a senseless tragedy to allow millions of Americans, especially children, to suffer the indignities of being homeless, and not have the Congress address the needless growing crisis." *Representatives Julia Carson and John Conyers join with National Coalition for the Homeless to Rally for the Bringing America Home Act, supra* note 107.

[114] Jencks, *supra* note 34, at 122. The situation that caused this reflection was as follows:
Our dilemma, both as individuals and as a society, is to reconcile the claims of compassion and prudence. When I ponder the problem I often think of a homeless woman whom Eliot Liebow quotes at the end of *Tell Them Who I Am*. 'I'm 53 years old. I failed at two marriages and I failed at every job I ever had. Is that any reason I have to live on the street?" No government program is very likely to solve Shirley's marital or employment problems. But we can keep her off the street. Because we can, we should.
Id.

Driving While Black and Flying While Arab:
The Complexity of Racial Profiling

Sarah Vatland
Department of Sociology
Furman University

The issue of racial profiling exploded in the 1990s and has since remained a very sensitive topic. Most of the political elite have denounced the action as a "morally indefensible, deeply corrosive practice" (Ramirez, McDevitt and Farrell 2000:1). The governor of New Jersey, Christine Todd Whitman, publicly forced the resignation of the police superintendent, Carl Williams, in connection with race-based policing in an interview with a prominent New Jersey newspaper (Toby 1999). However, there are those who believe that racial profiling does not indicate police prejudice, but instead is an efficient means of policing. The question of whether racial profiling exists has, for the most part, been answered; a majority of people believe that the practice of racial profiling is indeed a problem. According to Governor Christine Todd Whitman of New Jersey: "There is no question that racial profiling exists at some level" (as cited in Mac Donald 2001:6). However, the extent to which it takes place is under debate, as is whether it is a necessary practice for good police work.

Defining Racial Profiling

It is important to define exactly what is meant by the term 'racial profiling'. Most people today have heard of the slogan "Driving While Black" but cannot go any further in identifying a singular definition of racial profiling. There are numerous definitions of racial profiling--each center on the use of race in law enforcement. However, all have different ideas as to its scope. Some have broad definitions, while others have very specific definitions. According to Schott, in an article in the *FBI Law Enforcement Bulletin* (2001:24), "racial profiling refers to action taken by the law enforcement officers solely because of an individuals race." Carrick (2000:8) in an earlier *FBI Law Enforcement Bulletin* defined it as "the phenomenon of targeting 'people of color' in traffic enforcement as a pretext to further investigation or search." Palmer (2000:479) characterizes it slightly differently: it is when "police officers target suspects based on how closely they match what some think is a typical criminal."

Callahan and Anderson (2001:39) define it more specifically as, "the practice of stopping and inspecting people who are passing through public places—such as drivers on a public highway or pedestrians in airports or urban areas—where the reason for the stop is a statistical profile of the detainee's race or ethnicity." According to Ramirez, McDevitt, and Farrell (2000:2), profiling is "any police-initiated action that relies on the race, ethnicity or national origin rather than the behavior of an individual." For Porter (1999:1), racial profiling is "the practice of targeting people for police or security stops based on their race or ethnicity in the belief that certain ethnic groups may be more likely to commit a particular crime." Like Porter's definition, Carrick (2000:8) further states that it basically "amounts to the improper practice of selecting potential criminal suspects because of their race or ethnicity."

To define it further, Heather Mac Donald (2001:1) differentiates between "'hard' and 'soft' profiling." When race is the only factor used to assess a person's criminal suspicion, Mac

Donald (2001) labels this hard racial profiling. Many of the definitions discussed above are hard profiling definitions; for example, Schott (2001) and Porter (1999) both represent hard profiling definitions. However, when race is one among many factors used to determine a person's suspiciousness, it is considered soft profiling (Mac Donald 2001). For the purposes of this article, the definition of racial profiling will be the police-initiated practice of selecting potential criminals because of their race or ethnicity alone. Hence, hard profiling will be the main definition of racial profiling. If race is used in conjunction with other information, then racial profiling, under this definition, did not occur. This definition was chosen because it represents the crux of the debate. The most often disputed form of racial profiling is hard profiling; many times soft profiling is not seen as problematic. For instance, Schott (2001:24) reminds us that race coupled with other factors can be helpful in determining suspicion, but "race or color alone is insufficient."

Background to Racial Profiling

The discussion of racial profiling accelerated and gained media attention in the 1990s. According to Callahan and Anderson (2001), racial profiling can be linked to three tangible sources. One is the difficulty associated with policing victimless crimes and the need for intrusive police techniques. Another is the increased relevancy of the difficulty to police victimless crimes caused by the intensification of the drug war since the 1980s. The final source is "the additional incentive that asset forfeiture law gives the police forces to seize money and property from suspects" (Callahan and Anderson 2001:38).

Victimless crimes are difficult to police because there is not a victim to describe the perpetrator. Hence, intrusive measures are often needed in order to solve these types of crimes. For drug trafficking, a victimless crime, police will often resort to profiling because there is not a specific suspect in mind. Therefore, racial profiling appears to be the only method of fighting victimless crimes such as drug trafficking. However, it is not only an ineffective method but also overly intrusive into the lives of American citizens.

Although the New York shooting and killing of the Amadou Diallo, "an unarmed African immigrant" again ignited the debate in 1999 ("First Safety..." 1999:26; Leitzel 2001), most researchers on the subject blame racial profiling on the 1982 war on drugs during the Reagan administration (Harris 1999; Callahan and Anderson 2001). According to Holmes (2000:345), police assume "that blacks are naturally prone to criminality" and therefore, the profile of a drug courier has led to more African Americans to be stopped and searched.

The first reported incidences of racial profiling took place in the early 1990s on the New Jersey Turnpike, because it is considered a popular drug trafficking route (Leitzel 2001). The debate intensified with the torture of Abner Louima in 1997 and in 1998, with the police shooting of a minority-filled van after pulling it over for speeding on the New Jersey turnpike (Leitzel 2001). According to Harris (1999:1), the blame for racial profiling " can be laid at the feet of the government's "war on drugs"." He believes that the war on drugs was actually "a war on people and their constitutional rights" (Harris 1999:1).

Racial profiling is also encouraged within the police department because of the forfeiture rule associated with the war on drugs. The police retain a portion of the seized assets and, therefore, have the ability to augment their budget by seizure of drugs, money etc. Consequently, if it is true, as discussed above by Holmes (2000), that police believe minorities are more likely to be involved in criminal activities, then police officers might pull over more minorities in the hopes of discovering drugs. Thus, they focus on discovering drugs and believe that minorities are more likely to be in possession of illegal narcotics. This restults in pulling over more minorities than other racial groups, they seize more drugs, and, consequently, enhance their budgets. Hence, some experts argue that seizure of assets provides the police with an incentive to racial profile (Callahan and Anderson 2001).

Stereotypes and Labeling Theory

Racial profiling is a good example of stereotyping. Stereotypes are "unreliable generalizations about all members of a group that do not recognize individual differences within the group" (Schaefer and Lamm 1998:289). These generalizations are made widespread largely through the influence of the mass media; mass media often overrepresents minority groups as criminal offenders. This overrepresentation can cause people's perceptions of minorities to be skewed about their actual involvement in crime. Stereotypes are known to "contribute to prejudices and assist in the subordination of minority groups" (Schaefer and Lamm 1998:290).

The war on drugs has only strengthened the stereotypes that African American males are more likely to be involved in illegal activities than other racial groups—specifically with drug trafficking. During the onset of the war on drugs, police departments issued 'drug courier profiles' to help officers stop those believed to be more likely to be carrying illegal substances. This profile described the typical courier as an African American male driving a Nissan Pathfinder (Callahan and Anderson 2001). This is a very descriptive, yet inaccurate racial stereotype. However, that was not the first profile developed.

The first one was a behavior-based profile formed during the 1970s by a Drug Enforcement Administration agent ("Driving While Black" 1999). It was not until "the 1980s, with the emergence of the crack market" and a sequential heightening of the war on drugs that race-based profiles emerged ("Driving While Black" 1999:3).

The Debate: Good Police Work or Racism?

The debate surrounding racial profiling has traditionally been portrayed as a liberal-conservative dichotomy. Many conservatives believe that racial profiling has a functional purpose in society and is needed for effective police work. Often they have "dismiss[ed] such complaints [against racial profiling] as the exaggerations of hypersensitive minorities" (Callahan and Anderson 2001:38). Liberals find that race-based policing creates ill feelings between minorities and police and therefore should be eradicated.

In defense of racial profiling, "the police employ laws of probability to make the best use of their scarce resources in attacking crime" (Callahan and Anderson 2001:40). For the conservatives, it is not a racially prejudice action, although it is a racially discriminatory action. Some experts contend that profiling is a reasonable police procedure (Knowles and Persico 2001; Taylor and Whitney 1999; Derbyshire 2001; Toby 1999; MacDonald 2001).

According to former President Clinton, "racial profiling is, in fact, the opposite of good police work, where actions are based on hard facts, not stereotypes" (Ramirez et al 2000:2). Some people find that racial profiling is a breach of civil liberties, while others believe it is necessary for effective policing. Schott (2001) believes that there are both illegitimate and legitimate uses of profiling in law enforcement activities. According to the Supreme Court, laws that "curtail the civil rights of a single racial group" are not legitimate unless it can be shown to "serve a governmental interest" (as cited in Schott 2001:25). Those laws that on the surface appear to be race-neutral but are enforced in such a manner that race becomes a factor are, again, not legitimate uses of profiling.

Most recent claims are grounded on two constitutional provisions: the reasonableness requirement of the Fourth Amendment and the Equal Protection Clause of the Fourth Amendment. The Fourth Amendment states that "the right of the people to be secure in their persons, houses, papers, and effects against unreasonable searches and seizures shall not be violated" (Schott 2001:26). However, according to Schott (2001), most challenges of the Fourth Amendment do not succeed. The reason for this is because regardless of subjective motivation, if the officer has some reasonable reason for the stop or seizure, then the Fourth Amendment has not been violated. For example, if a police officer pulls over a person mainly because of race and partly because of a minor traffic infraction and receives consent to search the vehicle from the driver, the Fourth Amendment is not violated because the search was given consent. The motivation for the stop or for requesting a search is irrelevant.

Most of the successful challenges are fought under the Equal Protection Clause. The Equal Protection Clause states that every state must govern impartially to all races, sexes, etc. In the past, the Supreme Court has acknowledged three types of equal protection claims: the governmental adoption of a law or policy that classifies people on the basis of race (or gender etc); the racially discriminatory enforcement of an apparently race neutral law; and a facially neutral law enacted with discriminatory intent that has an adverse affect on certain groups (Schott 2001). The basis of the discriminatory policing typically lies within the second type of claim. A challenge based on this clause is more likely to succeed than one based under the Fourth Amendment.

Callahan and Anderson (2001) make an important distinction between two uses of race in policing: 'case' versus 'class' probability. Race is frequently used when victims describe their perpetrator. In this instance, it is logical to use race. Why would police investigate a Hispanic male if the victim described his/her perpetrator as an African American male? It is logical, instead, to search and question only those that fit the delineated description. This use of race in policing employs what Callahan and Anderson (2001:5) call "case probability." Case probability, as they define it, is the concentration "on suspects who fit the description you have of a suspect" (Callahan et al 2001:6). This use of race is reasonable and needed in police work.

However, there is another use of race, which angers most of the anti-profiling activists—when race is used to create a general profile of a criminal not based on any specific event or without a suspect in mind. They label this "class probability", which "refers to situations where we know enough about a class of events to describe it using statistics, but nothing about a particular event other than the fact that it belongs to the class in question" (Callahan et al 2001:5). Class probability is also referred to as "statistical probability" because it utilizes statistics in determining criminality (Knowles, Persico, and Todd 2001:205).

Class probability is where the racial profiling debate really lies. In cases of racial profiling on American highways, the police set forth to investigate a larger percentage of minorities without having evidence of a particular crime, only a profile of a 'typical' criminal. Most people agree that case probability is an essential part of police practices; " as long as this is based on evidence gathered from particular crimes, there is nothing untoward here" (Callahan et al 2001:6). Class probability however, is thought to be intrusive upon civil liberties and to " violate [the] basic principle of justice": innocent until proven guilty (Callahan et al 2001:7).

Making Sociological Sense of Profiling

Racial profiling has serious adverse effects on police/minority relations. The conflict theory best describes this viewpoint. To briefly explain conflict theory: it is the belief that the social world is in a continuous struggle between competing groups, typically those with power and those without it. The police often disproportionately target minorities because they feel threatened by them. According to Holmes (2000:349), the *minority threat hypothesis* indicates that "whites perceive racial and ethnic minorities, in particular, as criminal threats." Hence, whites, being the more powerful group, employ a greater amount of social control to lessen the threat of minorities towards the dominant white majority. This increased concentration on minorities leads to tension between this group and the police.

Racial stereotyping leads to parallel stereotyping of police *by* minorities (Leitzel 2001). Minorities feel that the police are more abusive towards them, while the police feel threatened by them and are, therefore, more aggressive. Thus, a cycle develops in which the "minority citizens...distrust the police, whom they view as threatening symbols of oppression," therefore causing the police to be more oppressive (Holmes 2000:350). In line with the conflict perspective, minority populations often view the police as a white man's structure of power (Davis 1990). Understandably, this "mutual threat" and parallel stereotyping of police and minorities leads to strained relationships between the two groups (Holmes 2000:350). According to Son, Davis and Rome (1998), minorities mistrust the police and are therefore uncooperative towards them. Consequently, the police then react to this 'threatening behavior' and perpetuate the cycle of mistrust and misconduct. Racial profiling undermines trust and creates a lack of cooperation between groups.

According to Leitzel (2001), in some ways profiling creates an inducement for minorities to participate in criminal activity, because there is no distinction between law-abiding citizens and criminals. Regardless of virtuous behavior, law abiding black males cannot easily overcome the profile placed on them, thus "reducing the incentive [for them] to be law-abiding" citizens (Leitzel 2001:43). The logic of this approach is simple: if you are going to be labeled as a criminal regardless of whether you are or not, what is the use of being good?

Racial profiling not only causes tensions between ethnic groups but it also has a "corrosive effect on the legitimacy of the entire justice system" (Harris "Driving While Black" 1999:2). Race-based traffic stops cause ethnic minorities to not only think that the police are prejudiced and biased, but that they are being dishonest about the reason minorities are stopped in the first place. These pre-textual stops further lessen the effectiveness of the criminal justice system (Harris "Driving While Black" 1999).

Flying While Arab

Racial profiling has turned its focus on Arabs since the attacks on the World Trade Center on September 11, 2001. Should Arabs be searched more than other ethnicities when boarding airplanes? Should their ethnicity be a criterion to single them out? Just as the war on drugs started the profiling of Black Americans on our nation's highways, the war on terrorism has intensified the profiling of Arab Americans in our nation's skies.

Since the September 11th terrorist attacks, more and more people have been in favor of racial profiling. In a Gallup poll taken a few days following the attacks, approximately six out of ten Americans "favored requiring people of Arab descent to undergo more-intensive security checks when flying on U.S. airplanes" (Dvailia 2001:1). Feingold (2001), the U.S. Senator from Wisconsin, reminds us that it is important to respect all American's civil liberties in the light of the September 11th tragedy.

Racial profiling can no longer be considered a "black" thing or even an "American" thing; the reaction since September 11th has shown it to be a "societal" thing. "Just like black men are stopped because police think they are drug dealers, now any Arab who flies is thought to be a terrorist," according to Michel Shehadeh, the West Coast regional director of the American-Arab Anti-Discrimination Committee (http://www.overgrow.com/news/news2793.shtml). For instance, Ashraf Khan, a Pakistani businessman was asked to disembark from a Delta Airlines flight on the Monday following the terrorist attacks "because the pilot and the crew did not feel "comfortable" flying with him on board" (Rajghatta 2001:1).

Is it fair to target the "three million Arab-Americans and the seven million Muslims living in the United States," the majority whom are innocent law-abiding citizens (http://www.overgrow.com/news/news2793.shtml)? Most experts would argue that it is not fair to profile, regardless of the reason. Many people claim that one cannot compare the two types of profiling—profiling created by the war on drugs and profiling created by the war on terrorism—since there is much more to lose with the new war. However David Harris, a professor at University of Toledo, reminds us that it is important to keep in mind that, although the hijackings of September 11th were done by people with Middle Eastern origin, "before these attacks, the single largest terrorist attack was done by a white man, [Timothy McVeigh]" (http://www.overgrow.com/news/news).

His pointing this out is important because following September 11th, people felt that racial profiling was justified, when in reality, profiling will not be successful in stopping terrorism.

Solutions

Most experts offer a few solutions to the racial profiling problem. Training is one of the most often cited solutions to racial profiling (McNamara 2001; Holmes 2000; Carrick 2000; Weaver 1992; Scott 1993). This solution is based on the belief that the causes of profiling involve a lack of knowledge and understanding of cultural issues. Some experts argue that training, including cultural awareness and intercultural communication will help foster understanding and sensitivity towards other cultures (Weaver 1992; Scott 1993; Carrick 2001). However, if the problem is not racist law enforcement agencies or officers, training alone will not solve the problem.

Policy changes have also been commonly cited as a solution to racial profiling. According to McNamara (2001), most police department policy on profiling is ambiguous and needs to be made more clear-cut and succinct. Inbau (1999) agrees with McNamara and believes that policy changes are essential to addressing the problem of racial profiling. But will training and policy changes solve the problem or make the problem go underground? Would officers still make the same decisions as before but, as a result of sensitivity training, not admit and take responsibility afterward?

Some researchers believe that the only way to solve the problem is by addressing the source of the problem. For Holmes (2000), that involves approaching the issue of segregation and depravation of America's minority population. His approach might be effective for race-based policing on the highways, however it would fail to challenge the racial profiling now taking place on a larger scale in airports around the country.

For Callahan and Anderson (2001), addressing the root of the problem would be to confront the laws put into place by the onset of the drug war. These policies and laws, they claim, create incentive to profile. As previously discussed, these researchers particularly oppose the potential abuses of the forfeiture laws.

One step that most agree would lead to a solution is the collection of data on all traffic stops, not just those in which a citation is issued. Many states, including Florida, North Carolina and Connecticut, have begun to require the officers to collect data on all their stops (Carrick 2001).

Videotaping all stops has also been enacted in some states since the problems of racial profiling became apparent. According to *The Economist* (1999), in Boston, leaders have made the decision to stop blaming crime on race and instead to "tackle the moral problems" ("First Safety..." 1999:26). Leitzel (2001), aligns himself with the idea that race should not be used as an excuse. Strict laws, and videotaping, he believes, would help reduce the number of racially based stops.

Carrick (2000) has a three-dimensional approach outlined in his article entitled "Professional Police Traffic Stops: Strategies to Address Racial Profiling." The first step would be organizational policy. Policy outlining what is acceptable officer behavior and what is discriminatory is needed to be an integral part of the process to clarify the situation. Second, he believes there needs to be officer training to bring awareness and sensitivity to the issue of profiling. Third, data collection must be required on each and every stop regardless of whether a citation was given.

The American Civil Liberties Union issued a special report in which they outlined a five-point plan for eradicating racial profiling (1999). Their plan, like Carrick's three-dimensional approach, includes data collection; it also includes ending the use of pre-textual stops as a crime-fighting tactic. Pretextual stops are believed to be the basis of mistrust among the minority populations and the police. Therefore, getting rid of this tactic would eventually lead to more trust among the two groups. The second point in their plan is to pass the Traffic Stops Statistics Study Act, which was introduced by Rep. John Conyers in 1998 and reintroduced in 1999. The Act would require "the collection of several categories of data on each traffic stop"(Harris "Driving While Black..." 1999:14). Third, legislation should be passed requiring states to collect statistics. Fourth would be banning racial profiling in all federally funded drug interdiction programs and "tak[ing] steps to ensure that racial profiling is not used"(Harris "Driving While Black..." 1999:15). Finally, as mentioned before, cities should voluntarily collect data, specifically the fifty largest ones.

Conclusion

There are still those who believe that racial profiling is an important aspect to police work. In regards to soft profiling, they are correct. However, hard profiling causes more anger and distrust in minority communities than "the extra arrests it purportedly leads to" is worth (Feldstein, 2001:4). Many solutions are cited to fix the problem of racial profiling on our nations highways; however, it is unlikely that any single solution will be effective in solving the profiling issue. Instead the recommended changes must be applied in conjuncture with one another for them to work. Race-based policing is a multifaceted problem and therefore needs a multifaceted solution. Perhaps the three-dimensional approach or the five-point plan mentioned earlier would be the most effective means to resolving the profiling problem because they employ the use of many solutions.

The government has recognized that racial profiling is a serious social problem and that it is increasing cleavages between groups of people. It has finally begun to take steps in correcting the profiling problem. However, the solution is not completely the responsibility of the government; citizens must work to rid themselves of their own racial stereotypes as well. This step might be the only real effective long-term solution to racial profiling.

REFERENCES:

Callahan, G. and W. Anderson. 2001. "Roots of Racial Profiling." *Reason* 33 i4: 37.

Carrick, G. 2000. "Professional Police Traffic Stops: Strategies to Address Racial Profiling." *FBI Law Enforcement Bulletin* 69 (11): 8-10.

"Cops Terrify President's Top Black Aides; Victims of Racial Profiling in Maryland." *Jet* October 16, 2000. 98 i19: 4.

Dvailia, F. 2001. "Judging Others by their Covers." *Seattle Times* October 10, 2001.

Davis, J. R. 1990. "Comparison of Attitudes Toward the New York City Police." *Journal of Police Science and Administration* Vol. 17 page 233-243

Derbyshire, J. 2001. "In Defense of Racial Profiling: Where is our Common Sense?" *National Review* 53 i3.

"Driving While Black, D.W.B." Online. Internet Explorer. Available: <http://www.wolfenet.com/~jneedlel/BLACK1.htm>

Feingold, R. 2001. "Feingold, Conyers: Making Skies Safer and Respecting Civil Rights are not Mutually Exclusive: Lawmakers Urge Immediate Action to Protect Civil Rights of Passengers." October 21, 2001. <http://feingold.senate.gov/~feingold/releases.

Feldstein, D. 2001. "City's Plan to Probe Racial Profiling Flawed: Some HPD Officers Ignore Form." *Houston Chronicle* April 15, 2001. <http://kpoa.org/news1.htm> (March 5, 2001)

------ 1999. "First Safety, the Civility" *The Economist.* May 1st 1999. 25-26.

Harris, D. A. 1997. ""Driving While Black" and All Other traffic Offenses: The Supreme Court and Pre-textual Traffic Stops." *Journal of Criminal Law and Criminology* 87 (2): 544-582.

------ 1999. "Driving While Black: Racial Profiling on our Nation's Highways." *An American Civil Liberties Union Special Report.* Online. Internet Explorer. February 13, 2002. Available: http://www.aclu.org/profiling/report/index.html

------ 1999. "The Media Awareness Project: Profiling-A Self-Fulfilling Racist Policy." *WallStreetJournal*Online.InternetExplorer.Available: http://www.mapinc.org/letters/1999/03/lte86.html

Holmes, M. D. 2000. "Minority Threat and Police Brutality: Determinants of Civil Rights Criminal Complaints in US Municipalities." *Criminology* 38: 343-365.

Inbau, F. E. 1999. "Democratic Restraints Upon the Police." *The Journal of Criminal Law and Criminology* 89 (4) 1429-1440.

"Is Jim Crow Justice Alive and Well in America Today?" Online. Internet Explorer. March 5, 2002. Available: http://www.aclu.org/profiling/index.html

Knowles, J.; N. Persico; and P. Todd. 2001. "Racial Bias in Motor Vehicle Searches: Theory and Evidence." *Journal of Political Economy* 109 (1): 203-229.

Leitzel, J. 2001. "Race and Policing." *Society* 38 i3: 38.

Mac Donald, H. 2001. "The Myth of Racial Profiling." *City Journal* Online. Internet Explorer. Spring 2001. Available: http://www.city-journal.org/html/11_2_the_myth.html

McGraw, S. 2000. "Blacks More Likely to be Searched, Cops Find: Michigan State Police Study Details Traffic Stops." Online. Internet Explorer. February 8, 2002. Available: http://www.apbnews.com/newscenter/breakingnews/2000/07/21/profiling0721_01.html?s=syn.yahoo.fc_profiling0721

McNamara, R. P. 2001. "Recruitment and Selection of Officers in Addressing Biased Policing." *Police Executive Research Forum* Washington, DC.

Miniter, B. 2000. "Video Vindication." *The American Enterprise* 11 (6): 7.

National Institute of Justice. 2000. "Examining Minority Trust and Confidence in the Police."Online. Internet Explorer. February 8, 2002. Available: http://www.ojp.usdoj.gov

Palmer, E. A. 2000. "House Judiciary Approves Bill Authorizing Attorney General to Study Racial Profiling by Police." *CQ Weekly* March 4, 2000: 479.

Porter, R. 1999. "Skin Deep: Minorities Seek Relief from Racial Profiling." Online. InternetExplorer.February8,2002.Available: ttp://www.atlanet.org/homepage/triaN99.ht

Rajghatta, C. 2001. "Racial profiling grounds Asians in US." *The Times of India* September 21, 2001. http://timesofindia.indiatimes.com/articleshow.asp?art_id=1276389720> (April 18, 2002)

Ramirez, D., J. McDevitt and A. Farrell. 2000. *A Resource Guide on Racial Profiling Data Collection Systems: Promising Practices and Lessons Learned.* Northwestern University.

Schaffer, R. T. and R. P. Lamm. 1998. *Sociology.* New York: McGraw-Hill Companies 6ed.

Schott, R. G. 2001. "The Role of Race in Law Enforcement: Racial Profiling or Legitimate Use?" *FBI Law Enforcement Bulletin* 70 (11): 24-32.

Scott, E. L.1993. "Cultural Awareness Training." *The Police Chief* 60: 26-8.

Sibert, A.. 2001, Cartoon. The Black Voice Newspaper. Online. Internet Explorer. Available: http://www.alternet.org/wiretapmag/Political_Cartoon.html

Son, I. S., M. S. Davis and D. M. Rome. 1998. "Race and its Effect on Police Officers' Perceptions of Misconduct." *Journal of Criminal Justice.* 26 (1): 21-28.

Taylor, J.and G. Whitney. 1999. "Crime and Racial Profiling by US Police: Is There an Empirical Basis?" *The Journal of Social, Political and Economic Studies* 24 (4): 485-5.

Toby, J. 1999. "Racial Profiling Doesn't Prove Cops are Racist." *Wall Street Journal.* March 11, 1999. Online. Internet Explorer. Available: http://www.frontpagemag.com/archives/racerelations/toby3-11-99.htm

"US: Arab-Americans Upset By Profiling." Bergen Record (NJ). Online. Internet Explorer. Available: http://www.overgrow.com/news/news2793.shtml

Weaver, G. 1992. "Law Enforcement in a Culturally Diverse Society." *FBI Law Enforcement Bulletin* 61: 1-7.

Will, G. F. 2001. "Exposing the 'Myth' of Racial Profiling." Online. Internet Explorer. March 5, 2002. Available: http://www.kpoa.org/news1.htm

The Police and Minorities

Robert Hartmann McNamara
Department of Political Science and Criminal Justice
The Citadel

Early one morning on February 4th 1999, a young immigrant named Amadou Diallo from Guinea was returning to his Bronx apartment when he was approached by four plainclothes New York City police officers. According to some accounts, Mr. Diallo fit the description of a serial rapist that had assaulted some 40 women in areas around Manhattan. What happened as the officers approached Mr. Diallo is unclear. The officers contend they identified themselves and said Mr. Diallo's behavior led them to believe he was reaching for a weapon. Others present at the time disagree with this interpretation of events. What *is* known is that officers drew their weapons and fired a total of 41 shots, resulting in Mr. Diallo's death (*The Economist* 1997).

In 1997, Abner Louima, a 30-year-old immigrant from Haiti, was arrested when he tried to intervene in a fight outside a Brooklyn nightclub. When Mr. Louima arrived at the police station, he was dragged into a restroom and sodomised by officers with the handle of a toilet plunger, which was then forced into his mouth. Eventually, he was taken to the hospital after having been charged with resisting arrest and disorderly conduct. Mr. Louima was critically injured with a perforated colon, a lacerated bladder, several missing teeth, and an assortment of other injuries (Puddington 1999).

On almost any given day, we hear of instances like the ones just described. These dramatic episodes raise questions about the role of the police in our society, particularly in their interactions with minority groups. Some minorities leaders, as well as others, have asserted that the police, and to some extent the entire criminal justice system, are prejudiced and racist. These individuals argue that situations like the ones described above are indicators that the police single out minorities and treat them differently. Is there any truth to these assertions? Are the police racist? Do they treat minorities differently? This article will review the information available about how and why the police treat minorities differently. Part of the explanation is found in the socialization of police officers as well as the labeling theory of deviance.

Public Opinion and the Police

According to a 1997 Justice Department report, an estimated 45 million people in this country, about 20% of the population, have some form of face to face contact with the police every year. In a review of the literature on the public's attitudes toward the police, Decker (1981) found that while race and ethnicity are the most important factors in shaping attitudes toward the police, the vast majority of whites have very favorable attitudes toward them. More recently, according to the 1998 *Sourcebook of Criminal Justice Statistics*, 85% of the people surveyed by the Department of Justice said they were very satisfied with the police who served their neighborhoods. Whites expressed the most satisfaction, with 90% being very satisfied or satisfied, while only 76% of African Americans felt that way. This differs from a 1993 report which found that 47% of whites had a great deal of confidence in the capacity of the police to protect them from crime and 9% had no confidence. Like the findings from the 1997 report, African Americans in this study generally held less favorable attitudes toward the police than whites: only 38% had a great deal of confidence in the police and 11% had no confidence.

There is also a difference in the way people feel about how the police treat other groups. According to the 1998 *Sourcebook for Criminal Justice Statistics*, in response to the question "Do you think the police in your community treat all races fairly or do they tend to treat one or more of these groups unfairly?", 59% felt the police treat all groups fairly, 33% felt they treated one or more groups unfairly and 7% did not know. When the race of the respondent is included however, a dramatically different picture emerges. Sixty-seven percent of whites felt the police treat all races fairly, while only 48% of Hispanics and only 30% of African Americans felt that way.

These figures show that, in general, a significant proportion of the population thinks the police are doing a good job. However, the problems between the police and minorities become clearer when other variables are accounted for. Minorities generally feel less confident in the police and are generally less satisfied with police services. Another important factor is the characteristic of the neighborhood. As Smith et. al. (1991) have found, people in general and minorities in particular living in high crime neighborhoods and low income communities tend to have more contact with the police and report less overall satisfaction with them.

Why do police officers have more contact with low income and minority neighborhoods? Part of the answer is that this group makes greater use of police services than other groups. As Walker (1996) describes, police departments assign more patrol officers to these neighborhoods because of greater calls for service and because minority groups in these areas have higher crime rates. Another reason cited by Walker (1996) is that minorities and low-income people are more likely to call the police to solve a variety of non-criminal matters. Compared to middle class Americans, for instance, people with low incomes are more likely to call the police for assistance for things like medical emergencies and family problems. This means that the police are more actively and intrusively involved in the daily lives of people from these areas. This greater contact also means that the decisions made by officers may not be what the members of these neighborhoods prefer, resulting in lower levels of satisfaction. Additionally, given the nature of the problems and the stereotypes used by officers of individuals from these environments, it is relatively easy to see how they can perceive the police as hostile, apathetic, and prejudiced.

Judging from the evidence, and while these topics remain controversial, there appears to be evidence to substantiate a differential treatment of minorities on a variety of indicators: violent crime, deadly force, arrests, and other minor forms of abuse.

Violent Crime

Many people, including the police, believe that minorities are more involved in violent crime than whites. Moreover, this perception affects how officers respond to violent crimes. For instance, Using data from the *National Crime Victimization Survey* from 1987 to 1992, Bachman (1996) examined the relationship between the victim and the offender's race on three police responses to robbery and aggravated assault: the response time to the scene, the amount of effort made by officers to investigate these crimes at the scene, and the likelihood of arrest.

Bachman found that officers were quicker to respond and invested more effort in the investigation (i.e. arrests and searches) when the incident consisted of African American offenders and white victims. This relationship held even when variables such as poverty, the victim's gender, and whether or not the victim was injured, were taken into account.

With regard to aggravated assault, particularly those involving strangers, officers were more likely to be more thorough at the scene if it involved a white victim and an African American offender. Officers were also much more likely, all other things being equal, to respond more quickly and to put forth a more determined effort if there was an injury to the victim and if the incident occurred in a public setting.

Arrests

Is race a factor in the arrest of a suspect? It seems fairly clear that minorities are arrested out of all proportion to their representation in the population. According to the *Uniform Crime Reports* in 1998, African Americans represent about 12% of the population but 34% of all arrests and 41% for all violent crimes. However, there is a great deal of controversy surrounding this issue. Do police officers arrest minorities more frequently due to racial bias or because minorities commit more crimes? What variables are considered in the decision to arrest?

Almost thirty years ago, Black (1971) in his famous article "The Social Organization of Arrest", found that, in general, the decision to arrest was predicated on a number of factors. These include: the strength of the evidence, the seriousness of the crime, whether or not the complainant or victim wanted the suspect arrested, and whether the suspect was disrespectful towards the officer. The decision to arrest was also based on the relationship between the victim and the offender. If the suspect was a stranger to the victim, the officers were more likely to effect an arrest.

Interestingly, Black found that race was not a factor in the decision to arrest. He did find that African Americans were arrested more often than whites, but this was mainly due to the fact that they were less likely to show deference to the officer. As he describes, this creates a vicious cycle, where African American men who are arrested often have negative feelings towards the police because they feel singled out. When these feelings are demonstrated, they are more likely to be arrested, which, in turn, increases the hostility felt by African Americans.

While Black did not find that race was a factor in the decision to arrest, since that time a great deal of research has found that it does matter. In the 1980s, for instance, race was considered in terms of the decision to arrest. Smith, Visher and Davidson (1984) found that in those instances where the suspect was African American and the victim was white, officers were much more likely to make an arrest. Similar to Black's (1971) findings, in these situations, officers were also more likely to arrest the suspect when the victim requested it.

Petersilia (1983) found that African Americans and Hispanics were more likely to be arrested on less evidence than whites. She also found they were more likely to be released without the case going to the prosecutor. While at first glance this may appear to be advantageous, arrest still represents a form of punishment even though formal charges are not forthcoming.

From another point of view, Son, Davis and Rome (1998), studied 718 police officers in Ohio and examined the extent to which a suspect's race influenced an officer's behavior. The results of the study showed that officers did not feel race was a significant factor in determining the officer's behavior. What was significant was the suspect's demeanor.

Use of Force

While the Rodney King example is perhaps the most visible and memorable reminder of the excessive use of force by police officers, which generated a great deal of interest in police brutality (Friedrich 1980; Cohen 1986; Adams 1995), one area of study on this topic that has been overlooked involves Hispanics. While the subject of police treatment of minorities has been discussed in a variety of ways, such as the aforementioned arrest rates (Sampson 1986; Smith and Visher 1981) abusive practices (Reiss 1971; Westley 1970) and the use of deadly force (Fyfe 1982; Sorensen, Marquart and Brock 1993) most of these have overlooked Hispanics. In one of the few studies on the subject, Holmes (1998) compared perceptions of police abuse of minorities by whites and Hispanics in a U.S./Mexico border community. He found that young, male Hispanics, and those living in the barrio, perhaps the group that poses the greatest challenges to police authority and the potential risk of injury to officers, were more likely to report having seen abusive practices.

Similarly, the police in these communities were more likely to view individuals in these communities with suspicion and rely on stereotypes to explain their behaviors. Other research supports this finding. For instance, Maguire, Pastore and Flanagan (1993) found that a higher proportion of Hispanics, compared to others, believed the police use excessive force. Thus, it appears that, like their African American counterparts, Hispanics are more likely to be perceived as threatening to the police and this creates a climate of fear, suspicion and hostility from both groups.

Deadly Force

A great deal of attention has been given to the frequency with which police officers use deadly force against minorities (Shoop 1998; Fyfe 1988; Dunham and Alpert 1992; Westley 1970). Minorities, both African American and Hispanics, are more likely to be shot by the police than whites. As Fyfe (1988) and Geller and Scott (1991) have found African Americans are disproportionately killed by the police. However, when compared with rates of police/citizen contacts, arrest rates and resistance to or attacks upon the police, there is no apparent racial disparity in the use of deadly force by the police.

Part of the reason for the general decline in the use of deadly force has come from more restrictive policies at the departmental level as well as from the Supreme Court's decisions. Sherman and Cohn (1986) for instance, found that between 1970-1984, the police use of deadly force declined substantially, particularly against African Americans. More recently, the data indicate that the racial disparity in the number of people shot and killed by the police has decreased from about seven African Americans for every white to about three to one (Walker 1996).

By the 1980s, a number of departments had changed their use of deadly force policy to one using a "defense of life" criteria. These are situations in which the officer is justified in using deadly force if the officer or another person's life is in jeopardy. Another situation in which deadly force is justified occurs when the officer prevents the escape of a person who is extremely dangerous (Roberg and Kuykendall 1993). One of the most significant changes in the use of deadly force came as a result of a Supreme Court decision. In *Tennessee vs. Garner*, officers used deadly force against an African American juvenile who was fleeing the scene of a burglary. At that time, officers were justified in using deadly physical force against a fleeing felon: someone who had committed a felony and was attempting to elude the police. However, the Court ruled that this was no longer acceptable. As a result, many departments were required to modify their policies concerning use of force against fleeing felons.

Minority Police Officers

While the study of the relationship between minorities and arrests is fairly well documented, another area that has not been examined in as much detail are how minority officers interact with people who live in low income neighborhoods.

According to Carter (1995) minority police officers are in an extremely difficult position. He contends that African American officers feel there are differences in the decision making process between white and minority officers. They believe that minority officers will be disciplined or fired if they use unnecessary force against a white or affluent person. Until only recently, white officers knew no such fear when they acted similarly in poor or minority neighborhoods. Carter also argues that an increasing number of minority officers have never lived in inner city neighborhoods. This lack of exposure may explain why some African American officers react too harshly--similar to their white counterparts. Additionally, the nature of policing contains within it a pervasive cultural influence: fitting in is an important part of being a police officer. Carter believes that, as a consequence, some minority officers overreact in their treatment of minorities because they want to fit in with their white colleagues.

There is an added problem for minority officers. Many minority officers are accused of "selling out" or being a traitor to their race by entering law enforcement. Because of the suspicion and tension between minorities and the police and because many of these sentiments are confirmed in interactions with the police, many minorities, particularly African Americans, dislike and mistrust other African Americans who enter the profession.

Moreover, as Peak (1995) contends, many African American officers feel as though they experience a double dose of marginality as police officers. Not only must they perform their duties at a high level, often times they are representatives of the feelings of their race. To complicate matters further, minority officers may also be prevailed upon by their superiors to maintain control in minority communities because they usually have higher crime rates and other problems.

Other Forms of Abuse

The issue surrounding discriminatory treatment extends beyond serious offenses however. In fact, one might argue that the minor forms of abuse create a climate of fear and hostility between the police and minorities. These indignities, or what Liebow (1999) has referred to as the "little murders of everyday life," characterize the attitudes the police have towards minorities in some circumstances. The difference between this type of abuse and the others discussed, however, is that there is no tangible reminder that the incident occurred.

Unlike the use of force, arrest, verbal abuse, profanity, or stop and frisk searches, or profiling, the problem usually ends with the interaction. These types of incidents typically occur on the street and involve no witnesses. This makes sustaining allegations very difficult and results in a painful but episodic way of sustaining tension between the police and minorities.

For instance, the New Jersey State Police are under investigation for allegedly ordering officers to concentrate on black drivers. Three state troopers have stated they were instructed by their superiors to single out African American drivers for traffic stops. The Justice Department is currently investigating these allegations. Additionally, a 1992 study of traffic stops in Florida found that while 5% of the drivers on the road were African American or Hispanic, nearly 70% of those stopped and 80% of those searched, were members of these two groups.

Further, according to Cole (1999), from January 1993 to August 1995, almost 90% of the individuals subjected to search and seizure operations on buses and trains were people of color. Another study of all reported federal decisions from 1993 to 1995 involving bus and train sweeps found that nearly 90% of those targeted were people of color.

Another example of this kind of practice was known as Operation Hammer in Los Angeles in 1988. This was an effort by the police to stop and search minorities. More than 1,400 minority youths were arrested, many of them were released later due to a lack of evidence. For two years, African American and Hispanic youth who were found in middle class neighborhood were very likely to be stopped, searched, and arrested (Crank 1998).

Browning et. al (1994) explored the extent to which there are racial differences in getting hassled by the police, which they define as the frequency with which whites and blacks are stopped or watched by the police when they have done nothing wrong. They also explored what they identify as *vicarious hassling*--knowing someone who has experienced this type of treatment by the police.

Their main argument is that African Americans are more likely to perceive that they are hassled by the police individually and vicariously. Nearly one half of African Americans in their study had experienced this type of interaction and two-thirds knew someone who had a similar experience. This compared to the 10% of whites who experienced this type of treatment in the same way. While they do recognize that it could be a result of different patrol practices, which focus on minority neighborhoods, they also recognize that some of these perceptions may be a result of frequent police contact. A third explanation may be that there exists a perception by officers that African Americans and other minorities are more likely to commit crimes and thus are potential offenders that warrant their attention.

Finally, there is verbal abuse. Many complaints are filed each year against officers who verbally abuse citizens. The Christopher Commission, created to investigate allegations of abuse in Los Angeles following the Rodney King incident, found that officers frequently use abusive language. This may occur during the interaction with citizens or it may happen between officers. For instance, the Commission's investigation discovered computer messages were sent between officers that contained racially offensive comments.

Research on police behavior suggests that derogatory comments and the stigmatizing labeling of people that occurs is a way for officers to control suspects. As White, Cox, and Bashart (1991) note, profanity serves several functions: to gain the individual's attention when interacting with officers, to keep them at a social distance while the interaction occurs, and to psychologically dominate the individual.

What does all this tell us? It should remind us that the relationship between the police and minorities is a complex one. And while minorities are disproportionately arrested, it may be due in part to the greater involvement in criminal activities. It may also have to do with the way they respond to police contact, and it may have something to do with the attitudes of police officers. Finally, it may have something to do with the perceptions of the police by the public, particularly minority groups, and this tends to inflame the nature of the interaction between the two groups.

Factors That Contribute to Police Decision Making

In its most essential form, the discussion of how the police treat minorities is essentially one involving police discretion. The topic of police discretion has been studied at length (Goldstein 1991; LaFave 1965; Mastrofski, Ritti and Hoffmaster 1987; Powell 1981). Brooks (1993) does an excellent job of conceptualizing the factors that contribute to police decision making. While there are a set of organizational factors that contribute to police discretion, such as the degree of bureaucracy, size of the department or the supervisors' span of control of officers, and while individual officer variables, such as age of the officer, years of experience and education level are significant, perhaps most important are what she describes as neighborhood and situational variables.

Neighborhood variables include the racial composition of an area. As was mentioned, generally speaking, the higher the proportion of African Americans in a neighborhood, the greater the likelihood of the police being called to that area. Also, officers tend to conclude that when they are called to such an area, there is a greater likelihood that an arrest will be made, that someone involved in that situation will resist, and the potential risk to officer safety is higher. Thus, the anxiety level for officers is higher and they will react more quickly to threats that they perceive as a danger to their safety.

Situational variables affect police discretion in that the decisions of officers are based not so much on structural characteristics, such as the racial composition of a neighborhood, but what a person does in the course of the interaction with that officer. Examples of situational variables include demeanor, age, gender, preference of the complainant, visibility of the encounter and the presence of others. Van Maanen (1978), in his seminal paper on the perceptions and attitudes of the police, found that the police tend to focus not on suspects, but on individuals who displayed a resentment about the intrusion of the police into their lives. He referred to these individuals as *assholes*. In response to the presence of people like this, the police feel that they exist, in part, to protect the world from assholes.

According to Van Maanen (1978), labeling someone an asshole involves an interaction between the person and the police. In other words, the process of labeling the person has more to do with what the individual does in the encounter with the police than with any characteristic or trait they possess.

Finally, officer attitudes about minorities is an essential ingredient to how and in what way the officer responds to the situation and the individuals in it. Because understanding the behavior of officers is, in part, a function of their attitudes, it is important to examine how those attitudes are shaped and influenced.

Some contend that police officers have very different personalities than people in other occupations. Others maintain that there is a cultural distinction that separates law enforcement from other occupations. Still others contend that officers have neither personality nor cultural differences from other occupations. In sum, what we know about the police culture and personality is dependent on how one views police behavior. While no single perspective provides a complete understanding of the varieties of police behavior, there is a long history of debate as to whether they have unique personalities or whether socialization and subcultures play a significant part in the behavior of police officers. What can be said with some confidence is that the roles and functions of the police set officers apart from other members of society (Radelet 1986). For the sake of time and brevity, the focus will be on the cultural aspects since they play a more important role in understanding officers' attitudes, values, beliefs, and behavior with regard to minorities.

The Socialization of Police Officers

A number of researchers argue that personality is subject to change based on different personal experiences and socialization. This school of thought focuses on the role of the police in society and how professionalization, training, and socialization influence an individual's personality and behavior. Researchers operating from this paradigm study how the work environment, peers, and academy training shape and affect a police officer's personality and behavior. Many of these researchers, such as Adlam (1982), still focus attention on an individual's unique experiences and the development of individual personalities.

A somewhat different approach contends that socialization occurs, but it is more of a group experience than an individual one (Stoddard 1968; Van Maanen 1973). For example, Van Maanen (1973) disagrees with the idea that police officers have certain personality characteristics, such as authoritarianism. He argues instead for a perspective based on both group socialization and professionalism. The latter is the process by which norms and values are internalized as an individual begins his or her new occupation. In this way, just as attorneys and physicians learn the values endemic to their profession, so too do police officers.

This perspective assumes that police officers learn their "social" personality from training and through exposure to the demands of police work. It follows then that if police officers become cynical or rigid, it is not because of their existing personality or individual experience, but because of the demands of the job and the shared experiences of others. Some research supports this idea.

For instance, Bennett (1984) found that while probationary officers' values are affected by the training process, little evidence was available that personalities were shaped by their peers in the department. Part of this explanation involves the legitimacy of newly hired officers, who do not become "real" police officers until they are accepted as a member in standing of the police subculture.

Other studies, such as Putti, Aryee and Kang (1988) find socialization into the subculture of policing may occur at different points in officers' careers. There is little evidence concerning the extent of how reference groups affect the personality of older officers, but it seems that in the beginning of his or her career, the officer's occupational values are shaped during the training and probationary process.

The idea of the police being a subculture is not new and has been well documented (see for instance Westley 1970; Rokeach 1971; Kirkham 1976; Bittner 1970). Entry into this subculture begins with a process of socialization whereby recruits learn the values and behavior patterns characteristic of experienced officers. The development and maintenance of negative attitudes and values by police officers has many implications.

Skolnick (1994) was among the first researchers to examine the influence of the police culture. In a study of two cities he called Eastville and Westville, he noted that police officers displayed prejudicial views toward African Americans. He distinguished however, between prejudiced and racist behavior. Though negative attitudes towards African Americans was common, these feelings were not often acted upon--racist behavior was uncommon. While there was no training conducted that told officers to treat African Americans differently, Skolnick states "from the point of view of the African American or the White who is generally sympathetic to the plight of the Black in America, most police officers--Westville and Eastville alike, would be regarded as highly racially biased" (pp.77-78). The essential question for Skolnick was not whether officers were racially prejudiced but whether racially prejudiced officers influence their judgment in the use of discretion.

Skolnick's work has made a significant contribution to our understanding of police-minority relations. Police attitudes towards minorities are filtered through a subcultural lens that has a significant impact on an officer's behavior. The attitudes, values, and beliefs that are strongly encouraged by the subculture have a major impact on how individuals will encounter and interact with all members of the community.

Making Sense of Police-Minority Relations

It seems that police officers discriminate against minorities and it seems that they learn this in the context of being socialized as police officers. And as Van Maanen (1978) has described, officers generally appear to have strong convictions about their assessment of these groups. This is similar in some ways to how most people in our culture understand things around them. It seems that once we learn something in society, whatever its source, it is often very difficult for us to break loose from that understanding. We all have what Leon Festinger (1954) called a fundamental "need to know" or understand the physical and social world around us. As such, we seek answers to questions around us.

We tend to take cues from people and things and when enough cues emerge, we tend to categorize the person. If a person acts in a particular way, he or she must be *that* type of a person. If they look or dress unconventionally, then people often make sweeping generalizations about who they are and what they believe. This simplistic understanding of the world around us and the people in it, leads to what phenomenologists call *typifications*. We put people and things into categories so that we are able to understand where they fit into our world, and, conversely, we understand our place in it as well. We label people and these labels can be negative ones. This categorizing is what Fritz Heider (1958) referred to as a *naive psychology* in that we all do this, and for the most part it is harmless. But is it? Does it reflect a myopic view of the world, in that everyone and everything must fit someplace into some category?

The reasons why we use a naïve psychology lies in part in people's perception. They tend to take their social world for granted, accepting their society and customs as unquestioningly as they do the physical world around them. Thus, while people want to understand their world, they do not want to understand too much of it.

Since people see the world narrowly, because they do not transcend their own experiences, many have very firm but erroneous beliefs about "how things ought to be." They have not taken that next step in understanding, and for the most part, they do not want to. This naïve psychology and "need to know" also affects police officers. They, like the rest of us, seek answers to questions in part because of their safety needs and in part because they are expected to solve the problems our society faces. Perhaps nowhere is this naïve psychology better understood than with the way the police perceive minority groups.

One of the best cues police officers use to identify and typify a person as well as their attitudes, behaviors, values and beliefs, is race. It is the most visible indicator, it is the easiest to identify and in policing, where the officer must make an assessment of the person quickly, it is often the only one used. But that initial assessment may lead the officer to draw a host of conclusions, which, in turn, influences his or her behavior. This behavior will be interpreted by the minority and he or she will react accordingly. Thus, if an officer concludes that African Americans or Hispanics are more likely to commit crimes, are more likely to pose a threat to their physical safety, and are more likely to jeopardize their authority, the officer will inevitably begin the interaction with these thoughts in mind. The minority member will respond to what he or she perceives as threatening behavior, creating a self-fulfilling prophecy. The behavior of the minority will confirm in the officer's mind what he or she thinks they already knew...minorities are potential trouble. When in reality, what may have happened is that the officer created the circumstances in which that outcome was derived.

Thus, the problems of tension between the police and minorities are based largely on the attitudes and perceptions of both groups of each other. These attitudes, values, and beliefs are reflected in the negative labels applied by each group. For the police, these attitudes and overall treatment of minorities is derived largely from the way officers are socialized and conform to the standards of the police subculture.

REFERENCES:

Adams, K. 1995. "Measuring the Prevalence of Police Abuse of Force." In William Geller And Hans Toch (eds.) *And Justice for All*. Washington, D.C.: The Police Executive Research Forum.

Adlam, K.R. 1982. "The Police Personality: Psychological Consequences of Becoming a Police Officer." Journal of Police Science and Administration 10(3):347-348.

Bachman, R. 1996. "Victims's Perceptions of Initial Police Responses to Robbery And Aggravated Assault: Does Race Matter?" Journal of Quantitative Criminology 12(4):363-390.

Bennett, R.R. 1984. "Becoming Blue: A Longitudinal Study of Police Recruit Occupational Socialization." *Journal of Police Science and Administration* 12(1):47-57.

Bittner, E. 1970. *The Functions of Police in Modern Society*. Chevy Chase, MD: National Clearinghouse for Mental Health.

Black, D. 1971. "The Social Organization of Arrest." *Stanford Law Review* 23:1087-1111.

Boydston, J. E. 1975. *San Diego Field Interrogation: Final Report*. Washington, D.C.: The Police Foundation.

Brooks, L. W. 1996. "Police Discretionary Behavior: A Study of Style," in R.G. Dunham and G. P. Alpert (eds.) Critical Issues in Policing: Contemporary Readings. Prospect Heights, IL: Waveland Press, pp.140-164.

Browning, S. L.; F. T. Cullen; L. Cao; R. Kopache; T. J. Stevenson. 1994. "Race and Getting

Hassled By the Police: A Research Note." *Police Studies* 17(1):1-11.

Carter, R. A. 1995. "Improving Minority Relations." *FBI Law Enforcement Bulletin* 64:14-17.

Cohen H. 1986. "Exploiting Police Authority," *Criminal Justice Ethics* (Summer/Fall):23-31.

Cole, D. 1999. "When the Reason is Race." *The Nation.* 268(10):22.

Crank, J. P. 1998. *Understanding Police Culture.* Cincinnati, OH: Anderson.

Decker, S. H. 1981. "Citizen Attitudes Toward the Police: A Review of Past Findings and Suggestions for Future Policy." *Journal of Police Science and Administration* 9:80-87.

Eisenman, R. 1995. "Is There Bias in U.S. Law Enforcement?" *Journal of Social, Political, and Economic Studies* 20:229-240.

Festinger, L. 1954. "Theory of Social Comparison." *Human Relations* 7:117-140.

Friedrich, R.J. 1980. "Police Use of Force: Individuals, Situations, and Organizations." *Annals of the American Academy of Political and Social Science* 452:82-97.

Fyfe, J. J.. 1988."Police Use of Deadly Force: Research and Reform." Justice Quarterly 5:165-205.

_____. 1982. "Blind Justice: Police Shootings in Memphis." *Journal of Criminal Law and Criminology* 73:707-722.

Geller, W.A. and Scott, M. S. 1993. "Deadly Force: What We Know." In Thinking About Police, C. B. Klockars and S. D. Mastrofski (eds.) New York: McGraw-Hill, pp. 446-476.

Goldstein, H. 1991. "Controlling and Reviewing Police-Citizen Contacts." In T. Barker and D.L. Carter (eds.) *Police Deviance.* 2nd Edition. Cincinnati, OH: Anderson.

Heider, F. 1958. *The Psychology of Human Relations.* New York: John Wiley and Sons.

Holmes, M. D. 1998. "Perceptions of Abusive Police Practices in a U.S.-Mexico Border Community." *Social Science Journal* 35(1):107-118.

Kappler, V.E., M. Blumberg and G.W. Potter. 1993. T*he Mythology of Crime and Criminal Justice.* Prospect Heights, IL: Waveland Press.

Kirkham, G. 1976. *Signal Zero.* New York: Ballentine.

LaFave, W. 1965. *The Decision to Take a Suspect into Custody.* Boston, MA: Little, Brown and Company.

Liebow, E. 1999. *Tell Them Who I Am.* Chicago: University of Chicago Press.

Maguire, K., A. L. Pastore, and T.J. Flanagan. (eds.) 1998. *Sourcebook of Criminal Justice Statistics.* Washington, D.C.: U.S. Government Printing Office.

Mastrofski, S., R. Ritti, and D. Hoffmaster. 1987. "Organizational Determinants of Police Discretion: The Case of Drinking and Driving." *Journal of Criminal Justice* 15:387-401.

"Only a Minority: Police Brutality." *The Economist* 344(8031):19, August 23, 1997.

Petersilia, J. *Racial Disparities in the Criminal Justice System.* Santa Monica, CA: RAND.

Powell, D. 1981. "Race, Rank and Police Discretion." *Journal of Police Science and Administration* 9:383-389.

Roberg, R. R. and J. Kuykendall. 1993. *Police and Society.* Belmont, CA: Wadsworth.

Peak, K. J. 1993. *Policing American Methods, Issues and Challenges.* Inglewood, CA: Regents/Prentice-Hall.

Puddington, A. 1999. "The War on the War on Crime." *Commentary.* 107(5):25.

Putti, J., S. Aryee and T.S. Kang 1988. "Personal Values of Recruits and Officers in a Law Enforcement Agency: An Exploratory Study." *Journal of Police Science and Administration* 16(4):245-249.

Radelet, L. 1986. *The Police and the Community*. 4th ed. New York: Macmillan.

Reiss, A. J. Jr. 1971. *The Police and the Public*. New Haven, CT: Yale University Press.

Rokeach, Milton, Martin Miller and Hohn Snyder. 1971. "The Value Gap Between Police and Policed." *Journal of Social Issues* 27:155-171.

Rubenstein, J. 1973. *City Police*. New York: Farrar, Strauss, and Giroux.

Sampson, R. J. 1986. "Effects of Socioeconomic Context on Official Reaction to Juvenile Delinquency." *American Sociological Review* 51:876-885.

Shoop, J. G. 1998. "National Survey Suggests Racial Disparity in Police Use of Force." *Trial* 34(1):97.

Skolnick, J. 1994. *Justice Without Trial: Law Enforcement in a Democratic Society*. 5th edition. New York: John Wiley and Sons.

Smith, D.A., C. Visher, and L. A. Davidson. 1984. "Equity and Discretionary Justice: The Influence of Race on Police Arrest Decisions." *Journal of Criminal Law and Crimniology* 75:234-249.

Smith, D. A. and C. Visher. 1981. "Street Level Justice: Situational Determinants of Police Arrest Decisions." *Social Problems* 29:167-177.

Son, I.S.; M. Davis, and D. M. Rome. 1998. "Race and its Effect on Police Officers' Perceptions Of Misconduct. " *Journal of Criminal Justice* 26(1):21-28.

Sorenson, J. R.; J. W. Marquart, and E. Brock. 1993. "Factors Related to Killings of Felons by Police Officers: A Test of Community Violence and Conflict Hypotheses." *Justice Quarterly* 10:417-440.

Stoddard, E.R. 1968. "The Informal Code of Police Deviancy: A Group Approach to Blue-Collar Crime." *Journal of Criminal Law, Criminology, and Police Science*, 59(2):201-203.

U. S. Department of Justice: Bureau of Justice Statistics. 1998. *Sourcebook for Criminal Justice Statistics*. Washington, D.C.: U.S. Government Printing Office.

Walker, S.; C. Spohn; and M. Delone. 1996. *The Color of Justice: Race, Ethnicity and Crime in America*. Belmont, CA: Wadsworth.

Westley, William. 1970. Violence and the Police: A Sociological Study of Law, Custom, and Morality. Cambridge, MA: MIT Press.

White, M. F., T. C. Cox, and J. Basehart. 1991. "Theoretical Considerations of Officer Profanity and Obscenity in Formal Contacts with Citizens." In T. Barker and D. L. Carter (eds.) *Police Deviance* 2nd edition, pp.275-297. Cincinnati, OH: Anderson.

Van Maanen, J. 1978. "The Asshole" in P. Manning and J. Van Maanen (eds.) *Policing: A View from the Street*. Santa Monica, CA: Goodyear.

Van Maanen, J.1973. "Observations on the Making of Policemen." *Human Organization* 32:407-418.

Who's History: Native Americans in U.S. History Textbooks

Maria T. Shelley
Department of Sociology
Vanderbilt University

What is it that makes one an "American"? What holds together a nation that cannot claim a common ethnic lineage, a single language, a unifying set of values, a shared past? Some of us come from Ireland, Russia, Britain, Iran, Germany, Mexico, Africa, China. Some speak Spanish, English, French, Japanese, Italian, Lebanese, Greek. Some light Menorahs or Christmas trees, celebrate Chinese New Year or Kachina rituals, worship Allah or Vishnu, commemorate Martin Luther King or St. Patrick. It seems as if the only things that hold us together are the Atlantic and Pacific coastlines!

The history books of other nations speak of hundreds of years of moral philosophy, unbroken traditions, the endurance of hardships, and feuds with ancient rivals. These nations compose hymns to folk heroes that every child learns by heart, and their museums echo a long, rich past. But our fledgling United States was officially born as recently as 1776. Thus, in addition to the fact that our country consists of people from other nations, we must also recognize the comparatively brief time we have had to construct our lives together.

Fortunately, for most of us, the question of America's identity is a rhetorical one rather than a pressing issue that demands an answer. We can go on with our day to day lives in this nation without fully understanding or defining what it means to be an American. U.S. History textbook writers, however, do not have that luxury. By virtue of the fact that students must learn about their country, writers must record *something* that describes the nation's past and its present condition. It is that "something" that is the focus of the debate over curriculum reform among educators. In a nation of many ethnic and racial groups, the relationship between multiculturalism and education is central in determining whose voices will be part of the historical knowledge that students will learn.

This study proposes that at the heart of the multicultural curriculum debate are two competing visions of America's identity. Educators are not merely arguing about how many lines of text to devote to a particular ethnic group; rather, they are contesting how future generations will understand who we are and what it means to be an "American." In short, textbook writers must reach some consensus out of conflicting interpretations of America's past. This task mirrors the debate between functionalist and conflict perspectives on society, making a sociological analysis an insightful way to understand the multiculturalism debate.

LITERATURE REVIEW ON THE MULTICULTURALISM DEBATE
Grounding the Debate in the Sociology of Knowledge:

The sociology of knowledge holds the question of "how we know what we know" at its core. Karl Mannheim, a classical figure in this area, explains that knowledge is a cooperative process, the result of group interaction (not individual thinkers) in which ideas tend to develop in response to common problems. These groups are not just economic classes, but also include occupational categories, status groups, religious organizations, and others. The groups with which one is affiliated help to shape the type of knowledge that individuals develop and then accept as "truth."

According to the sociology of knowledge, then, we can explore the process of constructing knowledge about America's past. More specifically, U.S. History textbooks are knowledge artifacts that make truth claims about the origin and development of the nation. Textbooks remain the centerpiece of public school education, making their content appear as objective, true "facts" about America's past (Gordy & Pritchard 1995). Foucault and other more contemporary scholars in the sociology of knowledge argue that such socially normative "truths" are actually reflections of the dominant group's interests and knowledge. Given that America is a country comprised of many racial, cultural and ethnic groups, *which* group's knowledge claims about America's past are found in textbooks is an important issue to explore. As Nelson, et al. (1993) suggest:

> Curriculum is political, and curriculum change is always a slow-moving political process. Be careful--, this is not a simple academic debate about textbooks or approved reading lists: The struggle over the curriculum is a political battle about the control of knowledge. Sort through the rhetoric carefully. Assess the arguments by asking which groups would benefit if a particular curriculum were pursued. (172)

Thus, this study uses a sociology of knowledge perspective in that it examines the compromises and decisions that result in a certain history curriculum as embodied in U.S. history textbooks.[1]

This study of a knowledge artifact, like all social products, can be analyzed through both a conflict and a functionalist theoretical approach. For functionalists, the sociology of knowledge explains how society is held together by a shared body of knowledge in order to interact and communicate with one another. Proponents of the conflict perspective, on the other hand, focus on the ways that certain groups in society use the production and consumption of knowledge to serve their interests. This study uses history textbooks as the knowledge object to be explored and reconfigures the debate over multiculturalism according to the arguments set forth between functionalist and conflict perspectives.

To date, the multiculturalism debate over history curriculum reform has its primary locus in the education literature and research forum. Most of these scholars' commentaries are grounded in government studies of students' skill assessments and on critiques of curriculum reform attempts. In addition, the exploration of multicultural curriculum reform has been largely neglected by sociologists, with the exception of a few noteworthy pieces. Accordingly, the debate has been argued without much theoretical or empirical grounding or systematic research. Therefore, in order to move the debate beyond philosophical criticism and political attacks on failed reforms, it is necessary to anchor the debate in theoretically informed empirical research that assesses the current state of history curriculum in schools. To that end, the purpose of this study is to provide a theoretical framework to the multiculturalism debate in education and to use content analysis of high school U.S. history textbooks in order to begin to address the following question: *What and whose knowledge is currently being taught as United States history in high*

---

[1] For purposes of this study, discussion of curriculum reform refers to textbook reform since textbooks still comprise a key part of public high school classrooms. It is important to recognize, however, that curriculum actually entails multiple components of which textbooks are only one part.

schools and how has that changed since the 1960s multicultural reform movement began to notably shape curriculum production?

Framing the Multiculturalism Debate with Sociological Perspectives:

Schlesinger explains, "The debate about the curriculum is a debate about what it means to be an American" (1992: 17). Many scholars agree with Schlesinger's claim that a relationship between American identity and education is what make curriculum reform such a contested domain. "If participation in a democratic society is essential to the good life, then it follows that education must foster democracy, but it also follows that just as people disagree about the nature of democracy, they will disagree about education" (Perry & Fraser 1993). As we shall see, the functionalist and conflict perspectives can be used to highlight two contrasting views of American identity and democracy as well as how those views then shape each side's attitude toward the multiculturalism debate in education.

Functionalist Perspective on American Identity:

Broadly understood, the imagery associated with the functionalist perspective is that of an organism comprised of many interdependent parts which work together for the survival of the whole. Functionalists focus, therefore, on creating and maintaining the social body by examining how each institution perpetuates social order and consensus. Accordingly, functionalism argues that schools are one institution that maintain social order by socializing students into the norms and values of the nation. In other words, schools produce students with an American identity. Functionalists understand American identity as a blending of cultures, races, and ethnicities all tied together by common political ideals of democracy. This "melting pot" vision of democracy permeates Arthur Schlesinger's, *The Disuniting of America* (1992). He argues that, "The point of America was not to preserve old cultures, but to forge a new American culture" (1992: 13). It follows, then, that any attempt to preserve racial or ethnic uniqueness is undemocratic because, for functionalists, being American involves stressing the "common social good."

Appleby (in Banks 1997) defines what I have described as a functionalist view of American identity in terms of "American exceptionalism." She explains that schools often teach history to students as if democracy has been attained in the United States and that any problems over multiculturalism were resolved in the sixties civil rights movement. In short, American exceptionalism presents democracy as a common American ideal that we have already achieved, unlike many "other" countries.

Functionalist Perspective on Multiculturalism in Education:

Consequently, although schools present a range of cultural voices, "these voices must be trained not for solo performance, but to be part of the chorus" (Nelson 1993: 179). So schools function to unite students by teaching them a common body of knowledge--the "core curriculum," or the "canon of Great Books," as it is often labeled (see for instance, Hirsch 1988; Bloom 1987). Thus, the challenge to include diverse perspectives and minority contributions has left many functionalists uneasy. The new mantra to go "back to the basics" and return to a national core curriculum is an attempt to preserve the schools' function of creating a common body of knowledge for all American students. Another way in which the melting pot view of democracy influences the debate is the functionalist's proposal that ethnic and minority groups should gain any specific group's knowledge from private schools or non-academic institutions like the family or the church; the assumption, therefore, is that all students must learn "basic" history, and that ethnic and other minority knowledge is only important to those for whom it is relevant (Nelson 1993).

The emphasis to incorporate multicultural perspectives into the curriculum or "canon" is often treated as the cause of educational decline. In 1983, the National Commission on Excellence in Education conducted an extensive research project on the nation's schools and declared that America was "a nation at risk" because of the students' low academic performance. E. D. Hirsch claimed that during the period from 1970-1985, the amount of shared knowledge among citizens in America was sharply declining. So concerned was Hirsch with this decline in common knowledge that he compiled his own list of "what literate Americans" should know (1987). Low scores on national standardized tests result from giving students too much "extraneous" information. Thus, the inclusion of more perspectives and interpretations of U.S. history is viewed negatively as a "dysfunction" that needs to be overcome by going back to the basics in order to regain social equilibrium.

In conclusion, functionalists regard the multicultural movement in curriculum reform to be a source of disruption in the functioning of schools. Those like Schlesinger and Hirsch argue that schools should serve to bring individuals into a common understanding of America. Therefore, those who wish to "fragment" a unified vision of America by perpetuating minority group experiences are attempting to destroy the nation's emerging collective identity. Although most scholars on this side of the debate acknowledge the need to incorporate women and minorities into the curriculum, they also maintain a commitment to establishing a single, common American identity.

Conflict Perspective on American Identity:

Critics of functionalism often site an exaggeration of consensus as a key flaw of the perspective. Alternatively, they focus on social conflict as the natural state of society. The conflict perspective basically argues that any apparent social consensus actually represents the domination of one social group and its ability to control competing groups. Therefore history is a series of conflicts between different groups, each struggling to gain power in society; these struggles are also the source of social change. For conflict theorists, then, any attempt to define a single, unified American identity is an oversimplification of reality (see for instance, Carlson 1997; Apple 1996). This perspective argues instead for the recognition of multiple American identities at best, or rather, that multiple cultural and ethnic identities exist in America but that they are often stifled and assimilated into the dominant Anglo hegemony. Thus, from this view, the functionalist vision of a melting pot democracy is an attempt to rid America of its diversity and its equally democratic ideals of individual liberty and tolerance.

Conflict theorists adamantly argue that notions of a "common identity" based on ideals of democracy and freedom are nothing more than a myth. They point out, that many scholars forget that although America is a nation of immigrants, some of those immigrants came in chains and faced centuries of repression, slavery and segregation (Apple 1996; Hu-DeHart 1993). Myrdal (1944) discusses this gap between American democratic ideals and the reality of American racism and discrimination, and he labels this discrepancy the "American dilemma." Building on Myrdal's concept, Banks (1997) argues that it the responsibility of educators to teach students how to better realize the ideals of the American Creed (i.e., liberty, equality, justice). Unfortunately, he admits, schools often teach democracy as American exceptionalism rather than as the American dilemma.

Conflict Perspective on Multiculturalism in Education:

Education scholar Michael Apple asserts, "The national curriculum is a mechanism for the political control of knowledge. In order to fully understand this, one must recognize its underlying logic of false consensus" (1996: 35). Some defenders of the Afrocentric approach to multicultural education also illustrate a conflict perspective on the debate. For example, Asante contends, "The reason Ravitch finds confusion [in history curriculum reform] is because the only way she can reconcile the 'many cultures' is to insist on many 'little' cultures under the hegemony of the 'big' white culture," (1990: 271). Many, like Apple and Asante, question the validity of having a "canon" at all because they see a canon as a way to perpetuate a dominant hegemony which marginalizes the contributions of non-Anglo Americans. But with an increasing amount of historical scholarship coming from women, African Americans and other minorities, some advocates of the conflict perspective simply seek more meaningful inclusion of minority groups into the "canon of Great Books."

In other words, the conflict perspective paints the debate over multicultural reform as an opportunity to overcome the imposed hegemony of white culture on America's identity. Schools currently serve as appendages of the state and attempt to assimilate and erase ethnic and cultural differences by promoting the idea of a "common consensus." But the conflict perspective argues that no such consensus ever existed and that attempts to coerce people into believing in consensus are merely attempts by the dominant class to preserve their position of power (Fullinwider 1996). Therefore, they support a multicultural reform agenda, which seeks to include minority perspectives in the construction of America's history, but they oppose textbook reforms that simply boil down to "token" minority contributions or other marginalized presentations of minority knowledge.

Limitations of the Perspectives:

From this brief outline of the two sides of the debate over multiculturalism, we see that both sides seek some degree of reform in the history curriculum. However, a key difference which prohibits meaningful communication between the two sides lies in their different visions of American identity. Those who embrace the "melting pot" image of democracy seek one common identity and, consequently, seek curriculum reform which incorporates minority contributions into the dominant canon in order to create a shared body of knowledge. Alternatively, the conflict perspective maintains that America is comprised of multiple identities competing with one another to define America's past; curriculum reform, therefore, is an attempt to recognize a plurality of voices which have long been silenced by a single, hegemonic understanding of America's past.

Regardless if we embrace a single American identity or multiple identities, textbook writers must reach some agreement over what content the books will contain and what image of America will be presented. Moreover, writers face monetary and spatial constraints over what information and how much information should be included in the textbooks. Historical scholarship has expanded and changed since the civil rights movement of the sixties making racial or ethnic minorities' and women's perspectives readily available for elaborating the presentation of America's past in high school textbooks (Davis 1986; FitzGerald 1979). However, little systematic research has considered the empirical impact, if any, of this "revisionist history" on textbook reform. As more and more interpretations of historical events surface, how are textbooks evolving in order to incorporate these ideas?

As I shall expand upon in the next section of this paper, existing research suggests that although minority scholarship in history has increased, textbooks have overwhelmingly ignored or marginalized such scholarship. One might consider advances in minority contributions to be evidence against the conflict perspective because multiple voices are being acknowledged. On the other hand, the fact that these voices seem to remain locked in the ivory tower, so to speak, suggests that textbooks still present an image of America's past as unified and uncontested. What this study will attempt to illustrate is a need for the multiculturalism debate to move beyond the simple "truths" of functionalism and the irresolvable struggles of the conflict perspective.

Textbooks confront finite amounts of available pages and students deserve a coherent grasp of historical accounts. Therefore, a meaningful resolution for the debate demands compromise between the functionalist and conflict camps. Some body of knowledge must be transmitted to students (yielding to the functionalist argument) and that body should *meaningfully* include multiple and diverse presentations of historical events (conceding with the conflict position). The question remains, however, as to what extent history textbooks have achieved this compromised position or if such a compromise has yet to be reached. As such, this study employs a longitudinal analysis of textbooks in order to shed light on whether and how attention to America's multicultural past has brought genuine history curriculum reform.

LITERATURE REVIEW ON TEXTBOOK REFORM

In her 1979 work, *America Revised*, Frances FitzGerald traces what history textbooks have taught students about America since the nineteenth century. *America Revised* examines information from an enormous body of texts from 1833-1977. FitzGerald suggests that books since the 1950s are distinctly different in that they have been influenced by the social sciences. However, the textbook adoption process has also had a political influence on the texts in that the three most powerful states--Texas, California, and Florida--set the standard for the publication industry as to what will sell and what will not. As a result, textbooks have become, "a kind of lowest common denominator of American tastes. The books of the seventies are somewhat more diverse than those of the fifties, but still they differ from one another not much more than one year's crop of Detroit sedans" (FitzGerald 1979: 46). Thus, textbook production tends to be based more on what will sell (politically neutral, non-offensive, etc.) than on the desire for increasingly refined scholarship (Stille 1998; FitzGerald 1979).

There have been very few studies of U. S. history textbooks since FitzGerald's work, and most have been minor in empirical scope. In "South Carolina Unrevised," Alan Wieder examines portrayals of race in two South Carolina history textbooks (1996). Onalee McGraw similarly examines how six American history textbooks portray the "Cold War" (1979). The Council on Interracial Books for Children analyzed thirteen texts from the early to mid-seventies, and they identify a number of "distortions and omissions" in references to Native Americans. Patricia O'Connor and Nancy Nystrom study images of Latin America in U.S. history textbooks and conclude that there is basis for the claim that Latin American topics receive less than adequate coverage and that distorted images of Latin America are conveyed through the texts (1985). Gordy and Pritchard (1995) content analyze multicultural perspectives in fifth grade history textbooks used in Connecticut schools during the early 1990s. Their study will be further discussed in subsequent paragraphs, but it is important to note that they found little evidence that textbooks adequately treat minority contributions and perspectives.

There have only been two fairly extensive studies of history textbooks since FitzGerald. O.L. Davis et al. (1986) analyzed 31 major U.S. History textbooks used in the state of Texas (of which only half were for high school students) and conclude that many improvements have been made toward integrating historical scholarship about minorities. In contrast, a study by the American Indian Historical Society examined over 300 books that were approved for classroom use in primary and secondary classrooms. The study concludes that, "...despite these new approaches [multi-ethnic integration, etc.] the basic content of instructional materials about the American Indian continues to be inaccurate and distorted. The situation has not changed" (8).

Each study discussed above, with the exception of FitzGerald, suffers from several limitations. All but two of the studies are based on samples of less than fifteen texts and most do not distinguish between primary texts and those for older students. Also, none of the studies offered evidence of a rigorous methodology (lack coding schemes, no mention of reliability, absence of rating criterion or measurements, etc). Finally, each of the studies offers only a cross sectional view of history textbooks. Since FitzGerald, there have been no attempts to systematically examine *change in textbooks over time.* Accordingly, content analysis research on U. S. history textbooks which explores changes in the treatment of racial and ethnic minorities over time is still necessary in order to empirically ground the multiculturalism curriculum reform debate. Thus, this study will focus on one minority group--Native Americans--in order to explore how writers portray their role in American history as a result of the multicultural reform challenges that developed in the 1960s.

METHODS

In order to discern if and how the Native American perspective has been integrated into U.S. history, this study content analyzes excerpts from 43 high-school American history textbooks published between the years of 1964-2000. Ideally, any attempt to assess the integration of minority contributions in American history would involve content analysis of each entire book for multiple minority groups, including women. As one can well imagine, however, such a mammoth task would take years and would likely require a full research team. However, since researchers have not attempted to systematically review textbook treatment of minorities since FitzGerald's 1979 work, even small contributions in this area are invaluable. Accordingly, while this study focuses on Native Americans during the Jacksonian Era of American history, future research on Native Americans at other historical moments (or research on other minority groups) is necessary in order to draw more meaningful conclusions about the representation of minority perspectives in American history textbooks.

Sample:

The 43 texts analyzed here consist of a convenience sample and were gathered from several different sources. It is interesting and important to note that obtaining less recent history textbooks is a difficult task to accomplish because no national or state repository exists for high school history texts published since the 1960s. Accordingly, books were collected from individual schools in the area, from inter-library loan of specific titles, and from contributions by some publishing houses who responded to a letter of request for these materials.[2] As is often common to content analysis archival research, the potential for selective survival bias of material is possible. However, this study makes no attempts to generalize findings or results to all textbooks published since 1960. Rather, this study intends to produce a reliable coding scheme that can be applied to other texts and to suggest ideas that may be theoretically generalizable and applicable to future research. Finally, one should recall that it is not the goal of content analysis methodology to assume how students would interpret such texts nor how teachers utilize the texts in classrooms; ethnographic and survey research could, therefore, enhance this study by considering the applications of history text lessons in the classroom.

Development of Coding Framework:

Although the dearth of research on multiculturalism and textbooks makes this study largely exploratory in nature, some coding guidelines are necessary in order to organize information that spans over three decades. Indeed, a major problem of longitudinal content analysis design involves creating a scheme to make unstandardized data comparable over time and across authorship. This study loosely combines James Banks' (1993) framework with that of Schuster, et al. (1995) to create a systematic set of measures on which to evaluate the textbooks.

Banks proposes that history textbooks fall into one of "Four Levels of Integration" of multicultural content. He arranges the levels on a continuum from marginal inclusion of minorities in American history to the most integrated level which genuinely incorporates each group's experiences into the history of America. Level one, *contributions*, includes token references to minorities, famous figures or holidays, and makes no attempt to view marginalized groups as a central part of American history. Next, the *additive* level brings in more minority group experiences and events but still discusses them form the perspective of mainstream society. The *transformative* level begins to present minority contributions from diverse perspectives and teaches history as a product of interaction among groups. Finally, in level four *decision making and social participation*, textbooks incorporate lessons on how to use history to act on current social issues and how to use historical knowledge to inform decision making and social criticism in the present.

Schuster, et al. (1995) present a related but somewhat different theoretical frame. Focusing on the inclusion of gender perspectives in textbooks, the authors suggest that there are six identifiable stages to curriculum change. Although I will discuss their theory according to the integration of women in curriculum reform, the basic framework can be translated to analyze the presence of racial or ethnic minorities as well. In the first stage, women are invisible; only male perspectives and actors in history are evident. Stage two brings in the "exceptional woman," a token instance of importance. Next, women (plural) are brought onto the scene and are discussed as a disadvantaged group but still within the perspective of mainstream knowledge. In stage four women are studied on their own terms, either by other female scholars or from a feminist perspective. Stage five uses the inclusion of female and feminist perspectives to

---

[2] I would like to thank Glencoe/McGraw-Hill Publishing and Holt, Rinehart & Winston, Inc. for their generous donations of textbooks for this study.

question the structure and content of curriculum outside of issues about women. Finally, in stage six, the curriculum is transformed when mainstream content has been reconceptualized and is sensitive to the intersection of race, class and gender.

Gordy and Pritchard (1995) applied Bank's framework to their analysis of fifth grade history textbooks' treatment of African Americans and found that all seventeen texts only reached Bank's second level (additive approach discussing African Americans as peripheral to mainstream history). If Gordy and Pritchard are correct, then their argument adds one more piece of evidence to the conflict perspective of the multiculturalism debate which suggests that although minorities are making contributions to historical scholarship, their knowledge is either being ignored or merely assimilated into the hegemonic representation of American history.

Although I cannot make such broad claims on the basis of one study's findings, the theoretical framework employed here does speak to the theoretical perspectives that divide scholars in the multiculturalism debate. Indeed, the purpose of creating another tool to measure the treatment of minorities in textbooks is to empirically assess the accuracy of the functionalist and conflict sides of the multiculturalism debate. Stopping at the "Additive" level in curriculum reform would suggest that textbook writers are buttressing the functionalist view of a melting pot democracy and the need for a common canon which avoids "fragmenting" the nation's past. Concerns about the neglect and assimilation of minority groups' knowledge and experiences would be justified. If texts reach the "Integrative" or "Transformative" stages, however, it would appear that the concerns of the conflict perspective are tenuous at best; textbooks which present multiple perspectives and treat history as negotiated and complex would suggest that writers are effectively challenging hegemonic understandings of the past.

To empirically ground the debate between functionalist and conflict perspectives on multicultural reforms in education, this study combines and reconstructs the frameworks of Banks and Schuster, et al. and focuses specifically on the textbooks' treatment of Native Americans during the Jacksonian Era. A four level scale which measures the degree of integration (no integration to high integration) of Native American perspectives is applied as follows:

Level 1:   No discussion of four key Native American (NA) topics in:
                    a) Cherokee assimilation b) Trail of Tears c) Resistance of
                    NA, and d) quotes from NA's

Level 2:   Discussion of key topics from white dominant perspective,
                    no quotes from NA or inclusion of their perspective

Level 3:   Include NA perspectives on some of the selected topics;
                    combination of levels two and four

Level 4:   Include NA perspective on all issues; inclusion of at least
                    one NA quote necessary

Unlike its parent tools, this four level scheme is a *continuous* measure (rather than categorical) comprised of four specific indicators that measure both what is present and the degree of NA perspective on the topic. The four components were summed and averaged, yielding an overall level of integration score for each case to assess how much voice is given to

Native American perspective(s). Although validity issues are often part of content analysis design, the four indicators used to develop the overall level of integration were derived from retroductively moving through the textbooks themselves as well as from concerns raised by existing research on the presentation of NA perspectives in history.

Each of the four components received a score of level 1 (absent), 2 (present but no NA view), or 4 (present with NA view) and each will be further described and illustrated with examples from the texts. Before preceding, you will note that no component was given a score of "3" because the scheme attempts to capture the evolution of textbook passages which often do not fall neatly into present versus absent perspectives on these issues. It may be that a particular passage discusses one component with a lot of detail and NA viewpoint, but completely ignores other components. Thus, as a statistical average of the four indicators, the overall level of integration score (OLI score) is a continuous variable that ranges between 1.00 and 4.00.

A final note regarding reliability is necessary. A pre-test of the coding scheme was employed to ensure that codes or coding rules were mutually exclusive and exhaustive. In addition to recognizing that most of the codes involve manifest terms that are easily identifiable in the text, an intra-rater reliability of 87.5% was assessed. Moreover, comparing identical excerpts from separate editions of the same textbooks yielded an intra-rater reliability of 93.8%.

Measures in the Coding Scheme:

Four Indicators of Overall Level of Integration

The OLI score is the main dependent variable derived from four indicators as mentioned above. The four indicators include Cherokee assimilation, NA resistance, Trail of Tears, and NA direct quotes. The first indicator discusses the "assimilation" aspects of the Cherokee, such as written language, established body of government, bilingual newspaper, etc. In order to integrate the NA perspective on this issue, however, the discussion must also mention the reasons that the Cherokee made these adaptations in order to remain on their ancestral lands and/or that even their concessions to Anglo ways of life were not enough to curb the greed of the white settlers who sought Cherokee gold mines and land. The following serve as illustrations of level 2 and 4 excerpts, respectively:

> In Georgia the Cherokee had developed a lifestyle that included schools, mills, and turnpikes. In the 1820s, under pressure from the state to give up their lands, they wrote a constitution, hired lawyers, and sued in the Supreme Court (Bragdon, et al. 1996: 317).

> Many Cherokee believed that they could avoid conflict with settlers by adopting practices similar to those of white society. For example, in the early 1800s, the Cherokee...establish schools...learned how to read and write English...created a government system inspired by the U.S. Constitution.... The adoption of white culture did not protect the Cherokee after gold was discovered on their land in Georgia. (Stuckey and Salvucci 2000: 342).

The second indicator involves Native American resistance by any group(s) other than the Cherokee. A text which discussed the opposition of the Seminole in Florida, for example, would receive a score of two; in order to increase to a score of 4, the discussion would need to explain that NA were defending their homes (as opposed to "attacking"), resisted because of broken treaties, or had no reason to trust the government because of bribe attempts, etc. Examples of level 2 and level 4 discussions of resistance are as follows:

In 1835, the United States asked the Seminoles to sign a treaty giving up their and. Osceola, a Seminole leader, refused to sign. Instead, he thrust his knife through the treaty. He had declared war! (Wood and Gabriel 1971: 332).

Black hawk refused to recognize the treaty, maintaining that the chiefs had been bribed with liquor and fancy clothes before signing the document.... In 1828, the federal government ordered the Indians to vacate the valley and to relocate to a reservation in the Iowa Territory. Black Hawk chose to defy the resettlement order. In the summers of 1829, 1830, and 1831--as had been customary for over a hundred years--the Sauk and Fox attempted to return to the Rock River Valley to plant their crops. But each time they were driven back across the Mississippi River by volunteers called out by the Illinois governor... The brutality of the Black Hawk War broke the will of many Indians to resist white encroachment on their lands (Todd and Curti 1986: 292).

The trail of tears is perhaps the single most obvious and well-known aspect about Native Americans in the Jacksonian era. Merely mentioning the phrase "Trail of Tears" earned a score of at least two, and discussion of at least three of the following characteristics about the trail were necessary in order to earn a score of four: removal was forced, NA left homes, many died, inadequate government preparation/food shortage, any quote about the destruction, NA tricked into moving, or use of detention camps. Two vivid examples that illustrate the distinction between a level 2 and 4 passage follow:

Jackson agreed with the Georgia legislature. In 1835, he ordered the removal of the Cherokees to Oklahoma. Some Cherokee moved, but others refused. In 1838, federal troops moved the rest of the Cherokees. Thousands of them died on the march west. The Cherokees called their tragic journey the *Trail of Tears*. Andrew Jackson was a strong and popular president (Reich and Biller 1988: 261).

The government thus furthered its goal of removal by dispossessing the native Americans of their land. Victims of wholesale fraud, trickery, and intimidation, the great mass of southern Indian had no choice but to follow the so-called Trail of Tears to the vacant territory of what is today Oklahoma. Subjected to disease, starvation, and winter cold, thousands died along the way. Military force gave a cutting edge to removal deadlines: in 1838 federal troops herded 15,000 Cherokees into detention camps. 'They are dying like flies,' various witnesses reported. As one Cherokee recalled many years later: 'Long time we travel on way to new land. People feel bad when they leave old Nation. Women cry and made sad wails. Children cry and many men cry, and all look sad like when friends die, but they say nothing and just put heads down and keep on towards West. Many days pass and people die very much' (Bailyn, et al. 1992: 252).

Finally, the clearest way to integrate minority perspective into the Jacksonian era involves the use of direct quotes from Native Americans. The previous example from Bailyn et al. on the "trail of tears" incorporates one such example of quoting Native Americans in text. Absence of a quote results in a score of one, unless the three previous indicators all score two or higher. For example, an excerpt which received a level 3 score for the Cherokee assimilation indicator, level 2 for resistance, and level 2 for trail of tears would receive a score of 2 for the absence of a quote (to avoid skewing the OLI score).

Other Variables:

In addition to the level of integration variables, texts were also coded for the total number of words on NA and the average number of words per page. Terminology used to refer to NA was also recorded (i.e., "Indians," "red men," etc.). In addition to the thorough coding of the integration indicators, other content terms were also recorded as "present" or "absent" and any additional terms that were present in the texts were added to the scheme. Examples of such content terms include references to specific individuals by name (e.g., Sequoyah, Henry Clay), treaties, tribe names, Indian Removal Act, and other manifest codes that were easily evident in the texts. For these content terms, however, level of integration of NA perspective was not assessed. The purpose of these variables is to assess change in the amount and types of references to NA issues over time.

Finally, five latent constructs were also coded as present or absent. First, discussion of the "Indian problem" as a state versus federal government issue was recorded (not including references to the Cherokee Supreme Court debate). Next, references to white advocates of Native Americans (or opposition to Jackson's policies) were noted as were the government's monetary provisions in the removal policies. Presentation of the settlers' desire for land as a central reason for moving the Native Americans was recorded. Finally, the scheme notes whether or not positive sentiments about Jackson's treatment of the NA people are evident (e.g., Jackson felt that moving the Indians was a compassionate and sensitive way to preserve Indian culture). Although each of these five content items are not simple, manifest "terms," each of them are relatively easy to discern in the texts.

RESULTS

The results of this study are twofold: they address first the content of *what* is present regarding Native Americans in the Jacksonian era, and secondly, *how* the content is presented with respect to integration of Native American perspectives. The manifest and latent content terms as well as the presence or absence of the four indicators of the OLI score indicate what information the texts are presenting over time. The OLI score and the degree of integration of each of the indicators addresses the extent to which Native Americans are given voice in these texts.

Content Changes Over Time: What do the passages discuss?

The first step in assessing the extent to which textbooks discuss Native Americans as a significant part of American history involves tracing what concepts are mentioned and how regularly they appear in the texts. Table 1 (see appendix B) indicates the percentage of passages in which the content term appears by the time period in which the text was published; the left half of Table 1 looks at content terms specific to the Cherokee, and the right half considers content terms on other Native American groups. According to Table 1, we see that textbooks have increasingly discussed topics related to the Cherokee with two exceptions. References to Corn Tassel have decreased, and the inclusion of Jackson's quote, "John Marshall has made his decision; now let him enforce it," has remained fairly constant. Similarly, references to non-Cherokee groups have also increased over time, except for the Seminole, which have been consistently mentioned in about 80% of the texts in each time period. It is interesting to note the curvilinear trends in the inclusion of the Sauk/Fox and Black Hawk (a Sauk leader), which peak in the eighties; note that references to Osceola (a Seminole leader) simultaneously dip in the eighties. It may be that textbook authors alternated which Native American leader received attention in each decade.

Table 2 (see appendix C) also indicates the presence of certain terms, but these are not specific to a particular Native American group. Recall that the first five content items in the table are latent codes, rather than simple manifest codes. If we consider the use of these ideas within each of the time periods, it appears that particular "themes" emerge regarding the relationship between Native Americans and whites. In the first period, we see that textbook writers explain that settlers wanted NA lands and that these land disputes were a state vs. federal government issue where the states' interests won because of Jackson's support of them. The seventies seem to suggest a different story line. The settlers wanted NA land, but there is much less discussion of "states' rights."

Instead, the authors seem to suggest that Jackson merely carried out the will of the white settlers as is evidenced by little discussion of white opposition to NA policies and a leap in references to Jackson's positive sentiments toward the natives. Finally, the nineties paint a more complicated picture in which the white settlers still desired the NA land but no dominant theme emerges to explain how or why the government's actions resulted in the removal of Native Americans. These themes could be more closely examined in subsequent studies in order to determine how the addition of content terms may complicate the discussion so much so that students are left with no comprehensible picture of the past. On the other hand, it may be that more recent texts present more balanced, competing themes, which give the student multiple perspectives on the same event.

As Tables 1 and 2 reveal, five new items were introduced in the eighties and nine additional topics were discussed in the nineties. Clearly, the sheer amount of content is increasing considerably over time. Moreover, as Table 3 suggests, inclusion of three of the four integration indicators also increased greatly over time; only discussions of NA resistance are consistently discussed in about three-fourths of the texts since the sixties.

TABLE 3. PERCENTAGE OF CASES WITH KEY TOPIC PRESENT
(regardless of level of NA perspective integrated into topic content)

	1960/70s	1980s	1990s
Cherokee Assimilation	55.6	85.7	85.0
	[5]*	[12]	[17]
N.A. Resistance	77.8	78.5	75.0
	[7]	[11]	[15]
Trail of Tears	33.3	100.0	100.0
	[3]	[14]	[20]
N.A. Quote	11.1	21.4	65.0
	[1]	[3]	[13]
N=	9	14	20

* frequencies in parentheses

However, the fact that *what* is discussed over time has increased does not address the issue of *how* such content is discussed. It is entirely possible, and indeed true, that texts can make many, many references to such content terms and do so without even offering the Native American viewpoint on this moment in U.S. history. Therefore, in order to explore if textbooks have truly integrated minority perspectives on the situation, we must turn to the four levels of integration analysis.

Integration of NA Perspective: How do the passages discuss the content?

One of the arguments of many educators in the multicultural curriculum reform debate has been that minority issues have been "added" but not "integrated" into American history. The difference between adding content versus discussing the content through a minority lens is addressed in Table 4, the average score of each indicator by year of publication as well as the overall level score by year.

TABLE 4. AVERAGE LEVEL OF NA PERSPECTIVE
(scores range from no integration to a high of level four)

	1960/70s	1980s	1990s
Cherokee Assimilation	2.38	3.29	3.35
NA Resistance	2.13	2.93	2.65
Trail of Tears	1.88	3.00	3.80
NA Quote	1.75	2.07	3.20
Overall Level Score	1.81	2.82	3.25

Recall that the cells can range from one to four (no integration of minority viewpoint to genuinely high integration). Three of the four indicators steadily improve in their level of integration of Native American perspectives. Although the sheer number of references to Cherokee assimilation jumped in the 1980's as evident in Table 3, the incorporation of Cherokee perspectives on assimilation increased much more gradually over time. Similarly, the inclusion of trail of tears content topped out in the eighties and remained at 100% in the nineties; however, the way in which NA perspectives were integrated into the discussion of the trail of tears again gradually increased over time and continued to improve into the nineties. Also, the use of NA direct quotes increasingly contributed to the integration of minority perspective over time.

NA resistance of non-Cherokee groups consistently falls between a Level 2 and 3 degree of integration. Accordingly, it seems that this area holds the most room for further improvement in the inclusion of minority viewpoints in the Jacksonian era. Likewise, 35% of the texts in the nineties still did not include direct quotes and could improve their overall level of integration simply by incorporating NA words.

Thus, overall, the level of integration increased gradually from a low score of 1.81 in the sixties/seventies to a high of 3.25 in the nineties. A chi-square analysis of OLI score by time period was moderately strong and significant at the $p < .01$ level ($X^2 = 8.869$, phi $= .454$).[3] Moreover, the sample of textbooks included several editions written by the same author and revealed a steady increase in the overall level of integration of NA perspective over time within these books. Table 5 illustrates a steady improvement of integrating Native American perspective over time:

TABLE 5. Level Scores of Texts authored by John Garraty in Five Editions

	1966	1975	1983	1991	1998
Cherokee Assimilation	4	4	4	4	4
NA Resistance	2	2	2	2	2
Trail of Tears	1	1	2	2	4
NA Quote	1	1	2	2	4
Overall Level of Integration	2	2	2.5	2.5	3.5

As the table indicates, including a nominal reference to the trail of tears in the eighties increased the OLI score. By the late nineties, the author discussed the trail of tears more meaningfully and incorporated quotes by Tushpa and John Ross, thereby increasing the score to Level 3.5. From this table, we see that the only deficit remaining in the Garraty text relates to his discussion of non-Cherokee resistance efforts. Though he discusses the Sauk, Choctaw, and Seminole, the author leaves the impression that these groups simply "refused" to leave, rather than offering an explanation to legitimate their reasons for defending their lands.

CONCLUSIONS

Perhaps one of the most striking findings of this research lies in documenting the sheer presence of more information on Native Americans in the Jacksonian era. Considering that America has seen dozens of new historical events since the sixties, incorporating more information about less recent events translates into that much more "new knowledge" that the textbooks embody today. Accordingly, the concern that most educators express--that students

---

[3] Both variables were reduced to dummy cases in which OLI score was reduced to low/hi (level 1 or 2 and level 3 or 4) and time period was transformed into pre-1990 and post-1990.

learn history rather than temporarily memorize thousands of meaningless "facts"--is a well-founded one (Hirsch 1988; Levine, et al 1995). This study proposes that merely "adding" content terms over time is not sufficient for either side of the multicultural reform debate because the end result is too much information (as Hirsch suggests) and token marginalizing of minority viewpoints (as Apple and Asante point out). However, as the data here suggest, textbooks not only are increasing what they discuss, but also are deepening the way in which they integrate minority perspectives with regard to Native Americans.

The functionalist arguments of those like Schlesinger, Davis, and Bloom that call for a return to "core curriculum" and a standardized national canon in order to create order out of so much information can be better understood if we recognize that the frequency of material being added to the textbooks in the eighties seems to be "additive" in light of the fact that the average overall level of integration of such materials was only 2.82. The result, therefore, might indeed have been too much confusing information without coherent explanations as to *why* the Cherokee assimilated or what the Native Americans had to say about the situation.

However, by the nineties, we see that the level of integration is approaching genuine integration of minority perspectives with regard to Jackson's treatment of the Native Americans. It is equally essential to recognize, therefore, that concerns expressed by the "conflict" side of the multicultural debate are also understandable because they struggle to point out that history textbooks often only paid lip-service to minority views even as they included phrases like "trail of tears."Thus, it appears that both viewpoints in the reform debate really have a common goal--to teach students history, *not* rote memorization of disconnected facts--but that they continue to speak past one another because they are ignoring the real obstacle which is the *additive* (rather than integrative) inclusion of minority information.

Perry and Fraser 1993 explain that resistance to dominant American society has been an almost constant part of African-American identity formation: slave rebellions, NAACP, Harlem Renaissance, Garvey's United Negro Improvement Association, Civil Rights Movement of the sixties, and much more. It is entirely reasonable, then, that the conflict camp in the multicultural debate emphasizes this need to resist dominant hegemonic treatment of American history. It is also essential, however, to acknowledge the changes in curriculum that are being made and to evaluate the academic contribution of making American history genuinely full of all Americans. There is still room for improvement in many accounts of Native Americans in the Jacksonian era as we move into the 21st century. More importantly, there is still need to ensure that other voices are also singing in our students' history texts with a voice that is memorable and inspiring and not easily forgotten.

SUGGESTIONS FOR FURTHER RESEARCH:

Consequently, an area in need of exploration involves conducting similar analyses on other minority groups and on Native Americans in other parts of U.S. history. It may well be that the finding reached here, which suggests integration of NA into American history is improving, is particular to this minority group or this moment in history. Similarly, studies are needed that examine how teachers actually use textbooks in the classroom and on how students understand or retain the information that they read.

Future research should also pay attention to what information is removed in order to make room for minority perspectives. For example, studies could address what Jacksonian topics are being dropped or minimized or whether other Native American perspectives in history are being neglected (i.e., during the Plains removals, etc.). What are the content costs of bringing in multiple perspectives in order to present a more well-rounded view of America's past?

Finally, in 1979, FitzGerald concluded that the fruits of revisionist history were not being incorporated into secondary education textbooks. She also emphasized that publishers were more concerned about writing non-offensive, politically neutral texts in order to appeal to the widest market possible. Unfortunately, in 1998, Stille replicated FitzGerald's conclusions. Such simplified accounts only exacerbate the problem of teaching history as trivia to be erased from the mind as easily as from the chalkboard. As Levine et al. express (1995), "What I find is a bland eclecticism where everything has equal weight. You add more facts...you add more people....You're left with a kind of unemotional, cold combination salad." One area in need of development, therefore, involves studying the extent to which publishers are resorting to token inclusion of minority "facts" and resisting deeper integration of minority perspectives because of their desire to sell as many texts as possible by appealing to states like Texas and California who employ statewide adoption and set the tone for what will sell in other states.

In conclusion, as Gary Nash, et al. emphasize, the future of high school history needs the fruits of revisionist history in order to create a more nuanced understanding of our past and to better realize our ideals of democracy. "This is nothing less than the story of the uncompleted project of making Americanism 'a matter of heart and mind rather than race or ancestry'" (Nash et al., 1997). Given the kaleidoscopic composition of our nation--past and present--if education scholars genuinely desire to create a common American identity, it should be one that unites us on the basis of responding to the "American dilemma" by educating students.

The Problems and Realities of Adoption in America

Raymond Godwin, Esq.

Ten-year-old Helen made an unusual discovery behind her parents' bed in their home in Kansas City: some worn and dated adoption manuals. When confronted with the simple question of whether she had been adopted, Helen's mother responded with a yes. Thirty-five years later in 2000 Helen Hill relates that the "yes" caused immediate confusion, bewilderment, even a big depression. Who was her birth mother? Who was her birth father? Why was she given away to total strangers?

Ten year old Helen was not provided with much information and for years she had no where to turn to get more. Some twenty years later, however, she had her file which contained snippets such as her birth mother was a Ahealthy, attractive girl who wears her hair in a long bob. The file which she added to over the years after spending thousands of dollars on private investigators also contained the critical piece to the puzzle: her birth mother lived in Des Moines.

The year was 1996 and forty-one year old Helen telephoned her sixty-four year old birth mother: "My name is Helen and I'm calling about a very personal matter. I was born on March 24, 1955, in Kansas City."

Silence, an extended silence, greeted this announcement. Finally, the birth mother responded, "I love you. I've always loved you." Helen Hill flew to Iowa and they met; it was a wonderful reunion. They have stayed in touch. But Helen was still not satisfied.

She found her birth father in Albuquerque and sent him a letter. He was a dashing lieutenant just returned from the Korean War when he met her birth mother. Their brief but passionate romance resulted in Helen's being born. He had not known that Helen even existed but upon receiving her letter, he called her immediately. "You were a love child," he happily related to Helen.

Helen Hill finally had a fair measure of solace as to her personal journey; however, her experience caused her to spearhead a ballot initiative in her state of Oregon granting all adult adoptees access to their birth certificates, which in almost all cases would have the birth mother's name on it. This initiative was approved in 1998 by the voters in that state and is known as Measure 58; it has been in legal limbo for two years after being challenged by a group of birth mothers who argue that such a measure strips them of privacy; a privacy they greatly wanted in the placement of children for adoption.

The debate has caused one birth mother to have flashbacks and nightmares; another birth mother says the fact that her ringing phone may mean her birth child is calling is like "a bomb held over your head." Another said that absolute privacy is crucial for her: she did not and does not now wish to see the child she placed for adoption as she was a product of rape.

Many professionals in adoption and other critics of Measure 58 favor birth parent and adoptee reunions only when all parties are in agreement. Such meetings can be healthy emotionally and very needful as to exchanging medical information. However, forcing contact between a child placed for adoption and his birth parent strikes many as unfair; particularly in cases involving adoptions which occurred years ago.

Critics also point out that not all adoptees share Ms. Hill's great interest in the past. Data would seem to indicate that a full two-thirds of adoptees make no attempts to locate birth parents even when the information is available. Of the one-third who do seek out a birth mother or birth father, 80% are women. There would appear to be no middle ground in the debate.

On May 30, 2000 Justice Sandra Day O'Conner agreed with Ms. Hill and refused to block the law as requested by the birth mother group. Oregon officials began gearing up for complying with the applications for the birth certificates which had been filed before the legal action by the birth mothers had thrown the law into limbo. Ms. Hill comments that "I've never believed in anything so much in my whole life. I grew up steeped in the secrecy and shame that the closed-record system perpetuates, and I don't want anybody else going through what I went through. It's as simple as that." (*New York Times, June 7, 2000*)

Is it really as simple as that? All other states have more restrictive laws on confidentiality than Oregon. Once an adoption is finalized in court then the records are sealed and can not be opened unless "good cause" can be shown, or in a majority of the states, upon the agreement of all the parties. Many states have a registry on which the birth parents and adoptive couple can place their names and addresses so that if either desires contact in the future or if the adoptee desires to search out her birth parents, then that information is available. "Good cause" to open sealed records usually only exists if medical information is necessary for the adoptee's best interests.

Measure 58 was an initiative made law by the voters of Oregon. The dialogue in the debate included the idea that sealed records and confidentiality are in the best interests of the birth parents who want closure on an unwanted pregnancy and the need for privacy surrounding the placement. The birth parents can get on with their lives with belief that they acted responsibly in seeing that their child was taken care of by a two-parent, financially secure adoptive couple.

Also during the debate it was emphasized that there is needed closure for the adoptive couple who have the confidence to take into their family an adopted child knowing that neither the birth parents or any of their family can interfere with the adoptee's life or that of the adoptive couple.

The best interests of the child to be adopted is also promoted by sealed records and confidentiality. Critics of Measure 58 argued that a child would suffer from psychological confusion if his birth mother makes contact shortly after birth and placement (*New York Times*, June 7, 2000). How do you introduce a three-year-old child to his birth mother? What does he or she call her? Should there be a limit as to how soon a birth parent can make contact after placement?

Is it really then as simple as that?

The year is 1965 and you are a birth mother or a birth father. You have just placed your baby for adoption with a couple from Portland, Oregon. You live in the same state but 100 miles away. You graduate high school, go to college, get your degree, get married and have children with your spouse. You have not told anyone, including your spouse, about the adoption plan and the events of 1965. You made it very clear to the social worker and to everyone else involved that you wanted no contact with the adoptive couple nor the adoptee: you wanted to put this "mistake" behind you and get on with your life.

The year is 2000 and you pick up the phone to answer it and you hear a voice asking whether you are her birth parent and did you place her for adoption in 1965? What do you think goes through your mind? Your heart? How do you respond?

Is it right to force someone to come out of their "closet" relative to being a birth parent. Why is the adoptee entitled to know her birth mother, or is she?

One final thought: Measure 58 simply allows an adoptee to obtain her original birth certificate which would normally contain the birth mother's name (and in many cases, the birth father's name). What if the birth mother desires to track down the adoptee. In other words, the complete reverse of the above discussion. Measure 58 does not address that issue. Is that fair?

This issue of openness and confidentiality is a critical one to discuss and bring to a resolution, if such a thing is possible. A lot of people would be affected by a Measure 58 if it were implemented on a national level or if a majority of the other states made it their law. In any given year there are an estimated 140,000 to 160,000 adoptions; the reference here to adoptions includes all types, including international, independent, agency, and relative adoptions. The former three types involve what is commonly referred to as "stranger" adoptions: that is, the birth parents who are strangers to the adoptive couple place their child with them. The later type involves mainly stepparent adoptions but also includes grandparents placements.

According to the National Committee for Adoption (NCFA), Adoption Fact Sheet (1998) the number of reported adoptions peaked in 1970 at 175,000 and decreased to approximately 100,000 in the late 1970's (see also Flango and Flango 1992). Unfortunately there is no consistent, structured mechanism to collect data on adoption placements either on a national level or in individual states. For example, the U.S. National Center for Social Statistics has not issued an annual report on adoption statistics since 1975.

There is also data collected to confirm the number of children accepted into this country because they have been adopted overseas by American couples. Also, California, Massachusetts, and New York attempt to maintain a system for confirming the number of adoption decrees filed with the courts each year. While it may be possible to only render estimates of adoptions in the United States, these estimates are more accurate than simply educated hunches as to the number and types of adoptions which occur in any given year. These estimates can be "ball parked" by indirect inferences from research dealing with fertility, childbearing, marriage and divorce rates and research relative to data involving unwed mothers and their children and to data involving the parties to an adoption plan.

From the media coverage and more heightened awareness in general about adoption, it would be easy to assume that of the estimated 140,000 to 160,000 placements each year, the majority involve stranger or third-party adoptions--the type that Helen Hill's story describes so poignantly. However, any such assumption is false. According to the NCFA Fact Sheet, the reality is that about 60% of adoptions each year are ones by relatives such as grandparents, aunts, uncles or cousins. This translates into 84,000 to 96,000 adoptions of the estimated 140,000 to 160,000 placements.

Adoptions by grandparents, aunts, uncle or cousins have always been common, particularly in ethnic communities, such as African-American or Asian, where the rearing of children has always been viewed as more of an obligation of the extended family than just the nuclear family. A study of American history would show that the hard life of the settlers and farmers often resulted in relative adoptions. Such adoptions occur frequently today due to the death of one or both parents from crime, disease, property, and, in cases involving termination of parental rights by the child welfare agency of the state, which then places the child with a grandparent or aunt for adoption (Hollinger 2000).

Due to the increasing numbers of divorces, remarriages, and out-of-wedlock births, the majority of relative adoptions are stepparent adoptions. According to Hollinger (2000), stepparent adoptions usually involve a stepfather who has married the mother of children who are typically over the age of one or two years old. The children usually live with the biological mother and stepfather, but who also have contact with the biological father. After an adoption by a stepparent, the biological parent who surrendered his parental rights in favor of the stepparent usually has no legal rights of visitation, except as to what is offered by the biological parent and stepparent.

Of importance for this discussion is the fact that only a very small percentage of stepparents ever adopt their stepchildren; however, this type of adoption is the most common and prevalent today. One reason for this small percentage is that the biological fathers do not often easily give up their parental rights. If a biological father does not sign a legal document in which he surrenders or relinquishes his parental rights or if the biological father does not go to court and renounce his parental rights to the children, then it is very difficult for a stepfather to adopt the children.

Most states have laws which allow the biological father's rights to be deemed abandoned if he does not pay child support and visit the children on a regular basis. In other words if the biological father does not pay court-ordered child support each month and does not visit with the children at least once a month, and more often in some states, then he can be brought into court and be made accountable for his lack of interest in his children. If his parental actions do not meet a minimum level as spelled out in the state statutes, then a court can rule that he has abandoned his parental rights and that the stepfather, or stepmother as the case may be, may proceed with adopting them. (For a complete discussion of birth father rights see *The Complete Adoption Book* by Laura Beauvais-Godwin and Raymond W Godwin, Adams Publishing,(2000), Chapter Eight and Appendix of state by state laws.)

A point of contention with blended families in the 1990's and into the 2000's is the biological father who is involved with his children on a very sporadic basis--just enough contact to not have his rights considered abandoned but not enough to really be involved in a child's life. Or to put it more cynically, just enough contact to confuse a younger child as to why he has two fathers and just enough contact to disrupt the older child's needed bonding with a father-figure such as the stepfather.

At what point for the sake of the children should the biological father be given the boot, as it were, relative his involvement in a child's life?

What if he visits once a month for three months and then misses a month or two? What if the biological father is in jail: some states take the position that his incarceration can not be held against him while other states stipulate that if he is in jail, it is due to his own actions, which, in turn, prevent him from being a father to his children, then his rights can be deemed abandoned. How about the father who pays $75 a month for one child (this is all he can afford per minimum wages) and he visits once a month for two hours at the McDonalds? Should he be allowed to stop a stepfather from adopting them, particularly if he has been the "father" to the children since they were one and two years old and they are now twelve and thirteen years old?

Most state laws on stepparent adoptions have been streamlined in an attempt to encourage the permanence of blended families. For example, most states waive the home study required in non-relative adoptions. A home study is an evaluation of a couple, their lifestyle, their home and overall suitability to be parents. It can cost anywhere from $500 (South Carolina) to $3,000 (Massachusetts) depending on the state. These home studies are done either by a private adoption agency or a certified social worker or by the state's child welfare agency. Before a couple can adopt in a non-relative adoption, they must be approved and recommended as a couple fit to parent a child by way of the home study (see Beauvais-Godwin and Godwin 2000).

After the child is placed in the home of a couple in a non-relative adoption, there is a required waiting period before the adoption is finalized in court. This time period can be one to nine months; also some states require two hearings, the first one to update the court as to the adoption and the second to finalize it. During the waiting period the agency or social worker who completed the home study will visit to conduct post-placement supervisory reports on the progress of the child to be adopted and on the adoptive couple's interaction with the child, in addition to reviewing doctor's records.

This procedure is in place to ensure that the couple has adapted well to the placement and do indeed show appropriate parenting skill, in addition to providing a nurturing atmosphere in the home. Some states only require one post-placement visit while others mandate that three or four be completed. The home study and post-placement reports are filed with the court and evaluated by the judge who will make the final decision as to whether the adoption is legalized. Also required is a listing of the expenses paid in any adoption situation; this is mandated to ensure that to the extent possible, no baby buying occurs.

Again, these somewhat intricate and time consuming requirements are waived by states in stepparent adoptions. To do otherwise would present a stepfather with a large expense and a mountain of paperwork to complete. Also, most attorneys charge more for non-relative adoptions than for stepparent adoption because all or almost all the usual requirements are waived.

Many professionals however are rethinking the stepparent process in light of what appears to be an increase in incidents of child abuse by stepparents. Some states waive all the usual requirements but still have a Guardian ad Litem or "friend of the court" appointed to represent the interests of the child or children being adopted. The Guardian will visit the home in which the child lives and interview the mother and the stepfather. The Guardian can also review medical records on the children and even contact references on the stepfather.

What is the reasoning for waiving the usual adoption requirements? What other means can be used other than an expensive home study to ensure as much as possible that the stepparent is a suitable for adopting? Some people believe that even if the stepfather is marginally fit to parent the children that they will be "ok" because their mother will be there. What is your opinion of this perspective? What about putting stepparents on a probation period or requiring counseling for them, particularly in view of the high rate of divorce for second marriages?

Because stepparent adoptions are so common and unregulated, they do not usually make the news, and while there have been many movies and television series dealing with blended families, a stepparent adopting the children is not often part of the story line. What does make the news however are non-relative adoptions. These contain more drama--a young unmarried woman caught in dire straits who must "give away" her child to total strangers. Or how about the young man who comes back to town after being in the Peace Corps or, better yet, the Marines and learns his Martha gave birth to a son (always a son, you understand), but she gave him away (never placed with a loving, stable two parent family but "gave away" or "put up") and he decides to fight for his son.

While this scenario plays out on occasion in real life, the reality that young unmarried women are routinely giving their babies away is becoming less and less common. According to Hollinger (2000), of the 140,000 to 160,000 estimated adoptions occurring each year, only about 20 to 30% of them, or 20,000 to 40,000, are ones involving childless couples who are not related to the birth mother. From the 1930s to 1960s, over 50% of all adoptions were non-relative ones. As an aside, the data shows that California, New York, and Texas are the states with the greatest number of children under the age of one who are placed for adoption with non-relatives.

While the number of children born in the United States who are placed for adoption with non-relatives has decreased, the number of out-of-wedlock births has increased dramatically since the 1960s with teenagers and women between the ages of 15-29 years, according to Usdansky (1996), in 2000, approximately 1,200,000 children will be probably be born out-of-wedlock in this country and only about 5% will be placed for adoption with non-relatives. This is a stark figure when compared with the 20 to 30% of out-of-wedlock children placed for adoption in the 1960s.

A study conducted by the Alan Guttmacher Institute confirms this steady decline in the availability of children for the purposes of adoption. For example, in 1973, 20% or more of the babies born out-of-wedlock to white women were placed for adoption. In 1990, fewer than 3% were surrendered for adoption. The percentage among women in the Black and Hispanic communities appears to be unchanged only because those numbers have always been much lower than those for white unmarried women. During the 1980s, less than 2% of Black children born to unmarried mothers were placed for adoption while less than 1% of Hispanic babies born were placed for adoption with non-relatives and this was so even though the childbearing rate among unmarried Hispanic and Black women is four times that of unmarried white women.

While the number of babies available for adoption decreased during the last several decades, the number of couples involved in some type of infertility treatment approached two million. That two million figure is often bandied about as the number of couples looking to adopt; Harvard Professor and adoptive mother, Elizabeth Bartholet, has researched the data and she feels that at any given time approximately 200,000 American couples are looking to adopt the estimated 20,000 to 40,000 children who are born in this country and who are placed each year. The *Roe v. Wade* decision allowing women greater access to abortion is often provided as the explanation for decline in the number of children placed for adoption. This may have been true for the 1970s, however, the steady increase in babies born out-of-wedlock means that there are babies potentially available for adoption but who are not placed. Instead, women are deciding to parent their children as single mothers--who in many cases do not receive any help or monetary assistance from the birth fathers. What are the reasons behind single women opting to keep their children?

It may be helpful to first discuss the reasons a woman places her child for adoption. According to the National Survey of Family Growth, as well as more recent studies, women who place their children usually have educational and vocational goals, which would be disrupted by their parenting a child. Also, they tend to have mothers who are college educated.

From this writer's own experience in approximately 400 adoptions since 1989, it seems that about 60% of the birth mothers fall into this category of having aspirations, which would be interrupted by parenting a child. Of the other 40%, the majority place because of dire straits related to lack of money and employment. A small portion place because of family pressure, addiction to drugs or other reasons. This data contradicts arguments that adoptions in this country have become a class issue: that is, middle or upper class adoptive families manipulating blue collar or low-income birth mothers. Many birth mothers are from middle or upper class families themselves.

According to Michael D. Resnick (1984), the reasons the birth mother does not place for adoption include pressure from family and friends; possibilities of marrying the birth father; promotion of self-esteem; and society's greater acceptance of single-parent families. There also appears to be a misunderstanding about and lack of acceptance of adoption in general in society. A study of crisis pregnancy centers in the mid-west shows that counselors were not trained in adoption issues nor were they encouraged to discuss adoption as an option for pregnant women who sought advice. It appears that there is a stigma involved in a young woman giving her child to total strangers for adoption.

Before reading this chapter, what was your knowledge about adoption? Did you know anyone in grade school or high school who was adopted? Is it strange to you that a 20 year old woman in a crisis pregnancy could "give up" a baby to a husband and wife she does not know and with whom she will probably have no contact with forever? What if you were in her shoes; what would be your response? Is it easier to counsel someone to get an abortion than to carry a baby to term and then place for adoption?

There can be no doubt that society accepts single parents more favorably than before, but is this a healthy trend? The acceptability of a parent who is single because of divorce is a reality because of society's acceptance of divorce in general; although, there is movement to rethink the liberal and "easy" no-fault divorce laws in several states. Social acceptance of the unmarried mother is a recent development, occurring in the last two decades. Every month or so the media reports on an unmarried celebrity who is pregnant and who does not name the father. In years past, shame and scandal would have accompanied such an announcement. Today, such announcements only register mild interest.

Apart from any discussions of morality, is it in a child's best interests to be reared by a single mother? Should our society provide more encouragement for an unmarried pregnant woman to place her baby for adoption with a two-parent family?

In "The Infertility Market", *New York Times,* (January, 1996), one out every six couples will not be able to conceive this year; the average infertile couple will spend $50,000 to $70,000 or more for infertility treatments. In vitro fertilization, embryo transfers, or some other related highly sophisticated reproduction technology can cost $10,000 or more per procedure. The success rate is only 25% and three-fourths of these couples go home not being pregnant. Often a couples' insurance company will not cover any of the costs, placing an infertile couple's desire for children in the same category as elective surgery .

In view of the approximate 2.3 million couples who are infertile and who will seek some type of treatment this year, and in view of the 1.2 million babies born out-of-wedlock this year, should society promote adoption over unwed women parenting their children? The issues here are not about fairness or entitlement; the issues relate to what is in the child's best interests. Is a child not better off with a stable, two-parent family than with a single, unwed mother who scrapes by with a number of sequential live-in boy friends? Again, the issue is not superiority of legal rights; there is no debate that the birth mother has absolute parental rights as to her child, unless of course she is deemed unfit.

The issue is have we as a society, in an attempt to be politically correct and sensitive to everyone's right to live as they chose, overlooked what is in the child's best interests in accepting single parent families which are the result of unmarried women giving birth and deciding to parent their children? For every Murphy Brown or Madonna, there are hundreds of single mothers struggling to make ends meet; they do not have high paying jobs with nannies at home. The average single mom drops her child off at day-care at 8:30 a.m. and does not return until 5:30 p.m. While it is true that many have family members, usually the child's grandmother, to baby-sit, is this still the best scenario for a child?

Should there be some type of media campaign to encourage young mothers-to-be to seriously consider placing their children for adoption instead of keeping them to parent? Are we talking about returning to a sense of shame to out-of-wedlock pregnancies? Maybe. Or at the very least, how about attaching responsibility and consequences to out-of-wedlock births. Think of the societal behaviors, which have been modified because people have been asked to take another look at certain behavior and its consequences. Smoking and driving while drunk are two recent examples of society rethinking its position on behavior issues. The use of seat belts and child seats in cars are another example of society's rethinking its positions.

In considering whether a societal change is necessary; look at the data in this paragraph about just the ages of the young women giving birth today. Since the mid-1990s, approximately 30% of all live births are those born out-of-wedlock, as compared with 10% in the late 1960s and 20% in the early 1980s. Teenage pregnancies number about 1,000,000 per year: about 400,000 end in abortions and about 500,000 result in live births and half of those are born out-of-wedlock. Approximately 250,000 babies therefore are born to unwed teenagers, of whom the vast majority decide to parent the child instead of placing her for adoption (Hollinger 2000:1-57). Is this wise?

Because there are so few babies to adopt in comparison to the number of couples who want to adopt, many white couples have adopted biracial or Black children. This trend really began very slowly during the 1950s and 1960s and became more accepted due to the number of children in the foster care system and to the lack of minority homes in which to place minority children. In 1972 however the National Association of Black Social Workers (NABSW) came out strongly against transracial adoption. Within a year the number of transracial adoptions was cut in half from 3138 to 1,569; by 1975 the number was down to 800.

The NABSW advocates that a Black child needs to be raised by Black parents in order to develop a positive racial identity, and only Black parents can help a child develop skills for coping in a racist society. To place Black children with white adoptive parents according to the NABSW is Black cultural genocide (see Beauvais-Godwin and Godwin 2000). Can this really happen or is the NABSW's position a relic from the early 1970s that should be evaluated and revised for the 21st century? Peter Hayes (1993), states that "To compromise a child's welfare in the name of culture, especially when the cultural benefit is slight or nonexistent, is inimical to the purpose of child placement and violates the best-interests standard mandated by the law."

Unless one is from a minority background, can a person really understand the fears of the NABSW? In 1972 when the Black social workers took this position, what events had transpired which may have caused such an absolute stance to be taken? Remember, the Civil Rights Act passed during President Johnson's "Great Society" took effect only in 1964. In the year or two just before the passage of the Civil Rights Act, Black young people were finally admitted for the first time to Clemson University and several other colleges in the South. In the early 1970s, Black young men were still being sent off to Viet Nam and the United States Supreme Court was ordering the neighborhoods in south Boston to integrate their schools. Less than ten years before 1972, restaurants in this country were still refusing to serve Blacks and there were Black and white water fountains in parts of the South.

Some would argue that not much has changed since then. The 1990s brought headlines showing white L.A. policemen beating a black Rodney King, Dennys refusing to seat Blacks employed by the U.S. Secret Service, and racial profiling by the New Jersey State Police.

But the issue remains: does placing Black children with white adoptive couples contribute to a dismantling of Black culture in this country. And even if this is true, shouldn't the best interests of the children prevail?

In discussing what many consider to be a delicate topic, consider these statistics: Blacks and people of color make up 12.3 and 17 percent of the total population, respectively, yet Black children and children of color make up 34 and 47 percent of the children waiting for homes. According to research by Elizabeth Bartholet in *Where Do Black Children Belong? The Politics of Race Matching in Adoption*, nearly half of the 100,000 children in the United States waiting for homes are children of color. In Massachusetts, for example, about 5% of the population is Black, yet nearly half of the children in need of foster or adoptive homes are Black. In New York City, 18,000 children are awaiting adoption, of whom 75% are Black. These children generally wait for two or five years, about twice the average wait for a white child. The numbers alone suggest that even if more recruitment efforts were made to find Black parents, there would not be enough such parents to fulfill the need.

According to Hollinger (2000), the number of children in foster care increased from 276,000 in 1986 to 450,000 in 1992 to well over a half million by the late 1990s. This tremendous breakup of families is the result of parental poverty, crime and substance abuse. These statistics wreak havoc on minority children.

Bartholet's research into the practices of adoption agencies responsible for placing Black children shows that agencies do typically practice racial matching, leading to delays in permanent placement. Six months may be a short time in the life of a bureaucracy, but for a small child it can have a significant impact. Racial preferences can also mean that a two-year-old child can be torn from foster parents who want to adopt him so that he can be placed with parents of the same ethnic background. Bartholet has documented cases in which foster parents have gone to court to contest such disruptions.

In response to such cases, Congress passed in 1994 the Multiethnic Placement Act (MEPA) which formally stated that race can only be a consideration in the placement of children and not the determining factor. The MEPA was amended in 1996 so that a child's or adoptive parents' race or ethnicity cannot be considered if it delays placement of that child. The question then becomes what is a delay? If a person subscribes to the NBSW's position, is it not easy to provide other reasons for a delay?

James S. Bowen, in his book entitled, *Cultural Convergences and Divergences, The Nexus Between Putative Afro-American Family Values and the Best Interests of the Child,* shows in several studies that so long as a white family totally integrates the child into their family and community that a child usually grows up with a strong sense of racial identity. This integration involves supporting Black culture and ethnic pride in children by way of providing books and music about Black culture, encouraging friendships with other Black children, and participating in Black historical and cultural events. Does this formula appear to require that white adoptive couples be educated and middle class? What if a single white mom working all day can not attend any cultural events or read many books about Blacks; should she be taken off the list? What steps can a state social services department take to assist families in adopting Black children and in helping them to maintain a sense of identity and pride?

It is interesting to note that the NBSW's position that only Black families should adopt Black children was issued during the time Congress was holding hearings about certain abuses occurring in Native American communities. What was presented before Congress seemed to indicate that state and local agencies were ripping Indian families apart. Evidence was presented that Indian culture was being wiped out on certain reservations.

To correct the situation, Congress in 1978 passed the Indian Child Welfare Act (ICWA), and it supercedes state adoption laws as they relate to the placement of children of American Indian heritage. In order to preserve the culture of the Indian Nations, a child who is of Indian descent and who is eligible (or who is a member) for membership in an Indian Nation can only be placed for adoption with adoptive parents of Indian descent and who are members of a specific Indian Nation. For example, a child of Cherokee lineage could only be placed with an adoptive couple of Cherokee Indian lineage.

A Congressional investigation revealed that the ratio of unwarranted removals of Indian children from their families by state child welfare agencies or social service agencies was excessively high compared to the number of children removed from white homes. To compound matters, two-thirds of the time the children were placed in most states in non-Indian homes. In some states they were placed in non-Indian homes 90% of the time. In addition, 25 to 35% of all Indian children were left for years in boarding homes run by the Bureau of Indian Affairs or in non-Indian foster homes, separated from their families and their culture. These Indian children placed in non-Indian foster homes or placements were found to often have serious social and psychological problems in their teenage and adult years.

Senate hearings were held between 1974 and 1977 and what tribal representatives, anthropologists, and experts in Indian culture presented was a decay and decimation of Indian family stability and culture. Non-Indian agencies were routinely disrupting Indian families and dictating non-Indian policy to them. The Indian Child Welfare Act was passed as a response; its effect today is still controversial and debated.

The issue surrounding the placement of Black and Native American Children with white adoptive couples will continue to be debated going into the 21st century, just as the issues involving adoption records and confidentiality will be considered in various state legislatures this year.

After reading this chapter on adoption, you will now have a background to form your own opinions relative to making adoption easier for stepparents or whether unmarried birth mothers should be strongly encouraged by our society to consider adoption. Perhaps after you have graduated and then marry (or then desire a family as a settled single person), you will return to this topic of adoption on a more personal level. If you do, hopefully the contents of this chapter will be one of the aspects of your student days, which will then be useful in your every day world.

REFERENCES:

Flango, V and Flango, K. R. 1992. "How Many Children Were Adopted in 1992", *Child Welfare,* Vol. LXXIV, No. 5, Sept./Oct.

Hayes, P. 1993. *"Transracial Adoption: Politics and Ideology,"* Child Welfare, Vol. 72, No. 3, May/June, pp. 301-310

Hollinger, J. H. 2000. *Adoption & Law Practice.* New York: Matthew Bender.

Usdansky, M. L. 1996. "Single Motherhood: Stereotypes," *New York Times,* Feb. 11, 1996, p. 5.

Teenagers in Foster Care and Aging Out:
Awareness and Action for the Lost Voices

Amy P. Hauser, J.D.

In his book, *Finding Fish*, Antwone Fisher shared his story about life in foster care as well as some of the struggles, challenges, and triumphs as a child in the child welfare system in Cleveland, Ohio. Fisher was under the supervision of over thirteen social workers throughout his time in foster care. (Fisher 2001) At the age of seventeen, he became what many teenagers in foster care become—homeless. ("Report to the Congress" 2001) Fisher recalls his initial feelings about being homeless:

> The first thing you notice when you're homeless is how long the nights are. It's hard to realize that a night can be so long; but in time you get used to it. You don't really sleep, especially in the beginning, because you wake up every fifteen minutes worried someone will come upon you. Your imagination runs wild with what terrible things would happen if you fell asleep and let that happen...In the span of this first long night in the alley I give up my other priorities, like finding a job to save money for art school and reuniting with my friends; instead, my focus now is on finding protection.

In reflecting on his years in a physically abusive and emotionally empty foster home, he comments, "You come to understand that you can be living in a house and still be homeless, as I was in the Picketts' home and in the institutions where I later went to live." When the time approached for Fisher to age out of the system, turning eighteen meant exiting the supervision and care of the child welfare system, he said: "...I would begin life as an emancipated minor in a YMCA men's shelter. Since my eighteenth birthday was two months away, I had only that much time to find my bearings in the adult world." (Fisher 2001) Fisher's story, though one of constant trials and pain, is one that ends happily: he is reunited with members of his biological family. This ending, however, cannot be the story of twenty thousand teenagers who transition out of the foster care system each year. (Greene 2002)

The very word "teenager" creates numerous images, all of which suggest incomplete or unformed individuals. Teenagers are still in transition in many ways, in the journey from childhood to adulthood. (Woodhouse 2002) Similar to Fisher is David Ahlgren, in foster care for four years, who "aged out" of the system and "was literally left on a street corner with his personal belongings" at the age of eighteen. (Newberger 2002) The foster care system was not intended at its creation to raise adolescents to adulthood, but many children are remaining in the system long-term or entering the system as teenagers. (Krebs and Pitcoff 2004) Each year, around 500,000 children are in foster care, and the H.R. Committee on Ways and Means reported in 1995 that approximately one-third of these children are teenagers. Nearly forty percent of the children exiting foster care each year are teenagers. When they leave the state's care, some do reunite with their family or may be adopted. (Mangold 2000) Other teenagers who exit the system are left to fallback on the training and skills they currently possess from independent living programs.

Former foster care teenagers often find themselves without a job, without a place to live, or in jail. According to information by the Children's Bureau of the Department of Health and Human Services, within two to four years of youth leaving foster care: only half have completed high school; less than half were employed; one in four were homeless at least one night during the year; a third do not have access to health care; and less than 20 percent were identified as self-sufficient. ("Youth Aging Out" 2001) One of the largest studies was conducted by Westat (1991), and it revealed that forty-six percent, of 810 teenagers, had not graduated from high school when they aged out. In addition, sixty-two percent did not keep a job for a one-year span of time. (Mangold 2000) Barth (1990) performed a study in the San Francisco Bay Area that revealed fifty-five percent of former foster care teenagers who had left care one to ten years ago had not graduated from high school when they left foster care. In addition, the study showed that thirty-eight percent had not even graduated at the time of the study. ("Statement of Fagnoni" 1999) A 1998 study, Courtney and Piliavin, conducted by the University of Wisconsin showed that only nine percent of former foster children enrolled in college after exiting the state's care twelve months or eighteen months earlier. (Gievers 2001) Teenage girls face additional problems: sixty percent gave birth within two years and the majority of the births were out of wedlock. (Mangold 2000)

Some teenagers become homeless or are arrested. The Westat study (1991) showed that one-quarter of teenagers who had aged out had spent a minimum of one night on the streets without a roof over their heads. Courtney and Piliavin (1998) found that incarceration was more prominent among the males who were former foster care children than females.[1] However, a good percentage of each had been in jail within the following twelve or eighteen months after exiting the system. (Mangold 2000)

Some teenagers run away from foster care. The Health and Human Services recently estimated this number at 10,000 children nationally that have taken such action. It is suggested that some teenagers believe they might as well try to "fend for themselves." This decision comes after being tossed around to different homes or never finding adults with whom to form meaningful relationships. ("Some Teens Flee" 2002) Those most likely to run away are the teenagers who are moved constantly, often when they should not be moved or are even sent home when it is not the right time. Generally, if older teens do not want to stay in a foster home, it is more difficult to keep them in it. Many states are having difficulty tracking teenagers who run away. Some child advocates believe the problem of runaway teens does not receive the attention it deserves from states. Richard Wexler, president of the National Coalition for Child Protection Reform, observed that, "'If your, or my, teenage child ran away, we would move heaven and earth to find that child. And when the state is the parent, it has the same obligation'" (Peterson 2002). There are many risks facing these runaway teens.

Youth leaving foster care may also be dealing with mental health problems. Courtney and Piliavin (1998) found that in their sample, scores on a mental health inventory for the former foster care youths were "significantly lower" than the same age individuals not in foster care who took the inventory. Additionally, in the previous year,

---

[1] The Courtney and Piliavin studies showed that twenty-seven percent of males and ten percent of females had been in jail at least one time. An older study by Richard Barth included thirty-five percent of teenagers who had been incarcerated at least once.

mental health services were obtained by only twenty-one percent of those in the sample twelve to eighteen months after aging out. ("Report to Congress" 2001)

Though the end result may not accurately reflect it, these teenagers have rights while they are in the foster care system. The Youth Advocacy Center in New York created a booklet called *Rights and Advocacy Guidelines* that informs foster care teenagers of their rights. One right each teen has is to be adopted. The teen must give consent to the adoption if he or she is over the age of fourteen. Therefore, teenagers also have the right not to be adopted. Additionally, teenagers are entitled to an allowance that is not to be used for basic needs.[2] If the allowance is withheld, the agency is to keep it in an account for the teen, and he or she can get it at the time of discharge. Teenagers have the right to participate in meetings that plan their future in foster care and after foster care and should have been attending these meetings since they were ten years old.[3] The teenager is also entitled to be notified in advance of this meeting and bring someone with him or her to the meeting. Teenagers also can have a lawyer who will speak confidentially with them and protect such rights as an appropriate placement, services such as AIDS/HIV testing, family planning, medication, preparation for independent living, visits with family, and a proper discharge plan. (*Rights and Advocacy* 2002)

Huge gaps exist in the child welfare system for teenagers in foster care. Over 20,000 children each year turn eighteen and exit the foster care system, (Mangold 2000) commonly termed "aging out." The problem is that many of these teenagers are not prepared to enter the world and are lacking the necessary resources and abilities to successfully survive. This article will evaluate the available programs and assistance given to teens while in foster care and after they exit, both nationwide and particularly in Kentucky.

In Part I, this paper will expose the difficulties that teenagers in foster care face, both while under the state's care and after they are released. This section will also evaluate the past legislation enacted to aid teenagers in the system. Part II will focus on state programs that are offered to teenagers before and after they age out. Kentucky programs will be specifically addressed to show what is available for teens living in that state. Part III will examine ways to improve and increase awareness about the problems facing aging out foster care teens. The final segment, Part IV, will examine recommendations to improve the present efforts and legislation for these young adults.

Part I. What Foster Care Does for Teenagers

Teenagers will usually be under the state's care due to one of two situations. The teenager may enter foster care while a teen or he or she may have grown up in foster care and never exited the system. Some may be in foster care as status offenders, but this is less likely. (Woodhouse 2002)

Life in foster care for a teenager can be filled with disappointment and instability. Even if it is not the case, teenagers in foster care are usually viewed as "'problem

---

[2] There is no set amount; instead, the amount given is determined by each agency. This allowance is statutorily enacted. Ten dollars a week is a typical allowance for youth in group homes.

[3] These meetings are likely given different names in different states, but some names include "case conferences," "service plan reviews," "treatment plan reviews," or "treatment meetings." Such meetings should occur soon after the child enters foster care and every six months after that time.

children.'" (Krebs and Pitcoff 2004) The issues teens encounter are numerous, including housing, emotional support, and a good education. As one child services director said, "'Teenagers probably do get the short shrift from the foster-care system.'" With regard to housing, there is not always available room for the teenagers to stay. When this occurs, teenagers may be placed in centers for delinquent youths. (Bjornstad 1990) Even if a good place to house them is located, the teens often need counseling of some kind and do not usually receive it. ("The Human Face" 2001)

Overall, things do not appear to get brighter for foster care teenagers following their exit from foster care. The kind of life that some teenagers lead following their life in foster care has earned them the nickname of "couch surfers." (Woodhouse 2002) This is explained as living night to night based on the generosity of friends and people they have met. Of course, when the couches are occupied and the doors to warm homes are closed, the likely bed for the night is the street.

Another difficulty for teenagers who have aged out is the lack of family contact. As it has been described, the teenagers are without a safety net. The teen may have not had contact with his or her family members for a long time or his or her parents may have lost their rights in a termination of parental rights proceeding. (Woodhouse 2002) Additionally, the issue of sibling contact is raised which may have involved a separation of the teenager and younger siblings. In one New York survey of foster teens, almost forty-three percent said they had not visited their siblings. (Chaifetz 1999)

Teenagers are also lacking an emotional and social support system. For a former foster care teenager, reaching eighteen and gaining independence is not a choice. (Chaifetz 1999) An aged out teen does not have the ability to call to ask questions or to get advice on decisions he or she is making. There is a clear contrast between a teenager turning eighteen with a stable home and family and an aged out teenager who wonders where he or she will sleep the next night and what he or she will eat the next day. In short, the aged out teenager must live day to day without the physical, emotional, and social security that is usually guaranteed by a family. Teenagers while in foster care are less likely to gain a family under the state's care through adoption. (*In the interest of Ashley* 1991) The typical parents, yearning to adopt, are not interviewing teenage kids to see if they would fit well in their family. The fact is, though, that teenagers need a loving family and home just as much as younger children in foster care. This realization removes only another hope for many teenagers in foster care that is likely to lead to a feeling of inadequacy. Also, bitterness and anger may develop because the teenager desires to be a part of a family and feels let down. (Garland 2002)

An additional obstacle is the low level of educational achievement that teenagers obtain. (Krebs and Pitcoff 2002) Research by the Vera Institute of Justice showed that children have a better chance of success in school if the child enters foster care at a younger age. The quality of education is affected by the stability of the home and constant transferring from school to school. Teenagers are sometimes placed in group homes to live; however, according to the Vera Institute, school attendance decreases when teenagers live in group homes. (Garcia 2002)

Other teenagers may be inappropriately placed in special education classes. For instance, in New York City, one-third of the foster care teens questioned by Advocates of Children responded that they were in special education classes, one half of which were not in these kinds of classes before they entered the care of the state. (Carter 2002) The purpose of placing them in these special education classes is to give them extra and more specialized and individualized attention. This is a valid concern since the teens are going through a lot of emotional strife at the time. (Earle 2002) However, most teenagers find that later changing out of special education classes is difficult once they are placed there. Remaining in special education classes at school may affect their chances to graduate as well as the overall quality of learning. (Carter 2002) In a group home, the materials being taught may not be meaningful nor actually helpful to increasing each teen's learning. Also in group homes, school may be separate from ordinary public school which affects the teens socially.

As was mentioned, young women face a variety of additional issues. (Krebs and Castro 1995) In 1999, the Children's Bureau in the Department of Health and Human Services reported that sixty percent of the teenagers had given birth within two to four years after leaving foster care. ("Youth Aging Out" 2001) The obvious fact is that many problems exist for older teens in foster care, and they each initiate a cycle that is likely to follow as they exit the system.

Legislative Efforts

Marion Wright Edelman, President of the Children's Defense Fund, boldly described the conditions of the child welfare system in the United States as "a national disgrace." (Chaifetz 1999) Early concern about child abuse and neglect led to the passage of the Child Abuse Prevention and Treatment Act (CAPTA), P.L. 93-247, in 1974. The main result of CAPTA was the introduction of initiatives in mandatory reporting, investigating, and record-keeping system of child protective services. (Mangold 2000)

The Adoption Assistance and Child Welfare Act (AACWA), P.L. 96-272, followed in 1980 with the goals of family preservation, reasonable efforts, and reunification. The Independent Living Initiative (ILI) focused on the specific needs of older children in foster care. This legislation passed in 1986 and demanded specific planning be provided to teenagers sixteen and older before they aged out. The stated goal of the ILI was "to help the individuals participating...to prepare to live independently upon leaving foster care." Programs through this legislation were aimed at education and daily life skills for the teenagers, which included a specialized written independent living plan for each teen. The Adoption and Safe Families Act (ASFA) of 1997, P.L. 105-89, was intended to generally address all children who were abused and neglected, with a special emphasis on child safety as a primary objective. With this act, the focus turned from family reunification and became adoption and permanent homes for all children in foster care. Since the passage of ASFA, it seems readily apparent that the needs of older children still have not been met. (Mangold 2000) The upshot of ASFA is that the only viable option for teens are independent living programs. One reason for this is that many teens lose the chance to reunify with their parents because termination of parental rights has occurred, making adoption unlikely at their age.

In 1999, Congress addressed the needs of teenagers aging out of the system with the Foster Care Independence Act, P.L. 106-169. (Mangold 2000) Some hailed the act as "monumental" for aging out foster children. (Guinn 2000) This legislation built on the principles of the 1986 ILI legislation, (Mangold 2000) with its purpose to produce self-sufficient young adults that do not fall into the trap of poverty. (Guinn 2000) Under this law, the age for provision of services was extended to twenty-one while teenagers make the transition from foster care into living on their own. (Mangold 2000) The amount of funding was also expanded to help states set up programs for those aging out.[4] The five goals identified by the Chafee Foster Care Independence Programs for aging out teenagers are as follows: 1) identify and give assistance; 2) provide proper training and services for employment; 3) prepare for post-high school training; 4) provide personal and emotional support; and 5) offer a range of services for former foster care children that are 18-21 to assist them in their success to independence. An important achievement of this program is that independent living is no longer a separate option for the teen because it can occur while the state seeks a permanent place for the child. (Guinn 2000)

Presented in the summer of 2002, two bills were introduced and supported by Senator Hillary Rodham Clinton named the "Fostering Service Act" and the "Opportunity Passport Act." ("Senators Clinton" 2002) The legislation advocates for support services and AmeriCorps community service opportunities for those aging out. The "Fostering Service Act" allows teenagers to gain job skills, establish a connection to their community, and earn an education award for school at a later time through service in AmeriCorps. As an incentive to programs, the "Opportunity Passport Act" will provide demonstration grants in the amount of ten million dollars to programs that support aging out teenagers. ("New Paltz Native" 2002)

The past is important to note and explore, but the present and future will best determine the future of many teenagers aging out of foster care. The studies and statistics show the past results of what many foster care teens did when they left the system. We know the difficulties they are facing and the weaknesses that exist.

Part II. What the State Can Give

Nelson sits in his caseworker's office. He'll be 21 in seven weeks. He has been in foster care for the past six years, has lived in three different group homes and one foster home, and this is his 11th caseworker. His disinterested and tough appearance hides the truth- he's scared of being discharged from foster care. The caseworker is sympathetic to Nelson, but there is not much she can do to help him at this point....Looking at Nelson, she asks, "'You got any plans?' Nelson is paralyzed by the question. No one has helped him make any solid plans. Nelson [says] 'I wanted to go to college. Now I got to learn to be independent. Pay the rent, food...You know, I really don't know how to do anything. I wanted to be someone but no one ever showed me how.' (Krebs and Pitcoff 2002)

Due to the above mentioned legislation and concern about teenagers aging out, programs have developed to ease the transition from foster care to living on their own as adults. However, these programs have been described by some experts as "few and far between." (Reyes 2000) Each state has its own programs, though most are teaching the

---

[4] Funding for Independent Living Programs, whose name was changed by the Act to the John H. Chafee Foster Care Independence Program, was doubled from $70 million to $140 million. The states are permitted to use up to thirty percent of the money for providing room and board for the those aging out at ages eighteen to twenty-one.

youth the same things and arming them with the same skills. A Missouri study by McMillen and Tucker (1999) supported the idea that providing appropriate services in transition improves the chances for positive outcomes following exit from foster care. The study found that those who participated in an independent living program while in care and graduated from high school had a higher rate of employment after they aged out. ("Report to the Congress" 2001)

In Kentucky, the primary provider of aged out youth comes under the Chafee Independence Program for teenagers. This program is federally funded, focused on giving these teenagers the life skills they so desperately need. ("The Chafee Independence Program") In 2003, Kentucky was receiving around two million dollars to operate its programs. Since the program uses federal funds, the state must follow the directive that all children in foster care that are twelve or older must receive these services despite the permanency goal for the child. (Conley 2003) The services are divided according to the child's age.

Foster parents are trained to provide the informal services to youth ages twelve to fifteen. The lessons taught involve "soft skills" such as anger management, problem-solving, and decision-making. For daily survival, the skills taught are how to cook, take care of the house, do laundry, and manage money. As the teenagers reach age sixteen, the child can then sign up for formal Life Skills classes that are handled by Independent Living Coordinators or private contractors. The classes focus on employment, money management, community resources, housing, and education.

Foster care children can extend their commitment with the state before they reach the age of eighteen. The state provides for this, extending their time under the Cabinet for Health and Family Services (CHFS) to the age of twenty-one. The CHFS has the discretion to deny this request for an extension. (Conley 2003) Once their time is extended, these teenagers can take formal Life Skills classes. Further, their education can be provided for in several ways. First, state funds can provide tuition assistance that federal funds have not covered for college or vocational training. ("The Chafee Independence Program") Second, tuition waivers occur under K.R.S. 164.2847, Waiver of tuition and mandatory student fees for Kentucky foster or adopted children. This waiver applies to tuition and mandatory fees at any Kentucky public university, technical, or community college. This is the last option for tuition help if no other method covers the educational expenses. Former foster care children who do not extend their time through the CHFS are still eligible for the same classes and education assistance.

Housing for aging out teenagers is arranged through contracts with private agencies. Another opportunity for any aged youth is the Kentucky Organization for Foster Youth (KOFFY). This group is composed of former and current youth in foster care who aim to increase awareness in the community, both to the public and policymakers, about their needs. This statewide group also has goals that include establishing a mentoring program and developing a speaker's bureau of youth. ("The Chafee Independence Program")

Kentucky also utilizes therapeutic foster care to target youth involved in juvenile crime. Similar to the independent living services, these teens are given chores to do, are required to keep a journal, have jobs, go to school, and attend counseling sessions. Foster care parents are specially trained to carry out this program, and the results have been successful. ("Ky. Uses" 2002) This, in effect, is associated with the teenagers in foster care and the effort to try new methods of rehabilitation and correction in these troubled teens.

New York has established several ways to assist its teenagers aging out. For former foster children ages eighteen to twenty-one, a housing subsidy is available. (*Rights and Advocacy* 2002) Several conditions attach for eligibility for the subsidy including a steady source of income, locating a place to rent, and getting approval from the landlord. The other housing option is a priority position for a Section 8 voucher. Those eligible are at least eighteen, committed to achieving independent living, have a plan for discharge from foster care in the upcoming six to eight months (or are under the age of twenty-four and were discharged within the last two years), and can prove they will have income at the time of discharge.

To successfully teach a teenager independent living, the foster care agency must give the teen access to college or vocational training, teach living skills, locate housing, and give a monthly stipend during the teen's participation in the program. The agency must also identify people and other organizations that can help the teen following his discharge from foster care. Further, the agency must assist in helping the teen to re-establish contact with family and friends. Following discharge, the agency must provide after care services that include contact and visitation by a caseworker, supervision of the teen, and further assistance with housing if the situation becomes unstable. (*Rights and Advocacy* 2002)

An innovative idea that some states have put into practice is providing foster children with an "eMentor." This involves pairing a mentor and an aged out foster child to communicate with each other through email. It is a very modern approach to meeting the needs of youth. It is easy on the mentor and mentee's schedules, and both are likely to benefit from the new relationship. This is a method to address the void of an adult role model and allows the mentor to share advice and help without the mentee feeling threatened. Plus, the two can discuss many things, from the bigger decisions to everyday issues. (Newberger 2002) This anytime, anywhere assistance seems like a beneficial and practical service to reach out to teenagers growing up in this computer age.

Some programs, such as the Youth Advocacy Center, focus on self-advocacy for teenagers. This includes setting short and long term goals, identifying those who can help and support, finding personal strengths and weaknesses, dealing with setbacks and rejection, making adjustments to strategies, and building on strategies and successes. With self-advocacy, the teenager is encouraged to always look forward to the future, because that is what one can advocate for. Self-advocacy also teaches the teens to be personally responsible and active. This program completes the message of self-advocacy to the teenagers through a seminar on the issue. The method of teaching involves assigning work for the teens individually and in groups and exercising Socratic methods for analyzing the skills and theories being taught. The Youth Advocacy Center even developed its own workbook to assist teens in their pursuit of self-advocacy. During the seminar, guest speakers give lectures and each student is required to complete a final project. (Krebs and Pitcoff 2002)

One issue that must be addressed by each state is the jurisdiction over the teenagers who extend their commitment or those still receiving services after they reach the age of eighteen. This affects not only the control and protection of the state over the teenager, but it also affects the ability of the teen to enforce his rights. For example,

Florida has decided that the circuit courts do not maintain jurisdiction over a teenager after he or she has reached eighteen despite the fact that he or she is still receiving services from the state. (Gievers 2001) Lawmakers should be sure that some court has jurisdiction over these former foster care children to address their needs, and this should be set out in detail to avoid uncertainty.

An ever-present obstacle that these kinds of programs face is financial support. In the midst of recent talk about cutbacks, programs to help foster care teenagers are not the best candidate for survival. Even three years ago, federal funding decreased for out-of-home placement, and state funds were unable to uphold the youth services being provided. (Lewis 2001) Therefore, any improvement resulting from the Foster Care Independence Act may be at risk in some states.

Part III. The Role Players

It is important not only for the teenagers themselves but also for society that these teens continue to receive assistance and be able to extend their commitment to the state. This creates a better likelihood that the teens will complete their education and make a smooth transition to living independently. (Gievers 2001) Society as a whole has an interest in this, but certain members of society have the ability to truly influence this result. These primary figures include attorneys, social workers, and policymakers.

A crucial aspect to mending these teens' lives is a role model. This role can be filled by an attorney, a social worker, and/or some other appropriate adult. One former foster care teen reflects on the woman who played this influential part in her life:

> She told me that in spite of all of those problems, not to let anything hold me back. Those words made all the difference. If one person was encouraging me, I knew that I was smart enough to go places with my life, and that the problems were not with me, but with the system. The way she talked to me and treated me and expected greatness from me gave me a firm push to put my goals into action. After talking with her, I decided that I didn't want to be one thing. I wanted to be many, and I could be them all. (Earle 2002)

This statement puts the effort needed and desired in perspective. It took only one person to make this difference, so if social workers, attorneys, and teachers really put some effort toward this, there should be more than just one.

Lawyers and judges should represent these teenagers and push foster care agencies to take action and help teens advance their goals through concrete plans for the future. (Krebs 2002) Lawyers should educate themselves regarding the opportunities and programs available for teenagers in foster care, particularly those who will age out in the next few years. If communication has broken down or has been nonexistent between the teenager and his or her social worker, then the attorney possesses an ideal position and ability to fill in the gap.

Policymakers must continually be educated, updated, and informed about the needs of these at-risk youth to ensure improvements in legislative efforts. Lori Rubiner, Vice President of Program and Public Policy for National Partnership for Women and Families, said the greatest barrier to passing the Chafee Bill was the lack of understanding among the elected officials on child welfare issues. ("The Human Face" 2001) This barrier must be brought down continually and hopefully permanently.

Part IV. Recommendations

It seems clear that the quality and quantity of services to all children in foster care are suffering due to the low attention foster care programs receive in budgets across the nation. ("NASW Stresses" 2003) President George W. Bush included foster care teenagers in his message regarding the nation's budget entitled "A Responsible Budget for America's Priorities" in 2001. He mentioned the need to strengthen families and included the educational and training needs of older foster care children. He specifically addressed an increase in funds through the Foster Care Independent Program to meet these needs. ("A Blueprint" 2001) This recognition is beneficial for foster care teenagers, but only if it is supported through actions and funding.

The recommendations can range widely from creativity to simplicity. One important suggestion is that the foster care system refocus on the futures in front of these teenagers instead of looking at past and present problems. (Krebs and Pitcoff 2002) This will enable the system to provide support to the teenagers in becoming participating citizens in society, a higher aspiration than ensuring they are self-sufficient. The Youth Advocacy Center believes that success will follow if the prejudices encountered by teenagers are tackled. The foster care teenager and the aged out teenager do not look that different from every other teenager or youth age sixteen to twenty-one in our country. Both share similar goals, needs, rights, and responsibilities. The primary difference is who has custody of the teenager. Since the state has taken these children from their homes, the state must also take the responsibility for meeting their needs and goals, while helping them acquire needed skills and protecting their rights.

Another recommendation is providing teenagers over the age of sixteen with additional options besides traditional foster care placement. One possibility could be placements that offer housing and an environment with career and educational guidance counselors. Another option could be transitional housing options for people aged eighteen to twenty-five that focuses on "learning by doing" in circumstances with real-life consequences. (Krebs and Pitcoff 2002)

Perhaps the easiest way to begin improvement is giving the teenager a voice in practice in his or her future. One author suggests that children are usually "treated as passive objects by the [foster care] system." (Chaifetz 1999) A teenager, or any child over the age of ten, should participate in decisions that affect day-to-day living and long-term permanency. Keeping teenagers quiet could be one reason that many teenagers will never truly become participating citizens, because this action becomes the first way to show them a lack of respect and care. (Chaifetz 1999) Thus, teenagers may see how they are treated in the system and be led to believe that they should never have a voice.

Another suggestion for improvement incorporates philosophy, planning, and accountability. The philosophy for foster care teenagers should be becoming participating citizens of society and not settling for self-sufficiency. This requires a higher expectation from policymakers and professionals for teenagers and what they can accomplish. Teenagers should then develop a solid plan for a future career, their education, and their personal goals that are unique to their desires and will extend to the age of twenty-five. To do this, teens will need adults to assist and support them in making and carrying out this plan. The next step will be accountability for the choices teens make. This responsibility should rest with foster care agencies and each state, since the teens cannot do it alone. (Krebs and Pitcoff 2002)

CONCLUSION

According to one child welfare agency, aging out of foster care is a "global issue." ("Youth Aging Out" 2001) Awareness is a definite key to improving the lives of each teenager in foster care. As Hillary Clinton stated, we must "make a greater investment in their lives." ("Foster Care Transitioning Event" 1999) These teens deserve nothing less than everything else that each person is entitled to and given. In response to the question of which she would choose between housing, healthcare, and education, one aged out teenager stated, "Why should I have to choose?" ("Foster Care Transitioning Event" 1999) She clearly made her point that an equal chance should be presented to every young adult in the foster care system. The problems facing foster care teenagers and aging out teenagers are readily apparent. Motivated through the federal government, each state must ensure that it is providing the skills and training to, at a minimum, meet the basic needs of this population.

REFERENCES:

"A Blueprint for New Beginnings- A Responsible Budget for America's Priorities." 2001. U.S. Government Printing Office. Washington, DC. Retrieved June 25, 2003 (http://www.whitehouse.gov/news/usbudget/blueprint/budtoc.html).

Bjornstad, Randi. 1990. "Teens Get Short Shrift in Foster Care." *Register Guard*. Retrieved May 22, 2003 (http://www.oslc.org/InTheNews/shrift.html).

Carter, Charlene. 2002. "Separate But Not Equal- Why Do So Many Foster Youth Get Stuck in Special Ed?" Youth Communications. Retrieved May 23, 2003 (http://www.youthcomm.org/FCYU-Features/FCYU-2002-09-6.htm).

Chaifetz, Jill. 1999. "Listening to Foster Children in Accordance with the Law: The Failure to Serve Children in State Care." 25 *New York University Review Law & Social Change* 1, 19-20.

Conley, Fawn. June 2003. Phone Interview. Director of Chafee Independence Program. Frankfort, Kentucky.

Earle, Ja'Nelle. 2002. "The Miseducation of Foster Youth- When Group Home teachers Expect the Worst." Youth Communications. Retrieved May 23, 2003 (http://www.youthcomm.org/FCYU-Features/FCYU-2002-09-2.htm).

Fisher, Antwone. 2001. *Finding Fish*. New York. HarperCollins Publishers.

Foster Care Independent Act of 1999, Pub. L. No. 106-169, 113 Stat. 1822. June 25, 1999. House of Representatives. H4962.

"Foster Care Transitioning Event- Remarks by Hillary Rodham Clinton." 1999. Speeches. Retrieved June 25, 2003 (http://clinton4.nara.gov/textonly/WH/EOP/First_Lady/html/generalspeeches/1999).

Garcia, Antwaun. 2002. "From Bad Boy to Bookworm: Foster Care Helped Me Focus." Youth Communication- Stories that Make a Difference. Retrieved May 22, 2003 (http://www.youthcomm.org/FCYU-Features/FCYU-2002-09-12.htm).

Garland, Rose M. 2002. "Teens Need Families Too." *The Roundtable*. Vol. 16, No. 2. Retrieved May 21, 2003 (http://nncf.unl.edu/foster/info/teenadoption.html).

Gievers, Karen. 2001. "Listening to Silenced Voices: Examining Potential Liability of State and Private Agencies for Child Support Enforcement Violations." 25 *Nova Law Review* 693.

Greene, Elizabeth. May 2002. "Fostering Smooth Transitions- Charities step up efforts to help young adults leaving foster care." *The Chronicle of Philanthropy*.

Guinn, Raudi P. 2000. "Passage of the Foster Care Independent Act of 1999: A Pivotal Step on Behalf of Youth Aging Out of Foster Care and Into a Life of Poverty." 7 *Georgetown Journal on Poverty Law & Policy* 403.

In the Interest of Ashley K., 571 N.E.2d 905, 919 (Ill. App. Ct. 1991). Kentucky Revised Statutes § 164.2847. Michie 2004.

Krebs, Betsy. 2002. "Foster Kids Need a Bold Plan." The Fortune Society. Retrieved May 21, 2003 (http://www.fortunesociety.org/fall0202.htm).

Krebs, Betsy and Nedda de Castro. 1995. "Caring for our Children: Improving the foster care system for teen mothers and their children." Youth Advocacy Center. Retrieved May 21, 2003 (http://youthadvocacycenter.org/reports.html).

Krebs, Betsy and Paul Pitcoff. 2002. "The Future for Teens in Foster Care." Youth Advocacy Center.

----------. 2004. "Reversing the Failure of the Foster Care System." *Harvard Journal of Law & Gender*. Vol. 27. 357.

"Ky. Uses Therapeutic Foster Care to Address Youth Crime." Feb. 26, 2002. Join Together Online. Retrieved May 21, 2003 (http://www.jointogether.org/gv/news/summaries/print/0,2060,548509,00.html).

Lewis, Tony. 2001. "The State's Challenge for Children in Custody." 24-DEC *Wyoming Law Review* 24.

Mangold, Susan Vivian. 2000. "Extending Non-Exclusive Parenting and the Right to Protection for Older Foster Children: Creating Third Options in Permanency Planning." 48 *Buffalo Law Review* 835.

"NASW Stresses the Importance of Adequately Funded Child Welfare Systems Nationwide." March 11, 2003. National Association of Social Workers. Retrieved June 25, 2003 (http://www.social workers.org/pressroom/2003/031103.asp).

"New Paltz Native Unveils Bill with Senator Clinton." June 25, 2002. Youth Resource Development Corporation. Retrieved June 24, 2003 (http://www.yrdc.org/Clinton%20release1.pdf).

Newberger, Julee. 2002 "Mentoring by Modem." Connect for Kids. Retrieved May 27, 2003 (http://www.connectforkids.org/articles/mentoring_by_modem).

Peterson, Kavan. November 2002. "State Agencies Search for Foster Kids." *Stateline.org.* Retrieved February 18, 2005 (http://www.stateline.org/stateline/?pa=story&sa=showStoryInfo&print=1&id=26 8782).

"Report to the Congress- Developing a System of Program Accountability Under the John H. Chafee Foster Care Independence Program." Sept. 2001. The Department of Health and Human Services' Plan for Developing and Implementing the National Youth in Transition Information System.

Reyes, David. 2000. "Something Lost in Transition for Foster Care Teens- Report cites need for young adults leaving system to have financial or emotional support to help prevent homelessness, pregnancy and joblessness." *Los Angeles Times,* February 10, B1.

Rights and Advocacy Guidelines. 2002. Youth Advocacy Center. Retrieved May 21, 2003 (http://youthadvocacycenter.org/pdf/RightsandAdvocacyGuidelines.pdf).

"Senators Clinton and Landrieu Call For Expanding AmeriCorps Opportunities for Former Foster Children." June 20, 2002. Retrieved June 24, 2003 (http://clinton.senate.gov/~clinton/news/2002/06/2002620C03.html).

"Some Teens Flee Foster Care to Fend for Themselves." Dec. 2002. CPS Watch. Associated Press. Retrieved May 21, 2003 (http://www.cpswatch.com/news/article.asp?Index=201).

"Statement of Cynthia M. Fagnoni, Director Education, Workforce, and Income Security Issues, Health, Education, and Human Services Division, U.S. General Accounting Office." May 13, 1999. Testimony Before the House Committee on Ways and Means Subcommittee on Human Resources.

"The Chafee Independence Program for Teenagers Currently In Or Aged Out of Foster Care." N.d. Cabinet for Health and Family Services, Commonwealth of Kentucky. Retrieved May 23, 2003 (http://chfs.ky.gov/dcbs/dpp/The+Chafee+Independence+Program.htm).

"The Human Face of Foster Care in America- Terry Harrak."Spring 2001. *Focal Point.* Vol. 15(1), 25-26. Retrieved June 25, 2003 (http://www.rtc.pdx.edu/FPinHTML/FocalPointSP01/pgFPsp01Human.shtml).

Woodhouse, Barbara Bennett. 2002. "Youthful Indiscretions: Culture, Class Status, and the Passage to Adulthood." 51 *DePaul Law Review* 743.

"Youth Aging Out of Foster Care- A Global Issue." 2001. Holt International Children's Services. Retrieved May 24, 2003 (http://www.holtintl.org/hifamilies/Philippines0201SB2.shtml).

The Police and Social Workers: Collaborations for the Future

Robert P. McNamara and Laura McBride
Department of Sociology, Furman University

There can be little doubt that child abuse is a serious social problem in this country. Since 1974, when the Child Abuse Prevention and Treatment Act was signed into law, the federal government has been spearheading efforts at the state level to confront the treatment (and prevention) of child abuse in the U.S. Three years later, The National Center on Child Abuse and Neglect (NCCAN) developed manuals to provide social workers with insight and guidance on how to adequately provide services to children and families.

Almost twenty-five years later, the nature and extent of child abuse and neglect has remained a salient feature of American life. According to data from the National Child Abuse and Neglect Data System (NCANDS) as well as the National Incidence Study of Child Abuse and Neglect (NIS-3), both sponsored by the Department of Health and Human Services, in 1997, child protective services (CPS) agencies investigated an estimated 2 million reports that involved the alleged maltreatment of approximately 3 million children in the U.S.

That same year, CPS agencies determined just under a million children were victims of substantiated[1] or indicated[2] child abuse or neglect. These figures only represent reported cases. There is ample evidence that more children suffer from abuse or neglect than are reported in official statistics. For instance, in 1995 the Gallup Organization estimated that three million children were victims of physical abuse alone. This number is 16 times greater than the number of children reported to authorities (Child Welfare League of America 1998). Further, while some data suggests that about 13.9 children per 1,000 (younger than 18 years old) were victims of abuse or neglect, the NIS-3 data estimates that 42 per 1,000 were harmed or endangered by abuse.

In attempting to explain why child abuse continues to be a problem, most experts cite two main reasons. The first has to do with our inability to adequately address the problem. Social workers and police officers, as well as the host of other professionals who deal with children, are ill equipped to contend with the severity or magnitude of abuse and neglect. Caseloads are high, many parents are substance abusers, and the system is designed so that only the most serious cases can be dealt with in any meaningful way.

The second reason is found in the recognition that abuse and neglect do not occur in a vacuum. The problems of poverty, housing, adult domestic abuse, lack of job opportunities, and inadequate education all contribute to high levels of stress for many families. In some ways, abuse and neglect become the visible manifestations of these larger issues (Child Welfare League of America 1998).

THE RELATIONSHIP BETWEEN THE POLICE AND SOCIAL WORKERS

It is obvious that the police and social workers play an integral role in addressing child abuse. While problems such as the maltreatment of children may appear to be only a law

---

[1] An allegation of maltreatment was confirmed according to evidence defined by state law.

[2] An investigation finding used by some states when there is insufficient evidence to substantiate a case under state law, but there is reason to suspect that maltreatment occurred or a risk of it exists.

enforcement issue or only a social work issue, in reality, there is a great deal of overlap between the police and social workers. Researchers have estimated that between 70 and 90 percent of police time is devoted to activities that are also performed by social workers. Examples include settling domestic disputes, protecting children, and providing information to community residents (see for instance Waddington 1993; Bell 1982). Fielding (1991), for example, argues that the functions of the two professions are so closely related that the police should be referred to as "all-round social workers." At the same time, social workers often find themselves in a law enforcement role. As Vernon (1990) and others have contended, the child protection movement, along with changes in state and federal laws regarding the safety of children, have required social workers to become more mindful of their role as law enforcers.

Despite these and other similarities, there are a number of organizational constraints that differentiate how each agency serves the public. The differing objectives and missions within each organization cause the individual working in these agencies to focus on different aspects of the problem. For instance, the police have a main mission to protect the entire society. This is not to say that officers are unconcerned about individuals or their problems. Rather, their focus must remain on the problems that are threatening to the entire community (Morgan 1989).

Police officers also tend to view child abuse and neglect cases only as a criminal matter. As a result, in these types of situations, officers usually spend time collecting evidence for criminal prosecution. Unless they have been trained in the philosophy of child protection, officers will generally see little value in family preservation. Most officers, in fact, would probably contend that a parent who abuses or neglects his or her child should lose those rights and privileges and be sanctioned through incarceration. This point is illustrated by Sireman, Miller and Brown (1981), who found that in cases of suspected child abuse, if the police were the first to respond to the scene, children were much more likely to be separated from their families than if social workers preceded them.

In contrast, the social work mission focuses on helping the individual. Social workers, also known as child protective services (CPS) workers in some states, maintain a focus on the protection of the child from further abuse and neglect, as well as maintaining the integrity of the family. When dealing with child endangerment cases, the primary objective of CPS workers is the protection of the family (so that the risk of endangerment is lessened). Consequently, the intervention strategies used by CPS workers are usually rehabilitative in nature. This mission is consistent with state and federal laws that support the preservation or the reunification of the family.

Since CPS workers operate under a different set of guidelines, these standards often put them at odds with police officers, who think they are ignoring evidence or are too lenient in their treatment of potential offenders. This lack of understanding has, in part, led to a long-standing tension between the police and social workers. Despite the fact that the two groups are similar (in terms of the populations they serve as well as a great deal of overlap of activities), each group often have negative perceptions of the other.

Perceptions of Police Officers and Social Workers

In addition to interagency problems relating to child abuse cases, there is an overall sense of professional animosity and conflict between the police and social workers. In policing, there has been a perception that the task of the police officer is to fight crime. Any activity that is considered to fall outside those parameters is not "real" police work and should be avoided.

In the minds of many police officers, social work is the type of occupation where well-intended individuals attempt to alter the attitudes and behaviors of others who have no intention of changing and who do not deserve society's help. The clients of social workers are said to be the type of people who are lazy, embrace the role of societal victim, and will exploit everyone and everything whenever the opportunity arises (Parkinson 1980; Treger, 1981; Bar-On 1995).

Police officers also sometimes perceive social workers as lazy, irresponsible and/or incompetent. The reasons for this stem from the poor salary, high turnover rate, and the bureaucratic environment in which social workers must operate. This perception is reinforced when officers interact with social workers who are, in fact, lazy, irresponsible, or incompetent. In short, while many police officers recognize the need for social workers, they rely on inaccurate perceptions and stereotypes to describe the profession and its members.

Social workers contribute to the long-standing tension between their agencies and police departments. The majority of social workers work for Department of Social Services (DSS) agencies and are guilty of the same type of stereotypical thinking as police officers. Many social workers feel that the police are too heavy handed in their tactics when dealing with members of poor families. Many workers also feel that the police do not have a real understanding of the issues surrounding the families and people they encounter. Far too often, they complain, police officers think that the reasons individuals are poor have more to do with a lack of motivation than the host of other structural factors that contribute to their situations.

Social workers sometimes contend that, because of this conservative view, officers believe that arrest or some other form of punitive intrusion will solve the problem. While arrest may indeed solve the immediate situation, many social workers feel that officers fail to recognize that their actions are little more than the treatment of a symptom (Brown, Unsinger and More 1989; Parkinson 1980; Bar-On 1995).

One of the main reasons these inaccurate depictions persist is due to a lack of understanding of exactly what each agency attempts to accomplish and the problems and issues each profession must face. This is why many police departments and DSS agencies across the country do not collaborate to solve problems in their communities.

Research on the Relationship Between the Police and Social Workers

These attitudes and perceptions between the police and social workers have been the subject of interest by researchers since the 1950s. However, the amount of research on this relationship declined after the 1970s. While there are some recent studies, most of the focus on this topic is dated. This is true despite the fact that the problems the police and social workers experienced in the 1970s remain a salient feature of both professions today.

One of the earliest studies of the relationship between the police and social workers was conducted by Penner (1954). He concluded that the police think of social workers as being "ivory towerish" and have little understanding or training in how to alter people's behavior. In assessing the differences between the types of people who become police officers and their subsequent attitudes, Trojanowicz (1971) found that police officers scored higher than social workers on scales measuring perseverance, orderliness, moral absolutes, and role conformity. Officers also preferred external control, directive leadership and routine operating procedures. In contrast, social workers scored higher than police officers on scales measuring planning ahead, independence, participative leadership, social interaction, intellectual achievement, and delegative leadership.

Finney (1972) found that police officers, when asked to identify a single term to describe social workers, used the term "wishy-washy." They also felt that social workers were too lenient in carrying out their duties. In describing themselves, many officers used the term "realistic" and "courageous." They felt that when the situation called for it, officers would do "whatever was necessary" to solve the problem.

Hogarth (1971) discovered a similar finding. In assessing consequences of behavior, he found that police officers were more likely to rely on punitive measures to solve problems than the rehabilitative methods preferred by social workers. Clearly, the two groups had frequent contact with the same families, but the explanations as to why the behaviors occurred, as well as what should be done to solve problems, were at different ends of the spectrum.

Police-Social Worker Cooperation

Despite the history of suspicion of each other, and despite the contentious relationship in the past and present, there is evidence to suggest a degree of cooperation and collaboration between the police and social workers. Most of the examples are problem-specific, such as partnering with each other to deal with the mentally ill, to address juvenile delinquency issues, or to deal with sexual abuse among children (see for example Stephens 1988; Roberts 1983; Conte, Berliner and Nolan 1980).

There is also evidence of a partnership between the police and social workers to deal with family crises. As far back as 1976, researchers were pointing to collaborative efforts between the two agencies to preserve families (Roberts 1978; Bard and Berkowitz 1969; Michaels and Treger 1973; Kowalewski 1975; Colbach and Fosterling 1976; Kilpatrick 1979; Bennet 1980; Holmes 1982; Fein and Knaut 1986; Findlay 1991; Schonborn 1976).

Generally speaking, these efforts were of two types. One focused on providing training for police officers so that they were better able to help people they encountered on patrol. This type of crisis intervention training focused on a number of issues, such as juvenile offenses, domestic violence, suicide, etc. This training was important since mental health professionals were not always available when a crisis developed.

The second type of police-social work effort involved the development of social work teams within police departments. These teams were staffed with veteran social workers who also had knowledge of police procedures and served as liaisons between the police department and other social service agencies. They also assessed clients referred to them by police officers and were responsible for providing in-service training to officers in crisis intervention (Roberts 1976).

Since the 1970s and 1980s, there have been a few instances in which social workers and the police have collaborated to deal with a variety of problems. While there appear to be logical reasons to work together and the value of these cooperative efforts appear obvious, there are a number of scholars who contend that this type of collaboration is not productive.

Parkinson (1980) for example, found that the problem of collaboration is based more on gender stereotypes than suspicion or organizational obstacles. He argued that since the vast majority of police officers are male and most social workers are female, the nature of the interaction between the two is mitigated by the stereotypes based on gender. He also argues that since gender distributions in each profession are not likely to change in the future, it will be extremely difficult for social workers and police officers to work together as long as these images remain.

Similarly, and more recently, Bar-On (1995) contends that the inherent differences between police and social workers: the different missions, organizational objectives, and different strategies, makes inter-agency cooperation between the two unfeasible and counterproductive. He asserts that it is more important for each agency to retain its own identity than to collaborate. While it is helpful to understand and increase the awareness of the other agency, if each is to perform its function adequately, the police and DSS need to have a clearly defined division of labor.

In sum, the research has identified similarities between the police and social workers. It has also shown that, due to organizational objectives, professional mandates, and cultural influences, tension as well as a significant amount of mistrust and suspicion is created between the two groups. Some researchers argue that this type of collaboration is not feasible and counterproductive. However, there is more evidence that indicates regardless of why they work together, greater contact between the police and social workers has led to improved cooperation, a greater sense of familiarity, and a better understanding each group's constraints.

While differences of professional opinion may remain, the nature of the relationships developed as a result of this type of collaborative effort has improved significantly (Schonborn 1976; Fein and Knaut 1986; Conte; Berliner and Nolan 1980 Treger 1976; Treger 1977). To that end, a rather unique experiment is taking place in Charlotte, North Carolina. This program is being used to bridge the gap between the police department and DSS, as well as between individual officers and CPS workers.

METHODS

The program on which we focus is Charlotte's Partners for Family Solutions (PFS) program. This is a collaborative effort between the Charlotte-Mecklenburg Police Department and the Mecklenburg County Department of Social Services. This examination consisted of classic ethnographic techniques of direct observation and semi-structured and unstructured interviews. In addition, a two-page survey was constructed, which was given to a random stratified sample of 200 officers, 100 of whom had not been involved in the PFS program. The latter group was selected at random from all sworn officers in the department and served as a control group. Of the 100 officers involved in the PFS, 25 were randomly selected from each of the four police districts involved with the PFS. The survey was designed to gain some sense of how effective the program has been in enhancing the relationship between the two agencies as well as between officers and CPS workers.

The Research and Development Division of the Charlotte-Mecklenburg Police Department was responsible for selecting the two samples of officers. There are approximately 400 police officers involved in the PFS, out of a total of approximately 1,400 in the department. Surveys were sent to the captains in each precinct where officers had been selected. The captain gave the survey to the officers, who returned them shortly thereafter. Once this was completed, the surveys were mailed to the authors of this report for analysis.

A similar survey was created and administered to 61 CPS workers and 64 social workers assigned to Mecklenburg County Department of Social Services. The latter group consisted of workers assigned to other divisions of DSS (treatment, case planning, foster care) and served as a control group. The method of distribution was identical to that in the police department. Supervisors were responsible for the administration and collection of the survey, which were then mailed to the authors for analysis.

THE PARTNERS FOR FAMILY SOLUTIONS PROGRAM

The PFS program began as an attempt to improve the training and understanding of family services for police departments. Family preservation has been the guiding principle of state and federal law for children and families since 1980, with the passage of the Adoption Assistance and Child Welfare Act. Since that time, family preservation training has focused on social workers, attorneys, and judges, but has ignored the police as a vital component of family preservation (Soler 1994). This omission is significant for a number of reasons.

First, the police and DSS usually have frequent contact with the same families in a given community, albeit for different reasons. Because of this, police officers could provide information, insight, and even protection to social workers when they visit homes of families at risk. Second, the efforts of DSS workers could be unnecessarily inhibited if the police are not aware of the theory and practice of family preservation in dealing with families.

Finally, without a clear understanding of the purpose and goals of family preservation, as well as training in how it is implemented, police officers are not able to take full advantage of collaborative efforts and problem solving strategies (Soler 1994). To that end, the PFS was designed to develop a training model for police departments to improve their understanding of family preservation, as well as to develop protocols to articulate how and in what ways police departments handle family preservation cases. At the same time, this model emphasized the development and enhancement of a collaborative working relationship with child welfare agencies.

To accomplish these goals, officers and social workers were provided with many opportunities to develop better working relationships through cross-training workshops, informal gatherings to share information and ideas, and by participating in a ride along program. This program consisted of CPS workers riding along with officers as they answered calls and conducted preventive patrol while officers also rode along with CPS workers when they made home visits. This allowed both groups to observe the problems and issues found in each agency.

RESULTS OF THE SURVEY

Recall that surveys were sent to 61 CPS workers and 64 social workers in other divisions of DSS. The response rate for CPS workers was 91.8% (56 of 61). The response rate for the control group was much lower, however 26.5% (17 of 64). Part of the explanation for the difference could be due to the fact that the Assistant Director of Child Protective Services was responsible for administering and collecting the surveys. Consequently, it is possible she was able to remind her staff about the importance of the study more often than other workers in different divisions.

One of the initial questions on the survey attempted to assess each group's knowledge of the PFS program. A higher percentage of social workers in the experimental group knew more about the program (25% vs. 0% rated it excellent or good). This may be due to the fact that the change in the name of the program may have caused some workers to believe they do not know about it. Interview data suggests that when the Partners for Family Solutions name was used, most workers seemed confused. When the qualification of Family Preservation project was added as a way of explaining the project, more workers (and police officers) seemed familiar with it.

We also asked workers how difficult it was to get in touch with a police officer. The rationale behind this was if workers had a personal and professional relationship with officers, contacting them for assistance would occur more quickly. Social workers in the experimental group found it less difficult to get in touch with a police officer than those in the control group (66% vs. 40%).

In an attempt to understand more about the professional relationships between the police and social workers that the PFS program attempts to develop, we asked both groups if they knew any staff members at the police department. Almost 64% of the experimental group said they knew staff members at the police department while only 29% of the control group knew officers, a statistically significant difference.

We also asked how responsive the police department had been in meeting workers' needs when dealing with a child-related incident. Although there were statistically significant differences between the experimental and control groups, both feel that the department does a good job in this area. Almost 81% of the experimental group rated the department as excellent or good while 47% of the control group felt that way. In fact, only one person in the entire sample rated the department as poor on this question.

One area of interest was the ride along component to the PFS program. While it is indeed an important tool for both the police and social workers, especially as it relates to understanding the issues and problems within each agency, it does not appear that this is happening with any regularity. Eighty-one percent of the experimental group, and over 94% of the control group said they had not participated in a ride along with officers within the last year. While the lack of ride alongs in the control group is to be expected, the fact that it is not occurring in the experimental group is surprising.

Another key component of the PFS program is cross training. We asked workers if they had participated in any training with police officers. Similar to the lack of participation in ride alongs, social workers in both groups indicated that they had not engaged in any cross training with officers (66.1% vs. 94%).

We also asked workers at DSS to rate their agency's relationship with the police department, their personal relationship with the police department and whether or not this relationship has improved or declined. Overall, workers in both groups felt that their personal relationship with the police department was a good one. In fact, the percentage of workers who felt this way was higher in the control group (69%) than the experimental group (57%).

Finally, we asked workers if they thought their relationship with the police department had improved or declined. This is a critical component to the PFS program: building and enhancing relationships between agencies. The majority of respondents felt there had been no change in the relationship. Almost 61% of the experimental group and 100% of the control group thought that their relationship had not changed, a statistically significant difference. One possible explanation for this finding is that workers felt that the relationship is a good one and has been for some time. Thus, while it is only speculation, no change is not necessarily a negative finding.

The Police Survey

Of the 200 surveys sent to police officers, 127 were returned for an overall response rate of approximately 64%. The control group's response rate was actually much higher than the experimental group, 84% compared to 43%. As with the DSS workers, we asked police officers about their level of knowledge of the PFS program. Unlike the DSS employees however, officers knew little about the program (54% of the experimental group and 68% of the control group said they did not know about the PFS).

We also asked officers how difficult it was to get in touch with DSS workers. Almost 44% of the control group found it difficult or very difficult to contact DSS compared to only

28% of officers in the experimental group. In an attempt to understand more about the professional relationships the PFS program attempts to develop, we asked both groups of officers if they knew any staff members at DSS. Most officers said they did not know DSS workers. This contrasts sharply with the DSS data in which 64% of CPS workers knew police officers. Only 21% of the police experimental group and 19% of the control group said they knew staff members at DSS.

We also asked how responsive DSS had been to meeting workers' needs when dealing with a child-related incident. Both groups felt that DSS does a fair job in this area. An almost equal percentage for both groups, 33%, rated the department as excellent or good and nearly 21% of the experimental group and 29% of the control group rated DSS as average in their responsiveness. As with the DSS data, the ride along component to the PFS program did not appear to be happening with any regularity. One hundred percent of both the experimental and control groups said they had not participated in a ride along with DSS workers within the last year.

Like the responses from the social workers, when we also asked officers if they had participated in any training with DSS, neither group had participated in any cross training activities (90.7% and 90.6% respectively).

We also asked officers to rate their personal relationship with DSS, their agency's relationship with DSS, and whether or not this relationship has improved or declined. A larger percentage of officers in the control group rated the relationship as excellent or good (20.9% vs. 28.9%) while a larger percentage of officers in the experimental group rated their relationship as average (49% vs. 40%). Still, responses to this question by both groups tend to indicate that officers feel that their working relationships with DSS varies quite a bit. Finally, we asked officers if they thought their relationship with DSS had improved or declined. Similar to the DSS responses, almost 89% of the experimental group and 76% of the control group thought that their relationship had not changed.

The results of the surveys suggest a few trends. First, the proportion of CPS workers responding to questions about the PFS program were more favorable than police officers. As Table 1 shows, whether it was knowledge of the program, the difficulty in getting in touch with the partnership agency, knowing someone in that agency, or assessing how responsive the partnership agency was to their needs, CPS workers exceeded police officers in their knowledge or evaluation on these issues.

Table 1
Comparison of Experimental Groups: DSS and the Police

| Question*** | Agency | |
	DSS	Police
Knowledge Of Program*	26%	11%
Getting in Touch**	66%	48.8%
Knew Someone At Other agency	63%	21%
Responsive to Needs*	81%	33%
No Ride Along	81%	95%
No Cross Training	66%	90%
Indiv. Relationship With Agency*	57%	21%
Agency Relationship*	58%	32%

*Responses are excellent or good
** Responses are not difficult or easy
*** p <.05

In sum, it appears that CPS workers clearly benefit from this relationship. They have better relationships with officers, know many more of them, and are fairly knowledgeable about the PFS. In contrast, few officers know anything about the program, have had difficulty contacting DSS and do not rate their relationship with DSS as highly. Additionally, fewer officers involved in the PFS felt that DSS was responsive to their needs in child-related cases.

DISCUSSION

Since these two groups are the ones that should benefit the most from the partnership, particularly since they comprise most of the PFS, one might wonder why the percentages differ so dramatically. One possible explanation for the differences between the groups is due to the fact that many officers currently involved in the PFS are less experienced. Anecdotal evidence from the interviews suggests that while supervisors are better able to "sell" the idea of a partnership with DSS to younger officers, it may also be true that these officers have not had the opportunity to work with DSS since they are new to policing.

Another explanation for the lower responses from the police department can be attributed to the criteria used to evaluate officers. As one officer stated, establishing and maintaining a collaborative relationship with DSS is beneficial, but becomes less of a priority when officers are not provided an incentive to participate. If supervisors continue to use traditional criteria to evaluate officers (i.e. arrests, issue tickets), less emphasis will be placed on developing relationships and understanding the problems and issues CPS workers face. This is particularly true since shifting priorities are common in both agencies. Perhaps more emphasis is being given to the PFS by DSS since they tend to gain more from this type of partnership.

Another factor that relates to the differences between the police and CPS workers is the lack of commitment to ride alongs and cross training. It appears that it is much easier for CPS workers to ride along with officers since there are more officers than workers. Additionally, CPS workers seem to gain a greater understanding of policing since a large part of the ride along involves answering calls for service. The same cannot be said for officers who ride along with CPS workers. Interviews with officers reveal that a main impediment to this activity is that officers find intakes and administrative duties of CPS workers boring. This means that officers are not excited about ride alongs with CPS workers. In short, because they are newer officers and because there are fewer opportunities to develop and enhance their individual and organizational relationships with DSS, officers tend not to know as much about the program and to rate the relationships with DSS as average or poor.

What does the future hold for the PFS? Since providing information about the program is a constant activity, and given that relationships need to be fostered, DSS has decided that one of the best ways to continually promote the program and its benefits to others is through the use of a training video. This video outlines the partnership, the benefits to each agency, and why it is such an important part of providing effective child-related services in the community.

While the future remains optimistic for the program and the people in it, the stakeholders also recognize the realities of the bureaucratic nature of each agency. The constant shifting of priorities and responsibilities is a fact of life for both CPS workers and police officers. One of the challenges will be to remain committed to one another during a time when employees from both agencies are being pulled in many different directions.

However, having said that, there is a strong commitment by the police department and DSS to bring officers and workers together informally to allow the development and fostering of relationships. The efforts in Charlotte represent a significant effort to collaborate between agencies. Were it not for the vision of the Charlotte-Mecklenburg police chief and the director of DSS for Mecklenburg County, the situation in Charlotte might mirror much of what was discussed in the literature concerning the animosity between officers and workers.

REFERENCES:

Bard, M. and Berkowitz, B. 1969. "Community Psychology Consultation Program in Police Family Crisis Intervention: Preliminary Impression." *International Journal of Social Psychology,* 15:209-15.

Bar-On, A. 1995. "They Have Their Job, We Have Ours: Reassessing the Feasibility of Police-Social Work Cooperation." *Policing and Society,* 5:37-51

Bell, D. J. 1982. "Policewomen: Myths and Realities." *Journal of Police Science and Administration,* 10:12-120.

Bennett, A. 1980. "Team Aids Police Officers, Works with Rape Victims." *Practice Digest,* 32(2):5-7.

Brown, J.A. and Daniels, R. 1990. "Child Endangerment: Social and Police Functions," in Brown, J.A., P.C. Unsinger, and H.W. More (eds.) *Law Enforcement and Social Welfare: The Emergency Response,* pp. 50-73. Springfield, IL: Charles C. Thomas.

Child Welfare League of America. 1998. *Protecting America's Children: It's Everybody's Business*. Washington, D.C.: Child Welfare League.

Colbach, E. M. and Fosterling, C. D. 1976. *Police Social Work*. Springfield, IL: Charles Thomas.

Conte, J.R., Berliner, L. and Nolan, D.1980. "Police and Social Worker Cooperation: A Key in Child Sexual Assault Cases." *FBI Law Enforcement Bulletin,* 49(3):7-10.

Fein, E. and Knaut, S. A. 1986. "Crisis Intervention and Support: Working with the Police." *Social Casework*, 67(5):276-282.

Fielding, N. G. 1991. *The Police and Social Conflict: Rhetoric and Reality*. London: Atholone.

Findlay, C. 1991. "Joint Police and Social Work Investigations in Child Abuse: A Practice Example from Central Scotland." *Children and Society,* 5(3):225-231.

Finney, R. K. 1972. "A Police View of Social Workers." *Police,* 16:59-63.

Hogarth, J. 1971. *Sentencing as a Human Process*. Toronto, CA: University of Toronto Press.

Holmes, S. A. 1982. "A Detroit Model of Police-Social Work Cooperation." *Social Casework*, 63(4):220-226.

Kilpatrick, A. 1979. "Police-Social Worker Teams Cool Down Family Crises." *Practice Digest,* 2(1):13-15.

Kowalewski, V. A. 1975. "Police and Social Service Agencies: Breaking the Barriers." *Police Chief*, 42:259-262.

Michaels, R. A. and Treger, H. 1973. "Social Work in Police Departments." *Social Work,* 18(5):67-75.

Morgan, R. 1989 . "Policing by Consent: Legitimating the Doctrine," in Morgan, R. and Smith, D.J. (eds.) *Coming to Terms with Policing*. London: Routledge.

Parkinson, G. C. 1980. "Cooperation Between Police and Social Workers: Hidden Issues." *Social Work,* 4:12-18.

Penner, G. L. 1959. "An Experiment in Police and Social Agency Cooperation." *The Annals of American Academy of Political and Social Science*, 322:79-88.

Roberts, A. R. 1978. "Training Police Social Workers: A Neglected Area of Social Work." *Education. Journal of Education for Social Work*, 14(2):98-103.

Schonborn, K. 1976. "Police and Social Workers as Members of New Crisis Management Teams." *Journal of Sociology and Social Welfare*, 3(6):679-688.

Sireman, J. , Miller, B. and Brown, H. F. 1981. "Child Welfare Workers, Police, and Child Placement." *Child Welfare,* 60(6):413-422

Stephens, M. 1988. "Problems of Police-Social Work Interaction: Some American Lessons." *The Howard Journal*, 22(2):81-91.

Treger, H. 1981. "Guideposts for Community Work in Police Social Work Diversion. " *Federal Probation,* 44(3):3-8.

-----------. 1977. "Counteracting Aggressive Behavior in the Community--The Police/Social Work Model," in P. J. Eck and B. Bradshaw (eds.) *Juvenile Justice Systems: New Directions in Policy and Programs.* Austin, TX: University of Texas Press.

Trojanowicz, R. C. 1971. "The Policeman's Occupational Personality." *Journal of Criminal Law, Criminology and Police Science,* 62:555.

U.S. Department of Health and Human Services. 1997. *National Center on Child Abuse and Neglect,National Child Abuse and Neglect Data System.* Washington, D.C.: U.S. Government Printing Office.

Vernon, S. 1990 . *Social Work and the Law.* London: Butterworth

Waddington , P. A. 1993. *Calling the Police: Police Interpretation of and Response to Calls for Assistance from the Public.* Aldershot: Avebury.

Do Magnet Schools Programs Meet the Goals of Desegregation?

By William Sakamoto White
Department of Sociology
University of New Orleans

In 1954, the United States Supreme Court handed down the most significant civil rights case in its history-- Brown v. Board of Education. Over forty years later, this society cannot honestly state that it has achieved the goals nor met the intent of that decision. In the arena of education, children still go to segregated schools. More importantly, the quality of the schools they go to is unequal. We have once again returned to a situation where schools are separate and unequal.

A number of strategies and programs were devised to provide "equal access" to education. Busing clearly was a political failure. Another program, though, has become the "cornerstone" for claiming victory for "integration." The magnet school program appears to be the measure which schools and courts use to evaluate the effectiveness of "successfully" integrating schools. But does the institutionalization of magnet school programs provide "equal access" to "quality education" across the community? Or does it provide "quality education" at specific sites? How can the institutionalization of magnet schools, just given the fact that there are so few of these schools in any given district, logically provide "equal access" to quality education? If magnet schools do not provide equal access to quality education, then have we met the intent of Brown? And if we have not met the intent of Brown with magnet schools, then shouldn't we be looking for other alternatives to providing equal access to quality education across our communities, as Brown intended?

Does segregation of children in public schools deprive minority children equal educational opportunities? In 1954, the Supreme Court held that it does. But the reality of education today is that forty years after Brown we have returned to a system of segregation in the schools. The segregation of schools is perpetuated by the continuing racial segregation of housing in America (Massey and Denton, 1993; Squires, 1994; and Fainstein, 1995). Schools today are not only "separate" but they are also "unequal." Given the institutionalized racism that exists as a force to retain neighborhood and school segregation, perhaps we need to revisit Brown and seek out the essence of that decision. Perhaps a new measure is needed when evaluating or establishing school programs. Based on Brown, are we providing "equal access" to "quality education?" If the white community is not willing to live with blacks in this society (Farley, 1993), and if they refuse to have their children go to school with minority children, then perhaps we should focus on providing minority children with quality education.

I will examine the emergence of the magnet school program as it relates to school desegregation and evaluate the program on two critical questions. First, do magnet schools provide equal access to educational opportunities to all of our children? Second, given the nature of schools today, does the net result of having a magnet school program in place provide all of our children an opportunity for a quality education? To place the issue into the proper context, let's first revisit the Brown v. Board of Education decision.

The Intent of Brown v. Board of Education

In Topeka, Kansas, Reverend Oliver Leon Brown, who was black, took his seven year old daughter to register at the local school (Brown-Smith, 1988). The child was turned away because the

Kansas educational system was institutionally segregated. With the help of the NAACP, Reverend Brown and several other families filed federal suit against the city. The case was settled three years later under the authority of Chief Justice Warren who went against the 1898 Plessy v. Ferguson ruling. The Supreme Court ruled that "in the field of public education the doctrine of 'separate but equal' has no place. Separate educational facilities are inherently unequal" (Brown v. Board of Education, 1954). Desegregation was mandated at a national level to uphold the constitutional moral of equality and reinforced by the same plaintiffs a year later (Brown v. Board of Education II, 1955).

The emphasis of the Supreme Court decision was equality in the *quality* of education. Segregated education was noted to (1) "generate a feeling of inferiority as to their status in the community," (2) "(have) a detrimental effect upon the colored children," and (3) "(retard) the educational and mental development of Negro children and to deprive them of some of the benefits they would receive in a racially integrated school system" (Brown vs. Board of Education, 1954). Brown II (1955) set up the rules for reviewing school desegregation suits. The Court ruled that the schools themselves would have to come up with a solution to the problem. It was the role of the courts to decide whether the school's actions were implemented in "good faith."

The twenty years following the Court decision saw several policy changes that emphasized equal access to quality education for Blacks and other minority groups. The Civil Rights Act of 1964 included Title IV which refocused attention to school segregation. "Title IV expressly authorized the U.S. Attorney General to initiate and intervene in suits to enforce school desegregation through the courts" (Darden, et al, 1992, p.477). The next year, Congress passed the Elementary and Secondary Education Act which provided money to school programs for low income families. In 1968, this Act was expanded to include bilingual education and drop out prevention programs. In order to facilitate desegregation, the Supreme Court institutionalized busing in 1971 with their decision on Swann vs. Charlotte-Mecklenberg Board of Education.
This decision, and the busing that followed, help influence the further "white flight" of middle and upper class families from urban centers.

The reaction to the Court's decision, at times antagonistic and violent, illustrate the deep-rooted individual and institutional racism that existed, and still exists, in American society. The wholesale closure of public schools for five years in Prince Edward County, Virginia illustrates one extreme reaction (Franklin, 1967). The violence experienced in Boston over school busing illustrates another. Since the Court's decision in 1954, white families have found ways to keep public schools from desegregating. Perhaps the most significant reaction was the exodus of white families out of neighborhoods with growing numbers of black families. Many chose to remove their children from desegregated schools, believing that the quality of education had declined with busing. Magnet schools and schools of choice were a response to this white flight. Designed first with the intent of integrating schools, magnet schools and schools of choice have become mechanisms to encourage white families to live in financially strapped cities.

Magnet Schools as an Intervention

Magnet schools are often cited by supporters as one of the most effective desegregation tools available (West, 1994). They are perceived as effective desegregation tools because they can offer special curriculum capable of attracting students of different racial backgrounds. As Henig (1989) points out:

Magnet schools traditionally have involved the assignment of extra resources, attractive programs, or special teaching approaches to schools in high minority neighborhoods in order to stimulate voluntary integration and moderate the conflict and white flight that might otherwise be generated under mandatory busing plans. (p.244).

Magnet schools generally consist of four characteristics. First, they provide a special curricular theme or method of instruction as the foundation for their "magnet." Second, they are a program initiated by school districts as a voluntary desegregation mechanism. Third, they are schools of "choice" for students and parents. Finally, they provide access to students beyond a regular attendance zone. As originally conceived, magnet schools were designed to accomplish two goals: 1) to enhance students' academic performance through their distinctive curriculum, and 2) to enhance the school's racial and social diversity (West, 1994). West further notes that magnet schools typically come into existence as a way of meeting the terms of court ordered desegregation (West, 1994).

There are also two types of magnet school programs: full-site and partial-site. The full-site magnet program constitutes an entire school. The courses offered by the school act as the "magnet." In full-site magnets, all students transfer into the school and are mixed together in the magnet program. Full site programs require that a school be dedicated to the magnet program and attracts a racial balance through admissions, lottery, or other selection methods.

Partial site programs offer a special magnet program within a "non-magnet" general school, although students still transfer into the school to participate in the magnet curriculum. Partial site magnets are often placed in schools that were predominantly minority prior to desegregation efforts, working to achieve a racial balance within the total school by attracting enough white transfer students. In both types of magnet programs, students and parents in effect make a "choice" to attend these schools.

The Social Goals of Magnet School Programs

Though originally intended to achieve more racial balance in public schools, magnet schools have also become the "poster-child" example for school choice advocates. They state that while magnet schools effectively achieve racial balance, they also increase educational quality. As the focus on magnet schools changed, so did the implied mission of magnet schools. Not only were they an intervention that led to more effective desegregation than busing, they also "satisfied" consumer demands. They could also be used to retain the middle-class in urban areas and central cities (Clune, 1990).

The early "successes" of magnet schools, and particularly the magnet school program in Prince George's County, Maryland (a suburb of Washington, D. C.), received a great deal of media attention. In 1988, President Reagan used a speech at Suitland High School, a magnet school in the Prince George County system, as the launching ground for a redefinition of magnet schools as schools of choice (Henig, 1995; Eaton and Crutcher, 1996). Magnet schools were no longer linked categorically to achieving the goals of desegregation. Rather, they were now examples of achieving educational excellence through a system of parental and student "choice" governed by "market forces." Magnet schools were to be the "miracle cure" for all educational problems, and choice would guarantee that the best students and the best parents had access to these hallways of success.

Urban governments also saw magnet schools as an attraction for potential homebuyers and joined in the efforts to solidify the permanence of magnet schools in central cities (Varady and Raffel, 1995).

Research on the Effectiveness of Magnet Schools

Though still touted as the "miracle cure" for educational problems, it is ironic that an extensive evaluation of the effectiveness of magnet schools has not been conducted to date. Rossell's 1990 study found that districts with magnet schools achieved two objectives: they were more likely to reduce white flight from schools, and they did improve the interracial contact of minority students over time than mandatory plans. Rossell concluded that, compared to busing and other mandatory desegregation plans, magnet schools were perhaps a more effective desegregation strategy. Eaton and Crutcher (1996), in their analysis of the Prince George's County magnet schools, point out that the claims of improved achievement from magnet schools were probably based on outdated and invalid measures. The appearance of "success" may have been the result of politics and public relations efforts rather than any real educational improvements.

There is much disagreement on the value of magnet school programs. The biggest skeptics exist within public schools themselves, namely professional educators and local school administrators. According to Finn (1990), their opposition is based on the fact that "choice is disruptive, costly, and logistically cumbersome; that choice ill serves poor, disadvantaged, and minority students."

Magnet schools take the "better students" away from their neighborhood schools, leaving the problem of educationally at-risk students behind in these schools (Finn, 1990; Rossell, 1990). Indeed, magnet schools are not generally instituted as a major solution for the problems of at-risk students (Blank, 1990). Providing spaces for middle-class students at magnet schools is viewed by many as denying others, especially poor minority students, equal access. As Moore and Davenport (1990) point out, magnet schools become new forms of educational segregation.

Running Away From the Social Intent of Brown

The major thrust of Brown v. Board of Education was to provide minority children with equal access to quality education. Indeed, the issue of equal access is the foundation for desegregation arguments. Forty years after Brown, this intent has been lost in the variety of policy initiatives intended to remedy segregated education.

As previously note, magnet schools have increasingly become a center point in the "school-choice" agenda. In this process, their utility as a means towards desegregating school systems have been diminished. As critics of magnet schools point out, they may well be serving the needs of powerful middle-class interests rather than meeting the needs of lower-class minority at-risk students (Metz, 1990). A number of key points need to be addressed in any reassessment of the magnet school/school choice/desegregation debate.

First, it must be recognized that magnets do siphon off the better students from a school district, leaving the problem of educationally at-risk students in the non-magnet neighborhood school. Second, magnets may be aimed at already well-served middle-class families. Third, removing students from a given school district removes resources from students most in need of this interaction (Metz, 1990). Fourth, magnets are not generally instituted as a major solution for the problems of at-risk students, the students most in need of any school reform initiatives (Blank,

1990). Fifth, even in partial-site situations, segregation continues within the walls of the school, especially in the classrooms (West, 1994).

One tragic outcome many times forgotten in the magnet school debate is the fact that providing seats for middle-class children in magnet schools denies at-risk students of equal access to those seats. Moore and Davenport (1990) found that the magnet school selection process is inequitable. In their study of magnet schools in New York City, they found that blacks, the poor and low attendees are more likely to wind up in nonselective neighborhood high schools. Junior High School counselors, for example, work more with students "likely" to succeed in magnet programs. Middle income parents are also a political force, insisting on programs and policies that benefit their children over at-risk youth. Though "lottery selection procedures" are a mechanism to check against any unfair influence in the selection processes by middle-class parents, Metz (1990) points out that lotteries "undercut the sense of parental control over children's fate that is a very significant benefit of choice" (Metz, 1990: 132). According to Metz's reasoning, magnet schools are a better alternative than no magnet schools at all because they do benefit "some" at-risk youth. Magnet schools begin to move towards a "tug of war" atmosphere where school boards must attempt to balance the needs of powerful middle-class parents with the real needs of at-risk children.

To be sure, it is not the sole responsibility of the schools themselves to remedy the situation of inequality in education. Perhaps this is where Brown made a significant error in demanding that only the schools were responsible for desegregating themselves. The institutionalized racism that exists in the housing market, perhaps the real foundation for educational inequality, must be addressed first.

What Are We To Do?

Desegregation efforts, both mandatory and choice oriented, have failed to provide an integrated, let alone an "equal," education opportunity for our nation's children. We can theorize all we want about the potential for integrating our schools and neighborhoods, and we can encourage policies that aid in the reintegration efforts. Indeed, studies continue to show that integration provides significant economic and cultural benefits when implemented (Massey and Denton, 1993). Logic, reason, and a national self-interest should lead us as a society towards working to integrate our schools. Personal self-interest, prejudice, and institutional racism, though, all play a major role in continuing to perpetuate a system of unequal and separate educational systems for whites and minority students. The Brown decision was significant because it opened the door towards creating an integrated society, but we have seen the process of integration failing in most every attempt. Though integration is a noble goal, and one which should be pursued from a variety of policy initiatives (Darden, et al, 1992), what are we to do *in the short run* with communities and schools that remain segregated? If we do nothing beyond magnet schools, aren't we relegating whole communities and children to a life of hopelessness?

First, we must recognize that there is a tremendous problem in our public educational system, one largely created by our social neglect in squarely addressing the needs of at-risk children and their families. There is a growing number of children living in poverty, for example, and this fact significantly contributes to their life chances. As Raffel, et. al (1992) state rather clearly:

> One could argue that America's urban educational casualties are high, the war is being lost, the future looks bleaker, we are not properly organized to achieve victory, and we are losing

this war in large part because we never made a commitment of resources (as opposed to rhetoric) to win (p.264).

Indeed, it can be said that magnet schools added to this rhetoric (Eaton and Crutcher, 1996). Promoted as schools of choice, magnet schools were not effectively measured for their academic performance nor for their lack of integrating school systems. Even without any strong evidence, magnet schools continue to be seen by many as a major strategy in efforts to increase educational quality. These hopes may be, at best, far-fetched.

We cannot neglect the findings from numerous studies that student background and attitudes influence school performance (Coleman, et al, 1966; Ogbu, 1986; Lareau, 1989; Farkas, 1996). Indeed, any sort of policy in educational reform must begin from these findings. Given these facts, and the fact that very little has been done to manage the gap between student background and school success, some researchers are skeptical of the future, speculating that the problems in education will only get worse (Raffel, et al, 1992). Poor and minority students (especially poor minority students) are affected by sets of liabilities that will influence their potential performance before they ever set foot in the schools (Jencks, et al, 1972; Bowles and Gintis, 1976; Ogbu, 1986; Farkas, 1996). Taken from an integrationist perspective, the interaction between high achieving and low achieving students creates the potential for the development of the positive attitudes necessary for school success. But, as W.E.B. DuBois clearly observed in 1935,

> The Negro needs neither segregated schools nor mixed schools. What he needs is *education*. What he must remember is that there is no magic, either in mixed schools or in segregated schools. A mixed school with poor and unsympathetic teachers, with hostile public opinion, and no teaching of truth concerning black folk, is bad. A segregated school with ignorant placeholders, inadequate equipment, poor salaries, and wretched housing, is equally bad. Other things being equal, the mixed school is the broader, more natural basis for the education of all youth. It gives wider contacts, it inspires greater self-confidence; and suppresses the inferiority complex. But other things seldom are equal, and in that case, *sympathy, knowledge, and truth*, outweigh all that the mixed school can offer (emphasis added).

If high self-esteem of minority students will help them succeed in school, and they are not getting it from either the magnet school or segregated school experience, then it is incumbent on society to help predominantly black schools raise it. A return to a segregated, minority-centered curriculum may indeed be a viable alternative for school success. The curriculum must integrate neighborhood, parents, and schools together to help change the attitudes of the students so that they could develop a positive self-image and believe that they can control their environment. Any discussion about returning to "segregated" education, though, must be tempered with the provision that it is a short run strategy to develop quality education for students who are currently being left behind in society. As Lerone Bennet pointed out in 1970, a return to segregated education must not mean a return to inferiority and subordination.

> "The fundamental issue is not separation or integration but liberation. The either/or question of integration or separation does not speak to that proposition; for if our goal is liberation it may be necessary to do both."

We, as a society, have not lived up to the promise of an equal opportunity to a quality education as demanded in the Brown decision. Magnet schools do achieve some racial integration, and this is positive. But it is not the "cure-all" for integrating our schools. Indeed, the focus on magnet schools as a mechanism for integrating schools probably ended in the late 1980s. As we continue to move further away from the intent of Brown, more children are being left behind. As a society, can we continue to wait for whites to integrate schools or neighborhoods? Can minority parents afford to wait for programs to reach them? Or do we need to engage in demanding quality education across the board to all students in a given community? Look into the eyes of an at-risk student in kindergarten, and see his or her eagerness to learn, to achieve, to be successful in school. The answer to our dilemma is there, if we only move to give him or her the opportunity to achieve the skills necessary to succeed.

REFERENCES:

Bennett, David A. 1990. "Choice And Desegregation." In *Choice And Control In American Education, Volume 2*. William H. Clune and John F. Witte, eds. London: Falmer Press. 125-152.

Bennett, Lerone. 1970. "Liberation." *Ebony* 25 (August): 36-43.

Blank, Rolf K. 1990. "Educational Effects Of Magnet Schools." In *Choice And Control In American Education, Volume 2*. William H. Clune and John F. Witte, eds. London: Falmer Press. 77-109.

Bowles, Samuel, and Herbert Gintis. 1976. *Schooling in Capitalist America*. New York: Basic Books.

Cibulka, James. 1990. "Choice And Restructuring Of American Education." In *Choice In Education: Potential And Problems*. William L. Boyd and Herbert J. Walberg, eds. Berkeley: McCutchan.

Clune, William H. 1990. "Educational Governance And Student Achievement." In *Choice And Control In American Education, Volume 2*. William H. Clune and John F. Witte, eds. London: Falmer Press. 391-423.

Coleman, James S., Ernest Q. Campbell, Carol J. Hobson, James McPartland, Alexander Mood, Frederick D. Weinfield, and Robert York. 1966. *Equality of Educational Opportunity.* Washington, D. C.: U.S. Government Printing Office.

Darden, Joe T., Harriet Orcutt Duleep, and George C. Galster. 1992. "Civil Rights in Metropolitan America." Journal of Urban Affairs 14 (3/4): 469-496.

DuBois, W. E. B. 1935. "Does the Negro Need Separate Schools?" *Journal of Negro Education* 4:328-335.

Eaton, Susan E., and Elizabeth Crutcher. 1996. "Magnets, Media, and Mirages: Prince George's County's 'Miracle' Cure." In *Dismantling Desegregation: The Quiet Reversal of Brown v. Board of Education.* Gary Orfield and Susan E. Eaton, eds. New York: The New Press. 265-289.

Fainstein, Norman. 1995. "Black Ghettoization and Social Mobility." In *The Bubbling Cauldron: Race, Ethnicity and the Urban Crisis.* Michael Peter Smith and Joe R. Feagin, eds. Minneapolis, MN: University of Minnesota Press. 123-141.

Farkas, George. 1996. *Human Capital or Cultural Capital? Ethnicity and Poverty Groups in an Urban School District.* New York: Aldine de Gruyter.

Farley, Reynolds. 1993. "Neighborhood Preferences and Aspirations among Blacks and Whites." In *Housing Markets and Residential Mobility.* G. Thomas Kingsley and Margery Austin Turner, eds. Washington, D.C.: Urban Institute Press.

Finn, 1990. "Why We Need Choice." In *Choice in Education: Potential and Problems.* William L. Boyd and Herbert J. Walberg, eds. Berkeley: McCutchan.

Franklin, John Hope. 1967. *From Slavery to Freedom.* Third Edition. New York: Knopf.

Henig, Jeffrey R. 1989. "Choice, Race and Public Schools: The Adoption and Implementation of a Magnet Program." *Journal of Urban Affairs* 11(3): 243-259.

_____. 1995. "Race and Choice in Montgomery County, Maryland, Magnet Schools." *Teachers College Record* 96(4): 729-734.

Jencks, Christopher, Marshal Smith, Henry Acland, Mary Jo Bane, David Cohen, Herbert Gintis, Barbara Heyns, and Stephen Michelson. 1972. *Inequality: A reassessment of the effect of family and schooling in America.* New York: Basic Books.

Lareau, Annette. 1989. *Home Advantage: Social Class and Parental Intervention in Elementary Education.* London: Falmer Press..

Massey, Douglas S., and Nancy A. Denton. 1993. *American Apartheid: Segregation and the Making of the Underclass.* Cambridge, Mass: Harvard University Press.

Moore, Donald R. and Suzanne Davenport. 1990. "School Choice: The New Improved Sorting Machine." In *Choice in Education: Potential and Problems.* William L. Boyd and Herbert J. Walberg, eds. Berkeley: McCutchan.

Metz, Mary H. 1990. "Potentialities And Problems Of Choice In Desegregation Plans." In *Choice And Control In American Education, Volume 2.* William H. Clune and John F. Witte, eds. London: Falmer Press. 111-117.

Ogbu, John. 1986. "Consequences of the American Caste System." In *The School Achievement of Minority Children.* Ulric Neisser, ed. Hillsdale, NJ: Lawrence Erlbaum. 19-56.

Raffel, Jeffrey A., William Lowe Boyd, Vernon M. Briggs, Jr., Eugene E. Eubanks, and Roberto Fernandez. 1992. "Policy Dilemmas in Urban Education: Addressing the Needs of Poor, At-risk Children." *Journal of Urban Affairs* 14(3/4): 263-289.

Rossell, Christine H. 1990. *The Carrot or the Stick for School Desegregation Policy: Magnet Schools or Forced Busing*. Philadelphia: Temple University Press.

Smith, Linda Brown. 1988. "Forward." In *Eliminating Racism: Profiles in Controversy*. Phyllis A. Katz and Dalmas A. Taylor, eds. New York: Plenum Press. xi-xiii.

Squires, Gregory D. 1994. *Capital and Communities in Black and White: The Intersections of Race, Class and Uneven Development*. Albany, NY: State University of New York Press.

Varady, David P., and Jeffrey A. Raffel. 1995. *Selling Cities: Attracting Homebuyers Through Schools and Housing Programs*. Albany, NY: State University of New York Press.

West, Kimberly C. 1994. "A Desegregation Tool that Backfired: Magnet Schools and Classroom Segregation." *Yale Law Journal* 103: 2567-2592.

Truancy and The Accountability Court in Charleston, South Carolina

Robert Hartmann McNamara
Department of Political Science and Criminal Justice
The Citadel

When most people think of skipping classes or school for the day, they typically do not think of it as a national problem with a host of social, economic, and political implications. However, every day hundreds of thousands of students are absent from school; many without an excuse. Although national data on truancy rates are unavailable, partly due to the fact that no uniform definition exists, many cities wrestle with the problem of truancy (Baker, Sigmon and Nugent 2001). In New York City alone, it has been estimated that 150,000 of its one million public school students are absent on a typical day (Garry 1996). In fact, so significant is the problem of truancy that a national review of discipline issues in public schools found that principals identified student absenteeism, class cutting, and tardiness as the top discipline problems on their campuses (Heaviside et al., 1998).

The implications for truancy extend far beyond simply the educational deficiencies for those students who miss school. Truancy has been identified as one of the most important gateway activities for additional problem behaviors. In fact, the U.S. Department of Education has gone on record, stating that truancy is the most powerful predictor of juvenile delinquent behavior. Many studies have connected truancy to dropping out of school, teen pregnancy, substance abuse, gang involvement, and serious forms of delinquency (Puzzanchera, et al., 2003; Rosen and Dynlacht 1994; Huzinga, Loeber and Thornberry 1995; Rohrman 1993). There is also a link between truancy and adult problem behaviors, such as violence, marital problems, welfare dependency, chronic unemployment, adult crime, and incarceration (Dryfoos 1990; Snyder and Sickmund 1995; Catalano et al., 1998). With regard to social class, race and sex, commonly cited demographic variables, a few trends are noteworthy. For instance, the relationship between race and truancy is not well established. Some data suggests that whites are underrepresented in petitioned cases (Bell, Rosen, and Dynlacht 1994; Puzzanchera et al., 2003). Other studies have found that African Americans and Latinos consistently have the highest drop out rates of all categories of students (Kaufman, Alt, and Chapman 2001). Additionally, while the relationship between income and truancy is not well known, it is generally believed that students from lower income families have higher rates of truancy (Bell et al 1994). Finally, there is some evidence that boys and girls are about evenly divided in the truancy statistics, with the peak age for truancy cases being fifteen years old (Puzzanchera et al., 2003). However, while girls tend to demonstrate a slightly higher rate of absenteeism in high school than boys, the latter are more likely to become chronically truant, especially in the later grades (Allen-Meares, Washington and Welsh 2000).

With regard to juvenile crime, in several jurisdictions, law enforcement officials have linked high rates of truancy to daytime burglary and vandalism. In Tacoma, WA, the police department reported that 1/3 of burglaries and 1/5 of aggravated assaults occurring between 8pm and 1pm on weekdays were committed by juveniles. In Contra

Costa County, CA police reported that 60% of juvenile crime occurred between 8am and 3pm on weekdays. Recent studies also indicate that truancy may be a precursor to serious violent offenses, particularly by males (Baker, Sigmon and Nugent 2001).

According to the Office of Juvenile Justice and Delinquency Prevention (OJJDP), adults that were truant at an early age were much more likely (than those who were not truant) to have poorer physical and mental health statuses, lower paying jobs, a higher likelihood of living in poverty, more reliance on welfare support, and to have children who exhibit problem behaviors. While these figures are central to understanding the impact of truancy, they should not overshadow the impact of the loss of Federal and State education funding (Baker, Sigmon and Nugent 2001).

A related phenomenon worth mentioning consists of students who simply refuse to attend school despite any efforts made by parents, schools, or the courts. *School refusal* is defined as a psychological condition in which the child is reluctant (and often outright refuses) to go to school. Children suffering from school refusal tend to seek the comfort of home and to remain in close proximity to parental figures during school hours. They also tend to display visible and emotional outbursts at the prospect of attending school, yet do not seem to have any other problems of controlling their behavior or aggressiveness for other matters. In addition to violent outbursts, some students also identify physical ailments at the thought of going to school, such as headaches, diarrhea, and stomach aches. While this disorder is more of an emotional reaction to leaving home than it is related to school per se, nevertheless, it has an impact on truancy (Berg 1997).

Finally, another dimension of truancy consists of students who are referred to as *push outs*. Many states are phasing in a series of challenging end of course tests that are required for graduation. This is part of a larger effort to improve public education. However, as more and more schools are being held accountable for educating today's youth, one strategy to ensure higher overall scores has been to convince poorly performing students that they should leave school. Critics of high stakes testing policies have charged that do-or-die exams prompt struggling students to drop out of school, either because they are discouraged by their failure to pass exams or because schools do not want their ratings decreased by lower scoring students (Rubin 2004). In other words, high stakes accountability testing has led some school districts to push students out of school illegally because of low test scores, low grades, chronic truancy, or other issues.

An example of pushing students out of school occurred in New York City. In January 2004, the New York City school system settled a federal lawsuit in which former students alleged that they had been pushed out of one of the city's high schools because of low grades, low test scores, and truancy. Under New York state law, students are entitled to attend public school until age 21. They can be legally expelled or suspended only for disruptive or violent behavior, not due to truancy, age, or poor academic performance (Rubin 2004). Part of the problem with the do-or-die testing is that schools often fail to notify students of their right to return to classes and to offer them extra academic help. In the case of New York City, the school district failed to inform students of their to return to school, told students the district could no longer afford to keep them in the school, or simply failed to provide any academic assistance to improve their scores.

Causes of Truancy

According to the National School Safety Center, in 2003 about 5% of students in grades 9-12 skipped school because they felt unsafe at school or on their way to or from school. Others miss school because of family health issues and financial demands, substance abuse, or mental health problems. Research shows that some of the most important factors contributing to truancy stem from three areas: school configuration, personal and developmental issues, the student's family situation, and community characteristics (Baker, Sigmon, and Nugent 2001).

School Configuration

According to the National Center for Education Statistics, large school systems in low income, inner city urban school districts have higher rates of absenteeism and truancy compared to suburban and rural school systems. Research consistently reports high absenteeism rates for urban schools, with approximately eight percent of these students labeled chronically truant (Epstein and Sheldon 2002).

Truancy is also more likely to occur in those schools that have not made it a priority in terms of policy, in those settings where there is little or no constructive interaction between teachers and parents, in those schools with a high percentage of uncertified teachers, and homework assignments that are lacking in academic rigor (Dougherty 1999; Epstein and Sheldon 2002). Truancy is also related to low teacher expectations, high teacher absenteeism, and inconsistency in school discipline (Baker et al., 2001; Strickland 1998).

Personal and Developmental Issues

Typically, the problems of absenteeism and truancy stem from the experience the child has while in the classroom. There is a wealth of research that suggests poor performance causes students to lose interest in school, which results them falling behind and begin to avoid class, then stop going to school all. The response by the school to the lack of attendance is usually punitive, which further alienates the student from the institution (Allen-Meares, Washington and Welsh 2000). The onset of this problem is particularly apparent in middle school.

Family Issues

There is evidence to indicate that the relationship of parental involvement and truancy is inversely related. When parents participate in their child's education, whether it be monitoring homework, helping to improve their reading ability, or attending PTA meetings, the probability of truancy decreases (Epstein and Sheldon 2002). Parental involvement is also related to social class. Research shows that parents with high Socio-Economic Status (SES) tend to be more involved with teachers and schools as well as being more involved with their child's educational and learning development. Part of the reason for this is that affluent parents tend to have more resources, time to spend with their children, and they place a high value on education. Youths from single parent homes tend to have higher rates of absenteeism and truancy than youths from two-parent households, which tend to be lower income families (Oman et al. 2002; Klein 1994). One study found that youths who lived in one parent households had a greater likelihood of skipping school, fighting, using alcohol or tobacco and participating in sexual intercourse (Rohrman 1993). Other studies show that where parenting styles are weak or nonexistent, meaning children are given too much autonomy in decision making and less corrective direction, truancy increases (Oman et al. 2002; Rohrman 1993).

Neighborhood and Community Factors

As was mentioned, social class is an important variable in understanding truancy. Children living in low income and/or inner city neighborhoods are more likely than suburban youth to experience acts of violence, maltreatment, neglect and abuse, and receive below average educations. This, in turn, affects student motivation about education in general and attending school in particular.

Related to social class, of course, are the physical conditions of the neighborhoods in which children live. The research demonstrates a substantial link between neighborhood context and truancy (Epstein and Sheldon 2002; Teevan and Dryburgh 2000). Exposure to mental and physical health stressors (e.g. abuse, neglect, domestic violence, family strife) and other signs of disorder (e.g. abandoned buildings and cars, condemned housing, illegal drug markets) are all related to truancy (Wandersman and Nation 1999)

The Costs of Truancy

Regardless of race or gender category, high school dropouts claim more in government funded social services expenditures than high school graduates. For men in particular, dropouts incur more in criminal justice costs. The average dropout costs society more than $800,000 over the course of his or her lifetime. Discounted for the current value of money, that amount is approximately $200,000. A study of the costs and benefits of three truancy reduction programs and three truancy courts operating in Colorado discovered that since one high school dropout costs $200,000 in current dollars, the truancy programs operating in Adams County and the City of Denver, each of which cost about $50,000 a year, can each operate for four years for the same cost. These programs serve about 85 students a year (National Center for School Engagement 2005).Therefore, even if those programs only encourage one out of 300 program participants to graduate from high school, they will yield a positive return on their investment.

The cost/benefits of truancy programs in general are readily self-evident: while cost assessment studies are limited, given their low cost of operation, and the high cost of dropping out, it is highly likely that all the truancy reduction programs and the courts pay for themselves many times over.

Strategies that Work to Reduce Truancy

While every state has its own set of laws regarding truancy, and national trends do not always reflect local policy, it is important to note that there is no single cause for truancy. This means there is no single model for each state to follow. However, there is substantial evidence to suggest that the most effective programs are those that can demonstrate an alliance between parents and teachers, systematic monitoring and recording of absenteeism and truancy, a consistent imposition of penalties for repeat offenders, support for intervention programs, and patience with regard to implementing new programs (Teasley 2004).

The evidence also shows that those highly punitive programs that place the problem of truancy on the individual have not curbed truancy rates. Zero tolerance polices have done more to alienate students from school than to improve teaching and learning (Civil Rights Project 2000). The best programs seem to be those that have a "carrot and stick" approach, whereby parents are involved, students are held accountable by both the school district and the courts, who are working collaboratively rather than trying to shift their burden of responsibility, a court system that can impose sanctions beyond school suspension on both the parent and the child, and some sort of positive reinforcement to the child. While the hard line approach to truancy would be that attending school is something students should simply do and not be rewarded for it, the realities of the lives of many students is that they need something to say "yes" to rather than being told about the potential negative consequences of their actions. This is not coddling kids, this is realizing that simply expecting this generation of children to do what they are supposed to do "or else" is an ineffective way of addressing truancy. Granted, there are some children for whom help is limited in effectiveness, however, the more proactive approach is designed to alleviate the problem before it becomes a chronic one. Positive reinforcement, even for small things like completing a life skills program, which is part of some anti-truancy prevention programs, can have a significant impact on a young person who is deciding which behavioral path to take: conformity, education and success or delinquency, crime, and substance abuse.

Innovative Ways to Combat Truancy

In an effort to address truancy in schools, many states have offered a variety of programs: suspension for missing a certain number of classes, fining the parents for each day the child misses school, and other punitive measures. However, a punishment such as school suspension, particularly for a habitual or chronic truant, actually rewards the problem behavior. Punishing a child who does not want to come to school with removal from the classroom is an illogical and counterproductive approach. Similarly, fining a parent for the behavior of the child, while clearly providing an incentive to motivate the parent to elicit the cooperation of the child, holds very little in the way of real accountability for the one who is failing to show up for school. The data clearly demonstrate that these programs have had very little impact on the problem of truancy. Consequently, many states are beginning to recognize that the best way to get school attendance to improve begins with making the problem of missing school painful to the student. They accomplish this by asking the obvious question: "What do kids want?"

From the time they become teenagers, most youth count down the days to when they can obtain their learner's permit and, ultimately, their official driver's license. Obtaining a driver's license is a teenager's symbolic sign of maturity, freedom, and a passport to adulthood. Given its social and practical importance for teens, many states have begun using it to improve school attendance. A number of states, including New Jersey, Minnesota, and South Carolina, have implemented programs that stipulate if a student has more than an allotted number of unexcused absences in a year, the student's right to obtain a driver's license is delayed for a fixed period of time, usually six months. In those cases where students miss school but already have their license, it is revoked/suspended for the same period of time. Additionally, some states are currently developing added punishments for repeat offenders (Jones 2005).

Critics contend that states do not possess the authority to revoke a driver's license for a school-related behavior. However, a strong argument could be made that a driver's license is not a right but a privilege extended to those who demonstrate sufficient maturity, responsibility, and trust. A student who does not attend school demonstrates a lack of all three of those ideals. That there exists legal precedent only reinforces the logic of the argument that a license is not guaranteed. For instance, many states, such as New Jersey, provide for the suspension of a driver's license if a parent is delinquent in paying their child support awards. A license suspension also occurs when a person fails to appear at a child support hearing or when an arrest warrant is issued for nonpayment of support (Jones 2005).

Another way to decrease truancy is to link welfare assistance to satisfactory school attendance (Wright 2005). Beginning in the late 1980s a number of states began implementing such a program that is similar to those of welfare-to-work initiatives. Linking welfare benefits to school attendance was said by proponents to reinforce the idea supporting the parameters and spirit of the Welfare Reform Act of 1999 (Wright 2005). As Wright (2005) discovered in her evaluation of seven different programs, case management services provided by welfare agencies are critical to the success of the programs in general and of school attendance in particular. However, it should be noted that there is a wealth of evidence that suggests truancy is not the primary issue of school absenteeism among welfare recipients: health issues are the major cause of the problem (Fein et al. 1999). Thus, students on welfare are not avoiding school for conventional reasons (e.g. poor performance, laziness). Rather, health conditions or related problems within the family explain why they miss school. Thus, the strategies to address truancy for this group should take into account the somewhat unique circumstances for this segment of the truant population.

Other communities, such as Houston, Texas, have implemented volunteer programs, where, in 2005, for example, school officials and community residents descended on more than 600 homes to persuade older truants and dropouts to return to school. Many students who had dropped out cited daycare and employment responsibilities as the reason they left school. Many, however, said they simply got into the habit of not showing up for school, particularly if their parents worked during the day (Stover 2005).

Still other communities have turned to technology to reduce truancy. In 1998 The Oakland Unified School District had an absentee rate of between 3,000 and 3,500 students per day, or 15% of the entire student population. At a loss of $19 per student per day, the school district was losing nearly $4 million in attendance revenue each year. This led the district to implement the PhoneMaster 2000 system. This system was developed to increase parents' awareness by calling the home of each student absent two or more periods each day. The system calls the parents or guardians of the children between 7 and 9pm on school nights. If the parent answers, they enter a PIN number, and the system informs them of the absences and allows them to excuse their child by offering an array of choices. The system also establishes an audio text message from each teacher. Parents can access information, such as what was covered in class that day or dates for assignments and tests. The overall objective was to allow parents a more active role in their child's education ("Case Study: PhoneMaster Systems 1998).

Boston has a new wireless system that allows police and truant officers access to student records. Given that nearly 5% of Boston's 64,000 students are truant for more than five days during the school year, this feature, which can be tied into an officer's cell phone, allows local probation and police officers to sweep "hot spots" with truant officers where they can immediately check court, police, and school records of the teenagers they locate (Trotter 2002).

SOUTH CAROLINA COURTS AND TRUANCY

Like many states, the courts have become the main strategy to address truancy. In fact, courts in general have been notoriously slow in dealing with truancy cases. For example, in Dallas County, Texas, one study found that truancy cases sat in courts an average of 73 days before a hearing was conducted, with some cases languishing for up to 160 days (Capps 2003). Moreover, many families are not intimidated by courts when it comes to acts of truancy (ABA 2001). Thus, even when the case gets to court, parents have a difficult time understanding the seriousness of the problem. Aside from this, the wisdom of the purely punitive approach should be called into question. Removing parents from the home by sending them to jail or putting children in non-secure detention or foster care is often counterproductive because such measures are traumatic for the families, are highly cost-prohibitive, and often end up taking students out of school, which is the main reason for a court visit in the first place (Mogulescu and Segal 2002). Rather, some other strategy is needed—one that helps parents to understand the seriousness of the activity while at the same time holding them accountable without completely disrupting the family.

In South Carolina, all children between the ages of 5 and 17 are required to attend a public or private school or an approved home study program unless they graduate from high school before age 17. There are a few exceptions to this rule, such as a child who has graduated from high school or received a GED; a child who completes the 8th grade and is gainfully employed and employment is important to the maintenance of the child's home. A parent or guardian who fails to make their children attend school can be charged with educational neglect (Children's Law Center 2005).

Truancy, as defined by the state, consists of three unexcused absences in a row or five all together during the year. The South Carolina Code of Regulations, R. 43-274, has three categories of truancy. First, a truant is a child who is 6 to 17 years old, who has three consecutive unlawful absences or a total of five unlawful absences. Second, a "habitual" truant is a child who is 12 to 17 years old, who does not comply with the intervention plan developed by the school, the child, and the parents or guardians, and who accumulates two or more additional unlawful absences. Third, a "chronic" truant is a child, 12 to 17 years old, who has been through the school intervention process, has reached the level of habitual truant, has been referred to family court and placed under an order to attend school, and continues to accumulate unlawful absences.

Initially, when the child meets the minimum number of absences, the school is required to meet with the child and the parents to develop some type of plan to prevent future problems with attendance. Failure to compel their children to attend school can result in parents being fined up to fifty dollars for each absence or incarceration for up to 30 days for each absence. Should the child fail to attend school and continue to miss classes, they may be brought to family court to appear before a judge. Should the child continue to miss school and defy the court's mandate, the judge has the authority to find the child guilty of contempt of court and detain the child through the Department of Juvenile Justice for a period of up to 90 days. It is at this point the child is considered a chronic truant and in need of some type of intervention.

Prior to the Fall of 2005, the nature of truancy in Charleston county was excessively high. There were no truancy officers in Charleston and School Resource Officers in each school were burdened with other responsibilities and obligations, so they could not keep track of truants. The school district had no intervention plan in place when a child became truant and virtually no referrals to other outside agencies. Essentially, school officials were not paying attention to truancy or were content to have students who failed to come to school, where they were often a disruptive element, to remain at home or in the community. What the school district typically did with truants was to refer them to Family Court for disposition. That way, the responsibility for truants and for truancy in general, fell outside the parameters of the school district (McNamara, 2005).

In response, a Family Court judge, a Solicitor, and several other key officials developed a program to address issues relating to truancy and drug offenses. Citing the research that attests to the fact that truancy is a gateway activity to long-term delinquency and crime, as well as recognizing that other agencies should be making truancy a priority, the Barrett Lawrimore Juvenile Drug Court and Accountability Court was created. The program is multi-disciplinary in fighting truancy and educational neglect. It is a collaborative effort between twelve different agencies ranging from the Department of Juvenile Justice, the Charleston County School District, the Department of Mental Health, the Public Defender's Office, Family Services, Inc. and the Charleston County Family Court.

According to internal documents, the program consists of three phases. Initially, once the child is brought before the court, he or she is placed on probation and the parent is placed under a court order to ensure their child(ren) attend school. If the parent and child successfully complete the program, the case is reopened and the charges are dismissed, which means that they are removed from the child's juvenile record.

In Phase I of the program, which lasts for twelve weeks, the student attends a life skills counseling program and their parent(s) or guardian(s) attend a parenting course. These courses are offered two afternoons each week. In addition, the truant and parent appear in court weekly. The parent pays a nominal fee for their counseling program, while the cost of the truant's program is billed to Medicaid. Both the truant and the parent are subject to any drug and alcohol testing ordered by the court. In addition to court appearances and the parenting course, the parent is required to make certain their child attends school each day and enforce a one hour homework session each night. The truant is required to attend school each day with no unexcused absences, skipped classes, or behavior problems. They also participate in any tutoring set up by the court or the school district and maintain satisfactory grades in all courses. The truant's curfew is 7pm as long as they are making satisfactory grades, have no behavior problems, and are following all the rules of the program.

If a parent violates the rules, he or she is subject to contempt of court, which carries a sentence of up to one year in jail, a $1,500 fine and /or 300 hours of community service. If the parent does not make sure the child gets to school, he or she can be fined the aforementioned fifty dollars each day the child misses school. In addition, if the court feels that the child's best interests are served by having the parent present with them in school, the parent is required to do so.

If the child skips school or a class, he or she spends each weekend in detention at the Department of Juvenile Justice, which continues until attendance is acceptable to the court. If the child misbehaves while in school, the child is subject to detention, community service, or counseling. Should the parent or child not complete Phase I successfully, they will be assessed by the Department of Mental Health to determine what should be added to the program to make their successful completion the second time around.

For those who have completed Phase I, they are required to appear in court once a month for monitoring. In this phase, their curfew is raised to 8pm. As long as they remain in good standing and comply with the rules of the program, Phase II lasts for twelve weeks. If they begin violating the rules, they return to Phase I and are assessed for additional services. If the participants complete Phase II successfully, their curfew is increased to 9pm and they do not have to appear in court as long as they continue to comply with the stipulations and rules of the program.

It should be noted that as of October 2005, there are 18 children enrolled in the program. This is partly because of the newness of the program, but it is also due to the fact that the Family Court has required the Charleston County school district to implement an effective early intervention program that prevents many children from ending up in court. As a result, the small number is somewhat of a testimony to the effectiveness of this early intervention. The remainder are considered the more difficult children, and the court addresses their issues on a continual basis. It is too early to evaluate the effectiveness of the Accountability Court, partly due to its recent implementation and partly due to the fact that so few children are enrolled in it. However, an evaluation component is being implemented by the school district in the form of a satisfaction survey of participants. Later, other instruments will be used to determine the overall impact of the program on truancy. What holds promise for this program is the evidence that suggests successful programs are comprised of a few key elements: multi-agency participation, parental involvement, consistent court intervention, and positive reinforcement for participants. It appears that the Accountability Court has all the necessary ingredients to be effective in reducing truancy.

CONCLUSION

The problems associated with truancy are significant and their implications have many far reaching consequences. There is substantial evidence that truancy is a gateway activity to an assortment of problems ranging from chronic delinquency, substance abuse, adult crime, teen pregnancy, unemployment, gang behavior, poverty, and dropping out of school. While there are a host of programs designed to reduce and prevent truancy, the most salient features of successful programs are those that involve parents, collaborate and coordinate with the local school district, court intervention for difficult cases, and positive reinforcement for participants along the way. South Carolina's experiment with the Accountability Court holds promise since it includes virtually all of these factors. Moreover, the use of Medicaid to pay for the costs of the program is an innovative idea that relieves the burden of finding financial resources to support it. What remains to be seen is how the program will grow and evolve and the evidence that it is successful in addressing the problems of truancy in Charleston County.

REFERENCES:

Allen-Meares, P. Washington, R. O. and Welsh, B. L. 2000. *Social Work Services in Schools.* Boston: Allyn and Bacon.

Baker, M. L., Signmon, J. N., and Nugent, M. E. 2001.*Truancy Reduction: Keeping Students in School.* Washington, D.C.: U.S. Department of Justice, Office of Juvenile Justice Programs, Office of Juvenile Justice and Delinquency Prevention.

Bell, A. J., Rosen, L. A. and Dynlacht, D. 1994. "Truancy Intervention," *The Journal of Research and Development in Education,* 27: 203-211.

Berg, I. 1997. "School Refusal and Truancy," *Archives of Disease in Childhood* 76(2):90-92.

Capps, W. R. 2003. "The New Face of Truancy," *School Administrator,* 60(4):34.

"Case Study: PhoneMaster Systems Reduce Truancy Costs and Headaches," 1998. *T.H.E. Journal* 25(9):68-70.

Catalano, F. R., Arthur, M. W., Hawkins, J. D., Berglund, L., and Olson, J. J. 1998. "Comprehensive Community and School-Based Interventions to Prevent Antisocial Behavior," in Loeber, R and Farrington, D. eds., *Serious and Violent Juvenile Offenders: Risk Factors and Successful Interventions.* Thousand Oaks, CA: Sage Publications.

Children's Law Center. 2005. *Frequently Asked Questions About Truancy in South Carolina.*

Civil Rights Project Harvard University Conference. 2000. *Opportunities Suspended: The Devastating Consequences of Zero Tolerance and School Discipline Policies.*

Dougherty, J. W. 1999. "Attending to Attendance," *Phi Delta Kappa Fastbacks,* 450:7-49.

Dryfoos, J. G. 1990. *Adolescents at Risk: Prevalence and Prevention.* New York: Oxford University Press.

Epstein, J. L. and Sheldon, S. B. 2002. "Present and Accounted For: Improving Student Attendance Through Family and Community Involvement," *Journal of Educational Research,* 95:308-318.

Fein, D. J., Wang, S. Lee, and E. S. Schofield. 1999. *Do Welfare Recipients' Children Have a School Attendance Problem?* Report prepared for the Delaware Health and Social Services Department, Cambridge, MA: Abt Associates.

Garry, E. M. 1996. *Truancy: First Step to a Lifetime of Problems.* Washington, D.C.: U.S. Department of Justice, Office of Juvenile Justice and Delinquency Prevention.

Heaviside, S., Rowand, C., Williams, C., and Farris, E. 1998. *Violence and Discipline Problems in U. S. Public Schools: 1996-1997.* Washington, D.C.: U. S. Department of Education, Office of Educational Research and Improvement, National Center for Education Statistics.

Huzinga, D. Loeber, R. and Thornberry, T. 1995. *Urban delinquency and Substance Abuse: Initial Findings.* Washington, D.C.: U.S. Department of Justice, Office of Juvenile Justice and Delinquency Prevention.

Jones, L. R. 2005. "Ending School Truancy in One Step," *New Jersey Law Journal,* March 7, 2005.

Kaufman, P., Alt, M. N. and Chapman, C. d. 2001. *Dropout Rates in the United States 2000.* Washington, D. C.: U. S. Department of Education. National Center for Education Statistics.

Kleine, P. A. 1994. *Chronic Absenteeism: A Community Issue.* East Lansing, MI: National Center for Research on Teacher Learning.

McNamara, R. H. 2005. Personal Communication with Court Official, October 7th.

Mogulescu, S. and Segal, H. J. 2002. Approaches to Truancy Prevention. New York: Vera Institute of Justice, Youth Justice Program.

"No Show, No License," *Scholastic Scope* 53(11):21.

Oman, R. F., McLeroy, K. R., Versely, S., Aspy, C. B., Smith, D. W. and Penn, D. A. 2002. "An Adolescent Age Group Approach to Examining Youth Risk Behaviors," *American Journal of Health Promotion*, 16:167-176.

Puzzanchera, C., Stahl, A. L., Finnegan, T. A., Tierney, N., Snyder, H. N. 2003. Juvenile Court Statistics 1998. Washington, D.C.: U.S. Department of Justice, Office of Juvenile Justice and Delinquency Prevention.

Rohrman, D. 1993. "Combating Truancy in Our Schools-A Community Effort." *NASSP Bulletin,* 76(549):40-51.

Rubin, H. G. 2004. "NYC Settles Lawsuit Alleging Students Were "Pushed Out" *Education Daily* 37(6):1-2.

Snyder, H. N. and Sickmund, M. 1995. *Juvenile Offenders and Victims: A National Report.* Washington, D.C.: U.S. Department of Justice, Office of Juvenile Justice and Delinquency Prevention

Stover, D. 2005. "New Ways, More Reasons to Fight Truancy," *The Education Digest,* 70(5):48-52.

Strickland, V. P. 1998. *Attendance and Grade Point Average: A Study.* East Lansing, MI: National Center for Research on Teacher Learning.

Teasley, M. L. 2004. "Absenteeism and Truancy: Risk, Protection, and Best Practice Implications for School Social Workers," *Children and Schools* 26(2):117-129.

Teevan, J. J. and Dryburgh, H. B. 2000. "First Person Accounts and Sociological Explanations of Delinquency," *Canadian Review of Sociology and Anthropology* 37(1):77-93.

Trotter, A. 2002. "Boston Will Use New Cellphones to Call Truants' Bluff," *Education Week*, 21(31):1-3.

U. S. Department of Education. 1993. *Conditions of Education: 1993*. Washington, D.C.: U.S. Department of Education.

Wandersman, A. and Nation, M. 1998. "Urban Neighborhoods and Mental Health: Psychological Contributions to Understanding Toxicity, Resilience, and Interventions," *American Psychologist* 53:647-656.

Wright, J. 2005. "Rethinking Welfare School Attendance Policies," *Social Service Review*, 79(1):2-27.

Tracking Matters

Vincent J. Roscigno
James W. Ainsworth-Darnell
Department of Sociology
The Ohio State University

Academic tracking is a common practice in most classrooms and schools in the United States. Beginning at early elementary levels, children are placed in unique reading groups based on what is seen as their intellectual ability or potential. It is often the case that schools set up distinct "gifted and talented" classrooms by later elementary grades for those who have performed well the first few years or who are viewed as academically advanced relative to their same grade counterparts. This process only intensifies--students typically end up on a distinct academic track by high school and are, more often than not, well aware of their track position and that of others. These tracks are typically deemed "academic/advanced," "general," "vocational," or one of a variety of educationally impaired tracks, most often having to do with a learning disability, emotional impairment, or mental retardation.

The reasoning behind tracking, and indeed its rationale, are relatively straightforward. Advanced students, when grouped together, spur one another along, will not become bored or have to wait for lower achieving students to catch up, and therefore will achieve at a higher level. Lower track students, in comparison, can work at a pace commensurate with their comfort and ability level and will not become overwhelmed by the brisk pace of high achievers in their classroom or at their grade level.

At face value then, the logic behind tracking is one in which all students benefit. Students work at their potential. They are not held back by slower learners, nor are they overwhelmed by material that is above and beyond their ability. These goals, however, as well-intentioned as they may be, mask some underlying and incorrect assumptions about the neutrality of the tracking process. One such supposition is that students are tracked solely on the basis of intellectual ability or innate potential. Another questionable assumption has to do with whether the quality of education received is equitable across tracks. Sociological and educational research has explored each of these questions, revealing relatively clear patterns of race and class inequality in tracking in U.S. schools.[1] There is also clear variation in the quality of education received across tracks.

Who Gets Tracked Where, and Why?

The institution of education in this country has historically been viewed as the "great equalizer," whereby individuals and groups can remedy disadvantages faced by previous generations. Inequalities associated with tracking, however, represent one way in which broader societal inequalities tend to be reproduced during the schooling process. Rather than a direct form of discrimination against poor or non-white children, the stratification dynamics associated with tracking, discussed below, represent *institutionalized discrimination*; discrimination that occurs without conscious intent, that is largely a function of institutional practices and rules, but that nevertheless works against and perpetuates inequalities for certain segments of our society.

Empirical evidence has been relatively clear regarding the social class and race character of tracking. Poor and non-white students are more likely than their well-to-do and middle class white counterparts to be low tracked through their elementary and high school years. Figures 1 and 2, derived from a national sample of U.S. high school students, offer clear evidence of these patterns.

White students are more likely than their Asian, Black, Native-American, and Hispanic counterparts to be on high, college bound tracks in both math/science and English/history. Racial inequalities in placement, as the reader can see, are most profound for African-American, Native-American, and Hispanic students. As a result, these students are more likely than white students to be placed in lower track classes in high school; classes that are usually general or vocational in nature.

[Figure 1 about here]

Track placement is influenced not only by race, but also by social class background. Students from poorer families are less likely to be placed high relative to their more well-to-do counterparts (see Figure 2). Middle class students fall somewhere between. Of course, these race and class patterns do not suggest that all poor and non-white kids are tracked low or that all well-to-do white children are placed high. What they do suggest, however, are general patterns and inequalities in where one is likely to end up, depending on race and socioeconomic background. Such evidence of race and class stratification in tracking is troubling not only because it represents a form of inequality perpetuated in the schooling process, but also because it has very real implications for the likelihood of dropping out and what students do after high school (i.e., go to college, obtain a blue collar job, etc.).

[Figure 2 about here]

Traditional social scientific reasoning associated with what has been called *Social Darwinism* would explain the trends presented above in biological terms, suggesting that low SES and non-white groups are disproportionately in low tracks due to inherent intellectual differences.[2] Historically, such pseudo-scientific views were used to first justify slavery then maintain racially segregated schools in the South. It also led to the placement of many Latino children in classrooms for the mentally retarded in the Southwest and, at the broadest level, led to the adoption of the Immigration Act of 1924. This piece of legislation severely limited the further immigration of certain southern and eastern European white ethnic groups (e.g., Italians, Polish, etc.), believed to be less intelligent and therefore more inclined toward criminal activity, into the U.S.[3]

Although most contemporary research has moved away from socio-biological explanations of class and racial inequalities, such views continue to garner attention. A clear example is the recent publication and publicity surrounding Hernnstein and Murray's *The Bell Curve,* in which the authors suggest that biology has more to do with achievement than do social factors.[4] Contemporary sociological and educational researchers rightly dismiss such overly simplistic viewpoints, especially when they are used to exclude one group to the benefit of another. Instead, research over the past thirty years has focused on how kids are placed on tracks in the first place. It is from this research that two clear biases in track placement have been uncovered.

First, children tend to be tracked on the basis of their performance on a standardized test. It is usually assumed that such tests measure innate potential or intellectual ability. Research, however, suggests that these tests measure much more. They tap into a child's experiences in life thus far and are biased in their construction, measuring more so the white middle-class normative standard than they do the day-to-day experiences of poor children and racial/ethnic minorities.[5] On comprehension portions of standardized tests, for instance, scenarios often depict that which is commonplace to middle-upper class white students, but which is quite foreign to a black child living in an urban ghetto, a Latino child living in a poor barrio, a Native-American child living on a reservation, or a white child living in a rural and poor agricultural area of the U.S.

Likewise, such tests capture one's educational experiences thus far, rather than merely potential. It is for this reason that children from higher socioeconomic backgrounds, who have had greater educational resources and opportunities in their homes from early on, tend to outperform poorer students. In fact, one's parents' education is consistently one of the best predictors of how low or high one perform in school and on achievement tests.[6] The relation between socioeconomic status and achievement is typically true not only for young children, but rather is consistent throughout the educational process, including performance on tests such as the SAT or GRE. It is no surprise then that when testing is used as a gatekeeping tool to see who is placed low and who is placed high, that broader patterns of societal inequality tend to be reproduced.

An important second mechanism that often comes into play during track placement is teacher expectations of a given student. Although we would like to believe that educators are capable of employing objective evaluation of student effort, intelligence, and potential, research over the past three decades has demonstrated that there is a subjective element that comes into play and which, like testing, places poor and non-white children at a unique disadvantage.

Rist, for instance, in his observations of reading group placement at the earliest educational levels in the early 1970s, found that teachers typically employ subjective judgments about potential.[7] Beyond student academic performance in front of the teacher, he found that teachers' judgments and conclusions about potential were also based on the student's ability to speak proper, middle class English and on the way in which the student dressed. Indeed, he found that by the eighth day of kindergarten, seating arrangements had been made along these lines, that those at the "fast learner" table received greater attention and privileges, and that students began to adopt their roles as "fast learner" or "slow learner" accordingly.

Alexander, Entwisle, and Thompson, undertaking more recent analyses with a similar concern in mind, uncovered similar results.[8] They found that class and racial biases in teacher evaluation, and consequently expectations, exist even at the earliest educational levels. Such biases seem even more pronounced when the teacher and the student are from quite distinct social origins. These biases, they note, are not only important for a student's experiences and performance in a given classroom. Rather, teacher expectations are crucial at early elementary levels due their effects on a student's long term educational trajectory, part of which is perpetuated through track placement. They conclude,

The evidence indicates that high status teachers, both black and white, experience special difficulties relating to minority youngsters. The perceive such youngsters as relatively lacking in the qualities of personal maturity that make for a 'good student,' hold lower performance expectations of them, and evaluate the school climate much less favorably when working with such students. As a result, blacks who begin first grade with test scores very similar to their white age-mates have fallen noticeably behind by years end.[9]

Thus, testing and teacher expectations represent two mechanisms through which race and class biases in the track placement process are played out. Non-white and poorer students tend to perform less well on such tests, due largely to cultural and class biases in the construction of the tests themselves, and due to the fact that such tests, in fact, measure one's background experiences and family educational resources as much as they capture intelligence. These students receive less in the way of expectations as well, often determined by subjective criteria rather than true academic potential. But what occurs once student track placement is determined? Is the educational experience similar across tracks?

Educational Opportunity and Why Tracking Matters

It is clear that children in higher track classes perform academically at a higher level than do their lower track counterparts. Not all of this difference, however, is associated with greater intelligence or academic potential among higher track kids. Rather, analyses of high and low track classrooms suggest that the quality of education received varies quite markedly by track level.

There are relatively clear differences across tracks in terms of the availability of educational resources, teacher quality, and expectations. As a consequence, classroom climate also differs as does peer encouragement of educational success. Figure 3, shown below, displays such differences across high and low tracks for our nationally representative sample of U.S. high school students. [Figure 3 about here]

Low track classes are less likely to have the types and quality of educational resources as do high track classes. Take, for instance, access to and use of computers as one indicator of educational resources. The percentages reported in Figure 3 reveal that high track students are almost four times as likely as low track kids to use and/or have such a resource at their disposal. Similar, if not more profound, is the association between track and teacher training. Fewer than two percent of low tracked students are taught by a teacher with greater educational training and experience. This is in contrast to high track kids, thirty percent of whom are being taught by teachers holding at least a masters degree.[10]

Typically, the newest and youngest teachers in a given school are asked to teach the low track classes. Those with the greatest credentials and seniority, in contrast, tend to avoid lower track classes. Research has suggested that teachers prefer to teach children who they believe to be more intelligent. One consequence is that those who teach lower track children tend to prepare less in the way of daily lesson plans and classroom activities, and hold lower expectations of their students. The reader will note this dramatic difference in expectations, displayed in Figure 3. Rather than seeing it as an opportunity to help "all grow to their potential," teachers given low track classes often see their job as one of "weeders, getting rid of the kids who can't make it..."[11]

The tendency to avoid low track classes and to hold lower expectations of students in such classes is unfortunate, not to mention unfair. Indeed, some research has demonstrated that these patterns lend themselves to a *self-fulfilling prophecy*; a situation in which people, in this case children, alter their behavior to conform to what is expected of them, thereby creating the reality others thought was true in the first place. Such an unfortunate causal loop of expectations and performance then serves to justify, in the eyes of policy makers and school administrators, greater classroom resources and teacher energy for high track kids.

A clear example of the processes we are discussing is reflected in the now classic "pygmalion in the classroom" experiment undertaken in the 1960s by Rosenthal and Jacobsen.[12] In this study, the researchers *randomly* selected 5 students from each classroom in a given elementary school and told the teachers these students were identified by a test as "potential academic spurters." By year's end, these students for whom the teacher expected great intellectual gains not only showed greater academic achievement than their non-identified counterparts, but were viewed by the teacher, as well as their classmates, as smarter, happier, and more likely to succeed. This example demonstrates that a self-fulfilling prophecy can work in a positive direction, and underscores the critical importance of teacher expectations for student performance.

Another problematic feature of the low track class, given lower expectations, less resources, and the self-fulfilling prophecy described above, is the resultant classroom climate. Students typically realize the tracks they are on, are *labeled* by teachers and other students, and often buy into this labeling themselves. Children understand where they fall on this continuum as early as second grade, and are effected not only in terms of their own expectations, but their self-esteem as well.[13] An unfortunate yet understandable consequence, some have noted, is the formation of a student subculture in low tracked classrooms; one that is antagonistic toward education and that has its own system of rewards, often valuing classroom rebellion and doing opposite of what the teacher desires.[14] As indicated in Figure 3, this obviously leads to a climate where disruption is more likely to impede on the learning process and a scenario in which one's peers lose respect for, and no longer value, the educational process and educational effort.

Achievement and Attainment Across Tracks

So what are the consequences of the patterns of track placement and inequalities in classroom resources, noted above, for student achievement over the long run? Does tracking shape one's likelihood of completing high school? And how, if at all, does the tracking process that begins early on in each of our educational histories effect our long term educational and occupational attainment once we exit the high school doors?

Figures 4 and 5 address the first of these questions by focusing on achievement levels throughout high school. As one can see, the initial gap in academic achievement across tracks in eighth grade intensifies and widens by tenth grade, and then again by twelfth grade.[15] Similar patterns are found for both math and reading. The widening gap between high and low track students, and depressed general achievement for those in low tracks in these subject areas, have clear implications for performance on SAT and ACT examinations and, therefore, one's likely admittance and/or success at the collegiate level.

[Figures 4 and 5 about here]

With regard to long term educational attainment and even occupational opportunity, being low tracked in high school is clearly consequential. Interestingly, although not too surprising, is the fact that students are relatively aware of where they stand. Expectations for low track students are depressed considerably by the twelfth grade, and this translates into a wide disparity among students in whether they expect to finish college. Figure 6 reveals this profound difference in expectations, with sixty seven percent of high track students believing they will complete college in contrast to only fifteen percent of low track students.

[Figure 6 about here]

Perhaps even more disconcerting are dropout rates, also reported in Figure 6. Only two percent of high track students drop out of high school by the twelfth grade. This is in stark contrast to students who are low tracked throughout high school, who are nine times more likely to drop out by the twelfth grade. Given the patterns and disparities in achievement, college expectations, and dropping out of high school, the practice of tracking should not be seen as merely something that happens in schools. Rather, it begins in school, but ultimately shapes one's life chances over the long term. It has consequences for the preparedness of our labor force in general, and the ability to eventually provide one's own children with adequate health care, food, and shelter. Given the consequences of tracking for the likelihood of dropping out, it also has very real implications for a number of other social problems including poverty and crime. Through tracking in education, inequalities by race and social class are partially reproduced and, indeed, passed from one generation to the next.

Why Track in the First Place?

Traditional functionalist theory in sociology has viewed the institution of education as critically important, not only because it socializes the younger generation and new immigrants into appropriate norms of conduct, but also because it represents a *meritocratic* sorting process; one based on ability, one that insures the "best and brightest" move on to the next level, and one that ultimately helps to decide who ends up in the most important societal positions.[16] Tracking clearly represents one aspect of this "sifting and sorting" function. Similar to assumptions made about tracking, however, this view of education and its functions put forth by social theorists rests on the assumption that the sorting that occurs is neutral, based solely on ability, intellect, and potential.

Evidence presented here, along with countless other studies of stratification and the schooling process, present a very serious challenge to this claim.

First, one's track placement (or the sifting and sorting that occurs, if you prefer) is shaped by more than simply ability or potential. *Ascribed characteristics* one is born with or into, such as one's social class or race, come into play during this process. Although they have no relation to intelligence or potential, they affect the likelihood of being of being tracked high or being tracked low and, therefore, one's educational and occupational trajectory and future success. Race and class biases in track placement, and the gatekeeping effects they have at initial stages, challenge the key assumption made by advocates of tracking and social theorists who suggest that the sorting that occurs is meritocratic in nature.

Secondly, it is typically assumed that the educational process is relatively neutral and equitable once track placement has been made. Low track classes, as we and others have shown, receive less in the way of important educational resources, are usually staffed by newer, less experienced teachers, and students in these classes are expected to do less than their higher track counterparts. It is no surprise that, under such circumstances, classroom climate less conducive to achievement and antagonism toward the educational process develop. Not only is the starting line different for poor and non-white students, but the race they run is on the outside lane of the track, and with a variety of hurdles that they must attempt to overcome.

Finally, the logic behind tracking itself, that high achievers will work harder and low achievers can work at a pace commensurate with their ability, is questionable at best. Recent evidence suggests that high achievers do just as well in heterogenous settings as they do when tracked with similar students. It also appears to be the case that those who are academically behind do better, and are spurred on to try harder, when grouped with high achievers.[17] So why track then, especially given the stigma and labeling of lower students? Who gains? These are perhaps the most fundamental questions of all. If there is little, if any, tangible achievement benefit for already high achieving students, but a very real, unjust cost for those at the lower end who are disproportionately poor and non-white, tracking in schools makes little sense.

What seems more practical, not to mention sensible, would be diverse groupings of students of varying abilities and backgrounds. Not only will achievement of otherwise low tracked students be raised in such a situation, but high achievers might also learn valuable leadership, creative, and communication skills that they might otherwise not. For education is not (or should not be) simply about grasping knowledge of English, math, science, and history. Rather, it should also be concerned with teaching students how to live and apply their knowledge and skills in a diverse world; one that is comprised of people and future co-workers of varying abilities, perspectives, and life experiences.

Notes

1. Class and race disparities in tracking placement are more apparent throughout the educational process, whereas gender disparities in tracking are more apparent in later high school grades, especially in math and science. See also Susan L. Dauber, Karl L. Alexander, and Doris R. Entwisle, "Tracking and Transitions Through the Middle Grades: Channeling Educational Trajectories," *Sociology of Education* (1996) 69:290; Adam Gamoran and Mark Berends, "The Effects of Stratification in Secondary Schools: Synthesis of Survey and Ethnographic Research," *Review of Educational Research* (1987) 57:415-435; Caroline Hodges Persell, *Education and Inequality* (New York: The Free Press, 1977); Terry Kershaw, "The Effects of Educational Tracking on the Social Mobility of African Americans," *Journal of Black Studies* (1992) 23:152-169; Jeannie Oakes, *Keeping Track: How Schools Structure Inequality* (New Haven: Yale University Press, 1985); Beth E. Vanfossen, J.D. Jones, and Joan Z. Spade, "Curriculum Tracking and Status Maintenance," *Sociology of Education* (1987) 60:104-122.

2. Similar arguments have been made with regard to differential gender effects in math or science, citing "proclivities" or "biological" tendencies which makes males and females each better suited for particular educational training and occupations.

3. Chinese and Japanese immigration was practically halted even earlier by the Federal Government via the Chinese Exclusion Act and the Gentleman's Agreement, respectively. For elaboration on white ethnic immigration, related legislation, and its justifications, see Stanley Lieberson, *A Piece of the Pie: Black and White Immigrants Since 1880* (Berkeley: University of California Press, 1980).

4. Richard J.Hernnstein and Charles Murray, *The Bell Curve: Intelligence and Class Structure in American Life*, (New York: The Free Press, 1994); for a response to the biological position, see Claude S. Fischer et al., *Inequality by Design: Cracking the Bell Curve Myth* (Princeton: Princeton University Press, 1996).

5. Jerome Kagan, "What is Intelligence?" *Social Policy* (1973)4:88-94.

6. For instance, see Annette Lareau, *Home Advantage: Social Class and Parental Intervention in Elementary Education* (New York: Falmer Press, 1989); Vincent J. Roscigno, "Race, Institutional Linkages, and the Reproduction of Educational Disadvantage," *Social Forces* (1998) forthcoming.

7. Ray C. Rist, "Student Social Class and Teacher Expectations: The Self-Fulfilling Prophecy in Ghetto Education," *Harvard Education Review* (1970)40:411-451.

8. Karl L. Alexander, Doris R. Entwisle, and Maxine S. Thompson, "School Performance, Status Relations, and the Structure of Sentiment: Bringing the Teacher Back In,"*American Sociological Review* (1987)52:665-682.

9. Alexander, Entwisle, and Thompson, 1987, p. 679.

10. The National Educational Longitudinal Survey, from which we draw the data used to generate these comparisons, surveyed two of the student's teachers. Teacher responses were combined in determing credentials and expectations for the student. Where both teachers have at least a masters degree or both have college expectations for the student, the student was placed into the high category.

11. Jill Rachlin, "The Label that Sticks," U.S. News & World Report (July 3, 1989), p.52.

12. Robert Rosenthal and Lenore Jacobsen, *Pygmalion in the Classroom* (New York: Holt, Rinehart & Winston, 1968).

13. Sheila Tobias, "Tracked to Fail," Psychology Today (1989) 23:54-60.

14. David H. Hargreaves, *Social Relations in a Secondary School* (London: Tinling, 1967); Paul Willis, *Learning to Labor: How Working Class Kids Get Working Class Jobs* (New York: Columbia University Press, 1981).

15. These figures actually underestimate the gap by twelfth grade, given the loss of dropouts in the sample, who tend to be disproportionately represented among low academic tracks.

16. For the classical functionalist position, see especially Kingsley Davis and Wilbert E. Moore, "Some Principles of Stratification," *American Sociological Review* (1942) 10:242-249.

17. John M. Peterson, "Tracking Students by Their Supposed Abilities Can Derail Learning," *American School Board Journal* (1989) 176:38; Jill Rachlin, "The Label that Sticks," U.S. News & World Report (July 3, 1989), p.52.

Enhancing School Safety Using
Student-Based Problem-Solving

T. Steuart Watson
Mississippi State University

H. Craig Huneycutt
Problem Solving Innovations, Inc.

Dennis J. Kenney
Policy Lab and John Jay College of Criminal Justice

The projects described in this article were supported by grants from the National Institute of Justice, Office of Justice Programs, U. S. Department of Justice (School Safety Program) #93-IJ-CX-0026, the Office of Community Oriented Policing Services (Bullying/Intimidation Project) # 98-SBWX0093, and the Office of Community Oriented Policing Services, U. S. Department of Justice (Kentucky Project) #397-CK-WX-0021. The views expressed herein are solely those of the authors and do not necessarily reflect the positions or opinions of the granting agencies.

During the 1994-95 school year, a project was implemented at West Mecklenburg High School in Charlotte, North Carolina that used student-based problem solving groups to address problems of crime, fear, disorder, and disruption. The project was labeled the "School Safety Program" because the focus was not only on reducing criminal and disruptive acts on campus, but also on making the school a safer place for both students and adults. It is our contention that the mere absence of, or reduction in, criminal acts does not make, in and of itself, schools safe. Rather, schools are safe when there is an absence of crime, disorder, and disruption and an absence of the fear of these acts.

This article provides an overview of the School Safety Program, its results, and the continued efforts in schools around the country that are using student-based problem-solving as a means for addressing many of the problems that create an unsafe atmosphere on campus. This article does not examine the statistics on school crime, fear, disorder, etc. There are many other more resources available that are replete with statistics on virtually every type of act imaginable and by whom they are committed (e.g., Kaufman, et al., 1998; National School Safety Center, 1999; Heaviside, Rowand, Williams, & Farris, 1998). Nor does this article provide a critical analysis of other efforts aimed at improving school safety. Again, other sources are available that provide a more thorough analysis of the benefits and limitations of these programs (Goldstein & Conoley, 1997; Goldstein & Huff, 1993; Kenney & Watson, 1998; Sandhu, 2000). Instead, we focus on the advantages of using a problem solving approach and provide recommendations for the development and implementation of similar programs.

Foundations of School Based Problem Solving

The idea for using student problem solving groups to address campus safety issues grew out of three distinct, yet related areas. The first of these areas is community policing. One of the central features of this movement within the policing and criminal justice fields is that the citizens (in the case of schools, the students) participate in decision making and share the responsibility for ensuring the safety of their community (i.e., the school). Citizens are seen as an integral component in crime reduction and prevention efforts because of their intimate knowledge of their communities - knowledge that is not always available to others (i.e., police and teachers). In essence, the students form a partnership with their teachers and administrators and work together to enhance safety for all students. This view is radically different from most perspectives in that students often view school as a place that someone else has made safe for them. Previous research on community policing has indicated that crime prevention and fear reduction are most effective when citizens and the police are working toward mutually derived goals (Lavrakas and Herz, 1982; Rosenbaum, 1982; Waller, 1979, Yin, 1979). Because schools are essentially a community where a variety of citizens come together daily, it seems reasonable that the concept of community policing applies to schools.

A second area that contributed to the development of the school-based problem-solving concept is problem-oriented policing (Goldstein, 1979; 1990; Eck & Spelman, 1987). Briefly, problem oriented policing is based on the premise that crime and disorder are best addressed within small geographic boundaries and customized solutions are applied to a specific problem based on where and when the problem occurs and what is known about it (Eck & Spleman). Quite obviously, there is a strong relationship between community policing and problem solving in that citizens often have in-depth knowledge about a problem that the police do not have and their cooperation is required in order for significant impacts on crime, disorder, and disruption to occur.

The third area upon which the problem solving groups were developed is applied behavior analysis, which was derived from B. F. Skinner's extensive research on operant conditioning. Although applied behavior analysis focuses on intervention at the individual level, there are several key principles that are closely related to problem oriented policing and problem solving. The first of these principles is that problems are identified with sufficient specificity that they can be observed and measured. Further, these problems are identified according to the context (i. e., geographical boundary) in which they occur. The second principle, and perhaps the most important, is that problems must be analyzed to determine why they are occurring. The analysis involves examining the parties involved, the location where the problem occurs, the conditions that do and do not occur before (antecedents) and after (consequences) the problem, and the coexisting problems (sequentials). Once a thorough analysis has been completed, a customized response can be developed that is based on the analysis. These principles are part of the foundation of applied behavior analysis and work as well for crime problems as those experienced by individuals.

Description of the School Safety Program

The School Safety Program was designed to implement the combined elements of community policing, problem oriented policing, and applied behavior analysis in a high school community. The primary feature of this program is that students, in this case 11th graders, working in cooperation with teachers and administrators, are assigned a great deal of responsibility for improving the safety of their school. The process the students used to address their concerns was a four step problem solving model referred to as

SARA (Scanning, Analysis, Response, Assessment). The acronym SARA is derived from the problem oriented policing literature, but shares many similarities with the problem solving model from behavioral psychology (Bergan, 1977; Bergan & Kratochwill, 1990; Watson & Robinson, 1996). Although a complete description of the SARA process is beyond the scope of this article, we will present the highlights from each of the steps. Readers interested in a more thorough discussion of the process are referred to Kenney and Watson (1998).

During scanning, the students identify the wide range of issues that are pertinent at their school. A number of methods may be used to assist in scanning including conducting direct observations, interviews, and surveys and examining school disciplinary data and official police data. Then, through a multiple step process, students eliminate issues, prioritize problems, specifically define one problem, set a tentative goal, and establish a working hypothesis for why the problem occurs. They then decide how and when they are going to collect data on the chosen problem. It is especially important for students to remember to specifically identify problems before moving to the analysis phase. For instance, "fear of the boys restroom on F hall" is insufficiently specific because it does not specify a behavior that is exhibited when students are afraid. A more appropriate scanning statement might read, "6th grade boys are afraid of the restroom on F hall as evidenced by their leaving F hall, using the restroom in I hall, and returning late to their next class."

Following scanning, students then begin an analysis of the identified problem while collecting baseline data. During analysis, students determine the temporally proximate antecedents, consequences, and sequential conditions that precipitate, maintain, and coexist with, the problem, respectively. Students must also determine the strength of the problem in terms of how often it occurs, the duration of each occurrence of the problem, and the length of time this has been a problem. After this part of the analysis has been conducted, students must then be able to tell why a particular problem exists in their school before continuing with the analysis. The final part of the analysis requires the students to establish a tentative goal, identify resources that can assist them with their problem-solving efforts, and discover what has been done in the past or is being done to address the problem.

The response stage is straightforward in that the goal is to design a response for the problem that is based on the analysis. This is a critical feature of the School Safety Program - implementing responses to a problem that are based on a careful and thorough analysis that determines why the problem exists - and is a radical departure from the way most schools address recurring safety problems. The typical methods of responding to problems are utilizing a procedure based on traditional practice (e.g., suspensions), because it is a "feel-good" or popular procedure (e.g., metal detectors), or because it is politically beneficial (e.g., zero tolerance policies) regardless of whether or not there are any data to support their use. During the response stage, students first brainstorm for possible responses. They are encouraged to be creative and at the same time remember the data information derived from the analysis. After brainstorming, students then carefully consider the feasibility of their ideas and select options for further development. Once students have selected their response(s), they outline the plan, determine who will be responsible for each part, plan for further data collection, obtain permission to implement the plan, plan for problems with either implementing the plan or an ineffective plan, and finally, implement the plan.

The final stage of problem solving is assessment. Part I of assessment actually begins in the scanning phase when students collect baseline data on the identified problem. The baseline data provide the standard against which the effectiveness of the chosen response(s) will be judged. As soon as the response is implemented, Phase II of assessment begins. Students continue collecting data on the identified problem to determine if the response is having the desired effect. If the plan is working, students determine if there are strategies that will enhance the effectiveness of the plan and how the plan is going to be monitored in the future. If the plan is not working, students must determine if the plan is being implemented accurately and consistently, if the analysis of the problem or the problem itself has changed since the response was implemented, or the responses chosen were not the most suitable based on the analysis.

It is important to note that the teacher have an important role in guiding the students through the problem solving process. Although the students select the problem and carry out the steps and substeps of the SARA process, it is the teacher who helps keep them focused and guides their efforts. The teacher must make certain that the students address each of the steps, even though they may not see the relevance of a particular step at the time. The teacher must also help the students maintain movement within the process. Students may become bogged down at various points and need assistance in determining when to proceed to the next step. They may also need to move back in the process when the problem has changed during the process. In essence, the teacher acts as a facilitator or guide by ensuring that students follow the process without dictating the content at each step (e.g., identifying the problems for the students, giving students the analysis information).

The teacher must also control and guide the group socialization. It is quite easy for one or two dominant students to control the group and limit input from the rest of the group. If this occurs, the problem selected may not be a group or community priority but only a pet project of the more dynamic personalities of the group. The teacher can also reinforce the problem solving process through curriculum exercises based on the current topics of instruction. As one example, a history teacher used this technique by looking at historical events (in this case, the Missouri Compromise) and then having the students identify the specific problem, determine the antecedents, sequential conditions, and consequences of the problem, determine the historical response that was used and then assess their efforts. This concept can be applied to many other topics including government, civics, social studies, etc.

Case Example

Perhaps one of the best examples of students using the problem-solving model to address a serious problem was the "Cafeteria Project." Our pretest data, and the observations of students in one of the classes, indicated that many students were afraid of the cafeteria and that there was a lot of pushing, shoving, and fighting occurring there. It is likely that the physical altercations were contributing heavily to the fear of the cafeteria. During the scanning stage, the students in this class chose this problem as their number one priority, with the goal being to reduce the number of altercations as well as the fear associated with the cafeteria. In conducting their analysis, the students carefully observed the behavior of other students in the cafeteria. Based on these observations, they concluded that the main reason for the fighting and fear was a lack of order maintenance. That is, there were no pre-established lines for the students to enter the cafeteria, get their trays, and get in line for food. Therefore, they embarked on a response that was based on their analysis; they built concrete stanchions with an eye hook at the top and looped ski rope through the hooks to create lines that would guide students, in an orderly fashion, to the tray table and to the lunch lines. Now that the response was in place, the students began conducting an assessment to determine if their plan reduced the fighting and fear associated with the cafeteria. Much to their dismay, their observations and interviews indicated that fighting and fear actually increased as a result of the plan. Quite obviously, the students were dejected and concluded that problem solving was not effective and they could not impact their school environment. The students were encouraged not to give up and were prompted to return to the analysis phase to determine the accuracy of their initial analysis.

The students again analyzed the problem but added methods that they had not used previously: a) interviewing those students who were observed to be pushing and shoving others and b) interviewing the cafeteria workers. Their findings in this reanalysis lead them to a much different conclusion than before, namely that a lack of sufficient amounts of pizza was the proximate cause of the altercations and resulting fear. That is, because the cafeteria manager did not order enough pizza to meet student demand, the larger and tougher students forced themselves, using physical means and verbal threats, to the front of the pizza line to ensure attainment of pizza. The previous response of increasing order maintenance actually made the problem worse because line breaking was more easily distinguished which heightened the likelihood of altercations.

After the second analysis, students implemented a much different response. They worked with the cafeteria manager to order adequate pizza, varied the types of pizza ordered, and advertised throughout the school that pizza would be available for everyone. When they conducted their second assessment, their observations indicated that fighting in the cafeteria was markedly decreased, as was the fear associated with the cafeteria. The data obtained by the students matched our post-test data which indicated a 50% decrease in the number of students reporting being afraid of the cafeteria.

Not all problems of fighting and disorder will be as easily addressed as the one cited in this example. We use this example for several reasons: 1) it illustrates how students can use the problem solving process to address a significant safety issue, 2) it shows how the process can be used when one response, that is based on an seemingly correct analysis, is ineffective, 3) it points out for adults that many of the safety problems experienced by students may be unknown to the teachers (that's one reason why the concept of community policing is so important in problem solving), and 4) it illustrates how creative responses may be necessary to fix problems that seem to demand a more traditional response (a traditional school response to this type of problem would have been to identify the line breakers and provide them with some type of punishment). The important points to remember are that the students were responsible for the entire problem solving process and they solved what was, for them, a serious safety issue - one in which teachers and administrators were unaware.

Overall Results of the Program

Two schools actually participated in the School Safety Program - West Mecklenburg High School and Garinger High School. West Meck was the school where the program was implemented and Garinger was the control school. Students at both schools were administered the Effective School Battery (ESB) at the end of their 10th grade year (May, 1994), the middle of their 11th grade year (December, 1994), and at the end of their 11th grade year (May, 1995)[1]. The ESB is a 115-118 item instrument that measures school climate and safety issues. We also examined school disorder, disruption, and disciplinary data and official police data. Together, these three sources of data allowed us to analyze the effects of the School Safety Program on fear and behavior.

Prior to the School Safety Program, slightly more than half of the students completing the ESB reported "almost never afraid of being hurt or bothered at school." By the end of the program, that number had increased to 74%. When broken down by race and gender, the results were even more pronounced for white males. Likewise, a high percentage of students reported being afraid of specific locations like the cafeteria, restrooms, and hallways and stairs. By May of 1995, there was a 50% reduction in the percentage of students reporting being afraid of these locations, including the cafeteria. There was also a 50% reduction in the percentage of students who reported that they had to fight to protect themselves while at school, a 33% decrease in the number reporting having witnessed a teacher being threatened, and a 50% reduction in the number reporting having seen a teacher physically attacked by a student.

The positive results achieved by the School Safety Program were not only experienced by the students but by the teachers as well. Teachers also completed the ESB at the same time as the students in order to analyze the effects of problem solving on their school experiences. Prior to the School Safety Program, 29% of the faculty at West Meck considered theft, vandalism, and personal attacks as problems. Only 12% did so at the end of the program. These reductions were even more pronounced for white teachers, female teachers, and those with more than 15 years experience. Reductions in self-reported victimization rates among teachers ranged from 30% (obscene gestures to female staff) to 72% (African-American teachers being verbally threatened)[2]. In addition to the reductions in victimization among teachers, student-teacher relations improved as evidenced by 14% more teachers reporting that they were not hesitant to confront a misbehaving student for fear of their own safety and a 17% increase in the number of teachers indicating that they wanted to continue working with these students. There was also a 17% increase in the number of teachers who reported being satisfied most or all the time with their jobs. An unanticipated finding was that only 2% of teachers after the program reported that students of various races did not get along well at school compared to 13% before implementation of the school safety program.

School data on suspensions were examined to determine the impact of the school safety program on school disorder and disruption. Compared with the previous year, student/student conflicts decreased by 66%, student/teacher conflicts by 33%, chronic disruption by 66%, and fighting by 36%. Examination of official police data provided further support for the efficacy of the program. For instance, aggravated assaults were reduced by 100% from the previous year, assaults by 80%, burglaries by 75%, theft by 80% and vandalism by 50%. It is important to note that the number of incidents in each of these categories, except for vandalism, <u>increased</u> at the control school during the same period. We are not saying that the School Safety Program was solely responsible for the positive impact on crime at West Meck. Because of the nature of the quasi-experimental design, it is impossible to separate the effects of various actions taken during the year. We can say, however, that the School Safety Program contributed greatly to reductions in fear, crime, and disorder and appeared to have a demonstrable effect on the students, teachers, and school environment.

Innovative Applications and Extensions of Problem-Solving

<u>Bullying/Intimidation</u>. Another project, implemented in both middle and high schools in the Charlotte Mecklenburg Schools, used SARA as a means of addressing problems associated with bullying and intimidation[3]. After collecting standardized school system data from all of the 137 elementary, middle and high schools in the system, 11 schools (7 middle and 4 high schools) were selected that showed evidence of significant levels of these behaviors. The variables that were examined to assess bullying and intimidation included: a) the number of reported assaults on students, administrators and staff, b) the number of out-of-school suspensions, c) the number of in-school suspensions, and d) the number of weapons reported on campus.

This initiative was different from the School Safety Program in that School Resource Officers (SRO), along with a teacher-partner, were trained in problem solving and formed problem solving teams at their school. The teams usually consisted of students and other school staff. These ad hoc teams then worked together to identify problems, collect data, analyze the problem, develop responses, and assist in the assessment. The students involved were given an overview of the process, but no formal training in how to carry out the individual steps in the model.

A computer was purchased for each of the schools and was linked to a web site that was developed to capture the documentation on each of the problem solving efforts in the schools. This secure web site had problem-solving templates for each step of the process and the school resource officer entered the information as he/she proceeded through the SARA steps. The SROs could also consult each other's efforts and assist each other when needed. Technical assistance was provided via the web site and monthly school visits by project personnel.

As of this writing, the final evaluation of the project is being completed. At the beginning (pretest) and end (post test) of the school year, randomly selected students at each of the participating schools completed a self-report questionnaire designed specifically for this project. One of the unintended consequences of surveying came from the SROs and provided a particular challenge. The SROs were aware that the pretest results might contain information that pinpointed problems within each of the schools. They believed that this information should be shared with them in an effort to assist with problem solving. We, on the other hand, believed that the SROs should follow the model and gather information on issues and school problems as they had been trained to do. We further believed that by going directly to the students for information, the problem solving teams would gain additional insight and support from listening to the students. In addition, it is likely that the teams would discover additional problems not revealed in the surveys.

We also believed that using the survey information was an unneeded shortcut to identifying problems. The problem solving process is a learned skill. We intended the officers and their teams to solve school problems and to come away with problem solving skills that could be used with other problems in other situations. Our compromise was a review of the initial data and a commitment that we would inform the individual SRO if there was a serious or dangerous problem at their school that warranted specific and immediate attention. The SROs were satisfied with this compromise and we were fortunate that none of the surveys pointed to a problem that required immediate action.

The SROs went about their problem solving efforts with varied proficiency. Most closely followed the model and selected specific problems at specific locations such as bullying in the boys locker room after 3rd period class, strong armed robberies of 6th grade students in the 6th grade hallway before lunch, and fighting at the end of the 300 building after school. We are happy to report that these officers efforts were rewarded with each of these problems being eliminated or significantly reduced within a short time frame.

Other officers were less successful, but not for lack of effort. While working with one talented school resource office in a middle school, the officer was leading us through a problem-solving project on which he had been working. The officer had identified several disruptive behaviors that occurred during the school day that seemed to revolve around the various class changes. The officer explained that, during scanning, he identified the problem as the school's failure to utilize the traditional bell system to signal the beginning and end of class. This was the first year that the school had elected not to use the bell system to signal class changes. The purpose for eliminating the bells was to avoid disruptions for teachers that were using alternative course schedules that did not conform to the regularly scheduled class times on a particular day. Some of the disruptive behavior noted by the officer included: 1) students taking up to twelve minutes to change class when five minutes was allotted, 2) students hanging out in the hallways for extended periods of time, 3) teachers having difficulty starting their next class, 4) students reporting late to class, 5) a large group of male students congregating outside of the girls bathroom forcing the females to squeeze through the crowd, 6) female students reporting that they had been pinched, fondled, and assaulted when attempting to pass through the group of male students, and 7) a large number of female students who could not or would not use the restroom during class change and then requested and received a hall pass during regular class. At this point, the officer set about convincing the school administration to begin using the bell system again. He gathered data on the disruptive behavior and compared the current data to the data from the previous year. The data indicated that there had been an increase in reported incidents.

Although it seems, at least at first glance, that the officer was correct in identifying the proximate cause of the disruptive behaviors - the lack of a bell system - we should first recognize the pattern that is being used by the officer. After identifying the disruptive behavior, the officer immediately went to the response phase. He then set about gathering data to support his intended response. This is what is called using the model backwards (i.e., scanning, response, analysis, assessment). It is very possible that the response of using a bell system would have been justified by a thorough analysis. It is equally likely, and perhaps even more so, that other effective responses would have been selected that would have had similar and lasting effects on the problem behavior.

Due to the lack of any meaningful analysis prior to selecting the response, the officer was prompted to gather more information that was related to the disruptive behaviors. Some of the analysis information that was gathered included:

- the clocks in the various classrooms were not synchronized and the times varied by several minutes;
- when teachers with fast clocks released their students for a class change, the other classes saw and heard the change which resulted in class time being shortened for the other classes;
- teachers allowed students to enter their next classroom, put their books down and then return to the hallways for additional minutes which resulted in teachers experiencing difficulty in starting their next class;
- the majority of the disruptive behavior was occurring in the eighth grade classroom building and predominately in one hallway;
- the teachers were supposed to stand at their doorway to help supervise the class change, but were often involved in other legitimate student contact or were often reluctant to perform this duty;
- the school was losing approximately 35 minutes of class time per day due to the extended class changes.

After looking at all of the information surrounding this problem, it is apparent that the problem is a bit more complex than not having a bell system. It is obvious that the lack of a bell system has contributed to several of the problems identified at this school and implementing the bell system again would appear to be a justified response. It is also noteworthy that many of the schools in this system function quite effectively without a bell system. It is also obvious that a bell system would not affect some of the problem behaviors nor address some of the other antecedents of the problem. By moving from problem identification (i.e., scanning) to a pre-determined response without a thorough analysis, the officer almost missed many opportunities for alternative responses to resolve the problem.

Kentucky RCPI Project.

The use of student-based and school-based problem solving is gathering momentum in different areas throughout the country. The Regional Community Policing Institute in Kentucky, centered at Eastern Kentucky University, is sponsoring a pilot program at four high schools across the state to evaluate the effectiveness of using problem solving to improve school safety and as a basis for their statewide school safety program. Two of the high schools area in rural counties in eastern Kentucky, one urban high school is in the center of Louisville, and the fourth school is in Paducah and was the site of the student on student shooting in 1997 that killed three students and wounded five others.

This initiative began with an orientation held with schoolteachers and administrators in the early spring of 2000. Training in the problem-solving model is scheduled to occur during the first few weeks of the new school year and each of the schools will receive follow-up technical assistance and visits throughout the year. Each school has been given the flexibility to implement the problem-solving model in the form that best suits their individual school. This is in keeping with our belief that rarely does a "one-size-fits-all" program actually work for every school. Some of the schools may rely on the SRO or teachers to be the problem solvers with input and assistance from the students (like the bullying/intimidation project) and other schools may infuse the concepts into the curriculum and have the students perform the problem-solving tasks (like the School Safety Program). A comprehensive evaluation will be conducted using a quasi-experimental design.

School-Based Partnership Conferences

Problem-solving has also spread to individual schools in every state through because of the innovative School Based Partnership Grants program sponsored by the Office of Community Oriented Policing Services in Washington, DC. At this time, approximately 300 schools and police departments have received grants to implement problem solving in their schools. Four national conferences have been held to assist the teams and problem-solving experts from across the country have trained and given technical assistance to these grant recipients.

Some interesting observations have been made during these conferences regarding the police officers, school personnel and students involved. Perhaps the most striking observation is the willingness of the schools and police agencies to work cooperatively in this initiative. It was not many years ago that schools resisted the interventions of police departments because it was perceived as "trying to tell them how to run their schools." Likewise, for many police agencies and police officers, working in the schools was not viewed as real police work. Community Policing has opened the doors to these relatively new partnerships where these different organizations find common ground and work together for the good of all concerned.

Another observation was the enthusiasm that the students brought to the process. These students were rarely satisfied with being passive in the discussions of the problems in their schools. They were quite willing to speak up and even challenge the teachers when their perceptions and/or opinions differed. On more than one occasion, the officers and school staff were heard to say "I've been at that school for six years and I didn't know that." A student in one class told the SRO "You should have asked me about that, I knew it all along." These pearls of wisdom from students who are actively involved in using problem-solving as a means for making their school safer brings to mind a line in a popular song that says, "When you walk in the shoes of a stranger, you learn things you never knew you never knew." At one point in time, police officers, teachers, and students were strangers in school based crime fighting efforts. With the advent of problem solving, problem oriented policing, and community policing, they have become partners to make schools a safer place in which to learn.

Yet another observation was the degree of difficulty that many of the participants had with the problem-solving model. Many, but not all, of the police officers had received some problem solving training in the past several years. Few of the officers and none of the school staff or students had ever used the SARA model to deal with an actual crime or community problem. They had often obtained books and/or problem solving guides but lacked any practical experience in using the model. This observation underscores the need for quality training in the mechanics of problem solving as well as training in supervising and facilitating the problem-solving process. There is also a great need for follow-up contact with experienced problem solvers. The officers, school staff and students need a forum where they can obtain additional advice, direction and validation of their efforts and so that they maintain confidence in themselves and in the problem-solving process.

Summary and Conclusions

In this article, we have outlined one method for addressing problems of crime, disorder, disruption, and fear that occur on school campus. The data that are available on student-based problem solving indicates that it is an effective method for reducing crime and associated problems, all of which are impediments to the learning process. Current efforts are underway to evaluate the effectiveness of problem solving for reducing bullying, intimidation, and their associated problems, and for its efficacy as a critical component of a statewide school safety program. Despite our enthusiasm for problem solving, we are by no means implying that schools with problem solving teams in place will have no shootings, assaults, robberies, etc. Problem solving is not a magic bullet that suddenly erases all of the problems that can and do occur on a school campus. Rather, it is a systematic means by which students can identify their most pressing problems, gain an in depth understanding of why those problems occur on their campus, design customized solutions that fit their school, and evaluate the effectiveness of those solutions.

In closing, it needs to be made clear that despite empirical evidence pointing to the effectiveness of problem solving for making schools safer and the commitment from the Office of Community Oriented Policing Services (in the form of about $40 million dollars granted to police agencies and schools to form problem solving partnerships), not everyone is a convert to new ways of dealing with school based crime and fear problems. During a training session in a midsize western city, one school resource officer was overheard to say, "I already have solutions to all of these problems that we are talking about. I have all the tools I need right here on my belt, but the people in this department want to SARAlize everything." If the train to the future is guided by community policing, problem oriented policing and problem solving, this young officer has yet to find a way to purchase a ticket. Without an open mind and a willingness to embrace tools not found on his utility belt, his traditional walking shoes will wear thin while he continues to just "cuff'em and stuff'em."

Footnotes
[1] Although both the experimental and control schools were evaluated simultaneously, we only presented the data from the experimental school here. Readers interested in comparing the data from both schools are referred to Kenney and Watson, 1998.

[2] 30% and 72% refers to the reduction in these types of victimizations, not the % reporting being victimized by a particular act.

[3] This project, called the Bullying/Intimidation Project, was funded by the Office of Community Oriented Policing Services.

REFERENCES:

Bergan, J. R. (1977). *Behavioral consultation*. Columbus, OH: Charles E. Merrill.

Bergan, J. R., & Kratochwill, T. R. (1990). *Behavioral consultation and therapy*. New York: Plenum Press.

Eck, J., & Spelman, W. (1987). *Problem solving: Problem-oriented policing in Newport News*. Washington, DC: Police Executive Research Forum.

Goldstein, A. P., & Conoley, J. C. (Eds.) (1997). *School violence intervention: A practical handbook*. New York: Guilford.

Goldstein, A. P., & Huff, C. R. (Eds.) (1993). *The gang intervention handbook*. Champaign, IL: Research Press.

Goldstein, H. (1990). *Problem oriented policing*. New York: McGraw-Hill.

Goldstein, H. (1979). Improving policing: A problem oriented approach. *Crime an Delinquency, 25*, 236-258.

Heaviside, S., Rowand, C., Williams, C., & Farris, E. (1998*). Violence an discipline problems in U. S. public schools: 1996-1997, NCES 98-030*. Washington, DC: U . S. Department of Education, National Center for Education Statistics.

Kaufman, P., Chen, X., Choy, S. P., Chandler, K. A., Chapman, C. D., Rand, M. R., & Ringel, C. (1998). *Indicators of school crime and safety, 1998*. NCES 98-251/NCJ-172215. Washington, DC: U. S. Departments of Education and Justice.

Kenney, D. J., & Watson, T. S. (1998). *Crime in the schools: Reducing fear and disorder with student problem solving*. Washington, DC: Police Executive Research Forum.

Lavrakas, P., & Herz, E. (1982). Citizen participation in neighborhood crime prevention. *Criminology, 20*, 3-4.

National School Safety Center. (1999). *The National School Safety Center's report on school associated violent deaths*. Westlake Village, CA: Author.

Rosenbaum, D. (1982*). Police responses: Conventional and new approaches to local crime problems*. Paper presented at the annual convention of the American Psychological Association, Washington, DC.

Sandhu, D. S., & Aspy, C. B. (Eds.) (2000). *Violence in American schools: A practical guide for counselors*. Washington, DC: American Counseling Association.

Waller, I. (1979). *What reduces residential burglary?* Paper presented at the Third International Symposium on Victimology, Muenster, West Germany.

Watson, T. S., & Robinson, S. L. (1996). Direct behavioral consultation: An alternative to traditional behavioral consultation. *School Psychology Quarterly, 11*, 267-278.

Yin, R. (1979). What is citizen crime prevention? In *How well does it work: Review of Criminal Justice Education, 1978*. Washington, DC: National Institute of Law Enforcement and Criminal Justice, U. S. Government Printing Office.